THE LOST SOLDIER

The Ordeal of a World War II GI from the Home Front to the Hürtgen Forest

CHRIS J. HARTLEY

STACKPOLE BOOKS
Guilford, Connecticut

STACKPOLE BOOKS

Published by Stackpole Books
An imprint of The Rowman & Littlefield Publishing Group, Inc.
4501 Forbes Blvd., Ste. 200
Lanham, MD 20706
www.rowman.com

Distributed by NATIONAL BOOK NETWORK

800-462-6420

British Library Cataloguing in Publication Information Available

Library of Congress Cataloging-in-Publication Data Available

ISBN 978-0-8117-3779-1 (hardcover)
ISBN 978-0-8117-6764-4 (e-book)

♾™ The paper used in this publication meets the minimum requirements of American National Standard for Information Sciences—Permanence of Paper for Printed Library Materials, ANSI/NISO Z39.48-1992.

Printed in the United States of America

For Grandma Ruth and her family

It is foolish and wrong to mourn the men who died.
Rather, we should thank God that such men lived.
—George S. Patton

Bottom fell out.
—Ruth Lynn, November 1944

There is a land of the living and a land of the dead and
the bridge is love,
the only survival, the only meaning.
—Thornton Wilder

Contents

Maps

INTRODUCTION

TODAY, A MEMORIAL TO THE GERMAN 116TH PANZER DIVISION STANDS outside a small village in Germany. It is situated on a knoll overlooking a World War II battlefield where the division once fought, and next to a cemetery filled with German soldiers, including some of its own. A low stone wall encloses the memorial. Entering through a steel gate that bears the division's greyhound insignia, a visitor follows a path past an information display about the 116th Division and stops before an iron gray statue depicting two men. One of the men, a healthy helmeted soldier, supports the second man, who is clearly wounded. The inscription says, *Soldiers Never Die Alone.*

It is a fine sentiment. But in the case of Pete Lynn, who died near where the statue now stands, it is not true.

This is his story, and his family's.

Today, library shelves bulge with books written by and about generals, soldiers, sailors, and airmen who fought, survived, and even thrived during World War II. Tales about men like Louis Zamparini of "Unbroken" fame, or the "Band of Brothers" of Easy Company, 506th Parachute Infantry, 101st Airborne Division, or famous leaders like Eisenhower and Patton are valuable and important, but something is missing from their stories. Veterans will tell you that the real heroes of their war died in the fighting. Unfortunately, we rarely hear much about those we lost. The dead are often faceless and nameless, and their deaths are often unlike the one depicted in the German statue. Yet the story of World War II, as with every war, is as much as anything about what was lost: the men who made the ultimate sacrifice and the families torn harshly asunder. If we ever get the chance to hear from the dead, we need to listen.

Indeed, the dead from that terrible war are legion. Of the 16 million Americans who wore a uniform, more than 400,000 died.[1] Pete Lynn's home state of North Carolina lost more than 7,000 of its citizens, his home county lost 190 men, and his hometown lost 33 dead.[2] Meanwhile, for every dead American, seven Japanese, twenty Germans, and eighty-five Soviets died.[3]

Pete Lynn was just one of the millions of Americans who served in World War II. When he died in the Battle of the Hürtgen Forest, he became just one of the hundreds of thousands of Americans who gave their lives during the war. It is not often that a biography of a common, regular, small-town man and his family appears. This particular man and his family could have been from anywhere, but one thing makes it special: their story is characteristic of so many people from those momentous days. Historian Gary Freeze fondly calls this postage stamp history because it describes tiny, postage-stamp-size places and the people who live there. Their stories are representative of larger historical themes. This book is postage stamp history, about regular people who lived in a small town and fought their own battles, both in Europe and at home, while the world burned around them. Through their eyes, we can see a world that no longer exists, lives that mattered, and a family that sacrificed and endured. We can hear from the dead—and from a man who in one terrible moment was in the forefront of the only offensive along the entire western front.

There is a lot more here besides World War II military and home-front history. At its heart this is a love story, between a man and woman who were made for each other. Meanwhile, Pete Lynn came of age during the Depression, working in a cotton mill in a small town; the story of the harsh existence in a cotton mill is not often told enough today. The way of life he knew then is a story in and of itself. Later, an element of mystery appears in this tale as his wife tries to unravel what happened to her husband. There's even enough irony to satisfy the sardonic.

I first learned about Pete Lynn from his wife. We called her Grandma Ruth. It was 1984, and I had just started dating Ruth's granddaughter. Laurie and I were married six years later, and along the way, I got to know Grandma Ruth much better, along with Ruth's living daughters, Bobbie Blake and Petie Bass. A silver-haired pistol, Ruth had a soft and shaky voice, but she always seemed to have a smile on her face. Her laughter came easily and often and her hugs were warm and firm.

Grandma was quite the character. She was a big baseball fan who lived in a senior residence village in Kings Mountain, North Carolina. On humid summer evenings, she used to sit in her easy chair by the window of her little apartment and watch the Atlanta Braves. She kept the window open so she could chatter about the game with her next-door neighbor.

She had a big and loving heart. When I was doing research for my first book, the need arose to visit the University of South Carolina. Since Kings Mountain is within easy driving distance of Columbia, Laurie and I decided to go see Grandma Ruth. My wife would spend the day with her grandmother while I drove to Columbia. We arrived late on a Friday and settled in for the night. I rose early the next morning so I could get to the archives when it opened. It was still dark outside. I tried not to wake anybody, but Grandma Ruth had other ideas. She met me at the door with a smile on her face and a bag of ham biscuits in her hand.

Later, I learned that Grandma Ruth had lived through some tough times. I did not know the full story then, but it was clear that she had every reason not to smile. She did anyway. When our first child arrived, Laurie suggested we name her after Grandma Ruth, and I was all for it.

We lost Grandma Ruth in 1993. It was just like her to take care of everything. She had already arranged her entire funeral. (I was half expecting a bag of ham biscuits to show up.) As the family gathered at the funeral home and later the cemetery, and she was laid to rest beside Pete, you could not think about Grandma without smiling, even through your tears.

Later, I discovered that Ruth and Pete's story was pretty amazing. It started gnawing on me when Petie showed me an old army duffle bag. Inside that aging, olive drab bag, I saw photos, a medal, and stacks of letters. Some of the letters in the bag were from Pete. Others were addressed to Pete and bore Ruth's return address on them: "Mrs. F.L. Lynn, Park Yarn Mill, Kings Mtn., N.C." On many of these letters, I saw the handwritten word "Missing" and a Return to Sender stamp. That did it; I went to work. First, I examined the content of the bag in detail and noted that some of the letters had not been opened since they were mailed in 1944. I found spelling that was quaintly poor, which I have largely preserved in the pages of this book except for some minor corrections in brackets for the sake of clarity. I also perused Ruth's diary; interviewed neighbors, millhands, friends, family members, and veterans; plowed through military records; and followed Pete's path from Kings Mountain to Germany and back. I was not disappointed. What emerged was a story of sacrifice and love that represents well the common people of those days.

World War II ended decades ago, but in many ways it still isn't over. The Lynn family still feels the loss suffered on a cold, wet day in 1944. Pulitzer Prize–winning author Rick Atkinson once said that his job as a narrative historian is to bring the dead to life. It is my hope that the pages that follow will do just that, and bring to life a brave man and woman so that we can know what they did and what they experienced.

Grandma Ruth, this is for you.

Chris J. Hartley
Pfafftown, North Carolina

I Love You Best of All

Ruth Lynn knew when her husband's workday was over. She could hear him coming.

First came the blast of the mill whistle announcing the end of his shift.[1] Then, as he walked the short distance from the mill to their little three-room gray house in the mill village, glancing occasionally at the distant 1,705-foot monadnock called The Pinnacle, Pete would whistle himself. He stopped only when he stepped onto the porch and opened the front door, ready to kiss Ruth hello.[2]

The man who walked from work to the little mill house[3] every day was not exactly good-looking. He was tall and slim: 150 pounds stretched taut across his six-foot frame.[4] Large ears leaned forward from his head, as if he was trying harder to hear. His long, narrow nose suited his body. Thinning brown hair topped his head. His blue overalls were covered with lint; he was a linthead, a man who spent every day working in thick cotton dust and breathing it too, among machines that could rip skin off a limb in seconds.[5] Hard as it was, the job did not erase his smile.[6] His wry sense of humor probably helped him cope, and his friendly personality made him hard not to like.

His waiting wife was a petite, cute brunette with a winning smile of her own. Her round cheeks, the sort that an overzealous relative might pinch to redness, held her smile like bookends. In Ruth's case, petite did not mean overlooked. She made up for her size with her sweet presence. Her laugh was infectious, and her caring nature was just as easy-going as Pete's. In welcoming Pete home, she probably had lint on her too, if she had not changed out of her mill clothes yet.[7]

For lintheads in the 1930s, life was better than it had been a decade before—but better was a relative term. They lived in a drab, postage stamp

A young Pete Lynn
Source: Lynn Collection

of a house that had morning glories sprawling across its trellis. Their house sat in a small town, where not much was going on. Their world scarcely stretched past the county line. Their jobs were monotonous and hard and barely paid a living wage. Very little came easy.

But Pete and Ruth did not see it that way.

Good friends surrounded them. So did parents, brothers, sisters, and cousins, who would be there in a heartbeat if needed. Not to mention their church family, and their God, in whom they believed deeply.

Pete and Ruth had dreams too: dreams of a better life—of a white house and a big yard surrounded by a picket fence. Most of all, they had each other.

For Pete, that was enough to whistle about.

———

Felmer Lonzo Lynn—thankfully, he went by Pete—was "born and reared near Kings Mtn," as Ruth later put it. He arrived on October 7, 1910, and had lived in Kings Mountain, North Carolina, ever since. Ruth was born in the next county in the town of Spencer Mountain. Her grandparents still lived there, but she had ended up in Kings Mountain too. She was five years younger than Pete, having greeted the world on November 4, 1915.[8]

Kings Mountain was, the local newspaper often proclaimed, "The Best Town in The State." It was on the map for one reason: the railroad, whose double lines split the main street right down the middle. Kings Mountain was incorporated on February 11, 1874, not long after workers drove the last spike into that section of the Atlanta and Richmond Air Line. A patriotic resident named the whistle stop after the Revolutionary War battle of Kings Mountain, which had been fought on October 7, 1780, just across the South Carolina line along a ridge that extends from The Pinnacle. Exactly 130 years later, Pete Lynn came along.[9]

Pete and Ruth lived in Kings Mountain for one reason: jobs. Textile jobs, to be exact. The railroad brought those jobs. The town's first mill appeared in the late 1880s, and cotton mill after cotton mill followed. The mills popped up beside the grade, where the yarns they produced could easily be loaded onto rail cars and shipped to market behind a huffing and puffing engine. Just a decade into the twentieth century, the count of mills reached double digits.[10] More people came and more mills were built; by 1938, nearly six thousand people lived in Kings Mountain, and two dozen mills were humming away in the town and surrounding countryside.[11]

It is hardly surprising that the textile industry thrived in Kings Mountain because it flourished across the South after the Civil War. That was especially true of the North Carolina Piedmont, which journalist Arthur W. Page once described as "one long mill village."[12] This was particularly clear to one visitor driving the state's byways. When the

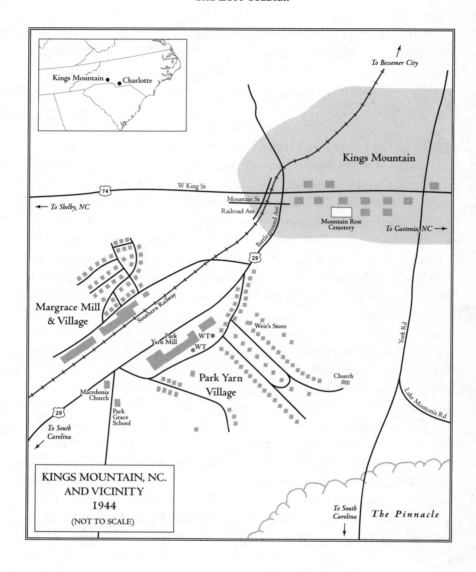

KINGS MOUNTAIN, NC.
AND VICINITY
1944
(NOT TO SCALE)

man pulled into a filling station to refuel, he couldn't help but query the attendant. "What do all these mills make, buddy?" he asked. "Never saw as many strung along one highway in all my life. Been passing 'em ever since we left Greensboro."[13]

Mills boomed because farms foundered. Declining crop prices, and failed crops from bad weather or pests, drove people away from field and furrow. Company recruiters, or family, or friends, told of the mills' steady paychecks, regular hours, and easier work—at least compared to plowing behind a mule. So farmers by the thousands traded their plows for the mill villages and went to work. In due course, North Carolina overtook New England as the leading textile producer in the country, with more than three hundred mills and over 50,000 workers statewide.[14] That included 2,145 workers in Kings Mountain alone.[15]

For Pete and Ruth, life revolved around two cotton mills: Park Yarn and Margrace. Although they were run by different companies, Park Yarn and Margrace might as well have been a single complex. Only State Highway 29 and the twin gleaming tracks of the Southern Railway separated them. They even looked a little bit alike, since both took architectural inspiration from New England mills. Woods and pastures surrounded the mills, while inside the two complexes it was equally open save for scattered chinaberry, oak, and maple trees.[16] Their location, some two miles southwest of Kings Mountain, was textbook: mill owners liked to build their factories away from towns to avoid taxes and separate employees from the potentially negative influences of town.[17]

Most workers lived in the villages that the mill spawned. The Lynns lived in one of the sixty-four houses in Park Yarn Village, arranged in an orderly fashion along oval streets that framed the mill complex.[18] That meant you couldn't really get away. The factory buildings of Margrace and Park Yarn were always there, wherever you went, every time you opened your front door. If you went to school, or to shop, or even to play, the buildings loomed, like sentinels, watching and waiting for another workday to begin. In the daylight, you could not miss the buildings; they were the biggest structures in sight. Streetlights kept the mill from disappearing completely after dark, but even if the mills were hidden from view you knew they were still there, black and large. The seductive humming of the machines told you so. This was all Pete and Ruth knew. "Growing up in a cotton mill village was a unique experience, probably unlike any other anywhere in the country," wrote one former Park Yarn man. "I read somewhere, 'You can take a boy out of the cotton mill village, but you can't keep lint from returning to his navel.'"[19]

Both Pete and Ruth had lint in their navels from birth. They passed their nonage in the shadow of those mill buildings and attended Park

Grace, the school that the mills shared. Built in 1928 to serve the children of both mills, the school stood next to Park Yarn and across the highway from Margrace.[20] Park Grace was no one-room wooden schoolhouse: it was a one-story brick building with white trim and a dozen rooms. Every school day, students crossed the narrow grass lawn in front, bounded up the school's five concrete steps, and passed through a rococo entranceway with double doors framed by four white columns, which held an open pediment atop a narrow entablature. Inside the pediment, the curved words "Park Grace School" proudly proclaimed both the sponsors and the purpose of the building. After entering, children found a classroom for each grade waiting for them. Four classrooms were in the front of the building, while three classrooms and a cafeteria were in the back. Pete attended the school through the sixth grade. Ruth made it through all seven of Park Grace's grades and then went on to Kings Mountain High School for two years.[21]

The fact that Ruth attended high school at all was a small miracle. Most mill schools were not part of North Carolina's town and county school systems. To avoid paying local taxes, mill companies typically subsidized their own schools. They often built the buildings and funded the teachers' salaries. That made the schools extensions of the factory.[22] Mill schools were free for mill families. The bad news came after the seventh grade, when Park Grace's curriculum ended. Under state law, children who had attended mill schools could study for four more years in a town or county high school, but not for free. They had to pay tuition. Most mill families could not afford that, so only 3 percent of students from mill schools went on to high school during the 1920s. Pete was not among them, but Ruth's family somehow managed to send her.[23]

When school was done, it was time to go to work. Pete started soon after he turned twelve years old. He did a stint at Cannon Mills in Kannapolis, North Carolina, about fifty miles northwest of Kings Mountain, but he spent most of his working life at Margrace and Park Yarn. That was the case for Ruth too.[24]

The larger of the two was Margrace Mill. People said the mill sat on a hill, but in truth it wasn't much of a hill at all. Charles Eugene Neisler was the man behind Margrace. He learned the business from his father, who ran a mill during the Civil War, and his father-in-law, who built Kings Mountain's first textile mill. In 1910, he founded Neisler Mills Inc. with a $10,000 loan from the wife of a local whiskey distiller, who unceremoniously pulled the money out of a large crockery jug. Small wonder that Neisler liked to name his mills after women. One was named for his wife, Pauline, and another for Patricia, wife of a company salesman. Neisler went on to acquire other mills in both North and South Carolina, but Margrace, built in 1919, was his crown jewel. Named after his two oldest daughters, Margaret and Grace, the mill manufactured bedspreads, tablecloths, and napkins. Neisler died in 1931, and his son, Charles E. Neisler Jr. took over, but Margrace and its parent company kept growing. More than four dozen houses, two apartment buildings, a stone-masonry clubhouse, and a two-story brick company store sprouted around Margrace, while the company's five mills and three affiliated spinning mills eventually produced 10 million yards of textiles annually. For its part, Margrace became one of the country's largest manufacturers of table napkins, with an output of 200,000 napkins a week. It even made the facing for the three-ton golden curtain at Radio City Music Hall.[25]

Pete only worked briefly at Margrace. Ruth started after her high school days, probably around her fifteenth birthday, and stayed throughout the 1930s. Like all women, she worked during the day. Regulations prevented nighttime work for women, mostly so that mothers could be home before school was dismissed. Ruth became a napkin hemmer: she sat at a sewing machine and hemmed napkins all day. Thanks to her job, in later life Ruth could wield a sewing machine like a paintbrush.[26]

Pete left Margrace for Park Yarn and worked there for fifteen years. Exactly when Park Yarn was built is unclear. Even the *Kings Mountain Herald* admitted that "information about the Park Yarn Mills Company is not very plentiful." Some records suggest it went up around the turn of the century, but it came into its own during World War I thanks to surging cotton demand. The Park Yarn Mills Company was incorporated on September 18, 1919, apparently after the original entity was sold. Its leadership included Charles Worth Johnston of Charlotte, a textile magnate in his own right, and Jacob C. Keller, superintendent. You might say that Park Yarn was Margrace's little sister. It was a single-ply operation

Pete Lynn beside Park Yarn Mill
Source: Lynn Collection

with about 175 employees and only fifteen thousand spindles that spun and twisted cotton into coarse single and plied yarns.[27]

The main mill building that Pete walked to every day was two stories tall. Its walls were made of red brick and mortar, its roof of tar and gravel. Outside stood two tall steel water towers, including one that held 5,000 gallons. Beneath, a rail siding connected a warehouse to the main line of the Southern Railway and passed a small water reservoir on the way. Inside one found pine-and-wood floors and walls painted mill white with paint from the Gilman Paint and Varnish Company. The mill even had indoor plumbing, complete with urinals in the men's restroom, as well as water fountains.[28]

Both Park Yarn and Margrace followed a manufacturing process that would have been familiar to any mill worker. The first step was opening and picking. In the opening room, workers removed binding from cotton bales and loaded them into machines that opened the bales, removed dirt, and fluffed the cotton. Next, the cotton was sent to the picker room, where pickers (or lappers) continued picking dirt out of the cotton and used machines to press it into flat sheets. In the card room, card hands fed sheets into carding machines, which had sharp teeth that removed more dirt, straightened cotton fibers, and turned sheets into a fluffy rope called a sliver. Next, the sliver was coiled into tall cans and sent on for further processing. That included drawing out, roving, and spinning, where slivers were thinned into single strands, twisted, and wound very tight. Spoolers then combined the yarn onto bobbins and wound the yarn into balls, or wrapped it around cones or onto reels for use in cloth making.[29]

The card room, spindles, and combers as well as some spinning frames were situated on the first floor, while the warper, spinning frames, and

A card room in a North Carolina mill
Source: North Carolina Digital Collections, State Library of North Carolina

twisters sat on the second.[30] Pete was a card hand, so he worked on the ground floor. In his words, he would "grind them old cards" for hours on end. Carding was a man's world. It required both skill and physical strength.[31] This was no antiseptic manufacturing environment; the card room was a place of dust, noise, and even danger. With machinery all around tearing at cotton, dust filled the card room. It settled on clothes, on hair, and on equipment; it crept into pores, into mouths, and finally into lungs. "Some of that dust was terrible," recalled Carl Durham, who worked in the card room of another mill. "Whew! That dust would accumulate and you had to strip them cards out every three hours, get all that stuff out. . . . It's a wonder I can breathe." Breathing the dust affected people differently. Some eventually contracted brown lung disease. "See, there was a continuous fog of dust in the carding department at all times," remembered another card hand, Grover Hardin. "When you hit the mill on Monday morning, you would have a tough time. You'd cough and sneeze and fill your mouth full of tobacco and anything else to keep the dust from strangling you."[32]

Carding was "the most dangerousest job in the mill," another man explained. Equipment with sharp teeth, pulleys, and belts surrounded the employees. "You'd have to watch yourself," remembered Carl Thompson. "There were so many things that you could do. Even cleaning up, if maybe your brush would get caught in a belt or pulley, it's going to jerk your hand. I've seen them jerked in the cards thataway and maybe get their whole arm and all broke and the skin pulled off, maybe slam through the bone."[33]

"The whole place was kind of dangerous," Park Yarn employee R. C. Pearson agreed. Born in 1927, Pearson lived in house number 32 on the middle row. He had moved to Park Yarn with his family in 1936 and attended Park Grace school before going to work at both Margrace and Park Yarn. He remembered the mill's belt drive system, powered first by steam and later by electricity, winding across the ceiling like a spider-web. Leather belts, each one about 3 inches wide and a quarter inch thick, stretched down to every machine. "If one would break it would go flopping around," he said.[34]

No matter where you went in Margrace, Park Yarn, or any other mill, you would also encounter thick dust, lint, heat, and humidity. To help control the heat, Park Yarn ran humidifiers that constantly filled the air with a cool mist.[35] Noise was just as pervasive, if not more so. "Working in a cotton mill town in the thirties and early forties was a nerve-racking experience," explained one man, whose father worked in a mill. "Throughout the mills, rumbling overhead shafts turned a belt and pulley system which, when combined with the whine of thousands of whirring spindles on the machines, produced a deafening roar that bombarded the mill hand long before he entered the workplace," he wrote. "The noise, which turned every conversation among the workers into a shouting match, was so much a part of the work environment."[36]

Each room housed a different step in the process, and each was a place of repetition as well: mind-numbing, unending repetition. Whatever your job, you did it over and over and over again. Chester Copeland, another North Carolina resident, described working in a mill as "nothing but a robot life." It was "just like [being] on a treadmill. There's no challenge to it—just drudgery. The more you do, the more they want done."[37]

Pete and Ruth Lynn came of age in an America on the verge of the Depression. Pete had just turned nineteen when the stock market crashed. Some historians have suggested that those Black Days only marked the beginning of the economic crisis but did not cause it since most Americans, including Pete and Ruth, owned no stock. Kings Mountain and the Lynns probably did not notice the gathering storm at all until 1930 when rural banks in many states, including North Carolina, began failing, and depositors flocked to teller windows to demand their money.[38]

By 1931, the Depression arrived full force nationwide, despite the well-intentioned efforts of President Herbert Hoover's administration. Unemployment spread like wildfire. The landscape was soon dotted with what Pulitzer Prize–winning historian David Kennedy has called "tarpaper-and-cardboard hobo shantytowns." None of these Hoovervilles appeared in Kings Mountain where the cotton mills still hummed, if uncertainly.[39]

On November 8, 1932, Franklin Roosevelt was elected president, and the following March he took office. When he rolled his wheelchair up to the *Resolute* desk, made from the timbers of a British ship, crisis waited in his inbox. The Depression had shredded America with the efficiency of the teeth on a card-room machine: some $7 billion in bank deposits had evaporated, 600,000 homeowners had lost their property, and 25 percent of the workforce had been furloughed. The Depression did not affect everyone in the same way, but to be sure it affected just about everybody. "To borrow from Tolstoy," wrote Kennedy, "every unhappy family was unhappy in its own way."[40]

Roosevelt answered, in the words of the Psalmist, with thunder. During the first, legendary Hundred Days of his administration, he introduced a flood of legislation to battle the Depression. Some fifteen bills were signed into law. "Taken together, the accomplishments of the 'Hundred Days' constituted a masterpiece of presidential leadership unexampled then and unmatched since," wrote historian Kennedy.[41]

Roosevelt's legislative volleys reverberated all the way to Margrace Mill and Park Yarn. For generations, if the noise, heat, dust, danger, and repetition of textile jobs were not enough, the textile industry had also promised long hours and low pay. Workers typically put in six twelve-hour days each week, and children worked alongside their parents, with many kids—Pete included—starting work in the mill full-time by the age of twelve. In return, workers could expect little, as Southern millhands were ranked among the lowest paid industrial workers in the country.[42] This began to change on June 16, 1933, when Roosevelt signed the National Industrial Recovery Act (NIRA) into law. Among the act's major components was federal regulation of maximum hours and minimum wages in several industries. In textiles, the act instituted a minimum wage of $12 per week, a forty-hour workweek, prohibited child labor, and approved collective bargaining. Another outgrowth was a new government agency, the National Recovery Administration (NRA), which was charged with overseeing production, prices, and wages in various industries.[43]

The Lynns thus saw both ends of the spectrum: long workdays and lower wages early in their careers, and then a transition to shorter hours and somewhat better pay. By the time 1940 arrived, Pete was working forty hours a week and Ruth just thirty-two hours. The Lynns also benefitted from the new wage rules, but only because it established a floor for the amount of their paychecks. In her job as a napkin hemmer, Ruth made $620 in 1940, while Pete made $624 as a card hand.[44] That amounted to a mere thirty cents an hour, or about $12 a week. Although this was an improvement from the years before New Deal laws went into effect, it was still minimum wage and arguably not even a living wage. According to one study, that fell short of the minimum needed for someone to avoid starvation—and the state of North Carolina did not help matters when it instituted a 3 percent sales tax in 1933.[45] (By contrast, Pete made less than half of the national average for a manufacturing worker, and far less than the $3,640 annual salary of Park Yarn superintendent Keller.[46])

The experience of one textile worker illustrates the problem. In a letter to the *Charlotte Observer*, the man explained his budget woes: start with $12 a week, and then subtract $8.40 for groceries, $1.50 for rent, another $1.00 for fuel, and $1.10 for insurance. That left exactly zero—nothing for medical bills, schoolbooks, clothes, and certainly not for luxuries. Nothing. The Lynns' expenses were greater still when children came along.[47] Yet thanks to dual incomes, the Lynns managed and even saved enough to buy a bedroom set. The red cherry chest of drawers, ornate makeup table and mirror, and simple bed boards must have been the pride of Ruth Lynn, even though her husband's feet dangled off the end of the short bed.[48]

The nation's income tax also had some impact on the Lynns. Since the minimum taxable level for a married couple was $2,000 per year, few households paid anything at all. The Lynns did pay taxes thanks to some odd jobs Pete took to supplement their mill income. The Lynns would also have seen their take-home pay shrink in January 1937 when payroll tax deductions began for the new Social Security system.[49]

The Lynns could take solace in the fact that they did have something many Americans did not. As financial historian Amity Shlaes once recorded, a saying at the time held that the Depression was not so bad if you had a job.[50] "When the millhands lay in bed in the dead of night," one millhand recalled, "they could hear the mills humming seductively, the sound providing the comforting knowledge that upon arising in the morning they had work." The only exception was Sunday, when the mills shut down and quiet settled over the complex. The lack of noise gave millhands "a strange uneasiness at the pervasive stillness," a mill town resident recalled.[51]

The decade of the 1930s was a difficult one for the textile industry. With new laws restricting hours and liberalizing wages, many mill owners cut hours, pushed their employees harder, and installed new, more efficient equipment. Other mill owners just avoided the problem altogether; as one textile union representative wrote, "no mills I know of are living up to the code." Layoffs hit many mill towns. For their part, workers answered. Some moved from mill to mill in search of better opportunities. Others organized and protested, and labor conflict rose across the South. By September 1934, strikes hit textile mills from New England to the Carolinas. Unrest came as close as neighboring Gastonia, which saw outbreaks of violence, protests, and a strike not long before Ruth started work.[52] Yet if the Lynns were among the dissatisfied, it has not come down across the years. Unlike many millhands of the times, Pete and Ruth showed no signs of restlessness. If they complained, it has been forgotten. Pete's real feelings about his life and job can be seen in how he responded later, when he found himself unexpectedly far from home: he spoke fondly of "Old Park Yarn" and dreamed of returning to the card room.

Low pay, repetitive jobs, and a harsh working world—Pete and Ruth had all of that. They were lintheads. But Pete knew the secret. Money, he observed, "[tain't] all that counts." Instead, Pete told Ruth, it "is love that makes the world go Round that is what makes yours and my go around sugar."[53]

<hr />

Love for each other they had, and in abundance—but the fact that Pete Lynn and Ruth Hawkins fell in love and got married was not unpredictable. They came together the same way just about everyone else did at Park Yarn or Margrace or any cotton mill for that matter: because of the closeness of the place. "We knowed each other from childhood," a millhand recalled. "Just raised up, you might say, together. All lived here on the hill, you see. That's how we met."[54]

Exactly how Pete and Ruth met is not known, but it certainly happened in or near the mill complexes. Perhaps it was at church, or the company store, or at school. Most likely, it happened at Margrace. Given their age difference, they probably did not pay each other much attention in their early years. However they met, their romantic interest in each other was hatched around 1931. Ruth was only sixteen at the time, and just starting work at the mill. Pete, already a mill veteran, noticed the cute brunette and decided he liked her.

In those days, card-room dust, tobacco, and the cares of adulthood had not worn on Pete just yet. He had an unquestionable touch of dash. His blue eyes shone from beneath a pair of bushy eyebrows. He kept his hair cut short, high above his ever-prominent ears, and slicked back, although his bare forehead hinted that his hair would not be around long. Pete was as wiry then as he would be later, but he hid it beneath the clothing of a dapper dresser—or at least he did away from the mill.

Petite and a bit dowdy, her hair parted to one side and doffed well above her neck, Ruth was every bit of a catch. What she lacked in height she made up for in spunk. At one point, she decided that her name was missing something, so she decided to tack Evelyn on to make it sound more elegant. In later years, she decided it had been a foolish thing to do, especially when she had to fill out paperwork and that extra name took longer.

Their courtship would have been closely supervised. Dating in mill villages followed a pattern. On Wednesdays, young men visited girls' homes, often with parents, brothers, and sisters around to keep an eye on them. On Saturdays, parents organized parties for girls and boys. Sundays revolved around church.[55] It must have worked, for Pete could not get her out of his mind during a trip to the North Carolina mountains that summer of 1931. As he walked the shores of Lake Junaluska, its blue waters shimmering and with tall, green, tree-covered mountains looking down on him, Pete decided to buy a souvenir and send it to her.[56]

The advent of automobiles changed dating. It enabled mill village couples to get away from the tight control of their families and enjoy picnics or outings to the mountains or parks.[57] Occasionally, Pete managed to borrow a car[58] or ride with friends so he and Ruth could take a few road trips. On one date, Pete, Ruth, and another couple drove to Bessemer City where they picked flowers and talked and laughed.[59] By the end of 1932, the two had a growing relationship. The Christmas season was special for the couple. On a Christmas card from Pete, Ruth jotted, "Best Xmas ever—and how!" They were still going strong a year later, when Pete gave Ruth a black leather pocketbook and gloves for Christmas.[60]

They were in love, with palms sweating and hearts pounding, but they lived in a time when people did not show it in public. Displays of affection came rushing in their rare moments alone, such as the night they went for a walk. It was dark, and nobody was around. They stopped at a railroad crossing, probably the one where the Park Yarn spur joined the main Southern Railway line a short distance northeast of the villages. As the rails at their feet glinted in the moonlight, Pete took Ruth in his arms and started singing. He liked to do that. His favorite was "I Love You Best of All," a song that had been around for years. "I love your eyes your fingertips, I love to kiss your dear sweet lips," he sang. "I love to hold you close to my heart, for I love you the best of all."[61]

He meant it. Another favorite song was "Carolina Moon," but its canorous words did not mean to the couple now what they would mean later:[62]

The moon was shining bright in Carolina
The night we said good-bye so tenderly
And now that I'm away from Carolina
Won't somebody tell the moon for me
Carolina moon
Keep shining
Shining on the one who waits for me
Carolina moon I'm pining
Pining for the place I long to be

How I'm hoping tonight you'll go
Go to the right window
Scatter your light say I'm all right please do
Tell her that I'm blue and lonely
Dreamy Carolina moon

There were all too few private moments. When they happened, Pete would "wonder what was going to happen next and then it would Happen[,]" he later wrote. Temptations came rushing at such times, but the couple did decide to wait to consummate their relationship when they got married.[63]

In those Depression-laden days, many young people put off marriage; by 1933, the marriage rate had fallen 22 percent in just four years.[64] Pete and Ruth ignored the trend but still waited to tie the knot until they could do so without parental permission. The day finally arrived on February 24, 1934. The venue was the twenty-room Mountain View Hotel at the corner of Railroad and Mountain Streets in Kings Mountain. While the hotel's stove radiated heat and its overhead electric lights glowed, the Rev. Harold M. Robinson, pastor of Park Grace Methodist Church, officiated. Pete and Ruth decided to keep the occasion discreet, so the wedding party was small. Only one of Ruth's sisters came. Three friends rounded out the party: Woodrow Wise, Lillian Eskew, and Rella Boheler. Pete was handsome and confident in his suit, tie, and white wingtip shoes; Ruth, petite as ever, wore a dress with a floral pattern and a white overcoat against the chill.[65]

There would be no honeymoon. It was right back to the mill for the couple. In fact, Pete and Ruth did not even tell their parents that they were now man and wife, and they did not live together.[66] It was only after they were caught holding hands in

The wedding party. Top, left to right: Pete, Rev. Robinson, Woodrow Wise. Bottom, left to right: Ruth, Eva Lynn, Lillian Eskew, and Rella Boheler
Source: Lynn Collection

public and people started asking questions that the truth came to light. Even then, Ruth remained reserved about their new relationship. The first night they stayed together, she asked Pete if she could turn out the light before they made love.[67]

Whoever got home from work first would cook supper.[68] The Lynns did not come home to much; they lived in one of the sixty-four houses the mill owned, just up the street from the main Park Yarn building. In those days, it was typical for cotton mills to provide employees with housing. Small towns like Kings Mountain did not have a large enough population to keep the mills going, so company housing helped mills draw workers from farms and outlying villages. It also gave the mill some control beyond the factory walls.[69]

The houses, made of plain weatherboard siding, sat on tiny lots along dirt streets. At Margrace, the streets were laid out in the same grid-like pattern seen in other mill villages. Park Yarn's houses stood along both sides of a road that curved behind the mill like a half moon, or alongside streets that branched off the main road. Tall, silver steel water towers lorded over both complexes. Wooden poles dotted the area and electrical lines hung tautly between them, connecting the factories and houses to some unseen distant power source. It was, a historian wrote, a place with a "strong character of sameness and repetition" that perfectly mirrored the repetitive jobs performed inside the mill buildings.[70] To journalist Lorena Hickok, dispatched from Washington to take firsthand stock of the Depression's sway, mill villages like these were "neat, if monotonous."[71]

But it was home for Pete and Ruth. Inside his little three-room cottage at "old Park," Pete liked sitting in his sway back chair.[72] The couple had lived there, paying $2 a month in rent, since at least 1935 but more likely since shortly after their wedding day.[73] The front room was where Pete sat in his chair and propped up his size 10½ feet. The bedroom and kitchen made up the rest of the house, except for a pantry and small front and back porch. That was it; there was little closet space, no indoor plumbing, and no telephone. You had to go to the well for water and to an outhouse to relieve yourself. When it came time to wash clothes, an iron pot waited in the backyard. Residents had to rely on a single fireplace for heat, but it could not always do the job. As a former Park Yarn resident joked, "A mill house couldn't be heated with a pipeline direct from hell."[74] Small wonder that Ruth, a cold-natured person even on hot days, called Pete her bed warmer.[75]

If the Lynns' mill house was typical, one could also expect to see a bare floor and a few other modest furnishings such as a dresser and some chairs. Knowing Ruth, there was probably a sewing machine sitting in the corner. Wall decorations likely included "the enlarged portraits of deceased relatives," a calendar, a Blum's almanac, and a few other framed pictures. That would be about it, except for maybe a small clock, any medicine Pete or Ruth needed, and a swing on the porch.[76]

If Park Yarn's residents had a luxury, it was electricity. They enjoyed access to electricity twenty-four hours a day, which was not the case with other mill villages. For the residents of Park Yarn that meant light after dark glowing uncertainly from electric streetlights and from plain overhead fixtures inside the houses. It also meant electric fans on hot summer days, and even entertainment by way of a radio or perhaps a Victrola.[77] By 1930, about 40 percent of Americans had radios, and the Lynns were among them. Charlotte's WBT-AM radio was the powerhouse in the region, and the Lynns tuned in regularly. No doubt they listened to Amos 'n' Andy, baseball games, and presidential addresses. Since the Lynns were fond of music, WBT's Saturday night programming, which included the Grand Ole Opry and local musician performances, certainly attracted them. Their favorite was Grady Cole, WBT's lovable and popular radio personality. Cole was so popular that across the southeast everything from babies to pigs, chickens, cows, horses, ducks, and other barnyard creatures had been named after him. He spoke with a "combination Will Rogers-Bob Burns drawl" and a "deep, slow, drawling voice," came across "as relaxed as a wet dishrag," and started each show with "Good morrrrrrrrning." Pete and Ruth loved listening to Cole's antics during his 7:00–9:00 A.M. Grady Cole Sunday Farm Club, which featured WBT's best talent and agriculture news.[78]

It wasn't much, but their Park Yarn village home was a place where Pete and Ruth could make memories. And they did.

———

The Lynns lived in a tight-knit world full of family, friends, and fellow congregants. "It was kind of a cliché: You grew up here and you knew everybody," recalled one millhand. "It was like one big family, and we all hung together and survived. It was a two hundred-headed family. Everybody on this hill, we looked after one another."[79]

Ruth did not have to look farther for support than her parents, W. Avery and Flossie Hawkins. Although he only had a third-grade education, Mr. Hawkins had done all right for himself. He worked at Margrace as a loom fixer, which historians in the seminal book *Like a Family* describe as among "the most autonomous and prestigious

Ruth (left) with her sisters, left to right: Mae, Betty, and Donna
Source: Lynn Collection

jobs in the mill." Thanks to his salary of $936 a year, Mrs. Hawkins could play the traditional role of homemaker. Besides Ruth, another Hawkins child had already left home: twenty-two-year-old Hazel was married and living with her husband Vic and their first child, Vickie. That did not mean that Mrs. Hawkins did not have her hands full. There was nine-year-old Betty Sue, eleven-year-old Donna Fay, and fourteen-year-old Joe. Another daughter, eighteen-year-old Mae, was also still living at home. She was the best-educated member of the family, having gone to school through the ninth grade. Now she worked at the mill as a battery filler. She was also Ruth's best friend.[80] Mae already had her eye on a young man, George C. Smith. She and Smitty planned to get married soon.

The Hawkins family lived in Margrace Village, but they also owned a farm out on Hoyle Road with a barn, a mule, a cow, and a garden. Farming was in Avery Hawkins' blood. His parents—Grandma and Grandpa Hawkins to Ruth—still lived on a farm in Spencer Mountain. Mr. Hawkins looked forward to quitting the mill one day and moving out to the farm, and he and Mrs. Hawkins stayed there occasionally, but as his youngest daughter Betty recalled, "He realized he couldn't make a living farming." For now, he kept fixing looms and leased some of the land.[81]

Pete's parents, Mr. and Mrs. C. C. "Charlie" and Ada Lynn, also lived in the Margrace Mill community, just a half block from the mill at 110 Fulton Drive. Their house, built about 1920, was a four-room, one-story weatherboard frame house with a brick chimney standing in the middle.[82] To this day, Ada is remembered as a wonderful cook. Her specialty was apple pie. Charlie was an inspector at the mill, for which he was paid $676 a year. He was a frail, little man, but everyone in the family agreed that he was "a bird." He liked to take a drink every now and then, so he kept some liquor hidden in the half basement. "Mama took care of him, though," Pete's brother later recalled. One day Charlie started punishing Bill for some indiscretion. Ada intervened. "You better not hit him," she told her husband. "Good Lord strike you down."[83]

Pete's parents were there for him, but there came a time when Pete had to be there for Charlie and Ada. That came on December 1, 1938, when their house caught fire. The roof was a complete loss, all of the furniture inside was destroyed, and the structure was badly damaged. Fire officials said the fire started in the oil stove. It made for a tough Christmas and forced Charlie and Ada to lean on their family, however reluctantly.[84]

Pete had three sisters named Lillian, Eva, and Marene, or Rene for short. He was close to all of them, but Rene most of all. One of their favorite things to do was to beat the heat of summer by going swimming together at Lake Crawford. The 13-acre lake was a part of Kings Mountain State Park, which was just across the state line in South Carolina. The park was developed during the 1930s by the Civilian Conservation Corps

Pete, Ruth, and a friend at Lake Crawford
Source: Lynn Collection

(CCC), one of President Franklin D. Roosevelt's New Deal programs that was designed to help combat the Great Depression.[85]

Pete also had a brother named J. C., but nobody knew what those initials stood for so he went by Bill. Although Bill was nine years younger than Pete, they got along very well, and hunted together often. Both Pete and Bill grew into tall men, but the similarities stopped there. "He was a good Christian man," Bill later said of his brother. "I was a roundabout man." Some went so far as to call him Wild Bill from Margrace Hill. On one occasion, Bill got into trouble for climbing one of Park Yarn's two water towers, which was off limits to such antics. Otherwise, Bill followed the pattern. He went to school through the eighth grade and then went to work as a dyer at the mill.[86]

Ruth's parents' farm was their refuge away from the ever-present, looming mill buildings. They loved to visit whenever they could.[87] The farm was also a great place to hunt. Pete, often with Bill in tow, would hunt for rabbit or squirrel.[88] And even if Pete could not get away, Ruth would sometimes spend the night at the farm with her parents anyway.

In those cases, Pete was always glad when she got home because he missed her terribly.[89]

To Pete Lynn, animals were family members too. He loved animals. He and Ruth owned two dogs named Joe and Bill. They were hunting dogs, and sometimes the high-spirited hounds got so carried away that Pete had to take a stick after them, but he never left home without keeping tabs on them.[90] Pete was also fond of Toodle, a little white dog that belonged to the Hawkins. Toodle looked nothing like a hunting dog, but he did not act that way. He was good at it, so Pete sometimes took him along on his own hunts.[91] If Pete loved any critter more than dogs, it was horses. He could not afford to own one himself, but he knew three different men—Charlie Hawkins, Mr. Ballard, and Mr. Walker—who did. Those men let Pete ride their horses just about every night after supper.[92]

Church offered Pete and Ruth another sanctuary against the trials of life. In those days, Kings Mountain was a "Sunday School Going Town," the *Herald* bragged, with over 38 percent of residents enrolled. The Lynns attended Macedonia Baptist Church. Although the church was not located inside either mill village, and was not officially a part of either mill, Macedonia might as well have been. Organized in 1920 and built on an old parcel of farmland, Macedonia stood across the street from Park Grace School and next door to Park Yarn. The clang of its bell added comforting notes to the whistle hum of the mills and the chugging of passing trains.[93]

It was common for mills to be deeply entwined with local churches. Many mills owned church buildings and even paid for minister salaries, church utilities, and church maintenance. Neither Park Yarn nor Margrace seems to have been quite so linked to Macedonia, but the companies certainly held some sway on the congregation. Employees of both mills worshipped there, and that doubtless included mill management, while from the pulpit sermons would exhort members to value hard work and thank God for their place in life, however menial and humble their roles may be.[94] The Hawkins family was prominent among Macedonia's membership. Ruth's dad was a deacon and had even helped build the church, while Ruth occupied her favorite pew every Sunday.

Pete was not beside her as often as Ruth would have liked. He believed in God, but it was hard to get Pete to church. If chores did not beckon, there were always rabbits to be hunted, fish to be caught, or horses to be ridden.[95]

There was at least plenty of opportunity for Pete to get to church, and Ruth managed to get him there when she could. Initially under the leadership of pastor Paul Horne and then pastor J. V. Frederick, Macedonia's services on Sunday began at 9:45 A.M. with Sunday School, followed by preaching at 11 A.M., Baptist Training Union at 5:45 P.M., and evening worship at 7:00 P.M. There were also services during the week, with prayer meetings on both Tuesday and Wednesday evenings. The church also sponsored a number of special groups and opportunities for study and worship. The Women's Missionary Union was a popular ladies' group devoted to the study and sponsorship of Baptist missions; surely, Ruth attended some if not all of its meetings. In March 1935, the church also brought to its flock an all-night prayer service that saw a number of ministers pounding on the pulpit, to be followed by an equally moving revival. Later, on a winter Sunday in 1937, the church welcomed Rev. R. L. Slater, a missionary from China, to its spate of services.[96]

Something as simple as shopping even connected mill residents. Although the concept of company stores was on the decline when Pete came of age, both Margrace and Park Yarn still had one. With many mills located outside towns, company stores saved workers from having to go into town to shop. Company stores also kept workers tied to the mills, as they could buy goods through paycheck deduction or on credit against future paychecks. The resulting debt weighed heavily on minimum wage earners. At one mill, people swore that the frogs along the river could be heard croaking "balance due, balance due" every payday.[97]

Company stores catered to just about every need and want imaginable. As one millhand recalled,

When you entered the store from the front, on the right there was a soda fountain, a glass showcase for candy, a sturdy wooden counter that concealed pullout bins of bulk sugar, rice, and beans, and wall shelves laded with canned goods, cigarettes, and snuff. Running nearly the length of the store on the

*left were showcases where dry good items were displayed and shelves loaded
with bolts of cloth, blue denim shirts, overalls, and other items. In the center
near the first support beam was a showcase that displayed an odd assortment
of items (for example, knives, harmonicas, and yo-yos) that seemed rarely to
change. Occupying the rear was a large showcase for fresh meats, principally
pork and beef, behind which were a chopping block and a walk-in freezer for
storage.[98]*

The Park Yarn store, at the end of the street that curved around the mill,
was among the most popular in Kings Mountain. The reason was thirty-
eight-year-old Ted Weir, the store operator. Weir's store had just about
everything a resident needed: gasoline; kerosene; hardware; staples like
meat, milk, canned goods, and vegetables; and clothing such as overalls
and long johns. Weir would also bring milk and hoop cheese right to your
doorstep. Merchandise aside, the store was probably more important as a
place where the locals—men more so than women—came to swap stories
and share a Coca-Cola, Pepsi, or Nehi out of the icebox. Ted himself was
a community fixture. He was not tall but he had a big belly, over which
he wore a white apron. He had opinions to share; that was true even
before he left home where he argued with his wife over their last name.
He pronounced it Ware, but Josephine, a librarian at the high school,
pronounced it Weir. The store was also a busy place on weekends. It was
also not unusual for company stores to stay open late on Saturday nights
so that customers could come and snack, drink, and play music or a game
of checkers. At one point Pete worked at Weir's store himself, but he was
always a customer. "Before the war, Pete Lynn used to pay me a nickel to
go to Ted's store for him," a mill resident recalled.[99] Ruth trusted Weir so
much that later she asked Ted to size up a suitor for one of the girls. "He
was a great guy. He helped mom so much," Bobbie remembered of the
storekeeper.[100]

If Weir's store did not have it, millhands could look in town. Logan
Dry Cleaners touted cash and carry prices for ladies' plain dresses at sixty
cents and men's pants at thirty cents. Over at Belk's department store,
during clearance, Ruth could pick up a house dress for eighty-seven
cents.[101] There were more choices at Schulman's and Keeter's department

stores or at Summers Drug, Summit's Nu-Way, and Plonk Brothers & Company. Best of all was Kings Mountain Dollar Days, one of the town's biggest annual events, which boasted great prices and free gifts and free movies for shoppers. Organizers even promised to release ten chickens at the top of Eagle five and dime store. "They are yours free for the catching," an advertisement bragged.[102]

If one did not peel back too many layers to consider the tiny paychecks, repetitive monotony, ubiquitous cotton dust, or endless noise, rose-colored impressions of this mill world could emerge. Jack Floyd was a reporter with worldwide experience who toured mill villages such as Park Yarn and Margrace and afterward shared his impressions with the *Herald*. In the villages, Floyd saw spic and span homes, most with cars parked out front and radios blaring inside. In the mills, he found "smiling faces, and moving trucks," which proved that Kings Mountain mills were doing their part to get the country out of the "red." Neisler's mills were the most impressive. Employees told Floyd that they were "well pleased with the general conditions, and all spoke the highest praise for the [mill's] officials."[103]

———

"What do you folks do here besides work in cotton mills?" asked a traveler. The gas station attendant did not hesitate. "Same as folks anywhere else," he said. "Baseball, fishin', a little frolickin' now and then."[104]

Thanks to new laws restricting work hours, Americans had more leisure time on their hands than ever before. In mill towns, there were few sounds as common as the crack of wooden bats or the pop of rawhide balls hitting leather gloves. If nothing else, the arrival of baseball season marked the return of spring. That alone was welcome after a long, dark winter, but the sport meant more than that for many millhands. Most mills sponsored teams that competed in city leagues with neighboring mills. Park Yarn's team, the Ragged Sox, battled clubs from Patricia, Margrace, and other mills. Other sports such as boxing and high school football and basketball gained a following as well, as the pages of each issue of the *Herald* attest, but baseball was king. Ruth's passion for baseball never dimmed, as late in life many summer nights found her sitting in an easy chair watching the Atlanta Braves and discussing the game through an open window with her neighbor.[105]

Pete loved baseball too, and he also loved movies. He could choose from two theaters in town. The Imperial was Kings Mountain's first movie house. The theater smartly ran promotions to keep business flowing. Who could resist buying Lux toilet soap so they could get a free ticket to see James Cagney and Pat O'Brien in *Devil Dogs of the Air*? In November 1935, the New Dixie Theatre—named in a contest by one of Neisler's daughters—opened for business. The Dixie, which sat on the north side of Railroad Avenue, lavished moviegoers with the latest in furnishings, including 591 seats "as comfortable as your parlor chair." Patrons were assured that the Dixie's air conditioning system would keep them warm in the winter and cool in the summer, and that whites and blacks would be properly segregated. For thirty cents, Pete could settle into one of the Dixie's maroon leather chairs and enjoy the opening picture, *It's in the Air*, starring Jack Benny.[106]

The annual Cleveland County Fair took place in Shelby every fall. It was not to be missed. The 1935 edition, which opened on October 1, featured Gertrude Avery's Diamond Revue, "a nightly pageant with wonderful scenic effects and colors, participated in by fifty beautiful girls." Attendees could also look forward to some bang-up car races with professional drivers such as Bob Sall, Ted Horn, and Chet Gardner, all of whom had driven in both the Indianapolis 500 and races at fairgrounds nationwide.[107]

The fun-loving Pete Lynn did not miss many parties either. He surely attended some of the square dances that Margrace sponsored at its Community House. The dance on Halloween night, 1935, featured music from Deward Wells and his string band from Spencer Mountain, so a strong turnout was no surprise.[108] Pete did not miss the 1935 wedding of his sister Eva to Austin Barrett, which was significant enough to gain mention in the *Herald*. The couple is "making their home at present with the groom's parents," the paper added. In 1938, Pete was also in on a surprise party for Wilma Rhea, who was moving away to study nursing. Partygoers enjoyed the ice cream, cake, and gifts immensely.[109]

The news of the day also captured attention, especially the local news. Big stories in those days ranged from a new stoplight at the intersection of the railroad tracks and Mountain Street, to a new highway to Gastonia, to the establishment of the Kings Mountain National Military Park.[110]

Residents were also proud to see a new public library open in 1937, and the Civilian Conservation Corps at work on projects not far from town.[111]

The biggest local event of the decade was President Roosevelt's 1936 visit to Kings Mountain. With his first term winding down and the Democratic nomination in hand, Roosevelt was just about to launch his reelection campaign. He had an appearance scheduled in Charlotte, and Kings Mountain was merely a waypoint on his journey, so it wasn't much as far as presidential visits go. It was more of a presidential drive-by, but to the locals it was huge. A blast from the fire siren announced that the chief executive was on his way, riding in a motorcade with the governor and fifty armed guards. Despite some intermittent rain, schools and businesses closed. People lined the streets from one end of town to the other, and the high school band struck up "Hail to the Chief." Down Mountain Street the presidential motorcade turned, and Kings Mountain roared. "With flags flying, whistles blowing and siren going at full blast, The President greeted the throng," a reporter wrote.[112]

Paying such modest attention to Kings Mountain no doubt helped as the president carried the town in a landslide during the November election.[113] When Roosevelt embarked on his second term the following January, the prophetic words he spoke during his nomination acceptance speech still rang in American ears. "To some generations much is given," he said. "Of other generations much is expected. This generation of Americans has a rendezvous with destiny."[114]

Soon, Pete and Ruth Lynn would learn exactly what the president meant.

CHAPTER 2

You Have Now Been Selected

SHIFT'S END AT PARK YARN or Margrace—IN THOSE DAYS, MARGRACE ran twelve-hour shifts while Park Yarn ran eight-hour shifts[1]—was a daily waltz. A writer named Mildred Barnwell toured similar Carolina mills in the 1930s and described the sights and sounds.

At Park Yarn, a whistle blast marked the end of the shift.[2] At that moment, Barnwell wrote, "The big outside door swung open, and out poured the textile workers." They emerged in groups: men here, women there. The men wore "overalls, wisps of cotton still clinging to them, [and they] walked with a firm step, heads up," she wrote. While the men talked mostly of baseball, the women evinced a similar garb but a different agenda. "Women, their gingham work frocks mussed from a day in the spinning room," some with "a fuzz of cotton lint showing on dark hair," hurried to "red up" the house or to get supper ready, Barnwell wrote.[3]

Pete, whistling as he walked, would have been in the middle of a throng just like that, streaming out of Park Yarn. Ruth, no doubt ready to "red up" her little house, would have been somewhere in the crowd of women flowing from Margrace.

They were a little like Israelites trapped in Egypt, hoping for a better life—but even if it was a hard life in their mill town, it was also a good one.

It might have gone on just like that for years. But it did not, for far beyond their small town, world events took a serious turn that would eventually be felt even in Kings Mountain.

⌒

It started slowly during the early years of the Lynns' marriage. In Asia, militaristic Japan occupied Manchuria and later attacked China. On the other side of the world, the Spanish Civil War erupted. Fascism and

33

Benito Mussolini claimed Italy, which in turn cast expansionist eyes outward and invaded Ethiopia. Germany rose out of the ashes of World War I under the leadership of Adolf Hitler and his Nazi Party. Then, with frightening and increasing speed, crisis after crisis followed. Hitler renounced the Versailles Treaty, and then Germany remilitarized the Rhineland, annexed Austria and Czechoslovakia, and kindled its wrath against Jews, taking their citizenship, their property, their dignity, and in growing numbers their lives.

Media outlets like WBT Radio and movie newsreels chronicled these ominous events, but Pete and Ruth did not worry much. While life went on as usual for them, with work and an occasional Sunday dinner with Pete's parents, America remained solidly isolationist. Public opinion demanded it, and congressional acts mandated it. When Japanese warplanes sank the American gunboat *Panay* in the Yangtze River, most Americans shrugged and wondered why their gunboat was even in China. Panzers rolling into Poland evoked little more response. "Very few Americans wanted to hear about trouble overseas," historian Shlaes wrote. The more important thing was "finding one's own way at home." President Roosevelt promised, "This nation will remain a neutral nation."[4]

This feeling pervaded Kings Mountain. The *Herald* did not print much in the way of war news, but when it did it was decidedly antiwar. One man returning from a trip abroad said, "We should stay at home and mind our own business." The paper's editor agreed. "The very idea of our getting mixed up in the European war should be ruled out entirely," he wrote. "It is not for us." Local events drew much bigger headlines, such as the resignation of Macedonia Baptist Church's pastor. Rev. J. V. Frederick's track record was admirable. During his tenure, the congregation had nearly doubled in size, installed a heating system and baptistry, and built a six-room parsonage. The church voted to reject his resignation and somehow persuaded him to stay.[5]

Pete and Ruth gave little thought to Nazi banners flying over Poland when they decided to start a family. One winter day in 1940, Ruth learned the happy news that she was pregnant. Sitting around the kitchen table, the couple faced many questions. How would they pay the bills? Where would the baby sleep? Should they look for another house? All they could do was trust in God and family. Ruth quit her job at Margrace and readied their nest. She acquired a crib and began knitting clothes and diapers. Pete redoubled his efforts in Park Yarn's card room; he would have to bear the entire financial load alone.

When the dogwoods around the mills bloomed, the couple began to realize that they could not ignore the world around them any more than Ruth could ignore her expanding belly. Ruth was well into her second trimester when German soldiers wearing coalscuttle helmets conquered Denmark, Norway, Holland, Belgium, Luxembourg, and France. President Roosevelt called the country to its altars to pray, as biographer Conrad Black wrote, "for the deliverance of civilization from the forces of evil." The war came into Park Yarn homes when the Battle of Britain roared in the skies over England. Whenever Pete and Ruth tuned their kitchen radio to WBT, they could hear broadcasters like Edward Murrow, his thin baritone voice accompanied by the howl of air raid sirens, describing the nightly siege of London. Not to be outdone, movie newsreels brought shocking images of war to the silver screen. Among the most watched films about the German Blitz was *London Can Take It*. Over 60 million Americans in theaters like Kings Mountain's Imperial and the Dixie saw the film. "These are not Hollywood sound effects," a narrator explained

A typical Park Yarn house. Lester and Nell Moss lived here.
Source: Cornelia Moss Davis

with a sad, matter-of-fact tone as antiaircraft guns banged away. "This is the music they play every night in London. A symphony of war."[6]

This uncertain world suddenly seemed even to menace Kings Mountain, especially when President Roosevelt—on the cusp of being reelected to a third term—finally shook the country free of neutrality. "America stands at the cross roads of its destiny," he said. "Time and distance have been shortened. A few weeks have seen great nations fall. We cannot remain indifferent."[7] It was enough to make Pete and Ruth question whether or not they should even have a baby at such a time, but it was too late for that.

There was much to do. America was completely unprepared. For one thing, America's army contained a paltry 190,000 officers and men. At the same time, army planners initially forecasted that the United States would need nearly 9 million men in 215 divisions if it became embroiled in war with the Axis. Although that estimate was later scaled back, America still needed men—yet the country was among the few in the world where citizens were not obligated to serve in the military, which meant that manpower could not easily be procured in the event of war. The solution was a draft. Originally introduced in Congress as the Burke-Wadsworth Bill, the concept of a draft sparked vigorous debate. The media editorialized, citizens demonstrated, and Congressmen argued, in one case to the point of fisticuffs. The outcome was inevitable. "Every time they bombed London we gained a vote or two in the House or Senate," a witness recalled. Congress finally passed the measure, and on September 16, 1940, the president signed the Selective Service Training & Service Act into law. It authorized Roosevelt to "set in motion the selective service machinery in each state and territory of the United States."[8]

Such machinery could fire its pistons only if young men came, as Roosevelt put it, "from the factories and the fields, the cities and the towns, to enroll their names." Registration Day—R-Day for short—was set for Wednesday, October 16, 1940, during the ninth month of Ruth's pregnancy; it required all males between the ages of twenty-one and thirty-five to register with their local draft board by filling out a questionnaire, signing their name on the dotted line, and receiving a draft number. Roosevelt issued a proclamation in support, while radio and press announcements and posters sounded the call.[9]

Pete could follow these developments in the *Kings Mountain Herald*. Having just celebrated has thirtieth birthday on October 7, he was among those required to register. Ruth doubtless did not like any of it. Her uncle, Arthur A. Jones, had served in Europe with the 56th Pioneer Infantry Regiment during World War I. Uncle Arthur had sent Ruth a photo and a postcard from the front. "Believe me it was terrible," Jones wrote of the fighting. "Guess you all was glad when it ceased."[10] But there was nothing she could do about it, so Pete went to register just like everybody else. America was not at war, so the idea that Pete could be drafted someday seemed at best a remote possibility.

Draft boards typically consisted of three or more persons at least thirty-six years old and living in their county.[11] Kings Mountain's draft board—Frank Summers, Arthur Hay, Hayne Blackmer, J. R. Davis, and medical examiner Dr. W. L. Ramseur—chose City Hall and the Cleveland Motor Company for the registration sites. Everyone knew those places not only for their regular capacities in government and car-buying, but also as the same places Kings Mountain would return to in November to vote in the election. On October 16, the sites opened at 7:00 A.M. A sense of historical importance was in the air. Flags flew proudly in the breeze while the queues filled with men who, wrote North Carolina governor J. Melville Broughton, gave "hardly a murmur of dissatisfaction or complaint." From that early hour until the sites closed at 9:00 P.M., some 1,400 men registered in Kings Mountain. Statewide, the number was 450,000; nationally, it was 16,816,822. Schools closed so teachers could help, and many businesses closed too. Registering took about twenty minutes per man.[12]

R-Day went smoothly, as these men in the line felt a surge of patriotism. One of the Kings Mountain men who came to register was blind. There were also men in line who celebrated their twenty-first birthday that very Wednesday. And though the questionnaire was designed to be simple, it still confused some. When one man listed his brother-in-law as his nearest living relative, an examiner asked if his father was still living. "Yes," the man said, "but my brother-in-law lives in the next block, and my father lives out of town."[13]

Eventually, it was Pete's turn. He sat down in front of the registrar, who took down his personal information. Name? Felmer Lonzo Lynn. Address? It had to be a place where someone would always be able to locate him. Park Yarn Mill, Route 2, Kings Mountain. Born? Cleveland County, North Carolina, October 7, 1910. Place of employment? Park Yarn Mill. Spouse? Mrs. Evelyn Ruth Lynn. Physical description? White, 6 feet tall, 150 pounds, with blue eyes, brown hair, and a dark complexion. The process concluded when the registrar gave Pete a registration card, DDS Form 2. He stuck the card in his pocket, as the law required him to carry it at all times.[14]

Just eight days later, Pete and Ruth welcomed their first child, Mitchell Ann. The joyous news even made it into the *Herald*. Yet, Pete still kept a wary eye open when Kings Mountain's draft numbers were tossed into an enormous glass fish bowl in Washington, DC, along with draft numbers from Charlotte, Cleveland, Kansas City, Los Angeles, and every state, city, and town in between. President Roosevelt stood in front of the bowl and drew the first names. With that, the draft had begun. Pete was a gainfully employed new father, and he was thirty years old to boot, so he probably felt safer than most, but the draft still became a major topic of discussion around Park Yarn. Years later, Park Yarn employee Robert C. Pearson would tell an interviewer that he remembered the fear of the fish bowl more than the news of Pearl Harbor.[15]

❧

So it was back to the Park Yarn card room for Pete, while Ruth stayed home to care for the little girl they called Mickie. America remained at peace, but as the months passed it looked like the country was inching closer to war. "We must be the great arsenal of democracy," Roosevelt told the country. That meant lots of work for cotton mills like Park Yarn and Margrace, especially when the army ordered a quarter-billion pairs of trousers, 250 million pairs of underwear, and half a billion socks.[16]

In May 1941, President Roosevelt declared a state of "unlimited national emergency." In September, the president announced that the U.S. Navy would attack any German or Italian vessel it spotted in waters American considered part of its defensive sphere. All the while, Roosevelt kept up the rhetoric denouncing the Axis, and America listened: according to a Gallup Poll that fall, 70 percent of Americans said it was more important to defeat Hitler than stay out of the war.

Pete, Ruth, and Mitchell Ann
Source: Lynn Collection

As author Conrad Black explained it, the president had largely succeeded in changing Americans' once fervent belief in isolationism.[17]

That was true in Kings Mountain. "The topic of conversation is WAR, WAR, WAR," wrote *Herald* editor Haywood E. Lynch.[18] Pete and Ruth were not deterred by any of this. About the time they blew out the candles on Mickie's first birthday cake, the couple decided to try for another baby. Ruth was pregnant by Thanksgiving.

December 7, 1941, dawned like any other Sunday in Kings Mountain. It was church-mouse quiet, with the mills shut down and a day of rest ahead for most. The Lynns spent the morning as usual, attending services at Macedonia Baptist Church. Around 2:00 P.M., radios across the little town started blaring reports of the Japanese attack on Pearl Harbor. The next day, the United States declared war on Japan, while three days later Germany and Italy in turn declared war on the United States. The United States returned the favor. The headline of the December 11 *Kings Mountain Herald* was stark and frightening: "U.S.-Japs at War." According to the *Herald*, "War, war, war, that's all we have heard since Sunday . . . Every person you meet on the street in the barber shop in the stores around the service station, that's all they discuss."[19]

Kings Mountain men, like those in hundreds of other communities across the country, responded. In the days after Pearl Harbor, many headed for the local army and navy recruiting stations to volunteer. They had no intention of waiting on the draft.[20] One man never forgot "the way people at the Park Yarn were reacting and talking. All the eligible men volunteered and were gone in no time," he wrote.[21]

Pete was not among these volunteers. After all, he was now thirty-one years old. He had a wife, a daughter, another child on the way, and a steady job. He and Ruth had other plans, other hopes, and other dreams that had nothing to do with Germany or Japan or the military. Conscription also seemed unlikely, thanks to his age and status as a parent. The war could take care of itself.

Home was indeed where Pete needed to be. On July 29, 1942—just days before U.S. Marines landed on a faraway Pacific island called Guadalcanal—Ruth gave birth to a little girl. They named her Barbara Jo. Pete was thrilled to be a dad for a second time, but he was just a little disappointed too. He was a man's man living in a man's world, and he desperately wanted a boy—a boy he could take fishing, play baseball with, and teach him how to be a man. Ruth shared that view. As if to underscore their hope, Pete and Ruth decided to call their little girl Bobbie. There was also little doubt that Pete and Ruth planned to keep trying for a boy.[22]

Boys or not, Pete loved his girls. He fondly called them his little "white-headed girls" or his "brats." As Mickie and Bobbie grew, playtime with dad in the little gray house was a raucous time of laughter and roughhousing.[23] He would march around the house with them, hollering "Hip Hop 3 4" at the top of his lungs. Or he might get down on his knees, plop Mick on his back, and give her a horsey ride. He called himself "Old Silver" after the Lone Ranger's horse.[24] When they visited the farm, Pete loved to put the kids in a wheelbarrow and wheel them around, or just sit back and watch them play.[25]

In more quiet moments, Pete and Mick would read together, although Pete had never been a good reader so he felt a little inadequate. One day Mick sat down in a chair, leaned back, stuck her little feet up on the bed, and started reading. Pete, listening in alongside, soon decided that she was reading faster than him.[26] Bobbie wasn't old enough for that yet but she quickly showed a personality of her own. Pete got a kick out of watching her sit in a high chair and eat pancakes. It wouldn't take long before syrup and butter were smeared all over her face and running down the front of her dress. When she finished one plate, Bobbie would start "Hollern for more," Pete smiled.[27]

Pete and Ruth soon felt the war come closer. It started at the mill as businesses and factories geared up to produce everything its military would need.

North Carolina fulfilled its role in the Arsenal of Democracy. Before the war was over, the federal government would spend some $2 billion in the state—and that did not include the money paid to subcontracted companies that sold goods to other companies for use in production. More than 1 million Tar Heels would work in factories manufacturing everything from rockets to radar components. Other businesses prospered as well. Timber flowed, dozens of ships were built in Wilmington, and construction companies did a brisk business building army and navy bases. Kings Mountain was as busy as any town. North Carolina mills doubled their payrolls during World War II, with 70 percent of their output going to the military as they churned out sheets, blankets, clothing, tents, bandages, towels, parachutes, shoestrings, polo shirts, tire cords, fabrics, and other goods. In fact, North Carolina would produce more textile goods than any other state during the war, so mills like Park Yarn and Margrace ran hard.[28]

The war reached beyond the factory walls as well, as the Lynns saw firsthand. "World War II had its impact on all of us," Park Yarn resident Tom Shytle wrote. "Almost everything was in short supply and rationed." Production of civilian cars stopped after February 1942. Official rationing ramped up in May 1942, beginning with sugar. Coffee was added in November with an allowance of one pound every five weeks. Then came rubber, gasoline, and shoes, the latter at a limit of three pairs a year. Later, the government also added other items including ketchup, canned foods, meat, fish, dairy, butter, and fats. Ration books were the only way to unlock access to these products; every civilian had a book of colored stamps to manage. You had red stamps for meat, fish, dairy, butter, and fats, and blue for canned foods. Each stamp carried a code so it could only be used at the allotted time.[29]

Ruth had to juggle the ration books for her household. It was never easy, and it required creativity. "We had chicken for dinner again today," a relative told Ruth. "One of the hens got out yesterday and they couldn't catch her, so Tom got mad and killed her with a stick. It saved us some money and points." Rare was the person who completely embraced this system. "Aren't those points the bears though?" the same relative wrote Ruth. "They worry me to death. I go to town half the time with out ours to buy groceries. I'll never get used to them." Scarcity did at least make one appreciate food more; when Ruth ate a chocolate bar for the first time in six months, she could not help but brag to her husband about it.[30]

To Kings Mountain mill workers, it seemed that the only thing the government had not rationed was fish tales.[31] Conservation was encouraged. The government asked civilians to collect scrap metals such as old tin cans. Young and old alike got involved, with kids even collecting bits of tin foil from cigarette packages and gum wrappers. Anything metal ended up recycled into armaments. The government also sought scrap newspaper, old cardboard boxes, hot water bottles, and rubber bands. The governor even asked citizens to reduce their use of electricity, coal, phone service, and bus service. A special song, courtesy of the famous crooner Bing Crosby, accompanied all of this collecting: "Junk Will Win the War."[32]

Everyday life was still there, but it was now framed by the purpose Crosby sang about—winning the war. The conflict now hovered over everything. Shopping was a challenge, especially if you needed bobby pins, can openers, or anything made of metal. Batteries were scarce. Gas and tire rationing forced you to get your car out only when necessary. Walking was a better choice. Ladies' stockings disappeared as their silk went for use in parachutes. Ruth probably opted for bare legs, although some women drew stripes down the back of their legs with makeup pencils. The war reached into schools too. Campaigns encouraged students to exercise, help around the house, and keep up on the news. Over at Park Grace School, the principal, who had a son serving in the Pacific, had her students recite the pledge of allegiance and have a short devotion daily. The regular duty of raising and lowering the flag on the pole in front of the building was an honor. Yet compared to civilians elsewhere in the world, Americans still had it easy. Collections of clothes and food for overseas refugees were a stark reminder of that.[33]

On February 9, 1942, a new word began circulating across the state: "Plant a Victory Garden: Our Food is Fighting." Victory Gardens were the idea of Secretary of Agriculture Claude R. Wickard. If citizens would plant gardens, the thinking went, then people would have a natural way to supplement what they could purchase through rationing. The concept was a rousing success. Americans planted more than 20 million gardens in 1943 alone. Before the war ended, North Carolinians canned 28 million quarts of food and dried 8 million pounds of fruits and vegetables from their Victory Gardens.[34] Kings Mountain joined in. Since many did not own enough property for a proper garden, mills came to the rescue. Margrace plowed up a big field and laid out garden plots for employees to use, and the Pauline followed suit. Soon enough, a local reporter "Found everyone planting 'Victory Gardens.'"[35]

If Victory Gardens were common, war bond sales were downright ubiquitous. War costs money, so Washington asked the nation's citizens to help pay for it by buying war bonds. The government also saw bonds as a way to fight inflation; with fewer consumer goods on the market and growing wages thanks to the war economy, bonds provided an outlet for excess wages. War bonds could be purchased in denominations from $25 to $1,000, or on an installment plan. Whatever your choice, bonds were easy to buy; from schools to movie theaters, war bond booths dotted the landscape like lampposts. North Carolina blew past its bond quota; in eight campaigns, state residents raised $85.7 billion. To generate additional funding, the government also instituted a 5 percent "Victory Tax" and started withholding money from paychecks. The personal exemption for taxes was $624, but thanks to odd jobs Pete's salary often exceeded that amount even when Ruth was not working.[36]

Kings Mountain and its mills became bond-buying dynamos. The First National Bank sold $90,000 in bonds in December 1942 alone, while Kings Mountain High School students hawked $15,000 worth. Employees of Neisler Mills did more than their fair share, purchasing an average of $1,455 bonds a week and some weeks even more. Margrace's credit union, which handled most employee bond transactions, sold enough to rank second in sales volume against total assets among all credit unions in the Carolinas, Virginia, and the District of Columbia. "Of that Record we are quite proud," a Margrace employee bragged. These investments became tangible when a trainer plane in honor of Kings Mountain High rolled off one assembly line and a B-17 emerged from another plant bearing the words "City of Kings Mountain, North Carolina" on the fuselage.[37]

Defense precautions made their way to Kings Mountain as well. A new national agency, the Office of the Civilian Defense, recruited men and women to handle duties such as airplane spotting, firefighting, ambulance driving, and first aid. Officials also made preparations for air raids, even though enemy planes did not have the capability to get anywhere close. The real focus for air raid preparation was in communities located up to two hundred miles inland. Kings Mountain was a little farther inland than that, but the town held blackout tests nonetheless. A typical test created an eerie landscape. All traffic lights and neon signs winked off. Window shades came down. Cars pulled off the road, their headlights switched off. Air-raid wardens patrolled to enforce the darkness. If you had a bomb shelter that was the time to go there, but most did not since building materials were scarce and few of Kings Mountain's residents could afford one. The other option, according to a civilian defense pamphlet, was to stay home and take shelter beneath a heavy table.[38]

"War changes the pattern of our lives," that same civilian defense pamphlet explained. "The kids still play baseball in the corner lot—but they knock off early to weed the victory gardens, cart scrap paper to the salvage center, carry home the groceries that used to be delivered. The factory whistle blows—but it calls three shifts of workers instead of one. The daily paper still has comics, but it's the front page that carries the answer to the urgent question 'how are we doing?' All over America there's a new tempo, a new purpose, a *new spirit*."[39]

By early 1943, one could hardly miss the new spirit around Margrace. "Nearly all the men have gone into the services, 'skirts' have taken up some of the jobs that men once did," explained the *Old Mountaineer*,

Margrace's wartime newsletter for servicemen. "The draft is cleaning out all of our 18–19 year old boys." By one count, nearly two hundred men had been drafted away from Margrace and Pauline.[40]

A walk through the mill told the story. "Went down to the mill . . . and found girls everywhere," a reporter wrote in Margrace's overseas newsletter. "They were running two of those big plush looms, running the cloth tables, skinning quills, doffing, running slubbers, running those Yo-Yo twisters, in fact they were everywhere and they all wore slacks." The same reporter assured the *Old Mountaineer*'s readers—Margrace employees to a man—that all was well. "You could not but be proud of them for they are fighting to hold down your jobs for you—and doing it with a smile. Sure its hard work. Tough work. Dirty greasy work—you ought to know for you had been doing it."[41]

Rationing also forced people to tighten their belts. "Our gasoline over here is running a little short, which makes it hard on our shoe leather—but what the Hell!!!" added the *Old Mountaineer*. "We're not grumbling about that—after all we weren't riding in a car when we came into the world."[42]

For all of these inconveniences, many felt that the war had not demanded any real sacrifices.[43] Pete and Ruth might have agreed with that sentiment. Work at the mill continued as usual, and Pete also continued to pick up odd jobs to supplement their income. He was good at painting, so he would just slide a paint mask over his head and go to work.[44] He still managed to get away and fish, and also took in movies; maybe he went to the Imperial the weekend it showed *Range Law*, *Week End Pass*, and *Outlaws of Boulder Pass*, along with some war newsreels.[45] Holidays were as special as ever; on Easter weekend 1943, the Lynns headed out to the Hawkins farm. Pete hid eggs for the girls, but he had to threaten Bobbie with a spanking when she stuck her tongue out at him.[46]

Still, the war slowly drew closer to home. Pete's brother Bill was the first family member to enter the service. He enlisted the summer before R-Day, at age twenty-one, full of bluster. "I received your cigarettes and just wanted to let you know I appreciated them very much, and in return I will bring you a big fat Jap," he told the *Old Mountaineer*. In truth, Bill had no desire to be a soldier. The army did not quite know what to do with him. It started with his name; when he could not say what J. C. stood for, the army called him Jeffery C. Lynn. He went to work in a motor pool at Fort Bragg, but Bill struggled. He was still a roundabout man. He had a heavy dose of homesickness, and health became a problem too. As his son later told an interviewer, Bill took too many "Dutch leaves," and the record shows that he took five of them in 1942, including one that stretched for six months. The army sentenced him to a corresponding five months in the cooler before finally giving up. Bill was discharged at Camp Hood, Texas, on May 27, 1943, officially due to chronic pulmonary tuberculosis.[47]

Meanwhile, in the spring of 1942, a close friend of Pete's left Kings Mountain to serve. George C. Smith, who married Ruth's sister Mae, left his job as a weaver at Margrace to enlist in the navy. Bespectacled with light brown hair and a ruddy complexion, the 6-foot-tall Smitty had a year of college under his belt, so the navy decided to send him to aviation and radar schools. He was found unfit to fly, probably because of his eyesight, so the navy turned him into an instrument landing equipment operator. He spent the entire war at naval bases stateside, although it appears that he was careful not to reveal his station to his family. "I recon he's on a ship somewhere," Ruth wrote.[48]

The Selective Service still had Pete's name too. At first, it appeared that he was safe from the draft. When the war began, the Selective Service's goal was to keep families intact, so it classified registrants with dependents separately from those without. It is hardly surprising that this spurred a deluge of weddings. A leading manufacturer of wedding rings saw a 250 percent increase in sales as an estimated 40 percent of twenty-one-year-olds married within six weeks of R-Day. Yet marriage alone didn't mean an automatic deferment from military service, so men turned to the stork. Babies were seen as "draft insurance" for the 8 million men of draft age who were "draft exemption" fathers. Men who had children before Pearl Harbor—pre–Pearl Harbor fathers—enjoyed the most protection. Congress even debated bills calling for the permanent deferment of pre–Pearl Harbor fathers, but those were amended to allow their drafting if the pool of single men emptied.[49]

By December 1943, the American military contained about 12 million men, but about 5 million had been granted deferments. Those men assigned Category I were deemed fit for military service. Other categories covered men who worked in occupations essential to the war effort, had dependents, or who were physically or mentally unqualified. Since the production of apparel and textiles was considered essential, some Park Yarn and Margrace family men fell into Class III-B for "Registrants with dependents, engaged in activity necessary to the war production program." However, not every textile job was protected, especially those that were more menial or required little training. The local draft board would rule on such jobs.[50]

As a pre–Pearl Harbor father with a spouse and children and also a textile worker, Pete found himself on the fringes of official, permanent deferment, but as a minimum wage earner in an unskilled job he did not technically fall into Class III-B. Even if he had, changes to Selective Service policies came frequently. One sea change, in June 1942, stemmed from the recognition that military service posed financial hardships on men with dependents. The Serviceman's Dependents Allowance Act addressed that by providing enlisted men with dependents extra pay. For men like Pete with two kids, the act would mean an extra $50 a month if he ended up in the military. That was significant for a man who made $12 a week, or $4 a week less than the national average.[51]

Battlefield realities drove more change to the Selective Service system. Allied landings in the Mediterranean in 1942 and 1943 met with success, but the resulting high casualties put stress on the system. Meanwhile, reports from the front indicated that individuals earmarked as replacements needed better training, so the army decided to extend basic training from thirteen to seventeen weeks. Suddenly, training centers couldn't keep up with demand. Draft boards fell short of manpower quotas. As the winter of 1943–1944 approached, a critical shortage of infantrymen materialized. The military simply needed more men for the sharp end of the spear. On July 31, 1943, Maj. Gen. Lewis B. Hershey, director of the Selective Service system, instructed draft boards to start reclassifying fathers and prepare to induct them beginning on October 1. Americans howled, Congress debated, and draft boards hesitated to the point that only 90,000 fathers were drafted by the end of 1943, but soon there would be no choice.[52]

The *Old Mountaineer* saw the handwriting on the wall and wondered when the army might call on "the real men for military service, the daddy's, and I don't mean the sugar daddy's either, you know who I mean, the guys who have something else running around the house besides a fence."[53] The run on pre–Pearl Harbor dads began in earnest as 1944 arrived. By the end of the war, one of every five fathers between the ages of eighteen and thirty-seven—1 million men altogether—would be on active duty. And in that segregated world, most of these men were white. These draftees were also older. The average age of draftees rose from twenty-two in 1940 to twenty-six.[54]

Like dirt tumbling from cotton sheets in the card room, the obstacles between Pete Lynn and military service were falling away.

———

In some respects, the new year of 1944 looked a lot like 1943 in Kings Mountain. At the mills, production moved along normally despite the absence of some workers due to colds and flu.[55] Another bond drive coaxed the locals to dig deep. Otherwise, things were about the same—unless you were a father of draft age.

A Margrace Mill newsletter called it the "Game of Fathers Vs Draft Board." Thanks to the military's demand for more men, the Kings Mountain Draft Board finally had no choice but to tap fathers. The first step was to send these men for preinduction physicals, and it now did so *en masse*.[56] While a preinduction draft physical did not necessarily mean a man was about to be conscripted, it was a sure sign that he was under consideration. Once the physicals were completed, the army would notify the draft board which men should be called to duty. The dreaded summons would follow.[57]

Pete was caught in the net. On February 8, 1944, he reported to the First National Bank building in downtown Kings Mountain with 139 other fathers. Worried about their futures, these men piled onto buses and headed south, across the state line and past the Kings Mountain battlefield.[58]

Their destination was Camp Croft, a Replacement Training Center (RTC). For most of the war, Kings Mountain's preinduction examinations had been conducted at the local high school gym, but now the process had been moved to the camp. Camp Croft sat on some old cotton and tobacco fields in Spartanburg, South Carolina, about fifty miles from Kings Mountain. Named for Maj. Gen. Edward Croft, a native of the area and a former chief of infantry who had died in 1938, Camp Croft had opened in March 1941. It trained about 70,000 men annually in basic infantry skills and also provided some specialty training in cannon, heavy weapons, antitank, headquarters, and other areas.[59]

These physicals were cursory at best as doctors looked for only the most obvious physical defects. They often found them, as rejection rates as high as 50 percent were not unknown in North Carolina, while nationwide more than 5 million men were sent home for various deficiencies. At a minimum, a man had to be 5 feet tall and weigh 105 pounds. Pete passed the height and weight requirement easily, unlike fellow Kings Mountain resident Hubert "Hefty" Davidson. Davidson weighed ninety pounds dripping wet. A Camp Croft doctor took one look at him and said, "My God, here comes Superman himself," before rejecting him. Pete's exam continued with little trouble. His vision was good, and he also had no flat feet or hernias. He was also literate enough to avoid reading lessons with the help of army primers like *Meet Private Pete*. Only one thing could have disqualified him: his teeth. A look at Pete's teeth surely gave the examining physician pause, because Pete had a mouthful of bad ones.[60]

Before the draft began, the army had rigorous dental standards. A man had to have six "serviceable natural masticating teeth and six serviceable natural incisor teeth, all so opposed as to serve the purpose of good incision and mastication." Men who had fewer teeth and dentures could only serve in a limited capacity. Those standards carried over into the early days of the draft when dental defects were the leading cause for rejection. Such standards did not last long. Authorities realized that the depression had led to poor dental care among many men. The army's leading dental officer, Brig. Gen. Leigh C. Fairbank, warned that "the safety of the nation should not be sacrificed just to maintain high dental standards," so the military ramped up its corrective dentistry capabilities. By October 1942, dental requirements for induction were virtually eliminated, and other requirements were loosened as well. The army needed men, and took them even if they had no teeth at all, or for that matter if they had no ears, only one eye, or were missing a thumb or three fingers on either hand. A doctor decided Pete's dental problems could be fixed, so he was certified as "physically fit, acceptable by Army for general military service."[61]

Then it was back on the bus for the return ride to Kings Mountain and Park Yarn. The next move was up to the local draft board, which would review the results from the physicals and determine what to do with each man.[62] In the meantime, Pete could only watch the mailbox and wait with what one historian has described as "more than casual interest."[63]

March arrived, and spring did too. "All the small grains are green; the yellow bell, jonquils, and buttercups are blooming and the buds on many of the trees are beginning to swell," wrote a Kings Mountain millhand. "Never have I seen as many robins as are here right now."[64] Pete paid less attention to the weather than usual as he waited for news from the draft board. He did not have to wait long. Soon an official-looking, ominous letter arrived at the Lynn cottage. It was addressed to Felmer Lonzo Lynn; the return address was the Selective Service, Local Board No. 2, Cleveland County. Pete opened it. Inside was a piece of paper that read, "Having submitted yourself to a local board composed of your neighbors for the purpose of determining your availability for training and service in the land or naval forces of the United States, you are hereby notified that you have now been selected for training and service herein." He was ordered to report to the draft board office in the First National Bank building in Kings Mountain at 7:30 A.M. on March 15, from where he would be transported to an induction station.[65]

Pete could have asked an appeal board to review his case. By the spring of 1944, as more fathers were being called up, such boards regularly heard cases of men with dependents. Men even had the right to appeal to as high an authority as the president.[66] In fact, Pete was almost certain that he could have arranged for a deferral with the help of Mr. Ballard, an acquaintance who apparently had some pull with the draft board, but he did not take that route. He was, his sister-in-law later recalled, "too proud not to go." Ruth agreed and understood her husband's decision. "I know you wouldn't be satisfied here thinking you weren't man enough to be in it," she told Pete. "If I had my way I[']d have you home any way I could get you, but I[']d want you to be satisfied. You have a nature to want in the middle of anything going."[67]

Pete was one of several Kings Mountain men who received draft notices that month. Among them were more than a dozen fathers. The government had given them just a few weeks to arrange their affairs and say goodbye to friends, family, and coworkers. They gathered early on the morning of March 14, nervously smoking and chatting with neighbors and new acquaintances, and then boarded a bus for Fort Bragg.[68]

Pete did not join them; he gained some extra time by arranging his own transportation. He spent his last hours at their little Park Yarn house. Ruth helped him pack. There was a party with friends and family; her sister Hazel was among the guests, and she tried to reassure Pete. Army life isn't so bad, she told him—at least that's what she had heard. The night before he left, Pete, Ruth, the kids, and Pete's mother had a quiet meal together. Later, some visitors stopped by to wish him well, including Pete's friends Blanchard Horne and Bill Shytle. What passed between Ruth and Pete is not recorded, but certainly it was a heartfelt day.[69]

Rising early on Wednesday, March 15, 1944, Pete found Mick already out of bed. He kissed her goodbye and then went into the back room and held Bobbie. (Apparently, a friend or relative had offered to drive him.) At 6:45 A.M., he said goodbye to Ruth and left Park Yarn for the next to last time.[70]

He was bound for Fort Bragg, one of the army's score of reception centers. After riding about four hours on the two-lane asphalt ribbon of U.S. Highway 74, past quiet pastures and roadside gas stations and through one-stoplight towns, the pensive passenger found himself among the pine trees and sand hills of Fayetteville, North Carolina. Fayetteville had seen soldiers come and go, from the uncertain days of the revolution, when a divided population supported both King and colony, to the Civil War, when Gen. William T. Sherman's Yankee host showed the locals that war is hell by razing the town. Pete discovered only a foreign world of Quonset huts, military vehicles, and drilling soldiers. Fort Bragg was an old army post, having opened during World War I. Now, it was the largest post in the state and would soon be the largest in the world. By war's end, some 3,135 buildings would be strewn across 122,000 acres, where 100,000 men prepared for battle.[71]

Feeling out of place in his civilian clothes, Pete reluctantly jumped into this new, drab world of barking orders and frippery. As he dropped his overnight bag, Pete probably heard worrying taunts from passing soldiers such as, "You'll be sorry!" Soon he found himself standing buck naked, in an endless line, with an ID number on a piece of cardboard hung around his neck. The line wound to the first station, where physical exams took place. This was the most thorough exam Pete ever experienced. A doctor checked his eyes, ear, nose, and throat, and then put him through a battery of X-rays and cardiograms. Somebody took his fingerprints and checked them against FBI files. Multiple injections against illnesses such as typhoid, smallpox, and yellow fever followed, and so did a genital exam and a blood test to make sure Pete was free of venereal disease. (For good measure, the men also heard a morality lecture in which the speaker would often admonish the men, "Flies spread disease, so keep yours buttoned." A film by Hollywood producer Darryl Zanuck and director John Ford called *Sex Hygiene* was also shown.) After being poked and prodded, Pete received a clean bill of health, although doctors may have spotted the effects of childhood labor they saw in many others.[72]

More testing followed, but of a different sort. It included an aptitude test to judge his IQ and mental capacity, a mechanical aptitude test, a radio code test, and the 150-question Army General Classification Test (AGCT). Then came interviews—guided discussions about background, interests, hobbies, abilities, and other things that might influence his future service. There was even a screening with a psychiatrist, which amounted to a series of questions to detect any phobias, emotional disturbances, or mental deficiencies. Nothing special emerged in Pete's tests and interviews. A clerk listed his civilian job as "semiskilled occupations in the manufacture of textiles" and his education level as grammar school. The results were coded by hole punch into WD AGO Form No. 20, which would be used by a classifier to determine his assignment. Through much of it, Pete remained awkwardly naked—until, at last, he received clothing, which likely as not fit him poorly. Shoes were a different story: the army made sure those fit well.[73]

The most alarming station of all was the one marked "life insurance," but he knew what he had to do. He signed up for a $10,000 life insurance policy, agreeing to have $7.40 deducted out of his paycheck every month. Ruth did not like the idea either and later asked him about it. Pete was characteristically blunt in his answer, but in his tongue-in-cheek style. "Well," he told Ruth, "if I Do get Bunked Off you will Have enuff to Do you and the Kids a while."[74]

The ten days that followed were a blur. Somewhere along the way, Pete heard lectures on military courtesy, close order drill, and a reading of the Articles of War (the army's criminal code). There were more films, and he probably received a copy of the pamphlet *Army Life* to review.[75] He also received his induction papers and a serial number, 34963373, to memorize.[76] Yet of everything he experienced at Fort Bragg, his swearing in surely stood out. It was a solemn ceremony. Pete would have been one of several recruits standing in a room. An officer came to the front, said a few words, and instructed the men to raise their right hands. Pete did so—perhaps his hand trembled at the implication of what he was doing—and repeated the oath. "I, Felmer Lonzo Lynn," he said, "do solemnly swear that I will bear true faith and allegiance to the United States of America; that I will serve them honestly and faithfully against all their enemies whomsoever; and that I will obey the President of the United States and the orders of the officers appointed over me, according to the rules and Articles of War."[77]

You have now been selected. Pete Lynn was a soldier, and his journey into the unknown had begun.

CHAPTER 3

This Sandy Place They Call Texas

"OLD MAN SPRINGTIME REALLY MOVED IN LAST WEEK," A MARGRACE millhand reported in late March. "The robins have come and gone, everything is blossoming, the leaves are beginning to sprout and the fellows are coming to work in their shirt sleeves."[1] Pete Lynn missed it all as he left Fort Bragg behind after a ten-day stay. A long bus and train ride later, he found himself staring at a land of brown sand and dust, of endless hills and swirling wind, and of marching, helmeted men in olive drab. The name on the sign read Camp Fannin. It was 900 miles from Kings Mountain, but it might as well have been on another planet.[2]

Camp Fannin, located nine miles northeast of Tyler, Texas, was officially a Replacement Training Center (RTC). Nearly 460,000 men passed through such facilities during 1944.[3] Named for Col. James Walker Fannin, a hero of the Texas Revolution who had been dispatched by Mexican troops, Camp Fannin had opened on May 29, 1943. A handbook someone handed to Pete described it as "15,000 acres of rolling hill country," but trainees would remember it more as a place where East Texas winds blew East Texas dirt around endlessly. The camp bulged with nearly 19,000 men, not including the prisoners of war who were also confined there. Lt. Col. Charles H. Brammel commanded.[4]

The army treated each RTC like an inflated division, organizing its soldiers into regiments, battalions, and companies. Camp Fannin had six regiments and two battalions. Each company bulged with 200 to 240 men, including 6 officers and 30 enlisted men permanently attached as the training cadre. The companies within each regiment or battalion were split into four platoons, and each platoon contained four squads.[5] Pete was assigned to Company C, 84th Training Battalion, 15th Regiment, which was under the command of a Lieutenant Keller.[6]

If Pete read the camp handbook, he would have gotten a glimpse of what to expect over the next seventeen weeks. "Replacement training centers provide you—the new soldier—with basic military training immediately upon your entrance into the service," the publication promised. "After you have undergone this training, you will be transferred and assigned to a permanent organization."[7] What the handbook did not explain was that basic training would be both challenging and jarring. It started innocently enough, with a short orientation lecture upon arrival in an assembly area or room designed to be comfortable, cheerful, and attractive, with posters on the wall.[8] Then, as a trooper recalled, the first day on post continued with a routine physical and introductions to non-commissioned officers and the company commander. Such moments could be memorable. Piling out of a bus, the trooper looked wide-eyed at all the hustle and bustle, hurry up and wait as an officer assigned the men to training companies. "That officer must have called off between 800 and 900 names and never faulted on one," the soldier recalled. After a break for chow, the men were assigned to a barracks, which would have been a two-story building with bunks for sixty-three men, and a bank of toilets, lavatories, and showerheads. Once each man was assigned a bunk, instructors ordered the new arrivals into the company street and lined them up by squad and platoon. "The training sargent [*sic*] called [us] to attention, then shouted forward march," he wrote. "That's when I found out I had 2 left feet. Most of the men were pretty good. But I was like training a wild horse. [The] Sargent . . . looked at me and said 'O Boy.' That's all for the first day at Camp Fannin."[9]

Back in Kings Mountain, an aching hole burst open in Ruth's heart. Those first days without Pete were very hard, including Sunday night, March 18, 1944. "Boy was it lonesome," she told her diary. A few days later her mood had not changed. "Dearest Soldier," she wrote him. "It still seems like a bad dream addressing you like that, if only we could wake up and the war was over."[10]

For Ruth, those first days away passed as slow as molasses. The lack of mail from Pete made it worse; she could only assume that his training schedule kept him from writing. "Honey I hope you're O.K.," she wrote him. "I think of you all the time and love you a bushel & a peck as Bob says." Friends and family tried to soften her grief. She spent a lot of time with Hazel, and Pete's dad came by almost every day. Focusing on the kids was another lenitive for Ruth, but nothing worked completely. It seemed that the very heavens shared her sadness. Rain pelted Kings Mountain that March, rendering it too wet to use a clothesline or work in the victory garden.[11]

Even innocent questions from friends, family members, and acquaintances bothered Ruth. It seemed that everybody wanted to know how he was doing. "Honey you have friends that won't forget you as well as me and the babies," she wrote.[12] The questions got so numerous that she hesitated to leave home. "Honey my heart nearly burst wishing for you," she wrote. "Sunday morning it was so bad we couldn't go to church so I read the paper & wrote letters & just sat & thought of you." She found comfort with a close circle of friends, parents, and in-laws, until she saw Pete's "cigs" and clothes lying around the house and burst into tears.[13]

Ruth worried about how the "brats" would handle Pete's absence. Though she was not yet two, Bobbie noticed. She liked to carry around a photo of her dad, and occasionally she would coo "Daddy" and kiss it. Mickey surprised Ruth. "Mickey understands better than we thought," she told Pete. "She hasn't cried for you, just talks all the time about her dad[d]y being a soldier and having a pretty suit. I think she's proud the way she talks."[14] If the service of her husband wasn't enough, Ruth also worried about her brother Joe. He was in the navy at a base in California, and Ruth knew that he would be shipping out soon. Joe returned his sister's concern and feared that she would have to give their little house up or get a job now that Pete was in the service.[15]

Weekdays passed easier with all of the chores she had to handle. That included meal preparation, with breakfast at around 7:30 A.M. each morning, dinner at noon, and supper at 6:00 P.M.; one night, she could not taste a fish supper she prepared thanks to a bad cold. In between, she washed their clothes and mopped and swept the house. On a warm day, the kids might go outside to play, but that meant Ruth would have some dirty kids to bathe. Ruth also had to manage their meager finances. "I hope you won't mind how I spend what I get," she told him. "You know how I hate being in debt, as soon as I go to town I[']m going to settle up with Dr. Ramseur then I know we can get a Dr. & groceries." She also planned to pay off their debt at the company store, and then she would try to save a little to celebrate with when Pete came home. Other chores included obtaining coal for the stove and buying shoes for the kids. Mick's shoes were worn out so Ruth had to go to the ration board to request an extra stamp.[16]

Single parenthood, Ruth discovered, was taxing. Soon she found herself writing Pete, "I'm so tired I don't know whether I'll write so you can read it or not."[17] But at least it kept her busy. In the quiet of a Saturday night, with her chores done and the kids in bed, Ruth missed Pete the most. "Darling I don't want to write you anything that would make you homesick or anything," she wrote him, "but I think you[']d like to know I miss you a lot and that's putting it mild."[18] To make things easier, Ruth and the kids stayed with her parents part of the time. It was common in those days for multiple generations to live under the same roof because it made daycare easier.[19]

One thing kept Ruth going: news from Pete, once his mail started arriving. "I live day to day waiting for the mail man," she announced. Ruth kept the postal service busy by writing every morning and every night, and she relished every reply of Pete's. "Darling, I'm so glad you write me so often, that's what I live for now one day till the next, your letters," she told him.[20] Sometimes Pete sent treats along with his letters, and the girls loved them. The arrival of a box of candy was a real cause for celebration. "It was the first real candy we've had in ages and it sure was good," Ruth told him. Ruth also cherished a photo her husband sent. "And honey I don't know what I thought you'd look like in uniform but I hardly knew you," she wrote. "As much as I could see of you, you look pretty swell in uniform."[21]

In return, Ruth filled her letters with encouragement and love. When Pete did not perform well on a test, Ruth assured him. "Don't worry about the mental test, you'll have plenty of chances to show how smart you are," she wrote. "It don't take book learning every time to be smart. What ever job they give you, do it well & learn to like it & get along good with your officers."[22]

Meanwhile, there was little going on in Kings Mountain to divert Ruth's attention. Maybe she went to the Hillbilly Jamboree at the high school one Monday night in May, since most of the town did. "Didn't realize that so many people liked to hear Hillbilly music," a Kings Mountain resident wrote. "They kept packing the cash customers in the auditorium until they had them everywhere except hanging from the rafters."[23] There was also some minor news about the draft board. Some members came and went, and the board's offices moved from the second floor of the bank to the first floor of the Fulton Building. "Since they had sent practically everyone in town who was able to climb those stairs, they thought it best to get down on the ground floor for the duration," a wag wrote. Ruth was beyond caring about the draft board since her man had already been shipped out.[24]

So passed the spring of 1944 in Kings Mountain. Although the tears eventually came less frequently, the days still passed slowly at the little cottage near the mill. Ruth kept looking for ways to make life without Pete more agreeable. Ever the able seamstress, she liked to sew all day long when she could.[25] She also tended to their victory garden, but the sweat and toil made Pete worry. "Don't you work too Hard in your victory garden," he chided her. "I want to Have the same sweet Little wife that I left the 15th of March."[26]

Pete had never seen anything this regimented and intimidating, even in the card room. Feeling trepid, he looked about and saw a collection of wooden frame buildings and prefabricated huts. Most stood only one or two stories tall, and the flagpole was easily the tallest object around. The buildings were all painted the same drab color, while the streets were laid out in orderly rectangles that gave the camp a sameness that was reminiscent of a mill village.[27]

Camp Fannin was also full of needles, crew cuts, and uniforms that didn't always fit. Every day called for calisthenics, unending marching, weapons practice, and kitchen police. The camp even had its own language, and Pete had to learn it. If some days proved to be mundane, others did not because Pete would be exposed to what an official army historian called the "sound and fury of actual combat."[28] The whole experience was designed to shift a man's mindset from civilian to military and to prepare him for war.

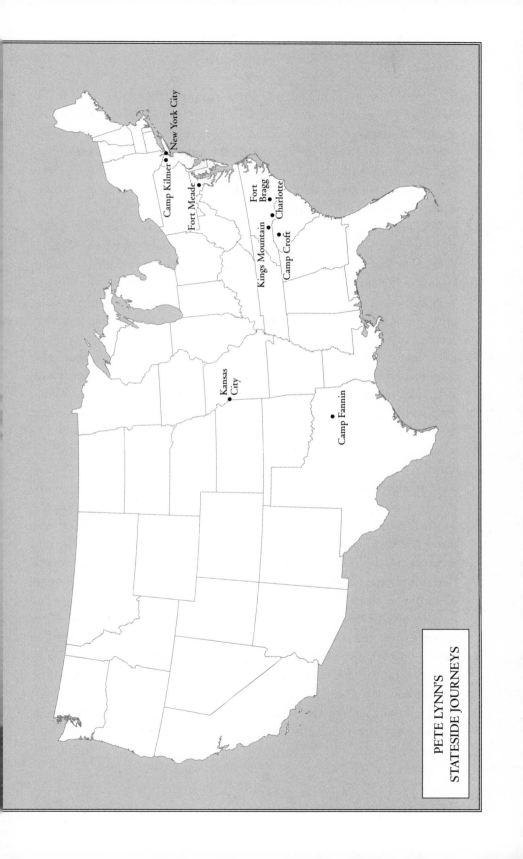

PETE LYNN'S
STATESIDE JOURNEYS

"Well I am in the infantry and this camp has the name of being one of the toughest in the country," wrote a Camp Fannin trainee named Ova Ratliff. "They are awful strict on us. They haven't let us go anywhere but where they have herded us." To Ratliff, the camp's purpose was clear: they were being trained as replacements to fill in "until some division gets enough of their men killed to need more and they send to one of those camps for whatever replacements they need."[29]

RTCs were a little like technical schools, as ground combat troops had to grasp multiple mechanical things and processes—with the singular difference that you were being taught to kill and not be killed. Training started with general military subjects such as military courtesy, guard duty, first aid, close-order drill, and care of clothing and equipment, along with physical conditioning. During the second phase of training, men learned to handle various weapons and also how to work with other squad and platoon members under strenuous, tense conditions. This phase also required gaining a basic understanding of camouflage and concealment, first aid, mine removal, booby trap detection, field sanitation, patrolling, map reading, living outdoors, and recognition of equipment, vehicles, and aircraft. During the third and final phase, training moved into tactics, scouting, patrolling, night operations, and combined-arms training where infantry, artillery, and armor worked together. It was capped by a 25-mile road march with full equipment, because a man had to be ready both mentally and physically: the war being fought in both Europe and the Pacific was a mobile war that would require strength, mental alertness, and leadership skills. "The intelligence, skill, and stamina of semi-isolated riflemen and small-unit commanders," an army historian wrote, "were to determine not only individual survival on the battlefield but also in many cases the outcome of battle."[30]

Ready or not—and it was more the latter than the former—Pete plunged into this new world. Everything was novel to him except for rising early, which Pete was accustomed to thanks to Park Yarn. At Camp Fannin, first call sounded abruptly at 5:55 A.M., which was followed by reveille and roll call at 6:05 A.M. (Unless Pete was on kitchen police, or KP, duty, which means he awoke an hour earlier.) By 6:20 A.M., the soldiers had to wash, dress, make their bunks, and march to the mess hall. They were allowed twenty minutes to eat breakfast, after which they policed the barracks and gathered their equipment. At 8:00 A.M., the real work began with calisthenics, field training, or classes on various topics. The program continued all day except for a break for the noon meal. Evening mess was at 5:30 P.M. Mail call and announcements followed at 7:00 P.M., along with chores such as cleaning equipment, polishing shoes, showering, and getting ready for bed. Last on the schedule was free time at 9:20 P.M. and lights out at 9:45 P.M.[31]

It was an eye-opener. Not long after arriving at Camp Fannin, Pete broke his watch. If that was not a sign that the days ahead would be difficult, there were certainly other visible omens. One trainee remembered being told, "that we were going over seas and we better pay attention because the little things might save our lives." Aches and pains also served as reminders of the challenge before him. Not long after he arrived at the camp, Pete got two shots in his left arm. About the same time, he hurt his right leg while exercising. When the men were ordered on a 3-mile march, Pete struggled. "I couldn't Hardly walk But I made it," he wrote.[32]

Then there were obstacle courses, and digging, and marching, marching, marching. "We just Cralid [crawled] under some Barb wire Fences and Run and Hide Be Hind Bushes and Dig a Hole in the ground Laying Down Flat you should try it some time it shure is fun Ha Ha," he wrote Ruth. "Darling you don't know How much fun we Do Have Down Here we march a while and then we march some more."[33]

Trainees like Pete also got their fill of spit and shine. One morning, the men got up forty-five minutes early to prepare for inspection. Pete didn't think they woke early enough. "[W]e Had to Shave Clean our Rifels and Shine our Shoes and Put on our uneeforms," Pete wrote. "Boy Did I have to get in a Hurry Some times Have to Be Super Man and then you Don't get it Dun Ha Ha."[34] To Pete, this part of soldiering was so much folderol. "[T]he only thing I Don't Like is shaving Every Day," he told Ruth. Still, he preferred shaving and shoe shining to the alternative. "Boy if you want to get your But chewed out you just Fail to shave or shine your shoes and you no How I Hated Both of them Ha Ha."[35]

The company's barracks had to be sparkling from top to bottom at all times, but it took practice for these rookie soldiers to learn how to clean the building just right. On one occasion, Company C received the dubious honor of having the worst barracks. "When we get that we have to work at nite," he explained. "They Have [a] sine [sign] they Hang on the Front of the Dirtiest Barrick and it says TS you [k]no[w] what that stands for if you Don't its tough shit Ha Ha."[36]

Rifle training was the centerpiece of the regimen. "Darling you ask me about shooting that Rifel Boy Me and it Has Had a time," he told Ruth. Fortunately for Pete he knew rifles, so he did better than most. The M1 Garand, a .30 caliber semiautomatic rifle, was the U.S. Army's main infantry weapon. "We are just Learning how to Handle it now," he wrote of the Garand in early April. "Boy it shure is Heavy it weighs about 9 pounds." When it was announced that prizes would be given to the best shots on the range, Pete's confidence kicked in. "Boy you no I will win Ha Ha," he bragged to Ruth.[37]

Monday, April 24 was his first day on the firing line. After shooting at targets 200 and then 300 yards away, Pete walked away encouraged. "I did Pritty Well," he told Ruth. He did even better on his second trip to the range, which included firing at 300 yards' range at a rapid rate, and then at 500 yards. There was a downside, though. "Tell Dad that my Rifel kicks worse than old tildis does," he wrote, referring to an animal the family owned. "I came in Monday with a Busted Lip and a sore arm." His lip swelled up "as Big as a Hen Egg."[38]

Four days later, the company went back to the rifle range and fired for record. The army awarded badges at three levels: Marksman, Sharpshooter, and the highest, Expert. Pete thought he had a chance to earn a Sharpshooter badge. "I made score of (84) Boy that is good," Pete wrote of one round. He even had six bull's eyes on the 300-yard range. However, the weather conspired against him. "The wind was Blowing the sand and Dust so Bad you couldn't see to shoot," he complained. In the end, Pete missed getting the Sharpshooter designation by a mere two points, but he did qualify as a Marksman.[39] He was disappointed, but he told his sister that "at least I will get a meddle [medal] any how" to go along with his busted lip.[40]

The men practiced shooting regularly, and Pete kept shining. On May 1, all thirty men in his platoon lined up to fire, but Pete was the only one to qualify. "Just think one out of 30," he bragged. "[Ai]n[']t that the stuff."[41] Rifle training meant more than just shooting on a range, however. It also required the men to learn to care for their weapon, doting over it as a parent does a child. Like many new recruits, it took Pete time to get the hang of it. One day in early May, he cleaned his rifle as thoroughly as he knew how, but an officer inspected his rifle and pronounced the chamber too dirty. Pete could only shrug and try again.[42]

Rifles, rifles, rifles. "Boy they shure Do think Lots About thise Rifel," Pete complained.[43] And Camp Fannin's training program covered more than just the Garand; it exposed the men to virtually every piece of American equipment the men might use on the battlefield. That included gas masks. Early in the training course, the men of Company C were issued masks and instructed on their use. Then, the men trotted into the middle of a gas cloud to test how quickly they could put the masks on. "Boy Did I Get it in nothing flat," Pete wrote. "[I]t was Easy for me it works about Like my Paint Mask Did just slides on over your head."[44]

A trip to the hand grenade range reminded Pete that this was a dangerous business. He learned that he could pitch grenades as well as he could pitch a baseball, although he had to learn that you threw grenades differently. "Boy you should Have seen me throwing them," he wrote. Then, to get an idea of what it felt like to be on the receiving end of a hand grenade, Pete went downrange. "[T]hey Put me Down in the Paster [pasture] about 250 yards I was standing there thought out of Range," he wrote, "But the Pieces Hit all around me[.] You should have seen me getting behind a big tree[.] I was standing Behind the tree and a Piece about the Size of my thumb Knocked the Bark off about 3 inches about my Head." It's no wonder that some posts erected mock headstones with warnings like, "Here lies Brown the Clown, who wouldn't keep his head down."[45]

Day after day, different weapons kept coming. On another range, Pete fired a weapon he could not spell. He called it the one that "Bob Burnes Invented," which meant the Bazooka, the antitank rocket launcher named for a prop comedian Bob Burns used in his radio programs.[46] Pete also fired an "anta tank grenade" from an attachment to his M1 Garand rifle that "nearly [k]nock[ed] my shoulder off." Next, he handled the Browning Automatic Rifle (BAR) and the M1 Carbine. Pete did not care for the BAR. "[I]t shoots to[o] Fast for me," he explained. "[It] will shoot 550 Rounds Per minute you will start shooting one and the next thing you no you are some where Else." Nonetheless, Pete excelled on the weapon. He tied another man for high score in the company. He also did well enough on the carbine range to qualify for that weapon.[47]

With all of this weapons training, the noise was ubiquitous. "There is hardly an hour of the day and a lot of time at night that there isn't rifles firing, machine guns firing, cannons firing and bombs going off, mines and booby traps going off and hand grenades going off all around the place," Ratliff wrote.[48]

Another important part of infantry training was fieldcraft: the art of living in the field. It required extended periods in the thick Texas woods that Pete described as Boy Scout camping trips. Having grown up hunting, Pete took to the field like he took to weapons. "We had a Big time yesterday Ramblen around in the woods," he told his sister. It was, he added, "Just Like Rabbit Hunting at Home Except we were the Dogs Ha Ha." Yet it wasn't long before Pete had his fill of hiking. "Boy that is all you Do," he wrote. The men marched between two and five miles daily, and his feet paid the price as angry blisters emerged on his size-10½ feet.[49] Longer marches were required as well, including a twenty-mile march at one point. Forced marching was the worst. "Boy these Force Hikes are the stuff," he told Ruth. "We march Rite fast and then we Run a Piece and when we get our cloes wet with swet we come home."[50]

Prepping all of the gear needed for an overnight maneuver took some doing. "Darling it shure is a job getting Redy to go," he told Ruth. "[Y]ou Have to Have all you[r] Equipment in First Class Shape and that every thing you got we sent our bed roll on the truck[.] But we have enough to cary on our back to we have a full Field Back and gass mask and Rifel," he wrote. Pete was still Pete. When Company C camped beside a lake, he stared at the shimmering waters and longed to go swimming or fishing.[51]

Some parts of Pete's training struck him favorably. One night, the whole battalion plopped down on a hillside and listened as officers pointed out the Big Dipper, the North Star, and other highlights of the dark Texas sky. "I enjoyed it more than any thing weve had yet," Pete said. "They Had 3 thousan soilders sitting on the Hill and when they gave them a Brake He told us all to strack [strike] our matches at the same time it was a Pretty site," he wrote. He told his sister, "It looked like a town lit up at a distant."[52]

Pete did not mention much about the classes he took. There were many, and much of it doubtless bored Pete. He would have endured six hours of lectures on topics such as military courtesy, discipline, and the Articles of War. Another ten hours covered sanitation, first aid, and sex hygiene. There were three hours of classes on protecting military information, an hour's lecture on army organization, and seven hours on progress at the front and on the nation's war aims. The latter would have included a viewing of *Why We Fight*, a movie by the legendary Hollywood director Frank Capra, which Pete the cineast probably appreciated more than lectures.[53]

In contrast, he liked dress parade. One Saturday afternoon, the men polished their weapons and shoes, formed up, and began marching. Pete loved almost every minute of it. "Boy was it Pretty," he bragged to Ruth. "Darling you should Have seen me marching Rite up on the front line of C Company Rite Behind the company commander." After passing the battalion commander, the men snapped their heads to the right. Then a bugle called retreat, and the men presented arms. Finally, they stood at attention for about ten minutes, and it was uncomfortable. "Boy was it Hot Drops of swet Run off me Big as Horse turds," he wrote.[54]

For Pete Lynn, the irony of those seventeen long weeks is that he discovered he had a natural inclination toward soldiering, but his heart was in Kings Mountain. "Darling you don't know how Home Sick I am But I ant gona Let it get me Down like that For it wont get you any where in the army," he wrote.[55]

Pete bore a number of fears through this experience, and they ranged from the silly to the serious. One concern was his height. He was so tall that his feet stuck out of his pup tent about 10 inches.[56] That prompted jokes and snide comments.

Pete's limited education troubled him as well. The average GI in those days had finished a year of high school. Having only made it through the sixth grade, Pete worried that he was intellectually behind his comrades, even though he was not entirely alone for about a third of his fellow soldiers had not progressed past grade school either. When he told Ruth that he felt like he was slower to grasp things than the others, she scolded him for it. "Darling you said to me to stop talking about Being Dum I am getting a Little Better," he admitted.[57]

Age was another worry. The average American soldier in 1944 was twenty-six, stood 5 feet 8 inches, and weighed 144 pounds. At 6 feet tall and 150 pounds, Pete was physically similar to many of his comrades, if a little taller. Age was the biggest difference. At thirty-three, and with a wife and kids to boot, Pete was wizened compared to many of the men at Camp Fannin.[58] Sometimes his age showed. One early morning, BAR class was particularly tough after he had stayed up all the previous night on guard duty. As a lieutenant lectured, Pete dozed. The officer noticed. "The first thing I [k]new He was waking me up I Had went to sleep," he wrote. "He ask[ed] me a question about the gun and I just told him I Didn't no sir and He just laughed and aske[d] some one Else."[59]

Pete and his comrades didn't always get off quite so easily. On another occasion, while the men were in formation, Pete missed a command. The sergeant noticed and called Pete "old man," much to the mirth of the rest of the platoon.[60] To his credit, Pete understood that getting dressed down was just part of this new life. "[T]hey Chew our ass out some times but we just laff about it at nite when we get Back to the . . . Barricks," he wrote. "[W]e have a Lot of fun at nite Laughing about the mistakes we make During the Day."[61]

If military training pushed the body and the mind, it also jolted his heart like an electric fence. Never before had he been separated from his family and his hometown for so long. "Darling I was standing out side the Dentle Clinik to Day next to a window and one of the nurse was singing Carolinia moon and when she said shining on the one that wates for you Don't know How I felt[.] I Rembered How we used to sing it to gether and I nearly cried," he wrote.[62] A couple of weeks later, the heartache seized him again. It came at the end of a long day as the men were trudging back to camp, the straps of their heavy field packs digging into their shoulders. Then the skies opened up with a heavy rain; the men could hardly see where they were going, but rather than complain the men started to sing. First, they gave a rough rendition of Gene Autry's "Springtime in the Rockies," a longtime hit song Pete knew from WBT radio. Then, the soldiers sang one of Ruth's favorites, "I Love You Best of All." Pete got emotional. "Boy did it Bring Back Memories," he told Ruth.[63]

Since the daylight hours were packed, gloomy thoughts usually flooded in at night when he had more time to think. One such night found Pete in a foxhole. He knew that he would not be able to sleep much in that uncomfortable little ditch, so he just sat and thought. Overhead, a beautiful moon shone in the dark sky, and Pete "thought of My 3 Little girls back home and told the moon to kiss you good nite for me."[64] In another bivouac, the family followed him to sleep. "I Lay Down in the warm sand Dozed of to sleep and Had the sweetest Dream," he wrote. "I thought I was just walking up the steps of our little 3 room Cottage to take you and Bob Mick in my arms[.]" Then a whistle blew and jerked him rudely awake.[65]

He survived with letters. In a style all his own, with poorly spelled words and homespun phrases, this man with a sixth-grade education became a prolific letter writer. Every day he could, and sometimes more than once a day, Pete wrote Ruth, his siblings, and his parents. The training schedule did not always leave enough time for a proper letter, but he figured a workaround: after lights out, Pete would sneak into the latrine, sit down on a toilet, prop his writing paper in his lap, and write away. He kept one such bathroom letter short because he had to get up at 4:00 A.M. the next morning for KP. One wonders whether his uncomfortable porcelain perch also had something to do with the letter being brief.[66]

Each letter was uniquely Pete: full of barracks chatter, stories of training, jokes—and love. "Just to take you in my arms and hold you would be Heaven to me Rite Now," he told Ruth.[67] The kids were constantly on his mind as well. "Tell Mick and Bob I still love them a Bushel and a Peck and a Hug around the Neck," he purred, not long after arriving in Texas. "Boy would I like to hug their Neck and yours to . . . Roses are Red violets or [are] Blue when this war is over I am Coming Back to you and I don't Mean Maby."[68]

Some days were harder than others. "Well Darling I cant think of any thing to say excep that [I] Love you with all my Heart," he wrote Ruth. "[Y]ou Bob—Mick is three of the Dearst things in if I could Just see and Hug you all as tite as I want to this army could go jump in the

Lake . . . Having to Be away From you and them some times I could take my Banette and stick it throw [thru] my Hart and not Hurt any worse . . . well I Had Better hush Before I Start Crying and Have the Boys Here [hear] in the Barricks[.]"[69]

His family was never far from his thoughts. "Just got caught up with my washing and Laying on my Bunk Listing to the Boy argie [argue] and thinking of you and the kids," he wrote. And he kept thinking about them, and loving them, despite regular interruptions such as barracks williwaws, loading trucks, or sitting down to a meal of roast pork, cabbage, carrots, syrup, peaches, and coffee.[70]

Some letters were quite mundane. In one, he told Ruth he needed envelopes and razor blades. In another, he asked Ruth for cigarettes and instructed her to tell Charlie Hawkins "not to plow too hard Be shure and keep that mule till I get home and I will ride him." He also told Ruth not to send him any more books, as he did not have time to read them.[71]

Pete Lynn at Camp Fannin, April 1944
Source: Lynn Collection

Once he even asked for string, which he couldn't get at camp. On the other hand, there were some items in plentiful supply at the camp, including candy and gum; he sent them home often. One of the packages he mailed home included a box of Milky Way candy bars, which surely left the kids' faces smeared with chocolate and a smile.[72]

Small wonder that mail call was Pete's favorite part of each day—he counted the hours until the time came. Family and friends kept the letters coming, to the point that it was not unusual for him to receive several at a time. On one of his best mail days, he went to the orderly room and found five letters waiting for him: two from Ruth, one from Bill, one from his parents, and another from a friend. "Shore was glad to Here from them all," he wrote. That same week, ten letters arrived over two days, and he devoured every one after the company returned from a hike. "Then I sit Down and Read and it is just Like talking to you," he wrote. "I just Picture you and Bob & Mick in my mind[.]" He could even hear Bob say "Daddy," and see her stick out her tongue. The hardest days were those when no mail arrived. He once told Ruth that if she stopped writing, he "would come over the Hill."[73]

Pete was careful to include his kids in his correspondence. Soon after he arrived at Camp Fannin, postcards began flowing toward Kings Mountain. His favorites were linen cards with cartoons on them, the ones produced by Chicago-based Curt Teich & Co. Inc., the world's largest printer of view and advertising postcards.[74] They showed everything from army life to famous Texas people, places, and things. One he selected depicted a soldier accidentally hitting another soldier with a rifle during drill beneath the headline, "Getting a Snootful of Army Life." Another showed two girls holding a jump rope for a boy under the caption, "I'm on the jump here every minute." Inside, Pete wrote messages that were, literally, short and sweet. "Just a card to cheer you up and hope you are fine and Dandy for your old Dadey shure loves you," or "Hello Micky, How is Dadies little girl to nite. Sweet dreams till I get Home."[75]

A pervading image from World War II is of Rosie the Riveter, the strong yet still feminine bandana-wearing woman who labors in American industry while the men are away. It is an image based on the fact that America did indeed turn to women—not to mention blacks, teenagers, the aged, the handicapped, and others—to keep factories and shipyards and farms running. In due course, more than 6 million women joined the workforce during World War II, though equality did not necessarily follow. Many grumbled, "Remember when women had to get married to get men's wages?"[76]

Although more than 50 percent of American women remained full-time housewives during the war, the trend of women in the workforce was still real. By 1943, women constituted nearly a third of the workers nationally, while in North Carolina the total was even higher with women making up about half.[77] Mills were part of the reason why North Carolina had a different total. Women employees were nothing new in mills. Kings Mountain had its own version of Rosie the Riveter long before the war arrived.

Ruth was among those Kings Mountain women who were accustomed to employment. On June 1, 1944, she decided to don work clothes once again and went to work at Pete's mill, Park Yarn. There is no record why Ruth did that, but money was undoubtedly a driver. Full-time work also gave her a distraction. She came to appreciate Mondays when she could go to the mill and think about something other than her separation from Pete.[78]

Kings Mountain's mills were somewhat unique in those days. The industrial work of World War II mostly funneled to large companies rather than small, yet both Margrace and Park Yarn thrived. "It isn't exactly a life of ease here on the Home Front," reported the *Old Mountaineer*. "You'd be surprised to see some of these that are 'too old to fight' pull two 8 hour shifts right along in order to keep production from lagging. And then to see some of these women holding down a man's job without complaining. They aren't getting any medals for their contribution to the War Effort, but that doesn't stop them."[79] Across the highway, Park Yarn ran just as hard as Margrace, and Ruth's decision to get a job was timely because officials were having difficulty staffing the mill.[80]

Ruth rejoined the workforce at a momentous time. Just days after she began working again, the Allies invaded France. "Kings Mountain citizens took the momentous day very quietly but stayed near their radios for last minute developments," the *Kings Mountain Herald* reported. "Church bells and mill whistles sounded early in the morning announcing that D-Day had arrived."[81] D-Day may have given Ruth some hope that the war would end soon. Until then, she could only pray for Pete while she focused on her family and work. "I'm keeping the home fires burning for one of Uncle Sam's soldiers and that's Private Pete L[y]nn," she wrote. "My soldier & my babies soldier dady."[82]

Pete harbored a special dread for one of Camp Fannin's nondescript buildings: the dental clinic. As a linthead, the man from Kings Mountain had not had the money to spend on his teeth, so years of poor dental care had left his mouth a mess. When he arrived for training, Pete did not have a complete set of teeth and those that remained were not worth keeping, so the army planned to correct that. The dental work was set to begin soon after he arrived at the camp. "I shore do dread it," he wrote. "I will get Be hind with my training and will Have to make it up at nite I gess."[83]

By that point in the war, 25,000 dentists—about one-third of all civilian dentists—had been recruited into the army because there were so many dental challenges to solve. The army based many of its dentists at RTCs because they had the needed facilities and recruits would be there long enough to undergo treatment.[84]

On April 21, Pete arrived early at the camp's dental clinic. The first step was to pull his bad teeth. It would take more than one appointment to pull them all, so the dentist started yanking on the teeth in the front and upper left side of his mouth. Fortunately for Pete, they put him to sleep first. "I counted up to Fore and then Last count I Don't mean I passed out," Pete told Ruth. "He was Pulling them so fast I couldn't count it Didn't Hurt a Bit[,] only when He was sticking that [needle] in . . . I nearly passed out." As Pete slumbered in the dental chair, the dentist took his tools and scraped Pete's gums "till they are as Level as you Please." Then, the dentist sewed Pete's gums up and sent him on his way. Pete's mouth ached after the appointment, but the medicine the dentist gave him helped. The pills could not control his embarrassment over the vast gaps in his mouth. "I will wait till they get my teeth Fixed now and then I can grin Ha Ha," he said.[85]

The next day, Pete's jaw swelled up "like I have the mumps." He felt weak and sick, so he had to take a day off from training. As he lay in his bunk, Pete hit rock bottom. He wished for "some body to simphize with me an Feel sorry," but "Down Here they Don't care if you Live or Die Ha Ha," he wrote. Fortunately the day of rest—and the gnawing concern that he would miss so much training that he would have to start all over again—did him good. He only missed one meal, and had to pass on some cake Ruth sent him, but sharing the cake with his barrack mates did not hurt his popularity.[86]

Pete's next appointment came almost two weeks later. He knew what to expect, but he dreaded it just the same. This time, the camp dentist extracted six more teeth. Pete's jaws did not swell, but the treatment made Pete so out of sorts that he still had to take another day off. He spent it resting in his bunk, writing letters, and spitting into a can. Only ten teeth remained.[87]

A week later, Pete returned to the camp dentist for another "Tooth Pulling Day," as he now called them. The dentist pulled six more, leaving his upper mouth empty and a mere four teeth on the bottom. His jaw was now hurting constantly, but nothing could sour his sense of humor. "I will Have to eat Mashed Potatoes for a while Ha Ha," he joked. Eventually, he learned that teeth were not always necessary at the dinner table. "Boy I can gum the houn[d] out of anything," he bragged. Pete even saw humor when a dentist announced that he would receive just one set of dentures; Pete said that he would not be able to send an extra set of teeth home for his dad to use.[88]

Pete kept smiling, gums and all, as his jaws puffed up again and again. A few days after his uppers came out, swelling returned and he had to take yet another day off from training. He watched his comrades leave the barracks, and then he hit the sack to write letters and swish warm salt water in his aching mouth.[89]

By now, Pete was running out of teeth so this stage of treatment could not last much longer. Once the swelling went down, the dentists finished the job, leaving his mouth as bare as the family bank account. "Darling you Have got a toothless Husban," he told Ruth. "They got the other 4 about 2 oclock and Boy am I glad it is over."[90]

That left one more appointment at the dental clinic, but for once Pete did not dread this one. It was time to receive his new teeth. He did not know what to expect when he settled back into the chair and the camp dentist leaned over him to fit his new denture. When he finished, the dentist gave Pete a mirror. "I Like to fanted to see Pretty teeth in my mouth Darling they did Look good," he wrote. Excited, Pete bounded to the barracks to show off his new teeth. His buddies were impressed and complimented him. It would take a few days for Pete to get used to them, but the newfound pride in his appearance would linger. Thanks to his improving physique and his shining new teeth, Pete was proud of his appearance for the first time in years. One night, he put on some khakis and a cap and glanced in a mirror. "Darling I Didn't realized how good looking your Husban was till to nite," he wrote. "The folks want no me when I come home."[91]

With that, Pete Lynn had played a small part in what a writer has called "the most momentous job in the history of dentistry." He had contributed a mouthful to the 15,189,936 teeth extracted during the war, and he was also the proud owner of one of the 2.5 million sets of dentures dentists fitted. Pete's treatment had taken longer than the military average of 38.5 days, and his "dental rehabilitation" had doubtless required more than the average cost of between $54.19 and $78, but to Uncle Sam it was worth it.[92]

The end of dental treatment did not mean the end of Camp Fannin's challenges. The training cadre kept up the pressure. One night, the men stayed in the field until nearly midnight. When they finally returned to the barracks, Pete collapsed into his bunk. "Boy was I tir[e]d," he reported. "I was the nearst gave out since I Bin in the Army."[93] The following week, Pete's platoon spent a whole day on the firing range. Practice continued into the evening, so the training cadre had food delivered to the range. It arrived at 7:00 p.m. Exhausted, the men pulled out their mess kits and plopped down to eat. "It is like a picnick to see us all Sitting around Eating Chow," Pete joked, but he didn't really mean it. The men still had to clean their rifles, and Pete had to get up at 4:30 the next morning to serve on a detail.[94]

Other days demanded even more of them, especially when the men awoke at 4:00 a.m. and did not go to bed until 11:00 p.m.[95] On another day, the men slept to 5:15 a.m. and then got up to scrub their barracks for inspection. The training that followed was worse; officers "tried to kill us this morning," Pete wrote later. The culprit was an obstacle course. "Boy was it Hard," he thought. "We Had to Run about a Half mile Jump in Holes and over walls and crawl under Rocks and every thing." Back at the barracks that night, the men found no rest. "Darling I Didn't [k]no[w] I could work so fast till I get in the army," he wrote. "We come in to nite we Had 35 minutes to change cloes [clothes] and stand Retreat[.]

I shaved changed close and cleaned my Rifel had 5 Minutes to spare"
before lights out.[96]

One day in late May, Pete had to march with his rifle on one shoulder,
a light machine gun on the other, and a full field pack on his back. He was
glad when the weekend finally arrived. "Darling we Have got some more
Hard weeks ahead of us," he told Ruth, "But I Don't think they can Be
any Harder than this one." Even KP left him beat: it started early in the
morning and lasted well into the evening. "Boy they shure Did work us
Hard today," he wrote Ruth of one stint in the galley. "Had me washing
Pots Pans and it aint little Pots Pans you Have at Home they were Big some
of them Holds 20 gallon." Sometimes KP extracted a price—especially
from the dishwashing detail. "Just got out of K.P. Boy I shure am tird,"
he complained. "They Had me washing Dishes and I never see so many
in my life my hands are Runt [ruined]." If KP had any benefits, it was the
fact that it kept Pete out of bayonet practice, which he disliked intensely.[97]

One of the roughest days Pete experienced came in early April. "We
went out Learnt How to jump in Big Holes and throw Hand grenades,"
he explained. "I hurt my Rite Leg to we Had to Run From one Hole to
the other then jump thrue a winder about 4 feet Hy and Boy you had to
take off Like Blalocks Bull and to cap that off we went on a 10 mile Hike
with a Full Field Pack and Rifel we Had to Pitch tents." To add insult
to injury, at the end of the day Pete sat squarely on a thorn. It felt like it
penetrated all the way to the bone and left him quite sore.[98]

Pete grew convinced that the army was trying to kill him. At one
point, he had to complete a four-mile march in fifty minutes. A ten-mile
march followed a few days later.[99] Pete called it the "death March" because
of the brisk pace they were forced to take. "We run half way nearly and
had my rifel and combat pack to But I made it like a top," he wrote. Pete
bragged that every man in the company finished, which pleased the battalion commander. The bad news was that another ten-mile march was on
the schedule for the next day.[100]

The men who guided the trainees through the course impressed Pete.
"We Have the Best in the camp," he wrote. He was especially fond of a
Lieutenant Watkins, a soldier from South Carolina. "Boy he is a swell fellow,"
Pete wrote. The officers reciprocated that feeling. "Darling I am on the good

side off the officers in our company," he told Ruth. "I ask for a week end pass and the sergeant yes sire Lynn you can get one." Rotation policy and the demands of the war often took those leaders away from the camp, though. "We are losing some more of our non coms But the ones that are taking there place seem to be good fellows they have ben across and sent back."[101]

While some noncoms received approbation from the ranks, it was not true for everyone. Consider the case of two sergeants. One was popular; when he was reassigned to other duty, the men from the platoon chipped in and bought him a $15 travel bag as a parting gift.[102] A Sergeant Harvey generated different opinions among the men. He was tough. During a hand-to-hand exercise, the sergeant came up behind a trainee, grabbed him, and threw him to the ground, breaking his ankle in the process. "No body don't like him and boy we give him all the truble we can," Pete wrote.[103]

Camp Fannin made everything harder, for it seemed that the army had put the camp in the worst place it could find. It started with heat: as spring 1944 arrived, Pete learned how warm Texas could get. "Boy the wether is getting Hot Down Here now," he wrote in early April. "I sure Do Dredd going out on the Field in about 3 weeks it will be Plenty Hot." Pete longed to jump into Lake Crawford back home to cool off but knew that was a vain hope. At least, the army issued the men summer uniforms. "Boy you just ou[gh]t to see me in them Do I look good," he joked.[104]

Camp Fannin was not always dry. Pete had always thought of Texas as a dusty place, so he was surprised to learn Texas received its fair share of rain, which quickly turned the soil into "shoe mouth Deep" mud.[105] Occasionally, powerful thunderstorms rolled across the plains. One morning, a storm caught the company as it marched through some woods. Pete's platoon was in the lead. Another platoon followed about fifty yards behind. As rain fell and thunder crashed, lightning struck a tree standing alongside the trail about halfway between the two companies. No one was hurt, but nobody forgot that electric moment.[106]

Texas had its share of bugs too, and the insects came in all shapes and sizes. Chiggers were everywhere, and they nagged Pete to no end. He called them "Red Bugs," and it was clear that he had little use for them. Another varmint, the "Blister Bug," was worse. The bug left blisters every-where it walked. "One got on my leg the other nite and walked about

3 in[ches] and the next morning [I] Had a Blister just like I Had Burnt it with a match," he wrote. Pete also complained about the mosquitoes and gnats that descended in clouds. He was not alone. Rumor held that Texas mosquitoes were so large that they liked to check a man's dog tags for his blood type before biting.[107]

"Boy they sure give us all Kinds of Difernt training Down Here," Pete concluded. All of it was tough, but Pete told Ruth not to worry. He was a man and he could take it. "This army is good For you if you can stand it it wont kill you[.] But you will think you are going to Dye Ha ha."[108]

As the weeks passed and he continued to perform well, Pete's confidence rose. "Darling this army Life isn't so Bad," he decided. "I am Beginning to Like it Better."[109] It showed, and both the men in his platoon and the training cadre saw it. As a pre–Pearl Harbor father, Pete had seen and experienced more of life than most soldiers. It was common for such fathers to have a stabilizing effect on younger men in their units, and Pete was no exception, despite his lack of schooling. One night, the company was ordered to pitch tents. As they worked, the men looked to him for guidance. "I Don't Have to Do any thing, I am the Leader and I tell them what to Do How to [put up] their tents," he bragged to Ruth. "Boy I make them Fix them so they Cant Be seen From any Direction . . . I think Be For the war is over I will be Running this army."[110]

⁃⁓

Boot camp was not all work and no play. During his seventeen-week tour at the training center, he formed new relationships that helped him endure. That's no surprise, for Pete Lynn was the type of person who never met a stranger.[111] A photo he sent home shows the ever-slim trainee standing with eight other soldiers. Pete looks a bit awkward on the edge of the group with his ill-fitting uniform hanging loosely from his spare frame, but his bonhomie is evident: this is a man who is well-liked and belongs. His helmet sits at a jaunty angle. A smirk is on his face. He stands at attention, his mill days long forgotten. Around him, the other men in the photo bear their own confident smiles as they brandish proud smiles and Garand rifles. Pete told Ruth a lot about the men in the photo and other friends he made. They included Walter Briggs, who is in the

Pete Lynn (back row left) with eight Camp Fannin trainees.
Source: Lynn Collection

photo, and a man named Nelson who occasionally accompanied Pete into town. Then there was Pete's "Big Buddy from Arkinsaw." Pete was in awe of the man. "Boy, He Shure is a whop[p]er," he wrote. Pete started calling him his Body Guard, but one day he learned that his Arkansas friend had a soft spot. After flunking a firing range outing, Pete's "Big Buddy" broke into tears. Pete felt so sorry for him that he felt like crying too.[112]

The antics of these men helped push back the tides of homesickness and anxiety that often washed over Pete. "Darling I [am] laghing so I cant Hardly Rite," he wrote in one letter. "[T]hese Fellows Shure is Funny when they get started ... we can Have a Hard Day and come in at nite Every Body seems Like they are as Happy as a Lark." Many of them were "Party Boys," Pete explained, especially the "Little Short Fellow" who was barely 5 feet tall. "Boy is He a mess He keeps us Laughing all the time He is a Darn good fellow tho." Such men even made guard duty bearable. Guard duty rotated each night among the battalions at the camp. It required each company to march around the camp, rifles in hand, for two hours, and then stand down for two hours while another company took a turn. Pete made the best out of it. "Here I sit in the gard House Ha Ha we have a big time when we are on gard 2 of the Lutenents just came in and are Laffing and joking with the Boys," he wrote.[113]

Conflict was just as much a part of barracks life as humor. One night as Pete came out of the latrine, a fellow soldier pointed a water hose straight at him. Pete warned the man not to turn on the hose, but his words fell on deaf ears. The man turned the hose on, full force. Pete "grab[b]ed a Rack [rock] Hit Him with it then He came Running up to me and I gave Him a Rite to the Jaw and Layed Him in the Company Street Boy I am gitting mean," he wrote.[114]

Among the other few pleasures of training camp, Pete relished food as much as anything. Neither homesickness nor dental care curbed Pete's appetite because Camp Fannin made him, as he put it often, hungry as a bear. "Boy they can Fix up some good Eates Down Here and I can eat any thing they fix," he bragged. His favorite meal of the day was the first one. Early or not, Pete started every day with a huge breakfast: after eating a bowl or two of Wheaties, he would go back through the line for a plate heaping with hot cakes and syrup, bacon, and eggs. Occasionally, he added strawberry jelly. Whatever the cooks served, Pete would go through the line more than once. "I might get fat yet Ha ha," he joked.[115]

Each meal was a highlight in series of otherwise long, hard days. He made it a point not to miss dessert. As training drew to a close, Pete decided that he had eaten more ice cream in the last seventeen weeks than he had in his entire life. To prove it, he told the story of a July night when he put away two pints by himself. Back at the barracks, the eating continued when the men found treats inside packages from home. Pete urged Ruth to send him cookies, chocolate fudge, cake, and candy, because they were his favorite and he also enjoyed sharing them with his buddies. Rigorous exercise and dental treatments notwithstanding, Pete did manage to put on a few pounds. By mid-summer, the scales tipped 155 pounds.[116]

Mealtime aside, one thing helped Pete through Camp Fannin more than any other: his belief in God. In his letters home, Pete described worship services often, which Ruth probably found heartening. For example, one Sunday morning in late April found Pete and about 200 other trainees at Camp Fannin's Chapel #2. Company C's commander read from Luke 24:13-35, and then the chaplain delivered a sermon. His words inspired Pete, and so did the deep voices of dozens of soldiers singing hymns together. "The chaplain shore did Preach a good sermon," he said. "I didn't cry but I shure did feel like it." It made Pete miss Macedonia Church. "I Don't think I will want to miss a Sunday again," he wrote. He also decided that he needed Bible study; when he learned that Camp Fannin offered only worship services, he started going into town to attend Sunday School. "Tell all my Sunday School teacher," he wrote, "that I shure would like to here him [them] teach." Most of all, Pete asked for the folks back home to lift him up. "I need the prarers," he wrote. Indeed, he said he could feel their prayers—especially his mother's.[117]

Camp Fannin's Easter services were possibly the most memorable Pete ever attended. Easter 1944 fell on April 9. The camp held a sunrise service; following church call at 6:30 A.M., the camp band gave a short concert. Chaplain Fred A. McCalley then delivered the sermon. The 11th Regiment Glee Club, directed by Pvt. L. S. Bullock, provided additional music. "Shure was a good service," Pete wrote. "They had a Big Band and it was good to the soldiers glee Club sung to." A huge Easter dinner of turkey and dressing, cranberry sauce, and sweet potato pie made the day even better. That night, Pete stretched out on his bunk and thought of his family, and remembered how different Easter 1943 had been.[118]

Every trainee looked forward to trips into town. Going off post required them to wear semi-formal attire: Pete would don his service uniform complete with a green jacket, khaki shirt and tie, and service cap. If no officers were in sight, he would give his hat a jaunty little tilt to the left. Then he and his buddies would hop on the bus, pay the thirty-five cent fare, and settle back for the short ride to town.[119]

About 30,000 people lived in Tyler, the seat of Smith County, Texas. A town of that size would have felt like a city to Pete, and to be sure it offered the diversions he used to enjoy back home and then some. True to form, Pete would head for the local eateries first to get "a square meal"; one evening, he relished a supper of calf's liver, French fries, tomatoes, potatoes, lettuce and bacon, and one "of the Best Cups of Coffee since I left Home." On another trip, he dined on barbecued steak and French fries. After eating, he often indulged in a movie. Among the several films he saw in Tyler was *Four Jills in a Jeep*, the story of a USO team entertaining American troops overseas. It starred Kay Francis, Martha Raye, and Carole Landis. Pete loved it. "Shure was good the Best I Have Seen Since I Left Home," he wrote.[120]

On occasion, Pete visited a local photographer to have pictures made and proudly sent them home.[121] He also loved to shop for his girls in Tyler's department stores. He bought baby dolls and dresses for the girls and a pin for Ruth. Although Pete was not a spendthrift—once he saw some pretty sun suits and sandals in a store window but steered clear after noting their price tags—he loved buying gifts. It also gave him the chance to joke around a little. "I Hope you like it if you Don't send it back and I will give it to some other woman," he kidded Ruth about one gift. "I will send it to Vergie White Ha Ha," he wrote in reference to a girl back home.[122] Best of all, shopping helped buck up his spirits. "Darling when you have a Blue Day just think about your Soldier Boy way out in Texas and give Him a grate Big Smile and For get about the Blues for He will Be thinking of you to Darling," he wrote, and then went into town and bought something for all his girls.[123]

Tyler's USO clubs were another draw. There were two in town. The National Catholic Community Service sponsored one, which stood on North Broadway Avenue. The other, underwritten by the Jewish Welfare League and the YMCA, sat along East Ferguson Street across from the railroad depot.[124] Pete's favorite club is not known, but he did leave a description of its interior. The first floor consisted of an open area with tables and chairs. If it was like most USOs, the space could function as either a reading room or a ballroom. This club also had a dining room, but Pete thought its meals were expensive. Upstairs was a balcony with a sofa and chairs, and probably a small library and rooms for meetings, games, and activities.[125] "Darling this is a swell place to Pass the time," Pete told Ruth. The men lucky enough to have wives nearby would meet them there. Pete watched them with envy and pretended Ruth could come too. "So," he explained, "I had to sit Down and talk to you all tho you are a long way from here and yet you are Rite By my side every where I go Darling you are rite here now." While he wrote, Pete would enjoy the club's music, and sometimes a friend would join him.[126]

The USO club became Pete's refuge. It had "all the Perty girls you want to look at," although he assured Ruth that looking "is all I do." He also enjoyed listening to the bands and watching couples dance. His favorite spot was a table to the left of the door where he could see people come and go, and he loved watching children. One night, he saw a cute baby boy sleeping soundly in a carriage. He also saw a little girl about Mickie's age "but she aint white headed ha ha." When he got tired of sitting, Pete sometimes joined in sing-alongs around the piano and sang until, he wrote, "my teeth nearly fell out."[127]

One night, Pete even had the chance to enjoy some female companionship, but of an innocent sort. He came to the club as usual and sat down to write a letter. Shortly, a lady sat down across from him. The two struck up a conversation that Pete later described as "swell." He learned that she had come to meet her husband, who was on guard duty. Apparently he had been delayed, for Pete and the woman talked until 10:30 P.M., when Pete had to catch a bus back to camp. There was something to be said for simply talking to a woman after months of living only with men.[128]

Indeed, to his credit, Pete steered clear of other women. If anything was for certain, it was that Pete loved only Ruth—not Vergie White or anybody else. "Darling you will never no How much I Do Love you and the Babys I will never Be able to tell you But when I get Back I will Show you."[129] He swore to Ruth that he would be faithful to her, and that was not the only promise he kept. Before leaving home, Pete swore that he would stay away from alcohol. He did just that. Trips to Tyler were safe because alcohol was not sold there, but Pete stayed sober even when he met up with some Kings Mountain boys at the beer garden in Camp Fannin's PX. His buddies wanted him to drink with them, but Pete resisted. If he found it hard to keep his pledge then, he did not at other times. Once, Pete watched a drunk bloody himself by breaking a beer bottle over his head. Pete just laughed. "Darling I am glad I have better since [sense] than to drink the stuff," he wrote Ruth.[130]

When Pete could not go into town, Camp Fannin also offered a few diversions for off-duty soldiers. For fifteen cents, Pete could see a movie at one of Camp Fannin's four theaters. The theaters had two showings nightly and also a Sunday matinee.[131] There were also two service clubs on base, but Pete did not like those as much as the clubs in town. Maybe it was the entertainment; once he walked in on a dance and sat down to watch. They "were Jitter Buggan I can't do that," he explained. Pete left to shave and take a bath.[132]

Pete also enjoyed shooting pool in the company's day room. Day rooms and regimental rec halls also usually offered other things for Pete to enjoy such as Ping-Pong tables, books, magazines, and sometimes a radio.[133] Pete also liked to read the *Camp Fannin Guidon* to keep up with the news. Issues that survive carry stories such as news from overseas, the official summer opening of Tyler State Park, of prisoners of war (POWs) being sent from the camp to alleviate a shortage of labor in the Texas lumber industry, and of famous visitors such as Ranger Col. William Darby and one of Jack Dempsey's sparring partners. Pete no doubt lingered over articles that related the results of rifle marksmanship tests or of candy prices hitting a new low at the PX. Or Pete might just sit back and listen to the radio, just like he and Ruth used to do.[134]

Camp Fannin offered its share of athletic competition, which suited Pete just fine. He was at his best on the camp softball field, and his company had a solid squad. He played right field and swung an able bat; in a game against D Company, Pete hit a triple and drove in two runs, paving the way for a 5–4 victory. His letters home brag of victories and hopes for future wins. "Boy we are good," he bragged. "We are going to Play the noncoms one of these Days and if we Beat them we are going to Play the officers if they will Play us[.] I g[u]es[s] they will they are a Fine Bunch of sports we have the Best officers in the Camp," he wrote. Those matchups apparently did not materialize, for Pete never wrote of them.[135]

❧

So the weeks passed, and the idea of going home never strayed far from his thoughts. "If I ever get out of this army and get back to civilian life us shore Is going to Have some swell times together and I Don't mean maby we will Paint old Kings Mtn Red from one end to the other," Pete promised. He began to count the days to the end of his training cycle, when he would be due a furlough. Pete figured the trip home would cost about $50, so planned to save all he could. "I am coming home if I have to hitch Hike all the way," he wrote.[136]

Thanks to Camp Fannin, Pete Lynn became a new man, inside and out. He may not have been the dapper guy he used to be—years of smoking, work, and age saw to that—but he was surely in the best shape of his adult life. His heart was different too; if he thought he knew what love was before, he had no doubt now. "Darling Life is going to be Different when I get Back Home," he told Ruth. "I Didn't No How Much you all Did Mean to me till I got way out here [to this] Sandy Place they call Texas."[137]

CHAPTER 4

The Best Little City in the World

DESPITE THE 900 MILES THAT SEPARATED THEM, PETE AND RUTH Lynn shared a dream. Maybe, just maybe, the war would end before Pete finished boot camp, and Pete could return "Home and Share the Little 3 Room Cotage [cottage] at the Park Yarn" with the "sweetest little wife and . . . the sweetest little girls in the world." Ruth had been very blue in Pete's absence, and neither of them could think of a better cure than that.[1] "Wont it be grand when this old war is over and we all get Back Home wont there Be a Bige time at the Park yarn Ha," Pete wrote from Texas. "Darling I Have Lay Here on my Bunk Lots of times and thought How it would Fiel [feel] to come Marching Down from the Park yarn Store and see Mick and Bob come Running up to Meet me and then you Be standing on the Porch waiting to take me in your arms and give me a Kiss."[2]

But Pete was not naïve. He suspected the war would continue, and that his chances of returning to the Best Little City in the World to stay were slim. So what would happen to Pete and the other replacements? It was a big war, a world war, and Camp Fannin's trainees worried that they would end up in a combat zone all too soon. That was the subject of conversation in every barracks and every mess at Camp Fannin.

Rumors gave him some reason for hope—at least, a hope that he would avoid combat duty, even if he had to remain in the military. Just a month after arriving in Texas, Pete heard that "us old men will never Have to go across the Pond." Although he shared this good news with Ruth, it did not strike Pete as definitive because his next duty station remained a matter of conjecture.[3] Pete's company commander also assured Pete that pre–Pearl Harbor fathers would not be sent overseas. "Boy I hope He is Rite," Pete wrote, but realized that the man did not really know.[4]

Barracks chatter was no different. "Here I am again . . . Laying on my bunk Listening to the Boys talking about the Japs and the war," he wrote. "Boy some of the Boys shure are worried about going across[.] I Don't think I will go tho of corse they want taught men Like me over there Ha Ha[.]" Pete did not want Ruth to worry to the point that she prematurely sprouted gray hair and wrinkles, so he reassured her at every turn. "Darling if I Do go across the war wont Last Long I will bit[e] there ass of[f] with my new teeth Ha Ha," he joked.[5]

Ova Ratliff heard another rumor, from a friend of a friend. According to this one, officials planned to start releasing pre–Pearl Harbor fathers over thirty years of age beginning July 1. "He said they had more men now than they knew what to do with and they just didn't need us," Ratliff wrote. "Of course that is second hand talk but I believe he was told that."[6]

It was hard to know what to believe. Amidst all these uncertainties, Pete knew one thing for sure: boot camp would end on July 22.[7] Like a man possessed, he looked forward to the ten-day leave that would follow. "Darling you Dond [don't] no what you are in for when I Do come Home For I am like the song I ant Had no Loving since January February June or July But the Last of August," he wrote. He expected furlough to bring "the sweetest Days of my life," and promised to make up for lost time. He would take the kids to get ice cream. He would march around the house with them. He would let them play with his dog tags. He also promised to take Ruth outside and read the stars to her, and he planned to show her "How much I Love you and then Let nature take its course Ha Ha," he wrote.[8]

As the days passed, Pete began planning. He warned Ruth that he would be bringing a lot of clothes and gear with him, so she might have to clean out the back room, or maybe his dad could find a spot in his coal house. The daydreams kept coming too; Pete could not wait to have a tea party with Mick on her little table.[9]

On July 21, the long-awaited day arrived, and the soldiers of Company C, 84th Training Battalion, 15th Regiment took the field one last time. Weighed down by olive drab field packs, helmets, web gear, and rifles, the men endured a hot, dusty ten-mile march. It left Pete's legs so sore that he could hardly walk, but somehow it did not matter; he was going home. Where he would be sent after that was anybody's guess. Perhaps his destination would be a post in Maryland, or possibly a base in California if he were bound for the Pacific. For the moment, he didn't care. Leave came first.[10]

In the best tradition of the army, Pete now had to wait, and wait some more. Each morning brought something of a shock when the soldiers did not have to fall in for roll call, dash to the firing range, or march off on a hike. For six days, Pete simply lounged around the barracks and waited for the army to issue shipment orders. Between writing letters and chatting with his bunkmates, he kept a watchful eye on the company bulletin board, where clerks tacked the latest orders. On July 24, a clerk posted the first set of orders, but only three men from Pete's platoon appeared on the list. Some men were dispatched to Fort Bragg, which was tantalizingly close to home. So Pete settled in to wait some more and began to worry that the army would never send him home. "Boy it get you Down in the Dumps to just thinking how you would like to [k]no[w] where you are going and whether you are gona get to go home or not," he wrote. To pass the time, he wrote three letters in a single day.[11]

While the men impatiently eyed the bulletin board, they surely kept up with war news. In France, over a month had passed since the D-Day invasion, but Allied forces remained bogged down among Normandy's hedgerows. American troops had only just liberated St. Lo after weeks of heavy fighting. Before the smoke cleared, the Allies would lose more than 200,000 men in Normandy. In the Pacific, marines and soldiers were hopping from island to bloody island, most recently splashing ashore at Guam and Tinian in the face of withering Japanese gunfire. Although this unabated fighting across the globe suggested otherwise, the replacements at Camp Fannin clung to the slim hope that their services would not be needed. They told and retold any favorable rumor, including word from a camp major who announced that pre–Pearl Harbor fathers would not be sent overseas. "Boy, Did all these old men take a fit" at that, Pete wrote.[12]

Pete surely took another fit when his furlough orders finally came through: at last, he could go home. It was Thursday, July 27. In Normandy, American troops pierced German lines and the breakout began; at Camp Fannin, Pete packed and wrote Ruth a hurried note. "If nothing happens by the time you get this letter I will be to where I can take you in my arms and hold you till I get ready to turn you loose," he promised. "[T]ell Mick she had better watch up the road for she will see me coming Down the Road on Charles Hawkings Horse Ha Ha well Darling Being as How I will Beat this Letter Home I will be si[g]ning off . . ."[13]

Pete Lynn bade his bunkmates good luck and left Camp Fannin behind. At the depot in Tyler, he boarded an eastbound train that chugged toward home.

———

Midsummer in North Carolina can be oppressive: so sticky and humid that you can almost see the heat shimmering from the pavement. In a mill town where air conditioning was rare, the heat could drive anybody under a leafy shade tree with a glass of cold sweet tea. For her part, Ruth Lynn could not afford to let anything slow her down. She had been working at the mill for only two months, and she also had a household to run. This particular Saturday, July 29, 1944, promised to be busy too. Ruth had a birthday party planned for Bobbie, who turned two that day. It was a smallish affair, and Ruth no doubt ran the party with a smile on her face and a firm grip on the children, but she could not help but occasionally turn away from cake and games to glance down the road. She knew Pete was on his way home, and she longed to see him coming. When her soldier did not appear, Ruth went to bed alone.[14]

The next morning, Ruth and the girls dressed in their Sunday best and walked past Park Yarn Mill—its machinery silent, its rooms empty on the Sabbath—to Macedonia Baptist. After Sunday School and worship, Mae, Hazel, and Hazel's husband Vic joined the Lynns for Sunday dinner. The afternoon passed slowly with no word from Pete, so Ruth and the girls strolled back to Macedonia for 7:00 P.M. services. Singing and preaching from the pulpit lasted well over an hour, and with each minute it seemed less likely that Pete would show up that day either. Then, at 8:45 P.M., the church doors swung open, Pete sauntered in, and Ruth and the kids exploded with joy. "Pete came & we disturbed everybody," Ruth told her diary. "One of the Happiest nights of my life."[15]

Indeed it was. "You had just been home a little while," Ruth remembered. "I can't even begin to tell you how sweet it was to have you where I could touch your hand or have you on my arm and put my hand on your hair, I get the biggest thrill just thinking of it now." Pete could not

Pete hugs one of his dogs while on leave.
Source: Lynn Collection

have agreed more. When he held her close for the first time in months, it reminded him of the first night they stayed together after they got married.[16]

Pete's orders directed him to report to Fort Meade, Maryland on August 12, so he had to make every minute of his furlough count.[17] Thus began a whirlwind of a week. "Bud worm at home at last—wish he could stay & not go back," Ruth wrote. She decided to take off work so she could spend all of it with Pete. Early on Monday morning, Pete, Ruth, and the girls walked across the railroad tracks to Margrace Mill village, where they visited Ruth's parents.[18] More visits followed, and there were many to make: at the Lynns', at Ted Weir's store, at the mill. Wherever Pete Lynn went, whether he saw his brother and sisters, his in-laws, his other relatives, or his friends, it was a reunion to be remembered. Surely he was bombarded with questions about the service, and if anyone asked him about his training he probably told them, "We were herded like sheep," or "We were handled like so many sticks of wood."[19]

Pete resolved to spend most of his furlough at the little gray cottage beside the mill doing exactly what he had intended since March. There were tea parties, and ice cream, and skylarking. The Lynns shared a juicy watermelon or two. They marched around the house together and enjoyed horsey rides with the kids bouncing up and down on Pete's back. In her diary, Ruth beamed about those wonderful days with "Dady Pete" at home. "Time sure flies when you're happy," she wrote.[20]

Best of all, Pete and Ruth found time alone. One night, the couple took a taxi into town, ate at the drugstore, and then went for a stroll in the moonlight. Pete surely kept his promise to show Ruth the stars and doubtless sang a verse or two of "Carolina Moon." Ruth was overwhelmed. "He is wonderful—love him so much," she wrote. "I[']m afraid it can[']t last." The entire night, Ruth thought, was "like a dream, too perfect to be real. I don't think I ever loved you like I did that night, you talked so sweet & I believe you really meant what you said to me." Later, Pete kept another promise, and let nature take its course. A "goodbye baby" would arrive nine months later.[21]

On another night, Pete and Ruth went to see a movie together. Afterward, they walked home. As the Carolina moon shone down, they talked about many things but mostly about their dreams. One day, they promised each other, they would settle down in a little bungalow house with a white fence around the yard and a big white horse in the stable.[22]

As the days passed, more visitors knocked on the Lynns' front door. The Moss family lived in house number 20, close to the Lynns. At twenty-two, Lester Moss was much younger than Pete, but the two men still had much in common. Lester was a grammar school–educated Park Yarn man who was now in the army. He was home on leave after undergoing training at Camp Croft. His wife, Rosanell, was just as giddy as Ruth to have her man home. The second of twelve children and a 1938 graduate of Kings Mountain High, Nell worked at Park Yarn. She had many hobbies, including writing and photography. Nell and Ruth were

Pete and Ruth with their neighbors, Lester and Nell Moss.
Source: Cornelia Moss Davis

becoming fast friends, and Mickie was growing close to the Moss's young daughter, Cornelia. Everybody called her Butch.[23]

Pete and Lester compared notes about their experiences, and then their wives coaxed them to pose in their uniforms for Nell's camera. Dutifully, the two men stood beside a mill house and grinned at each other as the camera clicked and morning glories climbed a trellis behind them. Another picture captured the soldiers with their arms around their wives: a pretty, smiling Nell wearing a flowered a-line dress, and Ruth in an ill-fitting, matching peplum blouse and skirt that she had probably made herself. All four squinted in the summer sun. The kids got in the pictures too. In one, Pete and Lester stand tall beside the porch, still in their uniforms, while Butch stands in front of Lester, Mickie smiles in front of Pete, and Bobbie looks a bit perturbed in Pete's arms. Mickie and Butch, wearing their short dresses, also posed in their dads' service hats

Lester Moss and Pete Lynn
Source: Cornelia Moss Davis

and saluted like Shirley Temple. Neither man appears to have a care in the world, but behind their facades worry weighed heavily on both. That was especially true of Lester; Nell had already lost an uncle in the war.[24]

Somebody also had a camera handy when Pete went horseback riding. He borrowed two horses during his furlough, including one from a man named Ballard and the other from cousin Charlie Hawkins. With leather reins held loosely in one hand, Pete relished every ride. There is no prouder sight than Pete Lynn sitting tall in the saddle atop a white horse. He might have passed for a cowboy had it not been for the army cap on his head and the mill houses and water tower behind him.[25]

Rosanell snapped other pictures: Pete, still uniformed, kneeling beside their little cottage, smiling so big that you can see his new, straight, pearly white dentures; a now hatless Pete, kneeling again, his right hand wrapped around one of his dogs, his left arm resting on his knee and words on his lips. These were moments in time—moments that the Lynns hoped would last forever but instead rushed quickly past. "Days long to be remembered just doing as we pleased with our Dady Pete with us," Ruth wrote.[26]

If Pete picked up a copy of the *Kings Mountain Herald*, he would have read that he and Lester Moss were among about a dozen men home on furlough that week. The newspaper also provided updates on local men at the front and told about the Kings Mountain Lions Club's plans to hold a Benefit Horse Show on September 6. Pete no doubt wished he would be home to see it. Otherwise, the *Herald* was light on news and used more ink promoting various remedies available at the Kings Mountain Drug Company, such as Petrofol Mineral Oil (thirty-nine cents) or Bismarex (fifty cents), which promised quick relief from acid indigestion. Other ads told readers to Say Yepsi to Pepsi-Cola or to take advantage of the clearance sale on summer sandals at Belk's department store. It all seemed so trivial to a man headed to war.[27]

On Sunday, August 6, the Lynns went to Macedonia for Sunday School at 9:45 A.M. and worship at 11:00 A.M. Rev. C. B. Bobbitt preached from the pulpit but it seems that Pete was the center of attention, standing tall in his crisp uniform. "Sure was proud of my soldier," Ruth bragged. A wonderful evening at home with the girls followed.[28]

As a new week began on Monday, Ruth was so busy focusing on Pete that she ignored her diary. When Wednesday arrived, the war seemed a little closer. "Not a care just enjoying each others company," she wrote, "not thinking of what is to come."[29] The next day it was closer still. "Just one more day with my soldier," Ruth explained, "can't think of the future & him gone so far away again."[30]

As each day passed, the specter of war descended more heavily. Even though his orders did not say so, the possibility that Pete would end up in a combat zone loomed, like a gathering storm cloud. Ruth's mother owned a piano, and the Hawkins family liked to gather around it and sing. Having Pete home was certainly a reason to sing so one day they stood beside the piano and sang again, just like old times. Some of the music, or maybe just the joy of being home, hit Pete hard. He slipped outside to cry.[31]

And so these twelve days[32] of bliss passed, but before they ended Pete had to get something off his chest. He wrote a letter to the *Kings Mountain Herald*:

> *Today I leave the best little city in the world, to me at least.*
>
> *I have spent 12 days at home and I know no soldier ever had a better time on furlough.*
>
> *I tried to get around and speak to all my friends. If I missed any I am saying hello to them here.*
>
> *Everybody was nice to me while I've been home. The Taxi drivers, dry cleaners, the new Jewelry store, Dr. Baker, and Dr. Griffin at the drug store were all especially nice. Also Charlie Hawkins and Mr. Ballard at Park Yarn loaned me their horses for several swell rides. I'm saying, thanks a million to everybody in our home town for helping make it a grand furlough.*
>
> *It really makes a guy appreciate his home town to be away for awhile.*
>
> *I read the* Herald *every week and especially like the news and letters from the other K.M. boys in the service. Hello and good luck to them all. Here's hoping we all meet again soon in our hometown.*
>
> *This letter isn't very long or of very much interest but I just want the home folks to know this is one soldier who really appreciates the kindness shown him. So long for now.[33]*

Mickie Lynn (left) and Butch Moss
Source: Cornelia Moss Davis

The dreaded day came: on Friday, August 11, 1944, the family saw Pete off at the Kings Mountain passenger depot. He was scheduled on the evening train, which usually ran late.[34] They waited beside the long, narrow brick depot building, which had been built in 1925 to replace the original depot. The building flanked Battleground Avenue, which linked Kings Mountain the town to the Kings Mountain where a battle had been fought exactly 130 years before Pete was born. Now, the tracks beckoned Pete to a new battleground in a faraway place.[35]

Bill Lynn was trackside. He was worried about his brother, and told him so. "Bill, I won a sharpshooter's medal," Pete reminded him, as if to convince Bill he could protect himself. Bill wasn't so sure. "I told him he was headed for the front lines," Bill recalled, then gave him his watch as a keepsake.[36] Pete's dad was there too, with tears in his eyes. That bothered Pete a lot. "You Don't know How I felt for I Had Never seen Him cry Before," Pete later wrote.[37]

The loneliest figure of all was Ruth. She hugged and kissed her soldier and waved goodbye as he boarded. She had one thought as the locomotive chugged into the night: "Hate trains!"[38]

It would be more than three years before Pete Lynn returned to Kings Mountain.

Pete stood at the train door for a long time. He whistled at her receding figure, but she could not hear him. "I will never For get how sweet you looked to me that nite," he wrote.[39] He watched Ruth standing at the depot until he could see her no more, but his emotions lingered. "Darling I Had a Feeling that it would Be a Long time Before I saw you and old Kings Mountain again," he wrote.[40]

Although it was getting late, Pete did not—could not—sleep much on the train. The cold he felt coming on had a little to do with it, but mostly his thoughts kept him awake. It had been a great furlough—"the Sweetest 12 Days of my life," he wrote—but Pete had no idea what lay ahead. The only thing he knew for sure was that a long road lay ahead and there was nothing he could do about it. As the train chugged through North Carolina and then Virginia, past towns shuttered against the darkness, he met other men who were also en route to Fort Meade. The sad journey passed without incident, and the soldiers arrived at 11:00 A.M. the next morning.[41]

Fort George Gordon Meade, named after the general who commanded the Union army at Gettysburg, was situated between Washington and

Baltimore. A military installation since World War I, the fort now served as a replacement depot and also boasted a school for cooks and bakers and a prisoner of war (POW) camp. Like Fort Ord in California, Fort Meade represented the army's last chance to get men ready for overseas duty. Here as many as 20,000 soldiers at a time endured more physicals, had their blood typed, and proved their weapons proficiency on the firing range while they awaited overseas transportation. The facility even included a live grenade course and a mock village for training. Replacements also received clothes and equipment from Meade's vast quartermaster stores. How long a man stayed depended on the commanders of nearby ports. Some soldiers would stay for just seventy-two hours, but on average most would linger for as long as three weeks. Everything depended on whether ships were available.[42]

Upon arrival, incoming replacements like Pete Lynn marched to an assembly point. Each man received a processing tag, ate in the battalion mess, and sat through an orientation session. Guides then directed the newcomers to the medical building, where physicians examined them for communicable diseases, administered immunizations for maladies like typhus and cholera, and checked eyes and teeth. After that the men assembled in groups and marched to the Receiving Building. With his personnel records in hand—including a card bearing the date of his arrival at Meade—Pete met with an interviewer who ensured everything was in order, and then Pete walked to another desk where he turned in his records and was assigned to a depot company. The Mileage and Rations section squared his furlough travel account, and then the Bonds, Allotments, and Insurance section advised him on financial affairs. Someone also checked his training status and made sure his pay was up to date. Finally, the men reassembled in groups and a guide led them to a regimental area, where their training companies issued bedding, clothing, and equipment.[43]

This process took the balance of the afternoon. By 5:00 P.M., Pete was finished and had settled into his company area. He found time to jot a note home, and at 9:15 P.M. telegrammed Ruth that he had reached Washington, DC.[44]

Pete did not expect to be at Fort Meade long, but he ended up staying for two weeks. He found he liked the place because it offered a number of diversions, including a movie theater. "Darling this is a Pretty Swell Camp," he told Ruth. "We walked around and Looked it over Before we went to the show." The camp also had a swimming pool behind the barracks. It even had washing machines, which struck Pete as odd. He had not noted a single washing machine at Camp Fannin, and heaven knew Kings Mountain had precious few.[45]

Ova Ratliff, who arrived at Fort Meade a few days after Pete, liked what he saw too. "This is a nice place and being here really makes a person realize how bad Camp Fannin was," he wrote home. "The weather is fine, the camp is much better, altho quite different and eats have been good so far." Like the men around him, Ova received new clothes and equipment including underwear, a pair of wool pants, two flannel shirts, two pairs of shoes, fatigues, and a coat.[46]

A soldier who passed through Fort Meade a couple of weeks earlier formed a different opinion than Lynn and Ratliff. "The whole place is rough and tough," he wrote, remembering endless maneuvers and house-to-house tactics training. "They just worked us to death."[47] Pete's experience was nothing like that, at least in the early going. The day after he arrived, Pete sat down in a "Pretty Little Pine grove Rite Behind the Barricks" and wrote another letter home. "Darling I have Found this to Be a Pretty good Place Here so far," he reassured Ruth. "It Reminds me of Fort Bragg a Lot for the Barricks are Built the same and we Don't Have to go out of the Barricks to take a Bath or Shave and we Havent Done any thing since we got Here[.]" The officers even gave the men a pass.[48]

The pass enabled Pete to visit Baltimore on Sunday, August 13, with some men he had met at camp. They left at 10:00 A.M. and returned around 5:00 P.M., and Pete, who had spent his entire life in a small town, was impressed. "Boy is it a Big town," he told Ruth. "You can walk for Hours and you will still be in town[.] [W]e went to a good show the Picture was wing and a Prayer it was really good," he wrote, speaking of a 1944 movie starring Don Ameche and Dana Andrews about an aircraft carrier in the Pacific. After the movie, Pete made a beeline for a local cafeteria. Separation from family did not curb his appetite now any more than it had in Texas. He devoured a hamburger steak, creamed potatoes, spaghetti, and a big piece of lemon custard pie, and washed it all down with a Pepsi. "I got to Have my Pepsi Cola Ha Ha," he explained.[49]

Dads and their daughters. Lester stands with
Butch. Pete stands beside Mickie and holds
Bobbie.
Source: Cornelia Moss Davis

Chances are, Pete could not taste his dinner because his cold continued to worsen. The next day he went on sick call to get some cold tablets and cough medicine. However, his cold was not bad enough to stop him from taking in an outdoor band concert. "It shure was good all except one girl that sang," Pete told Ruth. "She sounded just like one of Papis old Hens when she lays an egg Ha Ha."[50]

As he had at Camp Fannin, Pete quickly found Fort Meade's USO club and spent part of his free time there. On one visit, he found himself seated next to a young soldier, who had just come home from some unknown duty station, and his mother. The two enjoyed a turkey dinner together and chatted away. Pete watched with his usual uxoriousness. "That is the way you and I are going to Be one of these Days," he wrote. "Only you and Mick and Bob will Be in my arms and the Best thing of all I will Be Home to stay . . . I say again Darling what ever Happens where Ever I go just keep the Home Fires Burning till I get Back to the one I Love So Dearly."[51]

Not surprisingly, Pete connected easily with several soldiers at Fort Meade. The group included men he had known at Camp Fannin as well as some new acquaintances. Pete described one man, a bachelor from Oklahoma who only had his parents back home, as simply "a good old Boy to me." Pete also befriended a fellow Tar Heel from Raleigh, and an eighteen-year-old boy who he took under his wing. At camp a now-familiar barracks scene repeated itself, with Pete writing a letter in his bunk while his buddies tossed dice on the floor. When the players yelled "six" and "seven," Pete warned Ruth that she might "Run across a Lot of numbers in this letter Ha Ha."[52]

Meade was still the army, so there were duties to perform. At some point, the men watched additional training films, and staffers marked their records to indicate men had seen them. Camp officials also instructed the men about censorship and security, which would tighten as they moved to a combat zone. Training resumed about three days after the men arrived and continued until about three days before departure.[53] Inspections also came frequently—"It['s] tiresome as the Dickens," Pete thought—and the army also issued him a new M1 rifle and a winter uniform, complete with wool shirt, field trousers, high-neck sweater, field jacket, combat service boots, rain poncho, and M1 helmet. "I ges we are going to the North Pole ha ha," he joked. Once he received this new gear, Pete had to stamp his name on each item. Meantime, Pete's latest paycheck arrived. The $12 check, which included his furlough food allowance and the balance from the previous month's pay minus deductions for dependents and insurance, left his pockets comparatively bulging. Lest Ruth grow concerned, Pete assured his wife that he had not been gambling.[54]

Fort Meade offered these replacements another luxury Camp Fannin had not: the chance to call home. Pete telephoned Kings Mountain twice

Pete on horseback, with mill houses and a mill water tower behind him.
Source: Lynn Collection

during his stay in Maryland, but both conversations were awkward. For one call, he rang the mill and connected with Mr. Ballard—Pete was astounded at how natural Ballard's voice sounded—and then Ruth came to the phone. Neither had been on telephones much before, and they did not know what to say to each other. On another occasion, Pete called from the USO club. Within five minutes, Ruth came to the phone. Surprised that it took so little time to connect, he became "so Happy to Hear Her sweet voice," he recalled, "that I just fild up in the throat and my Heart was beating so Fast I couldn't talk."[55]

These conversations did little to ease Pete's mind. He was not worried so much about the kids as he knew they would be taken care of, but he was concerned about Ruth. He figured that going back to work after his furlough would be hard for her. Still, there was something to be said for getting "Back in the Harness again." Pete hoped he would be kept just as busy, for work would at least keep him occupied. What bothered him the most was the thought of Ruth being alone, so he kept wishing that he could go home.[56]

Then there was the biggest question of all: where would Pete go next? He had no firm orders yet. Even the most naïve of them knew that Fort Meade was a way station for men en route to Europe, but in the manner of a man who thinks something can happen to others but not to him, Pete stubbornly clung to the belief that he would not go. He made no secret of this feeling, but his new friends just laughed at him. "Lynn, have you still got that feeling?" they asked, every time they saw him. "Sure have, Buddy!" he replied, every time. A physical he received at Fort Meade gave him some reason for optimism. "Darling I still Don't think I will go across For we had a Feasible [physical] Examation and I Didn't look so good to them," he wrote Ruth.[57]

It had been a fool's hope all along. A few days later his shipping orders arrived, and he learned that doctors had not changed the army's mind about him after all. After drinking a Pepsi at the PX to collect his thoughts, he sat down in the company Day Room and broke the news to Ruth. "Darling you ask me to tell you if I thought I was going across," he wrote. "Well Darling I ant Never kep anything from you yet so I will tell you that I got my shipping orders to-Day but I Don't know where I am going." He expected to be leaving within the next two days on "a Big Boat." He asked for prayers from Ruth and his mother, and then offered a hollow assurance: "I Have got to Die at Old Park yarn and not over there," he wrote.[58]

On Saturday, August 18, Pete packed his clothes for shipment ahead to the port; he expected to follow that night or the next day. To kill time, Pete and one of his buddies went to an 8:00 P.M. movie. It offered scant escape from the reality that now faced him. "Darling I ges [guess] I will be on my way to a new destination in a few minutes so I will have to say good By till you Hear from me," he wrote.[59]

Pete's next destination was not a big boat but literally next to it. Camp Kilmer, New Jersey, was a Port of Embarkation (POE) facility. Named for the poet and World War I soldier Joyce Kilmer, the camp housed troops awaiting transport to Europe from New York Harbor. At most, a man would stay at Kilmer one or two weeks. Here he could expect to perform abandon-ship drills, endure gas mask checks, and receive a few more shots. The army did not overlook orientation at Kilmer, and for one soldier it was indelible when a colonel who had fought in the Pacific announced, "War's no damn fun; some of you are going to get killed." Training was limited since their equipment was now crated for the trip. If the camp was more boring than most, it offered a view that was among the best. From the confines of Kilmer, a man could see New York City's skyline in the distance, with the Empire State Building dominating all.[60]

Upon arrival, Pete would have been assigned to a reinforcement company that contained about 200 men and 4 officers. And with overseas movement imminent, censorship caught up with Pete in New Jersey. In his first letter from Kilmer, Pete told Ruth that he could no longer give specifics about his location.[61] Even when he was granted a pass for a night on the town, which certainly meant a visit to Manhattan, Pete had to save for later the story of a country boy seeing that massive city for the first time.[62] His itinerary is not known, but perhaps Pete saw Margrace Mill's giant curtain at Radio City Music Hall. He may also have visited Neisler Mills' sales office at 40 Worth Street. "Uncle" George Weber, who managed the office, promised a "good old Southern welcome" for Margrace servicemen visiting the city. Although Pete was not a Margrace employee, many of his relatives were. Pete only had to find the latchstring on the outside of the door to enter.[63]

Pete's letters home now became full of mundane details, like cleaning his rifle, which left more room for professions of his love. Mail call became more important to him than ever. "I can Have the blues so Bad every thing looks so Dark and Dreary and then thay Have mail call and I get a Letter from you or mother and it just Reminds me of what I have to fight for," he wrote. "Then I get Right Back on the Ball again and sing a Little song like I ust to at Home when John Richardson would come around and make me mad Ha Ha."[64]

In a happy coincidence, Pete met another man from Park Yarn at Camp Kilmer. David Eubanks was a thirty-year-old mechanic who lived close to the Lynns in House Number 56 with his wife, Virginia Lee, and two sons. Eubanks had joined the army the same time as Pete but had gone to basic in South Carolina. Not long after the two men connected, blackout descended on the camp: no one was allowed on or off the post and telegrams and phone calls were forbidden as the time for departure was at hand. On Sunday, August 27, as clouds of military police surrounded the area, the GIs lined up and received boat numbers. Then they boarded a train bound for New York Harbor, and after a short ride they arrived at an 1,100-foot pier in Hell's Kitchen on Manhattan's west side. This was Luxury Liner Row, where the famous *Queen Elizabeth* waited. Nicknamed the "Grey Ghost" after the way she could speed out of a fog bank and then disappear again, the *Queen Elizabeth* looked down-right Brobdingnagian. New York was the only port in the United States that could accommodate her, and boarding took so long that the process had to start the day before she sailed.[65]

She was quite a sight. Christened by the Queen herself in 1938, the passenger liner had been transporting soldiers to Europe for most of the war. Together with her sister ship the *Queen Mary*, the *Queen Elizabeth* would carry a million men during World War II. She displaced 83,673 tons, measured 1,031 feet from bow to stern, and had room for an entire division of 16,000 men. Her twelve boilers could coax the elegant lady to a maximum speed of 32.2 knots. With a pair of funnels and a pair of masts standing tall, the ship's profile hinted of gayer times when Cunard liners ferried leisure passengers on the high seas. For now, the *New York Times* called her the "Empress Incognito" because she wore a coat of dull sea gray paint, sandbags lined the bridge, and nearly four dozen guns pointed skyward.[66]

On the pier, an equally unforgettable sight awaited Pete. One man said it "resembled nothing as much as it did a packing house with little herds of men here and little herds there being driven thither and hither." Transportation Corps men wearing red and gold armbands barked orders. A band played patriotic songs such as "Over There." Red Cross volunteers handed out coffee, doughnuts, and cartons of cigarettes. In the midst of this throng, the soldiers queued up. Each man had a number chalked on his helmet and came forward when someone called his name and number. When Pete's turn came, he answered, "Lynn, F.," and ascended the gangway. Burdened by rifle, overcoat, full field pack, helmet, canteen, cartridge belt, webbing, and duffel bag stuffed with spare uniforms and personal belongings, each man tottered and huffed. To one observer, the stairs to the ship "seemingly went half way to heaven," but its actual destination was heaven's opposite.[67]

Other replacements joined Pete on the climb up the gangway, and so did the men of the 18th Cavalry Reconnaissance Squadron. Once aboard, these olive drab passengers settled in to wait for the voyage to begin. Their wait lasted through the night and the following morning, but the moment of departure eventually arrived. At 1:00 P.M. on Monday, August 28, the passengers felt a shudder below their feet; on the bridge, Capt. C. M. Ford gave the all clear, and the ship pulled away from the pier. Slowly she slid down the Hudson River and into the choppy, green waters of New York Harbor where she passed beneath the gaze of Lady Liberty and then through the Narrows.[68]

As the mighty vessel stood out to sea, the men stampeded for the deck to get one last glimpse of America. One man saw "New York in the sunlight, planes swooping overhead; tugs tooting occasionally, and a mute farewell to Lady Liberty." Another man, hugging the rail tightly, took "the last, lean, hungry look we would have of the sky-scraper city for some time," he wrote. "Those gleaming pinnacles of light were a long cry from the dark world into which we were to emerge on the other side." Eddie Slovik, later to be infamous as the only soldier executed for desertion during the war, was equally struck by the sight. "We all looked at the Statue of Liberty as long as we could see it and wondered if we would ever see it again," he wrote. Charles Haug remembered excitement on his ship. "For most of us it was our first real ride on the ocean and everything seemed so new. There was a big silence that grew over the ship though, as the U.S. coastline seemed to sink out of sight into the ocean." Behind the quiet facades, their insides churned like the waters swirling through the ship's propellers.[69]

U.S. Navy destroyers escorted the *Queen Elizabeth* to a point about 150 miles offshore. Then airplanes or blimps took over, until the ship passed the point where aircraft could not reach. From there, she sailed on alone. At 28 to 30 knots on a zigzag course, no ship could keep up with her, including U-boats. Adolf Hitler offered 1 million Reichsmarks to any U-boat skipper who could sink her, but it was a forlorn hope. At that speed, she would cross the Atlantic in five or six days.[70]

As the coast faded out of sight, Pete Lynn took stock of his new surroundings. He discovered that the *Queen Elizabeth* little resembled a luxury liner below decks. The unnecessary trappings of carpets, china, silver, paneling, and furniture had been removed to make way for as many men as possible. It made the spaces hot, dark, and confined, and even left the passageways crowded since the men carried weapons everywhere; to alleviate congestion, troops walked on the starboard side of the boat when headed forward and on the port side when going aft. In the sleeping areas, canvas and metal-frame bunks, stacked one above another, hung from the ceiling on long chains. Less than 2 feet separated each bunk—woe to any sleeper who forgot himself and sat up—and they were also a mere 6 feet long and 2 feet wide, so a man with Pete's length had to dangle his feet. The close bunks reminded some of shelves in a supermarket and gave others the feeling of being stuffed in the boat "like sardines in a can." A man could not even count on having his own bunk. The *Queen Elizabeth* did not have enough for everyone, so men rotated through her bunks up to three times daily or took turns sleeping on deck when weather permitted.[71]

Little on board was calculated to provide comfort or inspire confidence. Movement was restricted; the ship was divided into Red, White, and Blue sections, and GIs were issued buttons with the color of their section. There the men would stay, unless duty required otherwise. Upon boarding, Pete received a life preserver and a copy of the ship's Standing Orders, which explained what to do during an air attack or, God forbid, while abandoning ship. A letter from the president on official White House stationery offered no comfort either. "You are a soldier of the United States Army," Roosevelt wrote. "You have embarked for distant places where the war is being fought."[72]

Mealtime left chowhounds like Pete wanting. Given the number of mouths to feed, the *Queen* could serve only two meals a day. During the breakfast shift of 6:00 A.M. to 11:00 A.M. and the dinner period of 3:00 P.M. to 7:30 P.M., the men ate in forty-five-minute intervals. They used their own mess kits and had to wash them when finished. The ships only had English fare to offer, except for some sandwiches that were available between meals. Then again, not everyone cared to eat, as Roy Nix recalled. A draftee from a small Colorado town who would end up serving in Pete's unit, Nix never forgot the Atlantic passage. "You had all you wanted to eat but everybody was puking," he wrote. "The North Atlantic is rough in the fall of the year." Landlubbers could list more complaints: there were no showers. Smoking was restricted on board. And the ever-popular deck had to be shared because it wasn't big enough to accommodate everyone.[73]

"By the end of the second day," Haug recalled, "we had all explored every part of the ship and everyone felt like veteran sailors." That's when they discovered that life at sea was dull. To pass the time, men napped in every nook and cranny, or hung along the ship's rails to look for whales or schools of porpoises. Daily lifeboat drills and inspections required participation, while gunnery drills for the antiaircraft batteries gave the men something to watch. Lectures on tactics, equipment, and other topics were also conducted, but those were not nearly as appealing as the ship's modest library of movies. Readers could thumb through the copy of *A Short Guide to Britain* that every man received, while other soldiers preferred playing blackjack, poker, and craps despite regulations that forbade gambling. For the pious, the ship offered religious services. There was also some occasional entertainment, which might include a show organized by the soldiers or a concert by any unit bands on board. Such entertainment would be announced along with news in the ship's Daily Orders.[74]

Ruth never learned much about Pete's voyage. No letters from him during that period survive. What she did know was limited to a few words from a friend from Kings Mountain named Nelson, who Pete bumped into along the way, and an August 4, 1945, *Saturday Evening Post* article about the *Queens*. It seems that his journey was uneventful, and that the ship sailed over calm waters during a quiet part of a busy hurricane season that wreaked havoc in the Caribbean and also on Long Island. One may also assume that Pete's journey was no holiday. His experience was certainly similar to that of thousands like him: he was uncomfortable, bored, lonely, possibly seasick, and worried about what was to come.[75]

A week at sea passed, and then as September 4, 1944 dawned, the *Queen Elizabeth* approached Scotland's western shores.[76]

She no longer sailed alone. A Sunderland flying boat from the RAF's Coastal Command was the first escort to appear, when the ship came within 600 miles of shore. As the mighty ship drew closer to Great Britain, a squadron of Royal Navy destroyers joined the escort.[77]

Ahead, land came slowly into view, a distant thin line at first and then a growing mass of green. Past the Isle of Arran and into the Firth of Clyde the ship sailed, north up the firth and then eastward into the River Clyde. Around them, the shining waters now filled with ships: small ships, large ships, ships riding at anchor, and ships chugging toward port. On board, the helmeted passengers stirred. One soldier went to the *Elizabeth*'s deck and saw "a very green hill, on which the morning sun was falling, and what appeared to be a castle along the top." Landfall was a moment to remember for every passenger, no matter what ship they were on. "We were happy to see land," a veteran recalled.[78]

The *Queen Elizabeth*'s bow pointed toward the pierhead. Few of Great Britain's ports had the facilities the *Queens* required, and of those only Gourock, an ancient resort west of Glasgow, was beyond reach of the Luftwaffe.[79] A handful of tugs twittered up to the ship and took her in tow. Pushing and pulling, the little boats guided the mighty *Elizabeth* to the wharf, and then the massive job of unloading began. Soldiers in their military habiliments struggled down gangways that sprouted from the ship's A, B, and D decks. On the dock, a man holding a clipboard checked names off a list as men debarked. While a band of brass and pipers played, Scottish children made the V for Victory sign and men back from the war shouted, "Go back before it's too late!" and "What's your wife's telephone number?"[80]

It was afternoon before Pete's turn came and he made it off the *Queen Elizabeth*. His friend Nelson was still with him.[81] Back on solid ground at last, on a quay beside a "small, picturesque Clydeside town," the two men fell into one of four lines. Then they marched to some waiting trucks, which whisked them to a nearby train station where the troops were habitually welcomed by "friendly, smiling Scottish women volunteers [who] were giving us coffee and little meat pie[s]," a soldier recalled. "Although the pies were greasy and doughy we ate them, we would have eaten anything after 10 days on that ship."[82]

Hate trains! So thought Ruth, and Pete surely did too. Each time he boarded one, it took him farther away from his family and the Best Little City in the World. Now it was time for the itinerant soldier to board another. This train belonged to the London, Midland, and Scottish Railway and was blacked out against German air raids. Together, Pete and Nelson found seats as the train pulled out of the station. It chugged the rest of that day and all night long toward a port on the English Channel.[83]

Pete would never see more of the English countryside than what he could make out from the train window. "Scotland was green and manicured, with stone walls, thatched roofs and pastures, but not much else," recalled one soldier. "As the sun went down a few of us wanted to watch out the windows, but quite a few wanted the shades pulled and the lights on so they could shoot craps and play cards." Another remembered seeing the flashes of exploding bombs in the distance. Perhaps Pete drank in these sights, or maybe he was among the men who didn't much care about the scenery. "They sat," a rider recalled, "with eyes closed thinking about what they left behind and what was ahead."[84]

CHAPTER 5

I Wish the Ole Army Would Be Over

WHILE PETE SERVED HIS COUNTRY, HIS WIFE SOLDIERED ON AT HOME. Her task was just as lonely and hard.

On the August Monday after Pete left on a northbound train, Ruth went back to work.[1] Park Yarn did not keep her mind off of her husband. The sting of Pete's departure was too recent, and she did not have a scintilla of an idea of how things would turn out. Standing in front of her spooler, Ruth could not hold back the tears. They came in such a gush that she could not work. At home, she found no relief. The mailman had delivered two letters from Pete as well as his federal tax refund of $7.80. "I get worried about you & wonder when Ill get to see you again and I just go all to pieces," she admitted.[2]

Everywhere she looked, there were reminders of the war. At the corner of Mountain and Piedmont Streets, Kings Mountain erected an enormous board with the names of local men and women in the service.[3] Not to be outdone, Margrace Mill placed beside its main gate a 10-foot-tall, V-shaped sign that listed its servicemen above the words HONOR ROLL. C. E. Neisler Jr., president of Neisler Mills, also launched an occasional newsletter for mill employees "in the service of Uncle Sam." Christened the *Old Mountaineer*, with a masthead in the shape of the Pinnacle, the publication kept mill and millhands connected.[4] Margrace's patriotism was as logical as it was real: the mill was humming with military orders. During the war it ran around the clock, six days a week. Every morning, "the 5:30" mill whistle often shook Ruth awake so rudely that she could not go back to sleep. Among the goods Margrace churned out were large quantities of cotton duck, which the military used in body bags.[5]

There were more stark reminders. About the same time Pete left for overseas, bad news reached Kings Mountain. "Rene got a telegram that Fred Wiley had been killed in action," Ruth wrote of some friends. "Robert Mellon too. Nell [Moss's] brother you knew him. The whole family is nearly crazy. Nell was here tonight." If possible, such events made Pete's departure feel more ominous. His letters, the tone of which changed with censorship requirements, did not help either. "Darling your letters seem so strange, I know you can't but I miss you telling me little things that happen."[6]

For obvious reasons, mail from Pete stopped altogether once he boarded the *Queen Elizabeth,* but Ruth could not stop thinking about her soldier. The kids would not let Ruth forget either. One Saturday night, she took them to a Sunday School class social; maybe a little fun would get their mind off of things. They feasted on a supper of fried chicken, gravy, chicken rice, slaw, and cake, and washed it down with soda. Afterward, as they walked home, Ruth used a flashlight to guide them in the late summer darkness. When the threesome passed the mill, Mick looked up at Ruth. "Mommy, don't you wish my Daddy was here so we wouldn't have to go by ourself?" she said. "I wish the ole Army would be over."[7]

The girls talked about their dad constantly. Mrs. Hawkins often kept the girls while Ruth worked. "Mick told mama yesterday," Ruth wrote, "that she got tired staying here without her dady & mama teased her and ask[ed] her why she didn't go hunt her another & she said she'd rather have her old dady he was the best." Mickie even liked to wear an old soldier's cap while she played. Bobbie also noticed her father's absence, though she was just a toddler. On one occasion, when a taxi drove past, she remembered how her dad used them often and smiled, "That's my Daddy." Bobbie also associated the train with Pete. Spotting a train in town, she said, "Hey my Daddy."[8]

Like Bobbie, Ruth could not help but hope Pete would magically appear, even though she knew better. "Somehow today I've looked for you like I did the Sunday you came home," she wrote soon after he left. "Its raining & cool & every taxi comes by my heart skips a beat although I ought to know you aren't coming. But one of these days you will & I hope it will be right soon!"[9]

Pete even invaded Ruth's dreams. The day after the church fried chicken social was rainy and unseasonably cold, which made Ruth wonder if she needed to order coal. The damp chill also persuaded her to skip church. She spent the day writing letters and listening to sermons on the radio while Bobbie and Mickie played together. At 3:30 P.M., Ruth and the kids went to see Pete's mom, and then Ruth came home and wrote Pete. "Ive got so I dream about you all night, some times I wish I didn't have to wake up, they're so real," she told him. "Your Arms & lips are so swee[t] in dreams I can't express what they are in person . . . Good nite Soldier. I[']ll meet you tonight in dream land again."[10]

Indeed she did. Ruth's dreams were full of Pete for a long time. She dreamed of him three times the week he reached Europe, even though she did not know his exact location. Fortunately, these dreams were as pleasant as they were vivid; they were the kind that make you sorry when you wake up. "Its fun to dream of someone you love so much and dream about being with them." Small wonder that songs on the radio such as "It Had to Be You" bothered Ruth.[11]

At the same time, a new emotion emerged in Ruth: resentment toward men who avoided the draft. On one occasion, she even confronted a malingerer, and minced no words. "I hoped they got him & took him right over," Ruth said. "I didn't mean it but it don't look fair to take some & leave others especially the rough ones that don't amount to anything at home." Pete had the same attitude and asked for the address of a friend so he could berate him. Ruth said it wasn't worth it. "Sweet don't be bitter & hold grudges cause you're there & he isn't," she advised. "In your heart you know you're right & hese [he's] yellow but don't think about that just say you did your part & come home to us just like you left, sweet & loving & let the other fellow answer for his own cowardice." Of course Ruth wanted Pete to come home, but she knew he did not want to miss the adventure. She did wonder if he would change his mind the closer he got to the front. "You wanted to see the world," she wrote, "but you didn't want it this way did you?"[12]

After a while, Ruth's tears mostly came on the weekends, while around her life went on. The media reported local worries, such as a polio epidemic that hit North Carolina. It peaked between July and September and came quite close to home. Hickory had more than half the state's 878 cases, while Charlotte and Gastonia had large shares as well. As a result, the state decided to delay the opening of schools a week. There was also other school news when the state increased teacher salaries and added a twelfth grade. The tropical storms that delayed Pete's sailing hit the papers as well, but Kings Mountain did not receive any of their wind or rain.[13]

Harvest time also approached. "It's cotton picking time in the Carolinas again and believe me those white fields are beautiful," a Kings Mountaineer wrote as fall arrived. Mill men took heart at the sight, and so did hunters who noticed that rabbits were plentiful and itched to loose their beagles. Had he been home, Pete would have been among them. Only the summer's corn crop looked second-rate after a hot and dry summer.[14]

With the promising harvest and government orders still flowing in, Park Yarn and Margrace hummed. A few veterans, their service complete, returned to their looms.[15] Kings Mountain bustled with activity. "The Old Home Town is getting up in the world," crowed the local newspaper. The Lions Club put on a successful horse show. When school finally started after the polio scare, fifteen new teachers went to work at Kings Mountain High School, and its football team opened the season in a new stadium with a 25–6 win over Bessemer City. The city's sixth War Loan Drive also got underway. In the first ten days, locals bought $125,000 worth of bonds. Leaders from the local American Legion post, the Draft Board, the Merchants Association, the Lions Club, the Kiwanis Club, and even Mayor J. H. Thomson published thanks and salutes to the boys overseas. "Good Luck—and don't forget to duck when necessary."[16]

Ruth found comfort with friends and family. She made a point of visiting Pete's mom and other family members at least once a week. She also visited relatives such as her aunt Osie. "Nothing would do but us eat supper with them & they killed a chicken & boy did we eat," Ruth wrote. "She really had a good supper we just got home & I give the kids a bath & they had to have a biscuit & syrup before going to bed."[17]

Ruth complained that her parents did not visit enough, but she was glad that Pete's dad came around regularly. On one visit, Charlie Lynn showed Ruth his new $75 dentures, but admitted that he did not like them and could not eat with them. He was plainly jealous of his son's new army teeth. There was also some question as to who Charlie really came to visit: Ruth and the kids, or Pete's dogs.[18]

Ruth recognized that a busy house would keep her occupied, so she welcomed multiple houseguests while Pete was away. The regulars included a friend named Lois. Lois was good to keep Ruth and the kids company no matter what they did, which included trips to town. Once they stopped at the drug store. Bobbie made a beeline for the toys, and it took some coaxing to pry her away from the dolls and teddy bears. Eventually, Ruth made her way to the cash register, where she paid for some safety pins and elastic she could use to make a pair of drawers.[19] Other visitors included Nell, Lester's wife, who Ruth described as "good company to go anywhere with," and Verona Jones. Verona's visit prompted Ruth to invite her younger brother Joe and her mother and father to dinner. However, Ruth came down with a cold at the same time so she skipped church. Mae took Mickie and Bobbie to Macedonia Baptist so Ruth could rest.[20]

If being around family helped, so did work—despite the harsh environment of a textile mill. That was true especially as the summer of 1944 waned. "I got so hot in the mill today and spooled my 8 boxes & got done with the rest of them, but I smelled like Noah Caldwell when I got home I[']d sweated so much," she wrote after one shift. In fact, it was so hot that day that she only managed to cut part of the yard and spent the rest of it cooling the girls in a tub of water. Still, the paycheck and the distraction made the sweat worth it. She also welcomed the chance to put in overtime, which occurred on Labor Day as well as on odd Saturdays. Her hard work did not go unnoticed. A manager assigned Ruth a spooler of her own to manage. "I aggravated John till he's ready to give me one."[21]

Ruth's busy schedule did not end there. There was always something that required her attention. One day, Ruth grew concerned that Mickie was coming down with something so she took her to the doctor. Dr. Bill Ramseur reported that she "was OK, just run down," so Ruth and the girls strolled around town and shopped. Bobbie fell in love with a pair of red sandals, which Ruth bought for her. "You should have seen her eyes," Ruth told her father. The girls went to lunch and then made their way back to Park Yarn. Later, she got a sitter and went out with a friend. It was a good day, her best yet since Pete had gone overseas. "I felt so rested," she told Pete later. "It was the first time I[']d been out without the kids since you left."[22]

Other days were mainly about the girls. Occasionally, they went to town (usually by taxi) to eat their favorite meal, hot dogs. At other times, Ruth received a quick break when the girls went to a neighbor's house to play with their calf. Special occasions were not forgotten either. As October waned, Ruth planned a birthday party with a Halloween theme for Mickie. Afterward, Mick instructed her mother to write her dad and say that she "had a real good time." Among Mickie's presents were $1.50 in cash, two new dresses, a hairbrush and comb, two little cereal bowls, socks, and a red birthday outfit that Ruth made. Meanwhile, Ruth prepared for winter by purchasing a new heater mat, a double blanket, and some new pajamas for herself and Mickie. The pajamas would serve an especially important purpose. "Ive been sleeping by myself & it gets bad cold I don't know how Ill keep my feet warm," she wrote. "Mick sleeps with Lois, & Bob in her bed. I still turn over & miss the best bed fellow in the world, your place will always be waiting sweetheart."[23]

Ruth was smart to fill her days and nights with other activities as well. She started teaching a children's Sunday School class.[24] Chores such as mowing the lawn and chopping kindling for the winter also waited. One of her favorite pastimes was sewing. She pulled out her needle and thread every afternoon at 2:00 after her shift ended. Among her creations were dresses and a new pair of pajamas, after Lois told her "she was tired seeing my B—through my old ones."[25]

Little consumed Ruth's attention more than her pregnancy. It was the happy outcome of Pete's furlough. "Darling somehow I[']m glad you left a part of you with me to live, breathe & love till you're here again," she told Pete. "Does that sound silly to you. I don't ever worry about [this baby] like I did the other two. It just seems I know God will take care of everything for us. And you too," she continued, and then reminded Pete to trust in God and pray daily. "I've learned theres only one comfort in these days & that's faith in God & the hope of a future, which I'm hoping will be us together again very soon."[26]

Ruth tried not to worry about her baby. She felt good during the early stages of her pregnancy. There was the occasional back pain, but an afternoon off from work usually alleviated that. Her feet also swelled up intermittently, which prompted her to soak them. Otherwise, the only early indication she had that her body was changing was an urge to eat and eat some more.[27]

Ruth visited Dr. Bill regularly, and everything progressed well. The only thing he prescribed was a regimen of vitamins. Since Ruth took care of herself, she helped ensure a trouble-free pregnancy.[28] Meanwhile, she laid other plans. Ruth realized she would have to quit work when the baby arrived, so she started saving Pete's paychecks. Most of that would go toward the family's living expenses, but Ruth resolved to set aside $10 of each check for Pete. "I[']ll go back to work soon as I can & help you build that house and I[']ve already been picking out the kind of furniture I[']d like to put in it," she told Pete. "And maybe that $10 a month I save for you will make a down payment on that house you wanted. I can dream can't I." Then again, she decided she would be satisfied living in a barn as long as Pete came home.[29]

Since she wanted to work as long as possible, Ruth did not tell friends and family about her pregnancy at first. Her dad was certainly unaware, because he asked if she would come help on the farm. She wondered how long she could get away with it. In short order, Ruth began to feel that she looked like "Pa's Cow." By November, Ruth was "splitting out" of her clothes, and the time when she would have to quit loomed.[30] Lois planned to leave their house when she quit, so Mae promised that she would help take care of the kids until Pete returned.[31]

Her plans in place, Ruth focused on the children: the ones at hand, and the one to come. With relish, she watched Mickie and Bobbie grow. Mick now weighed 43 pounds and Bob 33 pounds. "They're real stout looking brats," she told Pete. "I sure don't think anybody can say they look starved to death." As for the member of the family that was on the way, Ruth hoped for a boy. "You never seemed excited like me over a new baby," she told Pete. "I recon its cause I[']m such a fool over their Dady & they're just another bit of him to love and pet and you always got tired of me petting you so much so I can just take it out on our babies."[32]

Most of all, she thought about Pete. At night, Ruth would look at the moon and stars and think of him. Above all, she remembered the "sweetest night I ever knew, the night we walked from town" during his furlough. "Darling I don't think I've ever loved and felt so near to you as I did that night," she told him. "You talked of our love & dreams & you never had quite like that before. You certainly left me with something swell to remember, Thanks a million, It[']s been a long time but to me it lives in my heart every night." Ruth dearly hoped that their little boy would be there when Pete came home. "The four of us will have a time together," she promised. "Maybe sometime then we can have the little white house with a fence & 3 kids a horse, dogs & all. Won't we have fun. I'm praying hard our dreams will come true, they just gotta darling."[33]

Yet Ruth worried, because news from Pete became scarce the moment he sailed. Indeed, not a single letter from him reached Kings Mountain during September, so most of the time Ruth did not know what he was doing or where he was. "I wonder if you're still traveling," she wrote. "I believe you're like the traveling salesman [who] just stopped in long enough to get me in trouble & then kept traveling with no forwarding address."[34]

Sometimes, it seemed that the only news she did receive was in the form of his paychecks. "Hon I got another $10 check on Saturday, does that mean you're fighting?" she asked, in reference to additional combat pay. Otherwise, she could only look at articles in newspapers and magazines and guess. "I saw a picture today of some soldiers in France, sitting on the ground having service and I wondered if somewhere over there you were in service of some kind and thinking of home," she wrote in late September. "Sweet sometimes I get the blues and wonder if its any use trying to carry on, I feel like quitting & sitting down & just crying my eyes out then I think of the times you were here and in writing you would say, keep your chin up & I find courage to keep going. How it seemed I always needed you to lean on so much more before our babies were born and this is that time again. If I could just feel you near to help out when Im feeling bad, Sweet I cant begin to tell you how much I love you. I sit and imagine all kind of things happening to you and I just lose my mind."[35]

Ruth Lynn
Source: Lynn Collection

Her busy schedule and the baby inside her helped, but Ruth never could fully escape the lingering sadness of Pete's absence. "I came by your mom[']s ... & we had a crying spell," she wrote Pete. "Its tough to go where you & I went together so much & you not with us." A church celebration she attended with another relative offered the best example of that. It seemed like a good idea at the time, thanks to some good food and good music, but then a trio sang "There will be no draft boards in heaven." Hearing that, Ruth broke down in tears.[36]

She channeled her love for Pete in other ways. Ruth, her brother and sister-in-law, and the kids met to make a Christmas box for him. "Seems so strange to be sending them in Oct.," she wrote. It was not the only package shipped overseas from Park Yarn. Another one addressed to Private Lynn bulged with candy, fruitcake, cookies, razor blades, powder "to hold your teeth in," and a fountain pen. Ruth kept the mail going as well. She wrote short letters so she could afford to send more via the more expensive airmail route. She and Pete also used Victory Mail frequently, which the U.S. Postal Service microfilmed to reduce the weight and volume of mail. It helped the war effort by saving shipping space, but frustrated correspondents with its smallish standardized paper.[37]

Some days, Ruth did finally get a glimpse of what was happening with her husband. On October 5, she received two letters. "Bet Im the happiest gal around her tonight," she told Pete. "They were both a month old, but after waiting 6 weeks any kind if it is old is welcome news. Helen Helms brought them to the mill and before an hour every body in the mill knew I[']d heard from you." After that, the mail stopped again. Pete's birthday came and went with no further word from him, and left Ruth started speculating and worrying all over again.[38] "We all work & sit & wonder just when it will all end," she wrote—and then in late October, another letter from Pete arrived. It was one month and 2 days old.[39]

The sporadic arrival of his letters became an unfortunate fact of life. "Here it is another night and bed time. It[']s pretty cold yet, I recon were in for winter time and having fire from now on," she wrote. "I dread it cause my feet won't get warm any more till spring especially without my man to sleep with. I bet it[']s plenty cold where you are. I think about you every nite sleeping in a tent or maybe in a fox hole and I nearly go crazy."[40]

"I still don't know where you are," Ruth added in another letter. "I believe you're the lost soldier."[41]

CHAPTER 6

Here I Lay in My Pup Tent
Many Many Miles from You

I BELIEVE YOU'RE THE LOST SOLDIER. RUTH WAS RIGHT. PETE WAS lost, in a sense—lost in the vast U.S. Army Europe military machine. He was serial number 34963373. He was an ant in a colony and a bee in a hive. Traveling to war, he followed the footsteps of thousands who had gone before him since June's invasion. Thousands more would follow him.

After the long, lonely, dark train ride across the English countryside, Pete arrived at a port on Britain's southern coast. It was probably Southampton, but his letters are silent on the point. Whatever the location, Pete and his fellow travelers would not remain there long due to the army's insatiable need for infantrymen. On September 5, just a day after the *Queen Elizabeth* docked at Gourock, Pete boarded a ship that slipped its moors and churned into the cold, choppy, gray-blue waters of the English Channel.[1]

Pete left no description of these days, but we can trace his footsteps. The vessels that carried olive drab-garbed soldiers from England to France varied; Pete may have sailed on a cross-channel steamer, a Landing Ship, Infantry (LSI), a passenger ship, or a small landing craft. His journey in that boat was brief; in mere hours, France hove into view. Men who crossed the channel found nothing to cheer them. One soldier, bound for the same division as Pete, saw ominous bomb flashes against the dark northern horizon, in the direction of London. Another trooper remembered weaving past dozens of ships that had been sunk to form a breakwater against waves and storms, while overhead barrage balloons, tethered by steel cables, floated in protection. "We were getting closer to the front," he wrote.[2]

Pete's destination was either Omaha Beach, the landing zone that had been made famous and bloody on D-Day, or Utah Beach, the other American invasion spot. Arriving offshore, his troopship dropped anchor, and landing craft came alongside to ferry the passengers to land. Unloading was a hazardous, awkward chore. "We had to jump with full pack, M1, and ammo from a door in the side of a ship down six to twelve feet (depending on waves) and land on the two foot square platform next to the ramp," recalled one soldier. "Some missed and went straight down and did not come back up."[3] Donald Hogzett, destined to join the same company as Pete, "left the ship by rope ladders (Jacob's Ladders) and were shuttled from ship to shore by landing craft. As we approached the beach, the waves got extremely high and bounced us around," he wrote. "One could only imagine what it must have been like to try to reach the shore under the conditions that existed on D-Day." Another man, his pockets lined with invasion Francs that the army gave him in exchange for his dollars, peered over the landing craft's gunwale. "As we looked up the coastline in either direction all we could see was wrecked ships and landing barges," he recalled.[4]

Disembarking, Pete and his fellow soldiers stepped onto French soil for the first time, combat boots and all. Some did so right on the beach, which was crowded with men and equipment but surprisingly tidy for a recent battleground. Others emerged on the busy quay that had been built right after D-Day.[5] Elzo N. Dickerson, who crossed the Atlantic aboard the *Queen Mary* and passed through Glasgow and Southampton before crossing the English Channel on a troop boat, was struck by the sights: "Seen a lot of burned equipment, left over from D-Day and the Hedge Groves (hedgerows) that we had been told about."[6]

Representatives from the 15th Replacement Depot met these new arrivals with a word of warning. "He said he couldn't tell us how to stay alive, as it was just luck or God, but he said, 'If you are not right with the Lord now, you better get right before you get in the first artillery barrage because you are going to ask Him for help then, so you better know the Lord as a friend now.'" Another veteran appealed to a higher power just as fervently. "We are not going to tell you how to live, but I heard several of you men using God's name as a curse word; please out of courtesy to us old-timers, don't use His name that way because we use His name in prayer all the time," he said.[7]

This was surely one of those moments Pete wanted to describe to Ruth, but censorship rules did not allow it. Leroy Schaller's arrival on Omaha Beach was certainly unforgettable. Schaller had completed basic training in New Orleans and went on to join the army's transportation corps. Now he was on his way to the infantry. Stepping ashore, Schaller saw ration boxes and other supplies stacked endlessly along the beach, and "a silly Captain . . . screaming about conditions urging troops to complain to congressmen."[8]

Guides led the new arrivals inland. They marched past the ruins of imposing concrete German pillboxes—some felt the urge to run inside one and hide—and climbed up the bluff overlooking the beach. "We carried our duffel bags, but even so, we were exhausted when we got to the top of the beachhead and one could only imagine what it must have been like to try to fight your way ashore," Hogzett remarked. A short breather atop the bluff gave little relief for a sobering sight awaited them. "As far as we could see there were little white crosses with a big American Flag at the far end," a soldier wrote. "As we looked at these thousands of crosses we realized for the first time just how many men can be killed in a single battle."[9]

After walking a few miles, the group arrived at the 15th Replacement Depot's transit area, where they would be organized for the next leg of their journey. Like beach and bluff, this was a place of small comfort. "The environment was bleak, the ground muddy," a witness wrote. "There were a few pyramidal tents and hutments of assorted types for cadre. Casuals and replacements pitched pup tents in the fields." An officer welcomed the men to the camp, but he did not have a pep talk planned or words of reassurance to share. Instead, he gave the obligatory speech about local rules, security, military discipline, censorship, and the black market. Ammunition was distributed, and someone warned the newcomers about hidden dangers like unexploded mines or abandoned ammo. Of most interest was the announcement that the men would be split up and sent to different units along the front, depending on their military specialty.[10]

Soldiers like Pete found an ample supply of advice at this camp. A medic named Robert Smith heard a captain say, "One in three of you will become a casualty in this war." Smith thought, "You poor guys, I wonder which one of you it will be." Clarence Blakeslee, another future member of Pete's division, heard a sergeant give a similar warning. "He told us we would be smart to shoot ourselves through the foot—anything to keep out of the front lines."[11] Even the simplest of security precautions were pregnant with reminders of combat. At one point, a sergeant led some replacements to a cluster of foxholes. "He pointed and said that the Germans are mostly in that direction so if something moves, shoot—anything from the other direction, challenge, then shoot."[12]

As darkness fell, the men discovered just how uncomfortable this camp was. Persistent rain kept the ground wet. Food was available, but only in the form of warm, unsatisfying C rations. A simple straddle trench served as the toilet, and there was no toilet paper. To pass the time, men could listen to orientation lectures about life in Europe. Sometimes a Red Cross Clubmobile appeared to show movies and distribute doughnuts and coffee. Otherwise, the men huddled around fires and talked, wrote letters, or read *Stars and Stripes*.[13]

At some point, Pete was separated from Nelson, his traveling companion. They would not see each other again. Alone with his fears, Pete spent an uncomfortable first night on this continent at war.[14]

Pete Lynn
Source: Lynn Collection

The next leg of Pete Lynn's journey to war began on the morning of September 6, 1944. That Wednesday, Allied forces waxed triumphant after their breakout from Normandy. While German troops retreated, Eisenhower's columns streamed into Belgium to the north and reached France's Moselle River to the east. Two more Allied armies approached from the south following their August 15 invasion of Southern France. More than 300 miles to the rear, Pete awoke at the 15th Replacement Depot's transit area in Normandy and wondered what his part would be. It was typical for soldiers to remain at the transit area only one night; the morning after usually found the men boarding trucks, probably GMC cargo trucks known as deuce-and-a-halfs. With only canvas tops and sides for protection against the weather, if that, the trucks departed for Le Mans, France. The bumpy, chilly 260-kilometer ride that followed, along roads crammed with other truck convoys, was just as eye-opening as their landing. "On our trip to LeMans we passed through hundreds of small towns in Normandy," recalled one soldier. "Everyone of these towns were completely destroyed. As we passed through St. Loo [sic] all that could be seen standing was a few battered walls. We saw very few civilians about and they looked in very bad shape. But even after all this these people were still able to smile and they waved at us as we drove past." Another man remembered seeing this same swathe of destruction, as well as dead bodies strewn about. "At first it got to us, but after a while we got used to it."[15]

Pete reached Le Mans on September 8th or 9th. Since 1923, the town had been home to the famous twenty-four-hour road race, but the event was on hiatus because of the war. To the average American GI, the Le Mans of 1944 served a much different purpose. It was an intermediate reinforcement depot—also known as a reception depot—which consisted of a headquarters and several reinforcement battalions, each of which was composed of four reinforcement companies.[16] "This was a collection point for infantry replacements headed for combat," recalled veteran William Meller. "We knew our fate would be dismal. We would be replacing those who didn't make it. All of us knew only a percentage would return in one piece."[17]

Officially, Le Mans was the home of Ground Forces Replacement Command (GFRC). GFRC had been based at Le Mans since late August because of its excellent highway, housing, and training facilities, although the headquarters was now in the process of moving to Paris.[18] New arrivals were assigned to companies and battalions according to their

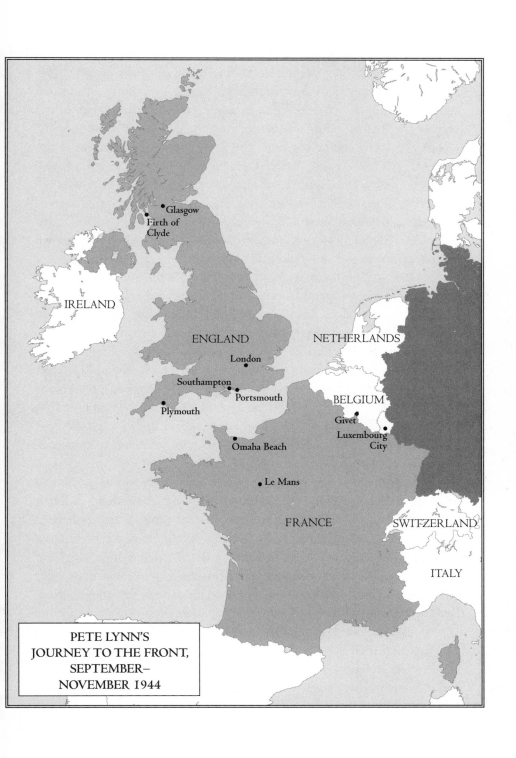

PETE LYNN'S
JOURNEY TO THE FRONT,
SEPTEMBER–
NOVEMBER 1944

branch of service and specialty. The Le Mans center had an important role to play. After languishing on board ship during the journey from America, men needed to sharpen their physical conditioning. In this foreign place, they also needed time to adjust to the climate, terrain, and prepare for the impending prospect of combat. That meant more training, replacing missing equipment, and zeroing their rifles. The men could also expect paperwork as clerks checked records and pay status, as well as more orientation lectures on topics as diverse as venereal disease, foot care, air-raid procedures, personal appearance, saluting, and the war's progress. Sometimes depots offered language classes or sessions on voting rights for soldiers as the 1944 election approached. Training films were shown too, to explain to the men their role in the war.[19]

Soldiers called these replacement depots "repple depples." Going through a repple depple was, one GI explained, like being "pushed out of a place blindfolded," because they knew little about where they had been and less about where they were going. At best, repple depples were unpleasant. "I had a feeling of some fear, but still some hope that maybe . . . the war would end very shortly there," a replacement explained. Small wonder that men found solace in bottles of Calvados, "a poor man's brandy" distilled from apples. Bill Meller traded soap with farmers to get his supply, until he heard tales of GIs going blind from the potent beverage. Pete does not say if the stuff tempted him; presumably, his pledge to stay away from alcohol remained intact.[20]

The time it took for a soldier to trek from ship to unit depended on many factors, including the tactical situation, the needs of different units, and available transportation.[21] It was not unusual for soldiers to stay at Le Mans for several days. William Meller would remain for a week. He was assigned a tent in what he described as a "tent city," and relished three hot meals a day of "American chow," while another soldier remembered bivouacking in open fields beside a small town just outside LeMans. Private Eddie Slovik, another replacement passing through the system about the same time, slept in a tent as well. "The place I'm in is all torn up," he wrote.[22]

Pete's experience was similar; with the front extremely fluid, he stayed in Le Mans for over a week. The pause gave him the chance to resume his letter-writing campaign. Pete had not written home since leaving

America. He may have found it difficult to find paper on ship, or perhaps he was in shock that he was on his way to the front, but mostly he had been too busy. "I Have Ben traveling so much that I couldn't Rite But I had a nice trip," he wrote Ruth on Saturday, September 9. "Darling I am some where in France[,] that is all I can tell you," he added. Clearly, Pete had taken the military's censorship rules to heart. He also began to admit to himself that he was now in it for duration and told Ruth that he would not be home in time to "Play Santy Clause." Instead, Pete promised, he would enjoy Christmas dinner in Berlin.[23]

During the days that followed, Pete wrote, and ate, and trained, and wrote some more. "Here I lay in my pup tent manny manny miles from you," he wrote Ruth the next day. "But my heart is at old Park Yarn with my three Carolina girls." Like Meller, he enjoyed the regular hot meals the camp served. In between, hard work was on the agenda. Pete did not say what he was doing, but he did confirm it included a good deal of walking. Most likely, the walking stemmed from the camp's training regimen. With all of the marching, Pete explained, he was not about to get fat. And if he had any complaint, it was the lack of light in his tent, which made writing at night difficult.[24]

Le Mans did have its share of recreation options. Pete could listen to a radio in the company area, or read *Stars and Stripes* or *Yank*. Around the camp, loudspeakers sounded news and announcements. But for Pete, the camp's ready supply of V-mail was most appealing since it allowed him to keep writing. Pete asked Ruth how everything was going at the mill. He also could not stop thinking about his amazing furlough with Ruth and the kids. Park Yarn was not far from his dreams, either; the army could not take those away. One night, he dreamed he was at home, playing with the kids and holding Mick in his arms. Pete also daydreamed about having a son—Little Junior, he called him—and the bungalow with the little white fence that he and Ruth would build. It is evident, though, that the army, the war, the distance from home, and the separation from Ruth and the kids was beginning to tell on him. Sitting in a tent in war-torn Europe, Pete finally admitted that he should have allowed Mr. Ballard to arrange a deferment for him. He also underscored his realization that it would be a long time before he saw his family again.[25]

Pete might also have benefited from a visit to town, but he never had the chance. It was just as well. "It wont Do me much good to go," he admitted, "for I cant talk to these People over Hear[.] I wish you had Learnt me How to talk French Before I came to the army[.]" Even in this strange world, Pete retained his sense of humor. "Maby I could Have caught me a girl Ha Ha[.] The girls over Hear aren't as Pretty as those were in Texas." Pete also enjoyed watching the antics of soldiers who tried to relate to the locals. "There is a Bunch of the Boy[s] Back Be Hind the tent trying to talk to two Little French Boys now it is Lots of Fun to try to talk to them," he said. "Thay will come up and shake Hand with you and talk and it just tickles them to Death when they Find one of the Boys that can talk to them in French."[26]

In military parlance, Pete Lynn and the other men at Le Mans were replacements. Between D-Day and November 30, 1944, 306,644 of them arrived in Europe to supplant individual frontline soldiers who had been wounded, injured, killed, sick, jailed, furloughed, or were otherwise unable to serve. They were spare parts in the vast machine, and the army needed them desperately because of mounting casualties.[27]

The U.S. Army's replacement system dated to 1917. During the Civil War, the army's policy was to keep units in combat permanently, but it had no provision for infusing fresh men into the ranks. Thus, regiments simply fought until they ceased to exist; new regiments replaced spent ones. When the United States entered World War I, the army created a replacement system that would keep experienced units, and their battle-tested men and leaders, at the front by sending new men to replace individual casualties. Army leadership preferred this approach to the British practice of rotating units out of the line to recover, because it kept veterans in the fight.[28]

The replacement system also preserved unit integrity, but it had its downside. "Too often, the system of individual replacements flung a lone man into a group of strangers, with no chance to get to know them before he entered combat with them," argued historian Russell Weigley. "Too often, the replacement arrived at night and did not even see his comrades' faces before the battle resumed. Not the least of the defects of a program that did not regularly rotate divisions out of line was the lack of opportunity to absorb replacements under conditions that allowed some introduction to the unit's members and history, to say nothing of a measure of training with the unit."[29]

Norman D. Cota, a general Pete would serve under, did not care for the replacement method either. "This was a cruel system, probably necessitated by the nature of the war, but it was cruel, nevertheless, and I never liked it," he wrote. "Men have a right to go into battle as members of a trained unit, flanked by friends and associates, and, if possible, led by leaders who have trained them and whom they have come to trust. To thrust an individual, no matter how well trained as an individual he may be, into battle as a member of a strange unit is in my opinion expecting more than many men are capable of giving." Cota would have preferred turning repple depples into training centers, where new men could be trained and sent to the front as squads rather than individuals.[30] Even Gen. Dwight D. Eisenhower, the supreme commander in Europe, admitted that a replacement typically arrived at the front with the "feeling of a lost soul" who would be "shunted around without knowing where he is going or what will happen to him."[31]

The media agreed. In the words of journalist William Huie, a replacement was "the lowliest, loneliest role of all . . . the man who would be trained with one group, shipped with another, assigned to a replacement depot, then led to the front one night and told to dig in, without catching the name of the outfit, without knowing even the names of the men on his right or his left." Huie also damned the makeup of these men. By this stage of the war, high casualties meant that the United States had to employ "those citizens who had no choice at all: the very young men who had waited for the draft, the older or married men, or the marginal men who had been passed over, who had not been wanted, but who now were summoned by the community, most reluctantly, only when the barrel was being scraped."[32]

Small wonder that each of these poor men was filled with trepidation. You could see it in the eyes of these replacements and read it in their expressions. "Unlike those in the path of an advancing hurricane who know there is at least a chance that it will veer away, the specter of combat for an infantry replacement is inexorable," a soldier recalled. "Our forward movement conveyed its own message, but if one needed a reminder, it was amply provided by the artillery, now no longer like distant rolling thunder, but clearly identifiable as distinct individual explosions."[33]

Veterans saw replacements as overwhelmed, "vague shapes, laden with packs and weapons, who were hurried away behind guides to their companies," a soldier recalled. "I felt an ancient among children, knowing and dreading what they were to meet." An officer remembered arriving replacements as bewildered and disheartened; the sound of guns in the distance only underscored the fact that they were about to taste combat.[34] Small wonder that a veteran described replacements as "walking bull's eyes."[35] If a man wanted to survive, he had to undergo a "serious psychological readjustment," an analyst explained. The replacement "began then to realize even more than ever before that he was to take on a job for which he had been trained, but for which he felt greener than greenest."[36]

A combat historian named Forrest Pogue gave his own estimate of replacements. "Their clean uniforms, shaved faces, and bewildered looks made their newness at the front evident, and the week-old veterans treated them like 'recruits,'" he wrote. "The old-timers assured me that the new bunch was awfully stupid."[37] Historian Lee Kennett has called them living "spare parts" that arrived at the strange, dangerous front alone, friendless, and more often than not improperly trained. "Not surprisingly," Kennett wrote, "a significant number of replacements fell victim to combat exhaustion in their very first engagement." As one characteristic complaint from the front went, "Don't send us any more replacements. We haven't got time to bury them."[38]

So America was running short of men at the front. Whatever the merits of the replacement system, it continued unabated. It did not matter that Pete Lynn had a wife and children. It did not matter that he was over the age of thirty, or that he could have helped the war effort in the card room at Park Yarn. America needed him, and thousands like him, at the front.

Pete wrote home on September 16, and then he stopped writing. That meant he was traveling again, and this journey proved to be even more uncomfortable and less conducive to writing than his last. On September 17, his week's stay completed, Pete said goodbye and good riddance to Le Mans and piled into a railroad boxcar called a "Forty and Eight." The nickname came from the forty men or eight horses a car could carry, and the words "*Hommes* 40—*Chevaux* 8" stenciled on the sides. Boxcars just like these—or possibly the same rickety ones, in the opinion of many—had transported Allied soldiers during World War I. A less agreeable way to travel could not have been devised. "If the eight horses were one half as uncomfortable as the forty men, there would have been grounds for an animal rights activist protest," one veteran observed. Inside the cars, the men sat with their backs to the walls, pointed their feet to the center, and pulled their knees up to make room. In good weather, the men could dangle their legs from the doorway and enjoy the breeze, but in wet or cold weather the doors had to be shut. Nights meant claustrophobic sleeping in tangled piles of arms and legs.[39]

It might have helped if the men knew their itinerary or destination, but in typical army style the men were given little idea of either. Alexander Hadden reported that his train underwent "seemingly aimless shunting . . . in every conceivable direction," so soon enough he had no clue where he was. Hadden only figured out his location once, when he saw the Eiffel Tower in the distance. The trip was nothing less, he explained, than "an interminable train ride toward the east." As another replacement wrote, "We had no idea where we were. We just went where they sent us."[40]

By September 21, Pete at least knew that he had reached Belgium.[41] After traveling in those cramped forty and eights, arrival surely came as a blessed relief. "When you ride for 5 days and 5 nights straight in them," Hadden explained, "you are mighty glad to get out and walk awhile." However, arrival also meant they were a step closer to the front.[42] Moving through the replacement system was like sliding down a funnel: the closer you got to the bottom that was the front, the smaller the depots became. The depot one went to from LeMans depended on one's classification. Infantrymen—62 percent of all replacements—went to intermediate stockage depots. Pete did just that and likely ended up at Givet, France, which served the First and Ninth U.S. Armies. From there, he moved to an army support depot, probably in Belgium. That would have put Pete at the Third Replacement Depot, which served the First Army, as part of a "package" of 250 men. Each arriving "package" found this depot quite large, with facilities for 10,000 men, although at times it housed many more. Next, replacements slid further down the funnel: to a forward regimental depot, which supported a corps; to a battalion depot, which supported a division; and then to a replacement company, which could usually be found near a regimental or battalion headquarters. From there, a replacement would be sent down to his final destination—a company— often by way of a subsistence depot, which allowed for an efficient delivery of both men and supplies in a single truck.[43]

Each stop also felt more like the front than the last, and proximity was not the only reason. The poking and prodding continued as medics checked immunization records and conducted final medical exams. The pace quickened too. Supreme Headquarters, Allied Expeditionary Force (SHAEF) set the number of men sent to each army. When a man came under army control—First U.S. Army in Pete's case—army headquarters dictated, in code, the number of men to be sent from forward depots to each division. When a man's name was placed on orders, he went on "will call" status and waited for a truck to come pick him up. In most cases, men were summoned in alphabetical order.[44]

En route, many replacements became scared stiff thanks to the stories veterans told. These battlefield anecdotes usually contained grains of truth, with legend and braggadocio added. The result? "The battle veterans scared the pants off the green boys," an observer wrote. Many replacements therefore decided that Germans were battlefield supermen, which meant that their personal chances for survival were slim. Eventually, army leaders took steps to counteract this by circulating combat veterans to assure replacements that German soldiers were not invincible, but it was too late in many cases.[45]

The journey down the funnel was frightening enough without the help of such yarns. Like Pete, Charles Haug found himself at Belgium's Third Replacement Depot. "This made us all quite nervous because now we knew that we would soon be in it," he wrote. "We were issued an apple, a stick of chewing gum, 2 boxes of 'K' Rations, and 8 clips of ammunition." Then the men loaded onto trucks for the next stage of the journey while a band inexplicably played "Deep in the Heart of Texas."[46]

Replacements could also hear the war as they drew closer to the front. Reaching Belgium, Alexander Hadden's group of replacements lodged in the gymnasium of a parochial elementary school. The school sat on a hilly avenue in a city, complete with tram cars clanging along the road outside.

It almost sounded normal, until Hadden heard "thunder-like rumbling from the east" as artillery fired at the front. He could also make out the "putt-putt" of German V-1 rockets flying overhead.[47] Indeed, the racket of rockets formed a common part of each replacement's experience. Clarence Blakeslee heard the buzz bombs fly overhead too. "They were small planes with a ton of explosives, and the rocket engines on them made weird lights on the clouds at night. When the rockets shut off, they would sometimes glide quite a distance and other times would dive immediately into the ground and explode. We watched one come straight toward us and then the rocket engine shut off. There was nowhere to go, just pray. It just cleared us and exploded, and I didn't realize how scared I was until I tried to walk. My knees were shaking so I could hardly walk."[48]

Charles Haug heard the clamor too. "The first thing we heard as we started to unload from the trucks was a series of loud, thundering, crashes at the edge of the town," he recalled. These replacements worried that they had arrived in the midst of a German attack, but veterans laughed and explained that the sound was from American artillery. Overhead, streaking German V1s made it worse. "They sounded very much like an outboard motor on a lake and as you looked into the still night you could usually spot a red flame moving rapidly through the air. As long as you could hear the motor you knew that there was no danger of the bomb landing. But once you heard a motor stop all you had to do was wait about a minute and the whole sky would light up as it struck the ground and exploded. Seconds later you could hear a thundering roar echoing through the valleys and woods."[49] Veterans acted like the noise did not bother them. "Most of the other soldiers were congregated in small groups playing pinochle, cribbage, shooting dice, reading their Bibles or paperbacks, talking, or just getting a few winks of sleep," wrote California native John Allard. But not everyone adjusted well. "One fellow, unable to endure the tension, shot himself in the foot rather than take another step toward front line combat."[50]

William Meller, trucked to a wooded area in Belgium, saw rather than heard evidence that he was approaching the front. The truck drivers looked scared stiff, and at night Meller could see yellow and red flashes against the dark northeastern sky. An officer told them that the flashes came from fighting in Aachen. "Maybe this is what hell looks like," Meller told a friend.[51]

— ◁▷ —

Pete Lynn's journey was similar—from army to corps replacement centers, subjected to these same sights and sounds. At some point, he was issued more clips of ammunition for his M1 rifle, but that surely did nothing to boost his confidence. "We were all feeling mighty green," Charles Haug wrote.[52] He finally found himself assigned to the 41st Replacement Battalion, almost the last stop before the front.

Pete started writing again when he reached Belgium. Although he had just arrived, September 21 found Pete "fixing to move again."[53] This time, he knew where he was going: he knew his division, his regiment, and his company. On September 22, he jotted its identification—which would also serve as his mailing address—on the envelope of a letter to Ruth: Company B, 112th Infantry Regiment, 28th Infantry Division.[54]

He would not go alone. After some tough September days fighting along the Germany border, Company B needed men. Pete was one of forty-three soldiers earmarked for the unit, and they were not the typical soldier of 1941 or 1942. Like Pete, almost half the men in the group were married. Nearly half had not worn olive drab prior to 1944; well over a dozen had joined about the same time as Pete. It was also an older bunch: the group's average age was nearly twenty-eight, just above the national soldier average of twenty-six. Pete was not even the oldest. Four were the same age as him, while Private Orion Smith of Comanche County, Oklahoma was older still at thirty-seven.[55]

There was not a professional soldier in the lot. They were taxi drivers and farm hands, filling station attendants and policemen, mechanics and salesmen. Their educational attainments were equally run of the mill: less than a dozen had only been to grammar school. Most had gone to high school, while only a couple of men had attended college. They came from across America: from cities like New York, Los Angeles, St. Louis, and Philadelphia, and from small towns such as Henefer, Utah, and Greenville, South Carolina. There were even other North Carolinians in the group. One of them was John J. Biddy, an Asheville native. He was the same age as Pete and had also enlisted at Fort Bragg in March. If he did not already know Biddy, surely Pete gravitated toward him since they shared a home state and a similar journey to the front.[56]

Fumbling with backpacks, overcoats, and rifles, Pete and his fellow replacements piled into a half-dozen trucks for the ride that would take them to the front. From the Belgium replacement center, the trucks bounced into the Grand Duchy of Luxembourg and through the streets of the country's capital city. Luxembourg City sits on a rocky plain that is enclosed on three sides by heights, at the foot of which flows the rivers Petrusse and Alzette. It is an ancient city, a place where roads joined and empires from Rome to Nazi Germany had marched. Now it was America's turn. From the uncomfortable vantage point of a deuce-and-a-half, Pete saw the city's mountains and valleys, rocky gardens and huge viaducts, statues and cathedrals, and fortifications hewn from solid rock. One trooper remembered how his army truck "meandered along the narrow winding road . . . in the shadow of ancient watchtowers that had guarded the city for centuries." It did not fail to impress the man from The Best Little City in the World. "Darling I had the pleasure of seeing Luxemburgs to day, it was such a pretty town to," Pete wrote.[57]

Leaving the capital city, the trucks carried the men into the countryside, where Luxembourgers welcomed them fervently. Many Luxembourgers wore homemade red, white, and blue buttons to honor their liberators—although the more practical among them put black on the back of their buttons in case the Germans returned. Pete's convoy drove to the headquarters of their new regiment, the 112th Infantry, which was in an old school building near Rippig, about twenty kilometers from Luxembourg City. The order of the day was resting and administration, and also preparation, for the regiment would be moving again soon.[58]

On the night of September 23, Pete wrote a letter home. "I am well But not Happy and want Be till this war is over and I get Back to the old Park Yarn and my love ones," he wrote from the scant comfort of his pup tent. "Darling I went to Preaching a little while ago Just got back the Chaplan Preached a good sermon to But I would [rather] Hear Mr Babbet tho at the Macedonia." Before sealing the envelope, he enclosed some French francs and a strip of cloth that bore the colors of the Belgian flag.[59]

The next day, the men got an early start. From regimental headquarters, they rode on to Company B, which was posted near Beidweiler, Luxembourg. For Pete Lynn, John Biddy, and the rest, the truck ride to the front must have been similar to Alexander Hadden's. "In the back of the truck no one spoke and each of us was alone with his thoughts," Hadden recalled. "Mine were chaotic, but dread was the overriding emotion, as I asked myself, 'How in God's name could I have let this happen to me?'" Pete probably thought about Mr. Ballard more than once.[60]

All too soon, brakes squeaked and the deuce-and-a-halfs lurched to a halt in a cloud of dirt and gasoline fumes. There was no ceremony as these forty-three overburdened men tumbled wide-eyed out of the trucks, and fell into formation. A clerk with a clipboard, the company commander, and various other bystanders in worn uniforms welcomed the replacements to Company B, 112th Infantry, 28th Infantry Division, and then assigned them to their respective platoons and squads. It was Sunday, September 24, 1944.[61]

Lynn, Felmer L., serial number 34963373, now found himself at a place he never expected to be: an infantry company at the front in the European Theater. Someone gave him a copy of the New Testament. In its pages, he wrote, "Presented to me in Luxeburg," and then signed his name, rank, company, and regiment. He did not say if the gift was reassuring or only added to his misgivings.[62]

That night, surrounded by other sleeping soldiers, Pete dreamed of home. It was Sunday morning: time to go to church. Ruth and Mickey were there, ready for the short walk to Macedonia. He held Bob in his arms, and she was wearing a pretty white dress and bonnet. "Boy, was she a Baby Doll," he wrote home. "I ges that is why I Have the Blues so Bad to Day." Pete then let Ruth in on a secret. "Darling this is not Like Being Back in the states," he wrote. "I could sorta stand it Back there But it is some what Differint Hear."[63]

Park Yarn, where he used to "grind them old cords" at work and then spend his leisure with his family, was gone, beyond reach. The front, its nimbus visible, was at hand. Pete Lynn was lost in the machine of war.[64]

Chapter 7

Gentlemen from Hell

EVERY DAY IN EUROPE, IN TRUCK BEDS OR THE CELLARS OF RUINED buildings, in bitter cold or blistering heat, while artillery thundered, public affairs officers published 3,000 copies of the 28th Infantry Division's newsletter. The *Invader*'s pages related war news, shared jokes, sold war bonds, warned against fraternization, explained how to prevent trench foot, and ran contests. One favorite was the sweetheart contest, where readers nominated the girl with whom they wanted to share a foxhole. The paper received 5,000 votes for forty-five nominees.[1]

To inspire the troops, the editors built several adages into the newsletter's masthead. These included the division commander's favorite saying, "Fire and Movement," and the unit's slogan, "28th Division—Roll On," which came from another newsletter contest. But the most telling of all was the other phrase on the masthead: "Gentlemen from Hell."[2]

It captured the past and present of the division best.

Upon assignment to the 28th Infantry Division, Pete Lynn endured the obligatory physical, equipment review, and interview with regimental personnel. Then, he placed the division's red keystone insignia on his shoulder and learned that he had joined a storied unit.[3]

The 28th Infantry Division was one of fifty-five divisions in Europe under Gen. Dwight D. Eisenhower's command, of which twenty-eight were American. The third American infantry division to arrive in Europe, the 28th was a Pennsylvania National Guard unit with a long history.[4]

The division, among the oldest in the U.S. Army, dated its origins to 1747 when Benjamin Franklin, among others, convinced Philadelphians to organize militia against the twin dangers of Indians and privateers.

From that humble beginning, the banners of what eventually became the 28th Infantry Division waved in every American conflict. Its early days included service in the Revolutionary War, the Whiskey Rebellion, the War of 1812, and the Mexican War. During the Civil War, Pennsylvanians served on bloody grounds from Bull Run to Gettysburg and donned the Keystone badge for the first time. Parts of the division fought in the Spanish-American War and the Philippine Insurrection. Then came World War I and four and a half terrible months. Fighting at Chateau-Thierry, St. Agnan, and in the Meuse-Argonne campaign, the 28th's doughboys lost over 14,000 men, including 2,874 dead.[5]

The company, battalion, and regiment Pete joined descended from the 13th, 15th, and 17th Pennsylvania Infantry Regiments, which had fought at Battery Wagner, Cold Harbor, Petersburg, and Fort Fisher. Those battles were bad enough, but a later generation suffered even more terribly in the Argonne when two companies from the regiment were wiped out by a German attack at Fismette, France. It remained a bitter memory. Only the spirit embodied in the regiment's motto, "Strive, Obey, Endure," ensured its survival. In turn, the 28th earned its own moniker when Gen. John J. Pershing dubbed it the Iron Division. Back home after the war, the doughboys kept the division alive as a National Guard unit. The division deployed only once in that period, to provide assistance during the 1936 Johnstown, Pennsylvania flood.[6]

When a new war suddenly loomed, President Roosevelt decided to increase America's readiness by federalizing eighteen National Guard divisions. The 28th was tapped on February 17, 1941. Company B, which hailed from Meadville, Pennsylvania, packed up and joined the rest of the division at Indiantown Gap Military Reservation. Training began in earnest and continued as the regiment shuttled to seven different posts across the country including Camp Livingston, Louisiana; Camp Gordon in Johnston, Florida; and Camp Pickett, Virginia. It marched in field maneuvers in the Carolinas and followed a procession of commanders that included Gen. Omar Bradley. These days were not without their challenges as many of the unit's best men left the division to help start new units. The division also had a poor reputation at first, but commanders like Bradley prepared it well. Camp Miles in Standish, Massachusetts, was the division's last stop before it crowded into troop transports at Boston Harbor and sailed for England on September 28, 1943. The 28th was not earmarked for the D-Day invasion, so its preparations for war continued apace in Great Britain via amphibious training and maneuvers.[7]

The Iron Division went ashore in Normandy in late July 1944. Assembling northwest of St. Lo, the soldiers marched straight into combat where, a journalist wrote, "they promptly got the hell shot out of them." On the 28th's first day of combat, it suffered 750 casualties.[8] In the days that followed, these Pennsylvanians bled and died profusely amidst Normandy's hedgerows. Its infantry regiments—the 109th, 110th, and 112th—soon lost much of their Keystone State character. Replacements flooded in, and the division became not one of neighbors who had trained together but one of strangers thrown together. (One replacement asked where the Pennsylvanians were when he joined the 112th. "We left them back in the hedgerows," came the answer.) The division also lost leaders; one division commander was relieved and a sniper's bullet felled another. Nonetheless, the 28th learned to fight and acquitted itself in Normandy. It also earned yet another nickname. "You must either be madmen or picked troops, so fiercely do you fight," a captured German officer said. Then, he pointed to the red keystone shaped shoulder patch, whose shape resembled a bucket. "We call you *Der Blutig Eimer.*" The Bloody Bucket.[9]

The Gentlemen from Hell fought across France to the gates of Paris. When French leader Charles DeGaulle asked Eisenhower to send American units into the City of Lights on a show of force, Eisenhower chose the 28th. "The trample of American soldier-feet echoed in Paris yesterday for the first time since the victory parade of 1918—and it was the trample of the feet of the sturdy fighting men of our own division," the *Invader* bragged. It was August 29, a "black, rainy Tuesday." Carrying polished weapons and wearing clean uniforms, the men marched "battalions abreast, with bayonets fixed and arms slung" past the Arc de Triomphe, down "broad, tree-lined Champ de Elysees, branching off at the towering memorial to Louis IV at the Place de la Concord." Bands played; throngs flung fruit and flowers at the men and cheered, "*Boche Kaput; Vive les Americans!*" Paris was free again! A star-studded cast of leaders watched from a makeshift reviewing stand. Then, the Bloody Bucket division marched back to the war.[10]

⌐◄—►

Settling into his new home, the 1st Platoon of Company B, Pete Lynn tried to get acquainted with the men around him. Many of them were very different, from many walks of life, but they were all so American.

Johnny Gregorio arrived at the front the same day as Pete. Born on Independence Day, 1924, Gregorio lived with his wife, Beatrice, in a two-story brick row house in Olney, a neighborhood in North Philadelphia.[11] Pete also met Albert J. Pesek, thirty-two, a city boy from Chicago who had enlisted on March 14, 1942. Still a private, Pesek was divorced and had two years of high school to his credit.[12]

Another new acquaintance, Vernon Bowers, was from Grantsville, a small town in the northwest corner of Maryland. The son of Mr. and Mrs. Charles Bowers, Vernon came from a family of six brothers and two sisters. He was among the youngest men in the platoon, having celebrated his twentieth birthday on September 18. In fact, Bowers had just graduated from Grantsville High School the year before; enlisted in the army a month after graduation; took basic training at Camp Haan, California, and Camp Carson, Colorado; and then shipped overseas on August 4, 1944.[13]

Thomas M. Floyd Jr. was a youthful twenty-two but he was a Southern boy. That, in Pete's estimation, made up for the age difference. His hometown was Sane Souci, South Carolina, a mere seventy-five miles from Kings Mountain. Back home, a full house waited on Thomas, including his parents, Thomas and Medra Floyd, and his three sisters. Like Pete, Thomas was easy-going and optimistic, so the two men surely had a lot to talk about.[14]

Clyde Edward Sprinkle, twenty-nine, was another kindred spirit, to a point. Sprinkle had enlisted at Fort Bragg the same week as Pete and had joined Company B with the same replacement packet. Sprinkle owned beagles back home in Lewisville, North Carolina, and without fail spent his limited vacation time away from his Hanes Knitting plant job to hunt for rabbit or squirrel. Sprinkle's little four-room house on Styers Ferry Road was also full of girls. Sprinkle and his wife, Lula, had two daughters, one of whom had just arrived. Pete understood more than anybody Sprinkle's hope for a son, which drove Sprinkle to give his baby girl a masculine name, Clydene Edwina Sprinkle. Sprinkle was also reticent and uneducated, having only graduated from Clemmons Elementary School. Unlike Pete, he was a man with little time for God. The only time his daughter could remember seeing her daddy in church was to attend funerals.[15]

Pete also got to know the organization he joined and the men who led it. The 1st Platoon of Company B was commanded by Lt. Ralph W. Spaans. Born in Medford, Massachusetts, Spaans spent his early years in Bergen County, New Jersey. He graduated from Bogota High School and then worked as a professional driver before he joined the army in Newark on September 10, 1942. At twenty-three, Spaans was younger than many of the men in his platoon. He was also single and had no children. In a different time and place, Pete would have had an avuncular relationship to Ralph, but the battlefield reversed their roles. The younger man was a combat veteran with a solid background. He had attended the infantry school at Fort Benning, graduated from Officer's Candidate School in May 1943, and had served with the regiment since it arrived in France. In European Theater terms, he was an old man. He also knew firsthand what war meant, having lost his father in World War I.[16]

On paper, each platoon contained three squads of twelve men each, but casualties often kept that total lower. Staff sergeants led squads. Company B, which had a muster roll strength of 186 men, contained three rifle platoons as well as a heavy weapons platoon. Lts. Gerald M. Burrill and Freeman W. McDonald led the other rifle platoons, while 1st Lt. John H. Garrity Jr. commanded the company. Normally a captain would have been in command, but the previous company commander had transferred out a few days before Pete arrived.[17]

Company B was a part of the 112th Infantry. The regiment contained three battalions. Each had a color code, with the 1st Battalion assigned red, the 2nd white, and the 3rd, blue. Red contained A Company, Pete's B Company, and C Company—all rifle companies—as well as D Company, which was a heavy weapons unit, and a headquarters company. Typically, a World War II army battalion contained about 900 men and 28 officers. Among the latter were regimental staff officers such as Capt. Victor Glider, the S-4, and Capt. Robert Holdsworth, adjutant. Maj. Robert T. Hazlett commanded the Red Battalion, and he was highly regarded. "Major Hazlett was a man who had the courage to do what he was told to do," one of his commanders later said.[18]

These were the *Gentlemen from Hell*.

<hr />

Maj. Gen. Norman Daniel "Dutch" Cota led the 28th Infantry Division toward Germany. He had lived an army life. Born on May 30, 1893, Cota was raised in a poor Episcopalian family in Chelsea, Massachusetts. He passed his early years in the Bay State until he matriculated at the U.S. Military Academy, where he graduated on April 30, 1917. Although the nation was embroiled in World War I, Cota missed the action. Instead, he went from stateside infantry regiments to a teaching position at his alma mater before ending up in the army's Finance Department.[19]

Shuttling through six different posts over the next five years, Cota commanded figures and ledgers, not soldiers. In 1924, he gladly returned to the infantry and went on to punch his ticket at the Infantry School, the Command and General Staff College, the Chemical Warfare School,

Maj. Gen. Norman D. Cota
Source: National Archives

and the War College. He also taught at Fort Benning and Fort Leavenworth, and tasted command with the 35th and 26th Infantry regiments. World War II accelerated the pace. Tapped as chief of staff for the 1st Infantry Division, he helped plan the invasion of North Africa and fought in it too, earning a Legion of Merit for his "perispacity, personality, and high degree of initiative" and for helping to mold the division into "an effective combat team." Afterward, he studied amphibious operations with Admiral Lord Louis Mountbatten at Combined Operations Headquarters.[20]

By the autumn of 1943, Cota had been promoted to brigadier general and given a job with heavier responsibility: assistant division commander of the 29th Infantry Division. Cota saw to it that the Blue and Gray Division, so named for its mixed Union and Confederate heritage, was readied for war, and nobody was surprised at his performance. In the words of a superior officer, he "contributed materially to the high order of esprit, unity, training, and general readiness of the division."[21]

Yet Cota's thoughts never strayed far from his family. He was a family man at heart, and his family shared his sense of call. His wife, Constance, lived with their daughter in Daytona, Florida, where she was active with the Red Cross. The men of the family joined Cota in Europe. Cota's son, Maj. Dan Cota, a recent West Point graduate, flew with the U.S. Army Air Corps while Cota's son-in-law, Capt. T. J. Norris, marched with the 90th Infantry Division.[22]

On D-Day, the 29th division rode into the thick of hell. At H plus fifty-seven minutes, Cota splashed through the surf of Omaha Beach and found a near disaster. Enemy fire tore his division apart, and for an hour the assault foundered. Cota stood against the onslaught and was seemingly everywhere. Ignoring bullets and shells, he vaulted the seawall and bellowed encouragement and orders. Cota personally supervised the placement of a BAR to fire on Germans along the cliff, and then he directed a Bangalore torpedo into the barbed wire. When the wire was blown, the assistant division commander was among the first men through the gap. From there, he led a column of troops to high ground from where they could shoot to advantage. Lt. Jack Shea, Cota's aide, ducked as six mortar shells fell into the knot of soldiers around Cota; when the smoke cleared, three men lay dead and two wounded, but Cota stood unharmed. Atop the cliff the attack bogged down again, but Cota again cajoled and pushed. Some witnesses swore he handled a BAR and Bangalore torpedo himself. He sent forces inland to take key objectives and then returned to the war-torn beach, which was still under sniper and machine gun fire, to help untangle the mess. Had it not been for Cota, many more men might have died on that beach.[23]

Cota's *ne plus ultra* combat performance continued after D-Day. In Normandy's hedgerows, Shea recorded, Cota led an "escapade across the

Vire River, where he fought for 35 hours against superior enemy forces while leading a force of less than 100 of our riflemen." After further experience fighting in the hedgerows, Cota developed some special tactics to help his men advance. Then, while leading "Task Force Charlie" on its drive into St. Lo, Dutch Cota stood manfully at an intersection as German artillery roared in and a shell fragment struck his arm. "He refused to be evacuated until he knew that the situation was well under control, which was hours later," a witness wrote.[24]

Small wonder that Omar Bradley described Cota as "a warm good friend" who "I admire greatly," or that his men came to swear by him. One GI was surprised when Cota showed up at his foxhole one day to chat and share some cookies. "He's sure as hell easy to talk to," the soldier wrote. On another occasion, the general's jeep screeched to a halt at the front. Dismounting, Cota walked from foxhole to foxhole, tapping soldiers on their helmets with his cane. "How's business?" he asked. "Everything going all right?" It was the mark of an approachable leader. During an exercise, Cota was wearing a combat jacket that hid his rank when a soldier asked for a light. When the general produced his lighter, the man could not help himself. "Bud, you look sorta old to be in the Army; how long yuh been in it?"

"About 28 years," the general replied.

"Lord!" said the soldier. "28 years in the Army and ain't got a stripe yet!"

Cota loved that spirit. One day, a division soldier named Bill Meller saw Cota in his staff car—a jeep he called "Fire and Movement" that had two small flags flying from the fenders. "This war will be won by the foot soldier," Cota told Meller as he drove away. "I had never seen a general close up before, and I was not impressed," Meller wrote, but in truth Cota had the right idea.[25]

When the smoke of Normandy cleared, Dutch Cota had won a chestful of medals: a Distinguished Service Cross with an Oak Leaf Cluster, Silver Star, Purple Heart, and a Distinguished Service Order from Great Britain. The accompanying citations were dotted with phrases like "gallantry in action," "constantly exposing himself to enemy fire without regard to his own safety," "outstanding courage and superb leadership," and "extraordinary heroism."[26] His reputation was equally bronzed. Combat historian Pogue wrote that Cota had become "almost a legendary figure," while author Rick Atkinson has named him the paladin of Omaha Beach and Saint-Lo. Even Cota's words became iconic. Standing in Omaha's sands, he yelled, "Rangers! Lead the way!" It remains the motto of the U.S. Army's Rangers.[27]

Thus, when Cota emerged from the hospital, it came as no surprise that a promotion awaited. On August 13, 1944, the same day Pete visited Baltimore, Dutch Cota took command of the 28th Infantry Division. The division's previous commander, Maj. Gen. Lloyd D. Brown, had just been relieved, and Brown's successor, Maj. Gen. James E. Wharton, was killed by a sniper hours after taking the post. Within a month, Cota was promoted to major general, in part thanks to the recommendation of corps commander Maj. Gen. Charles H. Corlett. Now fifty-one, with gray eyes, white thinning hair, a ready smile, and a paunch jutting from his 200-pound frame, the modest and quiet Cota tackled his new job amid high expectations.[28]

Having a man like Cota in charge of the 28th Infantry Division might have comforted soldiers like Ralph Spaans, Clyde Sprinkle, and Pete Lynn. Or it might have worried them, for a man with such a track record would surely end up in the thick of things, and soon.

———

Cota took the division's reins soon after the Allies, in the aftermath of Operation Cobra, finally broke the back of German defenses and surged out of the Normandy beachhead. In contrast to July's brutal yard-by-yard fighting, August and September 1944 were months of heady exultation. "It seemed clear," remembered one U.S. general, "that the Germans were beaten, badly beaten." Beneath the late summer sun, seven Allied armies, their ranks stretching from the North Sea to Switzerland, shot across France and Belgium. The conquerors breezed past the World War I battlegrounds where their fathers had fought. Soldiers of the Reich fled wildly before them, on foot and on bicycle, pushing handcarts and even baby carriages. From Allied headquarters to Washington to Whitehall, optimism reigned. Meanwhile, Soviet forces steamrolled in the east. Other Allied forces advanced inexorably in the west, while bombers pummeled German cities from the skies. American forces were also ascendant in the

Pacific. The end was "within sight, almost within reach," Eisenhower's headquarters reported. Even cynical Gen. George Marshall thought it was possible: "Cessation of hostilities in the war against Germany may occur at any time," he wrote.[29]

But a few men, including Col. Truman C. Thorson, were not so sure. A former commander of the 112th Infantry, Thorson was now the G-3, or operations, officer for the First U.S. Army, the 28th's parent organization. Thorson bet a colleague a dollar for every day past Christmas the war continued, and eventually collected a handsome payout. He saw what others missed: Allied momentum was slowing. The bastard child had many fathers. As summer turned to fall, colder temperatures arrived and rain turned roads to mud. Every step forward was also a step farther away from supply dumps at the beaches. The famous over-the-road truck shuttle called the Red Ball Express helped bring forward gas, ammo, and rations, but since the Allies had not yet captured a usable port it was not nearly enough. Fatigue in the ranks grew after long marches and hard fighting. The worst sign of all was the stiffening of German defenses the further east Allied armies pushed.[30]

The 28th Infantry Division, now a part of the First Army's V Corps, soon learned that firsthand. After Paris, the division marched nearly 300 miles, and along the way cleared the Compiegne Forest, where World War I's armistice had been signed and where France had surrendered to Hitler. Deeper in France, the Keystone men began to encounter resistance. "Our enemy stopped from time to time to fight strong delaying actions that caused many casualties and permitted me to learn my trade as a medic," recalled one Iron Division soldier. Among the casualties was the commander of the 112th, Col. Henry I. "Hammering Hank" Hodes. In his stead, Lt. Col. Carl L. Peterson took over. A forty-seven-year-old Zippo salesman and National Guard officer from Pennsylvania, Peterson had served in the same regiment as a private in 1916.[31]

Through Belgium and then Luxembourg, the Iron Division pushed and seized Luxembourg City itself. Beyond, the German border loomed. The 28th was among the first Allied units—and the first foreign soldiers since Napoleon—to enter the Reich, but barring the way was an ominous system of concrete, steel, and barbed wire fortifications. The Americans called it the Siegfried Line. To the Germans, it was the Westwall. The soldiers just thought it looked like hell. Thanks to Cota's leadership, the 28th Division had become a better division, but its reward was a chance to test those defenses.[32]

It came about when the V Corps received orders to conduct a reconnaissance in force of the Siegfried Line. Patrols judged the fortifications as not strongly held, so its commander, Maj. Gen. Leonard T. Gerow, decided to launch a full-blown assault. Peterson's 112th Infantry joined the fray. On September 14, the regiment, attached to the 5th Armored Division, found the Siegfried Line quite well defended. Hazlett's 1st Battalion and some 5th Armored tankers attacked into Germany, captured Wallendorf, and then moved east and secured Biesdorf and Wettlingen. The soldiers dug in on high ground east of the latter village, and then the Germans zeroed in. Heavy mortar and artillery fire came down, and German troops counterattacked. Casualties mounted. The Keystoners and tankers were forced to fall back, and army generals decided to call off the whole assault. Enemy artillery and infantry chased the Keystone men all the way back to Wallendorf, where on September 21 Hazlett's battalion recrossed the Sauer River bridge. Returning to assembly areas near Diekirch, Company B counted more than fifty men missing, wounded, evacuated, or killed; the 1st Battalion recorded a casualty rate of 37 percent; and the division tallied 1,929 casualties.[33]

In the days that followed, quiet descended on the front. On September 25, Cota received a telegram promoting him

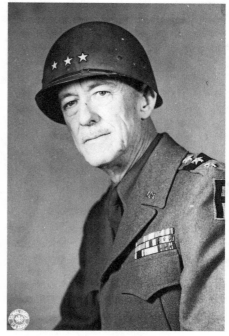

Lt. Gen. Courtney Hodges
Source: Library of Congress

to major general, but this did nothing to alleviate Cota's mounting troubles.[34] His concerns started with his superior officers. His immediate boss, the rarely unruffled V Corps commander Gerow, was a 1911 graduate of the Virginia Military Institute, a member of Pershing's World War I staff, and former head of war planning at the War Department. In Europe, Gerow had led his men well since the D-Day landings. He was also an old friend of Ike's, but his French-born wife, Marie-Louise was under fire because her family was suspected of collaborating with the Nazis.

Gerow's superior, Lt. Gen. Courtney H. Hodges, commander of the U.S. First Army, had enlisted as a private after flunking geometry at West Point. Despite this setback, he earned a commission only a year after his Academy classmates. A veteran of both Pershing's Mexico foray and World War I, Hodges was a calm, reticent, hard-working man who rarely visited his subordinates. They came to him. Hodges was also an intolerant panjandrum who fired men with little forethought. Paratrooper Jim Gavin once described the tall, erect Hodges as "colorless," but also "intelligent, thoughtful, studious," a man who "knew his trade well," and was careful

Lt. Gen. Leonard T. Gerow
Source: Library of Congress

with the lives of his men. Others called him a "soldier's soldier," in part due to his emphasis on precision and detailed planning. Then, there were his detractors. More than one man had difficulties with Hodges. Patton thought Hodges dumb. Others said he was a cautious, unimaginative man who looked like a "rumpled, unassertive small-town banker." Presiding over all of this was Bill Kean, the forty-seven-year-old chief of staff to whom Hodges delegated much authority. As the army commander's representative, Kean badgered and berated subordinates so much that they nicknamed him "Old Sam Bly." Cota felt ill-supported by this cast of characters and had little faith that he could work with them successfully.[35]

Cota was just as unhappy with his division's performance in Germany. He felt the Bloody Bucket's Siegfried Line attack had been too cautious, and the division had traded too many men for too little ground.[36] Meanwhile, more than 1,500 replacements flooded into the division to replace the casualties suffered during the fighting. (Pete Lynn was among them.) Not a fan of the replacement system, Cota worried about these green men, and the veterans in the division joined him as vilipenders. The replacements "were so inexperienced that, when I had to check them in at night before they joined the fighting groups, my heart was heavy," one soldier wrote. "I knew that ninety percent of the casualties the next day would be from this group who did not know what combat was all about." That was an exaggeration, but the lack of experience among replacements was clearly a handicap. There was nothing for it but to try to get the division battle-ready.[37]

Pete's first full day with Company B was Monday, September 24. About twenty kilometers to their rear stood Luxembourg City. In front of them loomed the Siegfried Line, pale, stark, and menacing with its concrete pillboxes, dragon's teeth, and barbed wire stretching into the distance. Nearby stood Beidweiler and Eschweiler, two modest villages of the Grand Duchy of Luxembourg. This spot constituted not only the 5th Armored's right flank, but also the right flank of the entire First Army. One might worry it was an exposed place. It was not, for the most part. The regiment's job was to patrol the Siegfried Line, but in the event comparative quiet reigned and allowed time for the men to rest, reorganize, and police themselves.[38] For the first time, Pete heard and felt the impact of enemy artillery fire, which fell on the 1st Battalion around 6:30 P.M. No one was hurt, but it was surely memorable for the man from Kings Mountain. Otherwise, the day passed quietly, although a few patrols ran into enemy forces and lost three men wounded and one missing, none of them from Company B.[39]

September 25 looked a lot like September 24. The company and the rest of the 112th Infantry spent the day in their foxholes while patrols ranged across the countryside and enemy artillery shells landed randomly. Three men were wounded, three went missing, and one man was killed during the day, and the regiment also suffered four "non-battle" casualties for reasons such as illness, accidents, or combat exhaustion. Neither Pete nor the official record say if he was tapped for a patrol, but he would certainly have gone if his squad or platoon received such an assignment. Meanwhile, word spread that orders had arrived for the regiment to move, and an advance party left as early at 6:30 P.M. to prepare the way. The time had come for the regiment to end its separation and return to the 28th Infantry Division.[40]

Moving day was September 26. Pulling out of the front lines by 9:00 A.M., Pete and his fellow 2,810 soldiers of the 112th Infantry slogged a short distance to the rear. (Troops from the 83rd Infantry Division took their place.) In a division assembly area near Beidweiler, the men found over 500 trucks lined up and waiting for them, their engines idling noisily. Company B and the rest of the battalion piled into eighty-five trucks, gear and all, shouting and cursing, while the rest of the regiment angled for the 421 other waiting vehicles. When everyone was aboard, the procession lurched forward. The trucks carrying the I&R Platoon led the way, while the rest of the regiment followed, in order. It was 11:35 A.M. when Company B's trucks pulled in behind Company A in a cloud of blue diesel smoke and churning mud. Drivers were careful to leave intervals of sixty yards between trucks and five minutes between companies. Guides stood at key intersections in Luxembourg City to point the way, and then across Luxembourg and Belgium the trucks lumbered. Like Gen. Stonewall Jackson's Confederate army in the Shenandoah Valley, the column paused for ten minutes before each even hour, and then the trucks roared forward again. At an average speed of thirty miles an hour, and with stops and starts, it took five and a half hours for the column to traverse the eighty kilometers to its destination near Steffeshausen, Germany and Burg-Reuland, Belgium.[41]

September 27, a Thursday, brought cloudy skies and anticipation. It was wash day, and Hazlett's battalion was happy for once to lead the way.

At 7:30 A.M., deuce-and-a-half trucks carried the battalion to a muddy field where a bank of showers sat that could handle 250 men at a time. The schedule did not allow for much lingering, but the hot water and the soap were a luxury for men who had been living in filth. The 1st Battalion emerged from the steam at 10:30 A.M., and the other battalions followed. After drying off, Hazlett's soldiers donned clean uniforms while the officers circulated through squads, platoons, and companies to conduct an ordnance inspection. Soldiers also cleaned vehicles and weapons. A few patrols marched out but saw nothing, and these men hurried back so they too could partake of the hot coffee and doughnuts dispensed from a Red Cross Clubmobile.[42]

This soapy, peaceful interlude felt a little like dressing a hog for slaughter. At 3:00 A.M. the next morning, more trucks arrived. This time they hauled Peterson's soldiers to the slopes of the Schnee Eifel, a high wooded ridge along the Belgian-German border. Just east of the ancient, stone-walled hillside village of Buchet, the Bloody Bucket dug in next to the 22nd Infantry. This was a dangerous place; enemy artillery crashed about, and brushes with German soldiers left one of Peterson's men dead. As the Keystoners dug deeper, officers planned an attack on the Siegfried Line near the town of Brandscheid. An officer with experience in fighting among the pillboxes toured units to share his experiences. Tensions rose at the thought of testing those stout German defenses again, especially for men like Pete who had not tasted a real battle yet. Then came a welcome reprieve: two generals, including assistant division commander Brig. Gen. George A. Davis, visited Peterson's command post and announced that the attack had been canceled, so on the morning of September 29 the men marched back down the Schnee Eifel, piled once more into those large, uncomfortable deuce and a halfs, and rode back to Steffeshausen and Burg-Reuland.[43]

The day they returned, September 29, saw partly cloudy skies in the morning and scattered rain in the afternoon. "The weather was bad," a clerk recorded, but Pete still found time between rain, trucks, and trenches to write.[44] "Darling there is a Lot I could tell you if I was Permited to," he wrote, but only disclosed that he was still in Belgium. Pete explained that he was "as well as can Be in fact I Feel just fine we are getting Plenty to Eat and Plenty of cigretts to." If he needed anything, Pete said, it was a pair of fur-lined gloves. Maybe Ruth could send him the gloves for Christmas. "Well Darling this is one 7 of October we wont be together," he went on, in reference to his birthday, "but my Heart will be with you and the kids to be Frank Dear that is where it stays it is Planted at the old PY where it will grow For Ever."[45]

Pete sounded pensive because the real war was here too. Six V-1 rockets sputtered through the gray skies, prompting corps to order the men to report the time and position of any flying bombs they spotted. In the distance, along the Siegfried Line, the Americans could plainly see the enemy. At one point, eight tanks lumbered down the main highway. Mortar and artillery fire exploded randomly, harrying the men along the lines. All of this lent urgency to the Americans' effort to lay mines, improve their foxholes, and run patrols.[46]

It was also a time of transition for Company B. Pete had never met Capt. Harold F. O'Neil, the regular company commander, because he was transferred to another company on September 19. When he joined the company, Pete did meet 1st Lt. John H. Garrity Jr., who took over the command from O'Neil, but Garrity's tenure proved short-lived. The lieutenant left the company due to illness on September 28 and turned the company over to Wayne T. Welch. Welch was promoted to first lieutenant about the same time.[47]

Such change was quite common throughout the command. Cota and Peterson also knew that the men had to be razor sharp and ready for anything, so training began anew on September 30. The topic was assault tactics against pillboxes. Companies divided into assault teams and flame throwers were trotted out. It was a forbidding sign of things to come. Fog lowered on the scene and rain varied from drizzle to hard showers until 2:00 P.M., but it did not deter training or the multiple Red battalion patrols that ranged through the hilly border area. For its part, Company B moved into an outpost position, while rumors and enemy movements charged the air: an enemy plane zoomed low over Peterson's CP, and it was said that a black Plymouth sedan was riding about with four black-coated Gestapo inside. Regimental clerks reported the loss of twelve wounded.[48]

So September passed. "As the month closes," a White battalion clerk wrote, "we are still here, high on a windy hill, amid the rain and dampness

ROTTERDAM

Arnhem

HOLLAND

RUHR

Lippe River

Niers River

Ruhr River

ANTWERP

DÜSSELDORF

Roer River

Erft River

COLOGNE

BRUSSELS

Duren

Aachen

Bonn

BELGIUM

Liege
Eupen
Roetgen

Hürtgen Forest

Remagen

Meuse River

Spa

Berg
Malmedy
Krinkelt
Wirtzfeld

Krinkelter Wald

Rhine River

A R D E N N E S

St. Vith

E I F E L

Burg-Reuland
Brandscheid

Mosel River

Lutzkampen

N

Bastogne
Eschweiler

Wallendorf

LUXEMBOURG

Trier

0   1.5   3 kilometers

0   1.5   3 miles

Luxembourg
City

GERMANY

PETE LYNN
AT THE FRONT,
1944

FRANCE

Source: MacDonald, The Siegfried Line

of which we have had more than a fair share this month, so, according to the law of averages, we are sure due for a lot of sunshine." Pete surely hoped so, and bedded down in his foxhole with a pocket full of German marks. It was payday, but his thoughts and dreams were like the song he used to sing for Ruth. He pined away for the place he longed to be and the Carolina moon shining overhead.[49]

———

As October arrived, it slowly dawned on the army's leaders that they faced "a bitter-end campaign," and that brought much consternation.[50] "Those early days in October were a time of utmost frustration in the Allied ground command," Gen. Omar Bradley later wrote. "We couldn't move."[51] Hodges and the men of the First Army learned that firsthand as they tried to capture Aachen. It was a bloody slog, but they finally managed it on October 21 after some tough fighting. Meanwhile, other First Army units not involved in the attack on Aachen, including the 28th Division, moved not east toward the enemy but north and south.[52]

Company B shifted yet again, this time from Burg-Reuland to the vicinity of Lutzkampen, Germany. Welch's Company B was assigned the task of clearing a designated area to its front three times daily. A machine gun unit and soldiers from the 60th Infantry lent a hand.[53] Most of the time, these patrols were uneventful, but not always. At 5:30 P.M. on October 2, a patrol from Pete's Company captured a German soldier. He turned out to be a deserter from the 526th Ersatz Division who had hid in a bunker until an Allied patrol passed. The prisoner's company, seventy men strong, had been formed in Bonn, Germany just a month before. A few weeks of serving with a noncommissioned officer, nine enlisted men, a light machine gun, and a collection of rifles and grenades had sufficiently cowed him. American intelligence officers learned plenty from the soldier, who identified the defending units in the area and the location of some mines.[54]

Here Pete began learning about the front lines, and there were heart-pounding moments to mark his education. Every so often, German gunners lobbed artillery shells into the American positions.[55] Usually the artillery was just a nuisance that hurt no one and damaged little, but all-out barrages from heavy caliber guns could be fearsome. "The big guns belched their shells with thunderous, unannounced, ear-splitting roars that reverberated against wooded hills and echoed and re-echoed until it seemed we were caught in the middle of some giant cauldron with hundreds of Satanic monsters banging sledgehammers against the side with fiendish glee," a veteran recalled.[56] Fortunately, Company B suffered no casualties during this period from artillery or otherwise.[57]

Meanwhile, new orders came down as the American army shifted and rearranged in its endless search for a force disposition that would produce victory. Maj. Gen. Troy H. Middleton's VIII Corps of Lt. Gen. William H. Simpson's Ninth Army, having completed separate operations in Brittany, was now available, so Bradley decided to reshuffle his lines. He planned to move Gerow's V Corps north and put the VIII Corps in its place, which meant the 28th would move to the Krikelt, Belgium area. A complex dance involving thousands of men, the reshuffling began on the night of October 3 when Pete's regiment, under cover of night and with radios silent, climbed out of their foxholes. Guides pointed the way.[58]

The Keystone troopers found a long line of deuce-and-a-half trucks waiting. On the bumper of the column's first and last truck was stenciled the convoy number, 2887; a driver and assistant driver manned each vehicle. With shouts and clanking equipment, soldiers loaded up and the convoy started rolling across the Belgian countryside. Military policemen stood at each intersection to point the way as the trucks clipped past at thirty miles per hour. They traveled Highways N-33, N-23, N-32, and some unmarked roads in between.[59]

It was a trip of only about fifty kilometers, but it felt longer. Those lumbering green trucks offered little protection against the "cold, biting rain" that fell and pelted them in the face. It seemed like hours passed before they finally arrived at a forward division assembly area near Wirtzfeld, Belgium. Disembarking, "the troops proceeded to pitch tents in an open country" and settled into their new surroundings.[60]

In some fashion, Company B lost one man, PFC Edwin C. Ross, to some light wounds. The records do not state how, but maybe a stray enemy shell caught him. Otherwise, the new assembly area was quiet. Some men sat down to read the October 3 issue of *Stars and Stripes*, which arrived on October 5. It contained a long article on the activities of the Keystone Division through September 20.[61] If Pete read the paper he did not say so; instead, he sat down in one of these tents and wrote home. He was frustrated. Thanks to his company's frequent moves, his name had not been called during mail call recently. "When it does catch up with me they will Have to stop the war till I get them Red Ha Ha." Changing topics, Pete looked around and felt unsure of his exact location. "Darling we must be some where in Belgium For I saw to grate Big Rabbits Down in the pasture Like the ones your Dad ust to Raze at margrace," he wrote. "I tried to Kill one But He got away we were gona Barbucue Him." There was still enough space on the page to share his real thoughts, of home and his girls. He could just see Mick with syrup and butter "all over Her mouth and Runing Down the Front of Her Dress and Hollern for more Ha Ha." One day Pete would go home, and when he did he promised Mick he would ride her on "old Silver," his back.[62]

October 6, 1944, dawned fair and hazy.[63] Hazlett's 1st Battalion deployed in an oblong half circle the men called Horseshoe Red. C Company took the left side of the circle, Pete and B Company the middle, and A the right. Hazlett put his command post behind the companies. The regiment's other two battalions set up similar but separate horseshoes with the 3rd Battalion in front and the 2nd Battalion directly behind it, meaning the 1st Battalion was in reserve. The 28th's other regiments deployed to the left while another division held the regiment's right.[64]

Thus arrayed, the Iron Division pushed east from the Wirtzfeld assembly area in column of battalions. Its objective was the Krinkelter Wald, a patch of dense woods along the German border that would serve as a line of departure for a future attack against the Siegfried Line. With equipment clanking as they trudged, elements passed through the quiet Belgian villages of Krinkelt and Rocherath, two months hence to be the scene of terrible fighting during the Battle of the Bulge. An occasional enemy shell exploded nearby. American artillery responded in kind, and P-47s flew overhead in support. Rain fell. "From authoritative sources comes the statement that the weather here is the worst it has been for 80 years, and far be it from anyone in our company to doubt it," a soldier moaned.[65]

During the push east, Company B lost another man wounded, although he was listed as a nonbattle casualty. The company, previously shorthanded in leadership, also welcomed a new officer, 1st Lt. Phillip Lord, probably to serve as executive officer. The addition of Lord brought the company to 163 enlisted men and 5 officers present for duty that Friday.[66]

Later, Pete once again pulled out some stationery. Ignoring the rain, he assured Ruth that everything was fine, but found a creative way to tell her he was advancing without alarming the censors. "Just a line as I sit Here to let you Here From your traveling Husban[d]," he wrote. "Darling I Don't ges I will stop till I get to Berlin[.] I am some where in germany now I wasn't joking when I said I would eat Christmas Diner in Berlin," he wrote.[67]

Saturday, October 7, was Pete's thirty-fourth birthday, and he spent it in a way he could not have imagined a year ago. Nothing, not even a birthday or the news of the World Series that reached the front that day, could distract Pete from reality. The advance resumed at 9:00 A.M. with the 3rd Battalion again in the lead; enemy soldiers in outposts and on patrol offered some resistance. That afternoon, a German Messerschmitt ME109E and an American P-51 Mustang roared through the skies above, locked in combat, and disappeared to the east. A column of smoke rose in the southeast. Closer at hand, fifteen rounds of large-caliber artillery shells exploded with mind-numbing noise in the regimental area, four rounds at a time and three or four minutes apart. Three buzz bombs flew overhead. When the sun at last set, the Americans had suffered four killed and four wounded, but in exchange they had collared about sixty enemy soldiers and now stood on their objective. They dug in on the edge of the trees about 500 yards from the German border, overlooking the barbed wire and concrete fortifications of the Siegfried Line. According to intelligence, the German 526th Ersatz Division and some home guards held those pillboxes.[68]

The flow of replacements was as constant as a river. Bivouacking, Company B received more fresh men from the 41st Replacement Battalion. There were nine new men in the packet altogether, and one of them joined Pete's platoon. His name was Guy Hardaway, and he was from Lincolnton, Georgia. Born on December 7, 1911, Hardaway's thirtieth birthday celebration had been spoiled by news reports about the Japanese attack on Pearl Harbor. Now, almost three years later, he found himself personally involved in the war. Guy and his wife, Bessie, had a son, James David, who was twelve years old. Grammar school educated, Hardaway was a professional truck driver who could back a trailer into a parking spot between two other tractor-trailers on his first try without a pause. Hardaway had been drafted on January 25, 1944. After training at Fort McPherson in Atlanta and Fort McClellan in Alabama, he went overseas in August.[69]

So passed Pete Lynn's last birthday. Back in Kings Mountain, Ruth noted the event in her diary, while from Horseshoe Red in Krinkelter Wald Pete told her all about it. "Just a few lines as I set Here Beside my Fox Hole to Let you no what a Hapy Birth Day I am Having," he wrote. "Just got thro cooking my Dinner[.] Had pork loaf and Bullion soop[.] Boy you should have seen us Milking cows yesterday when we pulled in here I Lay in my Fox Hole and made Hot coco out of a chocklet bar and milk and it shure was good it was Just like we ust to make Be for we would go to Bed you rember how me you Bob Mick would fight over the last glass Full Ha Ha[.]" By now Pete had determined he was still in Belgium, but expected to move again soon. He closed by explaining that he was using the stock of his rifle for a desk. "Don't find many Ritting Desks and Big arm chairs to set in and Rite over here [but] you may get on a cows back," he wrote.[70]

❦

Pete was right. He was still in Belgium, but this part of Belgium, known as Eupen-Malmedy, was very German. Before World War I, Eupen-Malmedy had been part of Germany. The Versailles Peace Treaty transferred ownership to Belgium, but then Hitler reclaimed the area by invasion in 1940. Small wonder that the countryside had its fair share of Nazi sympathizers around. Signs in German, including a smattering of Nazi propaganda posters, could still be seen on village walls. To avoid any potential problems with partisans and to keep civilians safe, the Allies decided to evacuate all civilians from the area that same month. Only a few caretakers stayed behind to tend to the herds of dairy cattle. Pete probably saw the procession of civilians, their most cherished possessions stuffed into suitcases or piled on carts and wagons, walking glumly west.[71]

Cota planned no further attacks on October 8, so the soldiers kept the horseshoe configurations in Krinkelter Wald. The 3rd Battalion, still in front, sent out a few patrols, which captured thirty-seven enemy soldiers. It was not enough for Cota, who called for more active patrolling to better pinpoint the front lines. The Germans responded with artillery. The 3rd Battalion took the brunt of it; ten shells hit company K, causing seven casualties, which prompted the men to start building overhead protection against tree bursts. A sign of the changing weather came when quartermasters started issuing cold weather such as overcoats, gloves, and wool caps. There was also plenty going on in the Red battalion area. Pete and his fellow soldiers could see black smoke clouds rising about 1,000 yards to the east, but no one could explain it. Men in Hazlett's command post did not really try. They were busy preparing for the visit Gerow and Davis paid to the command post at 11:10 A.M.[72]

In the Company B area, Lieutenant Welch welcomed ten more replacements from the 41st Replacement Battalion. The company did not net a full ten men, however, because two veterans were transferred to serve at higher headquarters, which left the company with a total of 176 enlisted men and 5 officers in its ranks. Otherwise, the men of the 28th Infantry Division remained in their positions, tried to dry out their clothing, and zeroed their weapons.[73]

Pete paid more attention to the calendar than he did to replacements or the brass or the distant smoke. It was Sunday, and that made Pete wish he was walking to Sunday School with the girls and not sitting in a foxhole in the Krinkelter Wald. Instead, he had to settle for a walk to a nearby creek to shave and bathe. "Was it Cold Boy I was shaking like you no what," he told Ruth. Once he dried off, Pete sat down in the freshly overturned dirt beside his foxhole to write home. He had trouble finding some paper, but when he did he gushed about "the Day I come marching Down By the old Park yarn store to the Little gray House and se you Bob and Mick standing with open arms waiting for there Dad."[74]

That day seemed impossibly far off though, and the only marching Pete did was in the Krinkelter Wald. The enemy stayed put in the

Siegfried Line, watching and waiting. The 3,185 men in Peterson's regiment maintained their horseshoe formations with the 3rd Battalion horseshoe forward, the 2nd Battalion in the middle, and the 1st Battalion in the rear. Within Hazlett's horseshoe, Pete and Company B still held the middle position. Patrols sallied forth and occasionally got into trouble; on October 9, machine gun and mortar fire pinned down one patrol, but with the help of reinforcements the men managed to withdraw with no casualties. The next day, another patrol exchanged machine gun fire with the enemy. Pete was not among the patrollers, so he and his comrades spent their time improving their shelters and foxholes against German artillery. Macedonia church was not at hand, but Pete could at least attend church services in a makeshift forest sanctuary. Rain made it all uncomfortable and there was limited visibility, so patrols could see nothing through the trees.[75] However, neither the weather nor the enemy stopped the replacement system as company officers processed in a lone replacement, which brought Company B's strength to 177 men and 5 officers.[76]

Together, the new man and the other 181 men of Company B tried to endure this place of mud and cold and rain, crowded by trees that were mostly barren from the twin causes of autumn and war. The place also stank of dirty, unwashed men, dying leaves, and cordite. October 11 was at least a drier day, and change was in the air too. The 3rd Battalion sent out more patrols, but found little. Only during the late afternoon did the war really return: Company L's mortars coughed and brought down thirty rounds on a pesky German machine gun nest that disappeared in shrapnel and flame.[77] Meanwhile, Hazlett's Red battalion started preparations for a move. It was their turn to take over the front from the 3rd Battalion. At 4:00 P.M., officers from Company B visited the Company K command post to discuss the transition and see the positions their men would assume the next day.[78]

The big news of the day was the visit of Army Chief of Staff Gen. George C. Marshall. Marshall, who had once served with the 28th Infantry Division as a lieutenant, was on a whirlwind tour of the European theater. He did not have time to visit every divisional unit, but he gave a memorable pep talk at Cota's command post. Wearing a garrison cap atop his graying hair and a tan trench coat around his thickening middle, Marshall talked of his days with the division, related some war news, and then turned to the issue at hand. "I want to thank you in the name of the Army for the fine work you have done in the past, and are doing now, and I am confident you will continue to uphold your proud record in the future," he said. "I was talking to your division commander here a moment ago and he had forgotten you were in Paris, you've moved so fast." Most soldiers, including Pete, did not get a chance to see the general, but they would have cause to rue Marshall's visit as it inspired Eisenhower and Bradley to resume the offensive in November. Marshall's old division and Pete's current one would figure prominently in the attack, and that would be to the detriment of Felmer Lonzo Lynn.[79]

As planned, Hazlett's battalion left its rear area position, marched forward two miles, and moved into the front lines at 8:00 A.M. It was Thursday, October 12. The skies were cloudy, and some light rain fell on the shuffle. Some scattered showers followed in the afternoon, so it made a perfectly gloomy backdrop for Pete's return to a frontline foxhole. It did not go smoothly. Three men were reduced in rank, one from sergeant and two from PFC. Surviving records do not say why. Four men were promoted to the rank of private. At least there was some respite granted when division did not ask the battalion to run any patrols, save a routine one by the Intelligence & Reconnaissance platoon. All remained quiet except for some light artillery fire and an unidentified plane that passed overhead at 10:00 P.M.[80] Maybe that allowed some men to read the *Invader's* predictions for upcoming football games between Army and Duke ("Army without even batting an eye"), Clemson and Tennessee ("Tennessee gets the nod"), and North Carolina and William & Mary ("the Tarheels look good"), among others, or stories about fighting near Antwerp and Metz and in Italy. Of particular interest was the article about the First Army's attack on Aachen: "A tremendous battery of 200 big guns were shelling Aachen," the *Invader* reported, "and the city was burning, thick, black smoke curling upwards from the town, often forming a screen around the community."[81]

The front is simply an alien world. Every sound and every sight is heavy with the chance, however random, that a threat to life and limb could materialize at any moment. Day two of this tour at the front fortunately passed in relative quiet, but the day still had a few events of note: at 9:45 A.M., three artillery rounds hit near C Company. No one was hurt. At 6:35 P.M., a V-1 zoomed past, while later a single engine plane flew over Hazlett's command post and dropped an unidentified five-foot-long object—probably a dud bomb—that landed harmlessly 1,000 yards away. None of these signs portended any real danger, and patrols reported nothing upon return to the lines. We do not know if Pete was assigned to a patrol this day, but it is likely that he did so at some point during this period. His letters were censored into silence.[82]

For Company B, the most significant event of October 13 was the arrival of a new company commander. Since Welch was a lieutenant and not a captain, it had just been a matter of time before a man of appropriate rank arrived. In this case, Hazlett and Peterson transferred an officer from Company C, and Pete and his fellow soldiers were quick to size up the newcomer. Born April 4, 1916, in a log cabin, Clifford Thorne Hackard was the valedictorian of Argyle High School, class of 1933. His intelligence notwithstanding, the Depression had kept Hackard firmly planted in Argyle, a little town tucked into the southeast corner of Iowa between the Mississippi and Des Moines Rivers. Under his father's watchful eye, he learned both farming and carpentry. Hackard also became quite the marksman during frequent hunts for pheasant, turkey, and quail to supplement his family's diet. In 1942, the draft wrenched him away from home. By September, he had been commissioned out of Officer Candidate School. The following July, he married a pretty school teacher named Mary Quisenberry, and then in June 1944 he and Mary welcomed their first child. Nothing in this whirlwind of events curbed his impish sense of humor. He would need it with Company B, along with his tendencies as a tinkerer and a perfectionist. Hackard inherited a company that now consisted of 176 enlisted men and 5 officers.[83]

October 14 dawned in Krinkelter Wald with lowering clouds and a steady drizzle. It was just another day of war for Pete Lynn: most of it proved to be dull and monotonous, but the threat of sudden death was always present in Horseshoe Red. Around mid-morning, observers from the G-3 (operations) section of General Bradley's 12th Army Group came to Hazlett's command post, to plan who knows what. The men in the foxholes paid these special guests little attention. They were more worried about high-caliber German artillery. Every few hours, German gunners fired short harassing volleys into the American position. Like freight trains, the shells came zooming low over the trees and crashed into the battalion area. Fortunately, the shells hurt no one but frayed plenty of nerves, so it was welcome therapy when Hazlett gave permission to open fire on a German machine gun position in the distance. Records do not show the outcome of the fusillade, but fighting back in some fashion surely made the men feel a little better. Later, Hazlett sent out three separate three-man patrols. Two of them went off routinely. The third patrol reached a gap in the triangular dragon's teeth and stirred up a hornet's nest of German small arms fire. The Americans wisely withdrew and returned to the horseshoe about midnight. There were no casualties.[84]

On October 15, a Sunday, Peterson reshuffled the deck: he sent the 3rd Battalion to the intermediate position and rotated the 2nd Battalion to the rear. Red stayed put, and saw more of the same. A rude awakening was in store for Pete. At 5:35 A.M., five artillery rounds exploded just behind Baker Company. That was enough to prompt a man to think about his mortality, but fortunately the guns stopped. The day also saw two different patrols from Hazlett's battalion, each composed of six or eight men, marching once again into no-man's land. And the result was the same. Just as the Americans neared gaps in the dragon's teeth, German soldiers opened fire. The Keystone patrol beat a hasty retreat. The day even looked the same, with low clouds and occasional drizzle. It did clear up in the afternoon, but rain returned after dark.[85]

By now, Peterson had set a formal rotation schedule that called for each battalion to undergo training in the rear for at least three out of every twelve days. Every fourth day, under the steady gaze of Peterson's blue eyes, the battalions swapped positions. It was an approach that allowed each company not only a way to sharpen its readiness with training, but also a chance to get some relaxation in the rear and gain some low-risk frontline experience.[86]

Peterson's schedule called for Hazlett's 1st Battalion to move to the rear on October 17. On October 21, the 1st Battalion would go back in the line to relieve the 3rd Battalion. Four days later, Hazlett's troopers would be relieved by another battalion and move to the middle area. Then, on October 29, the 1st Battalion would again head to the rear for more training and recreation. Optimistically, Hazlett's schedule extended all the way to November 18.[87]

From the forward horseshoe, the soldiers could keep a wary eye on the Siegfried Line. Occasionally, a man could see German soldiers moving around the pillboxes. One American spotted a Nazi walking around the Westwall wearing nothing but long underwear, and laughed when a few rounds of artillery sent him scrambling into a ditch. When the smoke cleared, the German jumped out of the ditch and ran for a pillbox, putting on his uniform as he ran.[88]

Given Pete's sense of humor he surely enjoyed sights like this as much as anyone, but when his smile faded he was left only with the spartan existence of the front. The men spent most of their time moving dirt, rocks, and logs to improve their positions, but they were still left with a crude abode. "Their foxholes are individual trenches the size of a small grave," a veteran wrote. "The soldier usually puts on shelter-half in the bottom and lays his blankets over that." Personal hygiene presented another challenge. If a man cannot bathe, "his hair becomes matted, dirty and stiff with the constant wearing of the metal helmet, and as he tries to comb it, it falls in tufts, and his scalp pains to the touch," a soldier recalled. "He picks up ticks, fleas, and body lice from sleeping in hay stacks, on open fields, holes in the ground, with animals in barns, and in demolished, filth-spewed hovels." Over time, soldiers learned to wash with cold water doled from their helmets—a whore's bath, they called it. Lice was immune to such pitiful washing. "Anybody who thinks high-explosive is tougher to take than lice just doesn't know how much he doesn't know," a soldier recalled.[89]

Except for routine patrolling, the men spent all of their time huddled in foxholes for protection against occasional German artillery and also against the Northern European weather. It was an uncomfortable autumn. "Old Jupe Pluvius is still favoring us with rain, rain, and more rain," one clerk wrote, using a popular term for the rainout of a baseball game. "We all agreed that this was the wettest country in the world," another soldier wrote. "The men spent most of the day improving their shelters and trying to keep dry."[90]

Thanks to Jupe Pluvius, keeping dry was a losing battle. "With the front now become static," a reporter wrote, "our men are pegged down in the rain and mud of autumn in northern Europe, which is the coldest, rawest, nastiest season imaginable. It cuts to the marrow." Indeed, those fall and winter months of 1944–1945 brought levels of wind, cold, and rain rarely seen before in Northern Europe. Standing water was everywhere, and "when one lives almost constantly in the open, a downpour causes not only momentary annoyance while it is coming down, but it wets the ground, one's food, one's clothes, and makes one's life generally unpleasant," a man wrote. "If it is hard, it drenches one, leaving no chance for a change to dry clothing, and it it is general, it forces one into the narrow confines of a pup tent or the overcrowded pyramidals." The luckiest managed to shelter in an abandoned house or cellar, but it remained a "mole-like" existence at best.[91] Such weather did little for morale. "Another day of rain dampened the spirits of the entire company," wrote a Company K soldier. "The ground was long past the saturation point and water just remained on the surface."[92]

In the midst of this wet, cold world, the men received issues of winter clothing including clean shirts, field jackets, overcoats, woolen gloves, wool knit caps, and shoes.[93] The American World War II soldier was at something of a disadvantage when it came to clothing. Their uniforms were bulky and did a poor job of repelling water. Typically, a man wore an olive drab cotton twill shirt and trousers. In colder weather, soldiers dressed in layers, starting with long khaki-colored underwear. Over that went wool trousers and then cotton trousers, a wool undershirt, and a high-neck wool knit sweater. He wore a wool cap under his helmet and wool gloves with leather palms. For outerwear, most men donned the thin, flannel-lined M-41 field jacket, which one man described as "the most impractical and at the same time sloppy and unmilitary garment with which soldiers ever were afflicted." The men also received woolen overcoats, but they were heavy, bulky, and soaked up water like a sponge. Soldiers often discarded them, but tended to hang on to government issue raincoats. And for all the inadequacies of this clothing, many men simply did not carry a full complement of it, either because supply was inadequate or because there was too much to carry. On October 19, some troopers received sleeping bags, and one man reported enjoying "considerable warmth during sleeping hours." However, sleeping bags remained rare because of their bulk. Most men preferred sleeping on just two blankets.[94]

Footwear posed another problem. It started with socks. Standard GI wool socks were thin and lacked enough wool to properly insulate a man's feet. Men tried to keep at least two pairs of socks on hand so they could change often; they typically wore one pair and stored the other pair in their helmet to keep it dry. Then there was the standard American combat boot, which simply did not keep a man's feet very dry. The boots had rubber soles and heels and a leather cuff, but the leather was not waterproof and the seams leaked. What was worse, many men wore snug socks and laced their boots tightly, but that restricted the blood flow their feet needed in cold weather and also provided no room for their feet to spread while walking. Overshoes were available, but they were bulky and hard to move in, so they were often discarded. It was a recipe for foot problems such as trench foot, which developed often. Some men even welcomed the malady so they could avoid combat.[95]

The M1 helmet and liner completed the uncomfortable livery. The steel helmet and the laminated phenolic liner weighed three pounds, but most deemed the weight well worth it because the assembly could stop a .45 caliber round fired from just five feet away. Helmets could also substitute as a water bucket, shovel, mixing bowl, and more.[96]

Uncomfortably adorned and living like a mole, a man in a front-line foxhole had few distractions. "The only things to look forward to," a trooper explained, "were chow and mail." At least this posting in a quiet sector had one benefit: it allowed for hot meals to be brought up often, sometimes three times a day.[97] Failing that, soldiers like Pete could fend for themselves with an adequate repast that was vastly better than what other armies enjoyed. C-rations were the main selection. These prepackaged meals came in six varieties: two for breakfast, two for lunch, and two for supper. Meat, vegetables, egg, or processed cheese came in gold-colored cans, which the soldiers heated over a makeshift stove, candle, or sterno flame if conditions allowed. Soldiers ate straight from the can to avoid dirtying their mess kits. C-rations also included packets of crackers, chocolate bars and caramels, coffee, lemon or orange juice powder, a pack of cigarettes, water purification tablets, a book of matches, bouillon powder, toilet paper, chewing gum, and a can opener. K-rations balanced out the diet. Intended for emergency use, K-rations were more compact and color coded. Brown lettering meant breakfast, blue stood for lunch, and green letters for supper. The entree, typically something like chopped ham and eggs or pork, came in a can. Other ingredients, packed in waterproof wax-coated cartons, included biscuits, chocolate bars, caramels, and Milky Way candy bars, hard crackers, and toilet paper.[98]

There was some relief for Pete Lynn and the men of the 28th Infantry Division: the middle and rear positions. Although rain still fell on both places (especially, it seemed, during meal time), they offered luxuries that made them a comparative paradise. The men could visit American Red Cross clubmobiles to enjoy coffee and doughnuts. They could shower and put on clean clothes. The occasional "darn good USO show" was also available. Movies showed four times a day, at 10:00 A.M., 1:00 P.M., 7:00 P.M., and 9:00 P.M. Church services were also held regularly. A makeshift barber shop offered free haircuts, and it lacked for no customers since Peterson stressed proper GI haircuts with a maximum length of 1½ inches on top and closely cropped sides. There was an officers' club with live shows. At the Red Cross Club, open to enlisted men, one could read books and magazines, pick up cigarettes, write a letter on a real table, and even buy beer. A few lucky men received time off in rest centers farther back from the front or even passes to Paris. All of this could make misery and the war feel a little farther away, at least until rain fell or a V-1 came streaking over. The rear horseshoe, one soldier noted, "seems to be on the Robot bomb route, and not an hour passes but what one goes by making its ungodly racket."[99]

Pete relished his days in the rear. He felt a little more at home in Krinkelt, which now housed the regiment's main rear facilities. Pete described Krinkelt as a "Little Town." During his free time, Pete was drawn to its Red Cross facility, where he could comfortably write a letter home on Red Cross stationery. With all of the moving back and forth, he had not had much time to write lately, so letters from Krinkelt often carried greetings to everybody he could think of. During his stays in the rear, Pete the movie hound certainly took in a few shows, although the theater lacked the lavish seats, air conditioning, and big screen of the Dixie Theater back home. On one occasion, Pete enjoyed watching the movie *Around the World*. A 1943 musical comedy starring Kay Kiser, *Around the World* follows Kiser and his band as they entertain troops overseas. Along the way, an American teenager named Marcy joins the troupe but learns that her father has been killed in action. If the idea hit too close to home, Pete did not mention it. He just thought "it was a Pretty good Picture."[100]

General Cota provided another spectacle as he made regular appearances to hand out medals and give pep talks. Members of the 3rd Battalion recorded a scene that was similar to what Pete probably witnessed. It was about 4:30 P.M. one October day when Cota appeared in Krinkelt. He handed out several awards, including three bronze stars. "During the ceremony, it showered while the sun was out creating a rainbow on the horizon beyond the Battalion," a clerk recorded. "After the formal ceremonies were completed, the General gathered the entire Battalion around him and talked to them like a 'Dutch Uncle.'"[101]

Pete did not care as much for another service found in the rear, even though it was necessary. Even at the front the U.S. Army did not over-look a man's teeth, so the rear also featured the regimental dental office. The 112th Infantry had two dental officers, including Capt. Robert A. Walborn of Sunbury, Pennsylvania. Described as "good soldiers and good dentists," these men had orders to check the dental condition of each man in the regiment once a month. It was a tall order that required the dentists to conduct about a hundred exams each day. The chance dis-covery of an abandoned dental office helped when they put its unused equipment to work. Given Pete's history of dental work, there's little doubt that he got acquainted with Walborn and his staff.[102]

Training also took place in the rear areas, and took different forms depending on a battalion's location. Peterson ordered the battalion in the "intermediate position" to break into platoon-sized "discussion groups." He wanted them to cover a number of topics, starting with a counterintelligence plan for operations in Germany. The groups also had to address German currency policies and spending money, the proper use of passwords, and the proper marking of weapons. There was more: Peterson wanted his troops to know that there were no extra M-1 ammunition clips available. "Present supply must, for the time being, suffice," he wrote. The groups also discussed censorship regulations, looting, conduct before the enemy, and the precautions they should take if captured. Leaders also had the responsibility of making sure the men wore their dog tags and carried no unauthorized equipment, and that insignia and chevrons are worn properly.[103]

In the rear horseshoe, more thorough training awaited. Daily, each rifle company went through a different nine-hour shift taught by instructors from regiment or battalion. One day called for two hours of current events and other topics, two hours of extended order drill, two hours of booby trap removal, and a two and a half hour period for showers. Day two called for a shorter half-hour lecture on current events, followed by one hour of camouflage discipline, one hour of weapons instruction and drill, and four hours' study of how to defend and how to attack a fortified position. The two and a half hour balance of the schedule was devoted to recreation. Day three brought another half hour on current events, four hours on patrolling, another hour on camouflage discipline, an hour of weapons and gun drill, with the rest of the time open. It was a lot to cover, and the curriculum was not always welcomed. "This list of subjects evoked Bronx cheers from our seasoned veterans," one of Peterson's men later wrote. Still, most men realized that replacements needed this training, so the catcallers eventually lapsed into silence.[104]

Pete drank in this instruction as best as he could, but as an enlisted man he did not receive the education awaiting Peterson's regimental and battalion leadership. Battalion officers and noncommissioned officers attended schools on river crossings and map reading. They underwent aerial photography training, using photos of the Siegfried Line before Krinkelter Wald. Other officers took communications security training at Peterson's command post and returned to their units to teach the field phone users there. Still more leaders saw a demonstration of "loading, characteristics, and use of assault craft, ferries, rafts, and other stream-crossing equipment" at a crossing of the nearby Warche River. The curriculum optimistically pointed toward an early crossing of the Roer Roer and the Rhine River beyond, but included little on forest fighting.[105]

—◦—

As scheduled, Pete and the Red battalion spent October 16 on the front. It was just another rainy day in the *Krinkelter Wald*. A patrol left the forward horseshoe at 2:00 A.M. and returned later with nothing to report and everyone safe. A few more patrols followed, with the same results. In the main line of resistance, the soldiers passed the time by working to improve their foxholes and overhead shelters. Happily, Pete and his buddies also packed up for the backward pending move.[106]

On October 17, per Peterson's schedule, the 1st Battalion rotated to Pete's favorite place: the rear. "Company marched back to Krinkelt, Belgium," a Baker Company clerk jotted on the day's morning report. "Marched 2 1/2 miles took over positions previously held for a rest period and training period." Here training resumed, and the rain continued.[107]

These static days did little to advance the war effort, and Norman Cota knew it. He itched to be more aggressive, so he ordered Peterson to plan a company-sized night raid of German lines, but apparently the raid never took place.[108] The routine beat inexorably on, leaving the soldiers time to attend to other mundane tasks. Some soldiers, for example, repaired camouflage nets by fixing holes, drying them, replacing faded garlands, and ensuring their colors met the 70 percent green, 30 percent brown army standard.[109]

When his work was finished, Pete occupied himself, as usual, with writing. At some point, he acquired a few trinkets, wrapped them up, and sent them home. One was an aluminum belt buckle from a German uniform. It had the words *Gott Mit Uns*, God with Us, inscribed on it. Pete also sent home an unusual red, seven-sided uniform patch that was emblazoned with a yellow griffon passant. It was the patch of a nonexistent unit that had been organized to help deceive German forces that the invasion would hit the *Pas de Calais* rather than Normandy. It later became a real unit, the 108th Training Command.[110]

October 19 brought no change for Peterson's regiment. One man was wounded that day, probably while on patrol, but otherwise those wooded hills stayed quiet.[111] The next day brought a little noise, but not much else. The brass also made the rounds. General Davis, the assistant division commander, visited Peterson's command post at 8:00 A.M. Four German shells exploded near the Krinkelt church a little after noon. Otherwise, nothing else of note occurred for the regiment, which now stood at 3,209 strong after the loss of a few men for both battle and nonbattle reasons (such as fatigue, exposure, or disease) and the arrival of replacements and men returning to duty from wounds or illness. The American line stayed in the same place, with the 109th Infantry to Peterson's left and the 22nd Infantry to the right. The Germans kept their heads down in their Westwall. For its part, Company B lost one man to either an accident or illness. Twelve replacements arrived, bringing Hackard's command to 188 enlisted men and 3 officers.[112]

October 21 was just as quiet, which was a good thing because Peterson's schedule called for another switch. Posted in some trenches in the intermediate horseshoe, the men of Company K rose at 5:30 A.M. to prepare to move. Later, Company K's men pulled out and headed to Krinkelt where they moved into some farmhouses and turned their attention to Red Cross clubmobile and movies. The sun even came out for the first time in several days.[113] Pete and his fellow Company B men took over Company K's trenches, having marched a short two miles forward from Krinkelt. Now 188 men and 6 officers strong, the company over a line of trenches in the intermediate horseshoe. "Morale of men was good," a clerk reported.[114]

Light fog, haze, and a little rain prevailed during the night of October 21 as Hackard's men settled in. The morning brought fog and drizzle followed by afternoon showers, and also some frontline violence that left one American dead and two wounded. After lunch, some news arrived that portended changes that Pete and his buddies would not like. "All battalions and special units 'confidential,'" the orders read. "You are hereby alerted for a move in the immediate future. You will pack up at once all 'Loose Ends' in anticipation of this move."[115]

What lay in store for the regiment and division? The men wondered. Nothing was said about their destination, but rumors and scuttlebutt buzzed in the foxholes. Nobody seemed to know the truth. The consensus was that the division was about to move to a spot near Aachen, where the war was worse.[116]

The men would find out soon enough, sooner in fact than they wanted. On October 23, a clerk in Company B reported that the unit withdrew from the Krinkelt area for good. It was about 3:30 P.M. when the soldiers departed, and marched seven miles to a new assembly area in some woods west of Wirtzfeld.[117] The entire regiment went too, having been relieved by the 22nd Infantry. The tapestry that framed the move surprised no one: thick, gray clouds scudded overhead, scattered rain fell, and V-1 rockets zoomed past from time to time. At 4:45 P.M., Colonel Peterson opened his command post in the little Belgian village of Berg and reported that his 3,192 men were ready for their next duty, whatever it was. A clerk also recorded the loss of one killed and three wounded in the transition.[118]

While Peterson's staff did paperwork, Pete camped on a hillside and watched some cows graze. The mail had finally found him, so he enjoyed a letter from his parents. Looking up, his thoughts drifted back to the cows and he wondered if he could milk them and then toss in a chocolate bar to make chocolate milk. He snapped out of his reverie when he remembered it was Micky's birthday. As a present, he sent her a "gearman pin" he had picked up somewhere. Shaped like a shield and with a green gem in the middle, the pin was reminiscent of those from the early middle ages. Pete also remembered that Ruth's birthday was just around the corner. Pete went on to share what he could about his situation. The company has "moved Back a good ways from the Fronts Lines but I Don't know where we will go from Here," Pete wrote. "Even if I Did I couldn't tell you we Have Ben so many Places I cant Rember them all if I wanted to." With that, Pete ended his letter because it was time to get ready for inspection.[119]

He meant the "showdown inspection" that Peterson ordered for October 24. It began at 8:00 A.M. as squad and platoon leaders checked each of their men. At 1:00 P.M., company and battalion commanders repeated the process. Noncoms and officers verified that each man possessed a raincoat and overcoat as well as leggings, woolen underwear, socks, gloves, and shoes, and that all items were in good condition. The inspection also covered shelter halves, weapons, and vehicles. Everything had to be clean, serviceable, and ready for action.[120]

For battalion and special unit commanders, the day ended with a 9:00 P.M. meeting at Peterson's command post to discuss training and future operations. The gist of the meeting was that the Keystone men would stay put for at least one more day. All agreed that they were in a good place that was quieter and safer even than Krinkelt. Movies were available here too, and a Red Cross Clubmobile was parked nearby to dole out gallons of coffee and dozens of doughnuts. The weather even turned a little better, although drizzle and fog still came and went. Except for some V-1 rockets that flew past with regularity, glowing red in the sky, the war felt a little farther away, although there was renewed attention to military punctilio, and training covered patrolling, river crossing, and assault. In Company B's bivouac, paperwork and promotions flowed. First came the announcement of Company Order No. 18, which promoted Pete and 54 other men to PFC. Captain Hackard published an order of his own promoting nine soldiers from private to PFC. Hardaway, Sprinkle, and Gregorio were among the men tapped on Hackard's order. Pete was not impressed. He calculated that the promotion would put an extra $4 in his pocket every month and joked that Ruth could use the money to buy the girls ice cream.[121]

October 25 turned out to be the regiment's last day near Wirtzfeld and Berg. They still managed to get in a little training, mostly in patrolling, river crossing, and assault, while at least one company held a conference on tactics in wooded areas. Some units also searched for men with experience in handling mules and horses. The weather was fair for a change, but also cold. Peterson's regiment, now some 3,189 strong, was as ready as it would ever be for whatever came next.[122]

That was not entirely the case in Company B, as one soldier, Pvt. Raymond Mazurek, went missing in action. It was a sure sign that combat was near. Pete was troubled too, but he diverted his worries by going rabbit hunting. "I miss one . . . Boy was He a Big one He was a Big Jack Rabbit," he wrote. Then he told Ruth that he would be moving the next day but he had no idea where they were going. "That is about all we Do is Jump From one place to another But I Don't mind it as Long as we stay of the Front Lines," he wrote. "Boy I Hope we nevr go Back on the Front For I Just Don't Like it up there."[123]

Pete's hopes were about to be dashed, for the Gentlemen from Hell were headed back to the real war.

CHAPTER 8

I Will Always Love You till the Day I Die

ON A FOGGY, DAMP, AND COLD OCTOBER DAY, PETE LYNN AND THE MEN of the 28th Infantry Division marched into a forest.

This was not just any forest. "It was a forest out of a German fairy tale—dense, forbidding, and hostile," recalled Dr. Bedford Davis, one of the new arrivals. "It seemed filled with dark secrets, evil, and the ghosts of the dead . . . One could imagine that a wicked witch might live in its shadows, waiting to snatch some unfortunate soul." It reminded another soldier of wading into the ocean. "You walk in it all right, but water is all around you," he wrote. The big evergreens, an officer complained, "with thick, dripping branches almost engulfed us" and exuded a "cold, eerie, uninviting" feeling. The 28th Division would grow to hate this place, a reporter wrote, for all its "stately Douglas firs with their epaulets of snow ranged like frosted grenadiers, close-ordered on the hillsides, immutable, impenetrable and cold." About them, the arriving Keystone men saw the detritus of war: shell craters, splintered trees, totaled vehicles, scattered equipment, discarded ration cartons, battered road signs, and piles of mines and shell casings. From the direction of the front shuffled files of tired, unshaven men, wearing torn and muddy uniforms. Bloodshot, vacant eyes peered from beneath dirty helmets. They reminded one soldier of a line from an Edwin Markham poem: "The emptiness of ages in his face, and on his back, the burden of the world." As Colonel Peterson put it, "It was unnecessary to ask if they had had a tough fight or if they had reached their objective." These veterans from the 9th Infantry Division had been in hell, and the men of the 28th were taking their place.[1]

Pete Lynn had arrived in the Hürtgen Forest, or as the Germans called it, the Hürtgenwald.

Infantrymen of the 28th Infantry Division in the Hürtgen Forest
Source: National Archives

The Hürtgen Forest was a fifty-square-mile mass of trees that lay along the Belgian-German border south of Aachen. Technically, it contained the Wenau, Roetgen, Konigl, and Meroder woods as well as the Hürtgenwald proper, but the Americans just called the whole mass the Hürtgen. It was also part of the Ardennes-Eiffel demesne. The men of the Bloody Bucket did not care. They only saw fir trees towering from 35 to 100 feet, in spots so densely packed that their branches hid the noontime sun. The soldiers also saw rushing creeks and rivers, imposing heights, and ruined villages. A series of three ridges lay ahead, with each succeeding ridge higher than the one before it. In the deep gorge between the first two ridges, the shallow, cold Kall River meandered. A part of the Siegfried Line since 1938, the Forest was dotted with camouflaged bunkers and barbed wire with thick belts of mines lurking beneath blankets of pine needles. Its timber had been pruned to create clear fields of fire, or cut down to fashion obstacles. It was a place that smacked of terrible past American battles like the Wilderness and the Argonne.[2]

A less hospitable place to fight could not be imagined, and the men of the Bloody Bucket knew it immediately.

The Battle of the Hürtgen Forest was the stepchild of "the Big Bust." That was Lt. Gen. Omar Bradley's name for the autumn days of 1944 when logistics and German defiance stopped the Allies' rapid advance from Normandy. Eisenhower, who liked to push his armies forward on a broad front, realized that his forces could not do everything everywhere on a shoestring so he reluctantly selected a main effort. FM Sir Bernard Montgomery's 21st Army Group got the nod. It would aim north of the Ardennes, toward Antwerp and the German Ruhr.[3]

Montgomery accepted the task eagerly—the ill-fated Operation Market-Garden was the result—but asked Eisenhower for American troops to guard his right flank. Bradley's 12th Army Group was the logical choice. Bradley's command, which contained Hodges's First Army and Lt. Gen. George Patton's Third Army, already sat on Montgomery's right. Hodges's First Army was the closest, so Eisenhower directed two of Hodges's corps, the VII and V, to drive northeast along the British flank toward Aachen and the Roer River.[4]

When this order arrived at First Army headquarters, the West Wall was within sight but Hodges's ammunition was so depleted that he contemplated a short pause. V Corps commander Maj. Gen. J. Lawton "Lightning Joe" Collins demurred. Collins feared that a halt would give the enemy time to ready their bunkers, so he asked his boss for permission to send a "reconnaissance in force" to try and quickly punch through the Siegfried Line. Hodges agreed, but went one step further: he instructed both Collins and Gerow to probe the German defenses. This led to the 112th Infantry's incursion near Wallendorf, which battered Company B so much that Pete Lynn was sent as replacement.[5]

Collins's part of the reconnaissance brought American soldiers into the Hürtgen Forest for the first time. Although the VII Corps's main advance would be through the natural, narrow invasion path below Aachen called the Stolberg Corridor, the Hürtgen Forest loomed to the south. As World War I veterans, both Hodges and Kean remembered France's Argonne Forest and how it had menaced the American left flank during Pershing's 1918 offensive. They worried that German forces would charge out of the Forest and hit Collins. Yes, the Forest's terrain looked harsh, but its steep ridges also sat behind and above the Siegfried Line. Owning that ground might help the Allies clear the West Wall and serve as a natural egress for further advances. "Somebody had to cover the Huertgen Forest," said Collins, a forty-eight-year-old West Pointer and Guadalcanal veteran. "Nobody was enthusiastic about fighting there, but what was the alternative?" Hodges's G-3, Colonel Thorson, the skinny, chain-smoking, peanut butter addict nicknamed Tubby who had predicted the slowing of the Allied advance, shared Collins's concern. "It was a horrible business, the forest," he wrote.[6]

There was a better reason to conquer the Hürtgen. Along the Roer River, which framed the eastern edge of the Forest, sat seven hydroelectric dams. The most important of them, the Schwammanauel and Urftalsperre dams, restrained more than forty billion gallons of water. To the Germans, these earthen and concrete dams were as much a part of the Siegfried Line as pillboxes and dragon's teeth. "We were very much worried about the enemy's flooding the Roer River," recalled Col. Benjamin "Monk" Dickson, First Army G-2. "Since the Roer flowed directly across the front of the 9th U.S. Army and the 2nd British Army as well as ours these two big catchments and two other dams had to be in our hands or empty before we could safely cross over the Roer." Reporter Iris Carpenter thought the dams were the key to the whole Siegfried Line. "The 'damn dams' we came to call them," she explained. Publicly, however, the Allies would not even admit that the dams existed, and they barely mentioned the dams in their fall 1944 attack plans. "It was sometime before First Army realized their capacity to flood the southern part of the army zone of action," Collins recalled. "That was an intelligence failure, a real combat intelligence failure, on the part of the top intelligence people."[7]

So the Forest (but not the dams) remained an objective, albeit a secondary one to the Stolberg Corridor. On September 12, Collins's reconnaissance in force began. Elements of Maj. Gen. Maurice Rose's

3rd Armored Division captured Roetgen on the Hürtgen Forest's edge. It was the first German village to fall to American forces. Then, Maj. Gen. Louis A. Craig's 9th Infantry Division came up to clear the Forest and secure Rose's flank. Craig's men captured Lammersdorf easily but then emerged from the town and found themselves in a brutal battle among concrete pillboxes and Christmas trees. Places named Deadman's Moor and *Jagerhaus* entered the division lexicon. "It did not take long to discover that, far from mopping up the forest, the forest was destined to mop up them," opined reporter Carpenter. When the smoke cleared, the 9th Division had traded 4,500 casualties for a few thousand yards of trees and the village of Germeter. By October 26, Carpenter wrote, "They had had enough."[8]

Meanwhile, Collins's reconnaissance in force into the Stolberg Corridor penetrated the Siegfried Line and captured Aachen but then turned into a bloody stalemate as well. "We ran out of gas," Collins explained; "we ran out of ammunition; and we ran out of weather."[9] With that, the American advance came to a halt. Eisenhower's fifty-eight divisions had now been in Germany for over a month but had hardly advanced more than twelve miles past the border. The fighting around Aachen, in Holland, and elsewhere had left the Allies bloody. Clearly the war had changed. "We have facing us now one of our most difficult periods of the entire European war," Eisenhower told Marshall. "Deteriorating weather is going to place an increased strain on morale."[10]

From October 16 to 18, Eisenhower convened his senior commanders in Brussels, Belgium. With winter approaching and the enemy standing fast, they debated what to do next. The supply picture was improving, so the commanders' decision was an aggressive one. "We would hammer the enemy with all possible force in an effort to splinter his Armies west of the Rhine," Bradley recalled. The brass planned to begin the attack in early November. Ike reverted to his favored broad front approach. In Supreme Commander Allied Forces (SCAF) Directive no. 114, he ordered Bradley's army group to attack toward the Rhine, Montgomery's to clear the approaches to Antwerp and then proceed to the Rhine on Bradley's left, and Devers's 6th Army Group in the south to also push east. Eisenhower wanted Bradley to start the assault between November 1 and November 5.[11]

Bradley started planning. First, he transferred the XIX Corps from the First Army to his new Ninth Army, under Lt. Gen. William Simpson, and then inserted Simpson's command between Hodges and the British. This put Hodges squarely in front of the Hürtgen Forest, so Hodges moved his headquarters to Spa. It was October 25 when the army's headquarters, codenamed MASTER, reached the famous Belgian resort town. Soon it was anything but a resort: muddy, drab, hustle, and bustle. Trucks and jeeps tore up boulevards and halted in once-pristine parks. Messengers bearing papers came and went. Overhead, V-1 rockets streaked toward distant targets. Bradley remembered how soldiers "tracked red mud into the stately Hotel Britannique where MASTER set up shop. Field desks were scattered through the casino where Europe's rich had once gambled under the huge crystal chandeliers that hung from its high ceilings," he wrote. Perhaps it was poetic. Hodges took for his office the same room German FM Paul von Hindenburg had once used, and the army's war room opened in the salon where Kaiser Wilhelm II had abdicated. Here, Hodges and his staff laid the plans that took Pete Lynn to the Hürtgen Forest.[12]

With the Rhine a mere twenty miles away, Hodges wanted Collins to lead the main drive through the Stolberg Corridor. Somebody else should worry about the VII Corps flank and the Hürtgen, and that somebody was Leonard Gerow and his V Corps. The V Corps contained one armored and four infantry divisions, but only one of those units was rested and ready: the 28th Infantry Division. Granted, the Bloody Bucket was brimming with replacements, but its time in a quiet part of the lines had given Cota a chance to prepare his men. Orders sped to the Iron Division: the 28th was to move north, relieve the 9th Infantry Division, and attack into the Forest. The objective was to clear the Germeter-Hürtgen Road and adjacent wooded areas as well as the Vossenack-Schmidt-Lammersdorf triangle down to the headwaters of the Roer River. The assault would pave the way for the main attack by Collins's VII Corps.[13]

When "Dutch" Cota received these orders, he explained the plan to his regimental commanders. Preparations began immediately, and in short order army trucks and jeeps were rumbling across the Belgian countryside.[14]

Cota rode in one of the lead vehicles. On October 25, he and his staff drove to Rott, a German village the 3rd Armored Division had just captured.[15] Halting his jeep alongside the gently sloping Quirinusstraße, he chose for his command post a two-story stone *gasthaus* across from the church of St. Antonius. As he settled in, Cota probably felt like singing. The general was a character. He always kept a cigar in his mouth. He usually carried a cane too, but why was anyone's guess because he did not need one. For all that, Cota's most eccentric habit was singing songs he made up on the spot. The tougher the situation, the more he crooned. Once, when under heavy artillery fire, he sang, "If I knew the answer to this what a hell of a smart guy I'd be!" At Rott, the same uncertainty applied because he did not like the looks of things one bit.[16]

Neither did his men. After Cota moved into the Rott *gasthaus*, the rest of the division followed in a larger convoy. Equipment and bed rolls in hand, the men rode north across a Belgian countryside sheathed in a light fog and a pesky, cold drizzle. Regimental reports described the roads as fair, but that did not tell the full story of this or any other trip. "Convoy travel was usually irritatingly slow and fitful," remembered one American soldier. To the frustration of its passengers, the long line of trucks halted frequently but nobody ever seemed to know why. Waiting was at least more comfortable than moving. "Once we started up again the wind whipped through the open cabs of the trucks and the jeeps and bit right down to the marrow," he recalled.[17]

The journey was not without incident. One man died and a passenger was wounded when their vehicle hit a Teller mine. Pete's Company B also lost one man from its roster of 186 enlisted men and 5 officers due to a nonbattle injury. Otherwise, after traveling about thirty-five kilometers, the convoy crossed into Germany, passed through Roetgen, and reached Rott safely late in the afternoon. Relief of the 9th Infantry Division began. Regiments, battalions, and companies detrucked and bivouacked in wooded assembly areas east of the little village. Immediately they started digging new foxholes or improving old ones and building overhead shelters. A few amenities awaited too, in the form of company kitchens preparing hot food, mail clerks delivering mail, and a showing of the 1944 romantic comedy *Cassanova Brown* starring Gary Cooper.[18]

PETE LYNN IN THE
HÜRTGEN FOREST
NOVEMBER 1944

NETHERLANDS

Antwerp

GERMANY

Brussels

BELGIUM   map

Bastogne

LUX.

U.S. Line, morning of Nov. 2, 1944

Stolberg

GERMANY

Kreuzau

Roer River

Vicht

Hürtgen

Nideggen

XX
28th ID

Germeter
Richelskaul   Vossenack   XX
275th ID   Kall River

Rott

Deadman's Moor

Jagerhaus   Simonskall   Kommerscheidt
Kall Trail   Schmidt

Roetgen   Lammersdorf

Schwammenauel
Dam

BELGIUM

Simmerath

Urft Dam

N

Roer River

0   2   4 kilometers

0   2   4 miles

Monschau

source: Rick Atkinson, Guns at Last Light, 316

In Rott, Cota pondered the coming attack. Craig's 9th Division had failed here. Normally, it would have been up to General Cota and his staff to determine a better approach, but Hodges and Gerow and their staffs had already planned the coming attack. This was unorthodox, but First Army leadership had micromanaged its formations more than once that fall.[19]

In fact, the plan had even more hallmarks of micromanagement than usual. As author Jade Hinman suggests, Pearl Harbor may have had something to do with it. Gerow had just returned from Washington where he testified before the Army Pearl Harbor Board, which had been convened by the Army Adjutant General in response to an act of Congress. In 1941, Gerow had been chief of the War Plans Division, which had some oversight of the army's Pearl Harbor command. When the hearings concluded, the board censured Gerow for not keeping Pearl Harbor army leadership properly informed before the Japanese attack. Resuming command of V Corps, Gerow felt he had lost the confidence of both Eisenhower and Bradley. He became overly cautious and dictated much of the attack plan while ignoring concerns from Cota. Hodges's staff lent a hand, perhaps out of newfound concerns about Gerow.[20]

The resulting plan was nothing less than gormless. The division main effort fell to Lt. Col. Peterson's 112th Infantry. The attack would begin with the 2nd Battalion investing Vossenack, a German village to the east atop the first ridge. Three hours later, Peterson's other two battalions would bypass Vossenack, navigate the wooded Kall River gorge, and climb the higher ridges to the east to capture Kommerscheidt and Schmidt. "The Roer Dams never entered the picture," Peterson wrote.[21]

Schmidt was a logical objective, but the tasks given the rest of the division made less sense. The 109th Infantry, under future division commander and future Pennsylvania lieutenant governor Lt. Col. Daniel B. Strickler, had orders to attack north toward a treeline facing the village of Hürtgen. In October, the 9th Division had endured a savage counterattack from that direction, so planners felt compelled to take this step. Meanwhile, two battalions of Lt. Col. Ted Seely's 110th Infantry would march southeast through thick woods toward Simonskall and Steckenborn to provide flank protection and secure the roads in the area. Except for the Vossenack attack, Cota later wrote, "the infantry units were directed to operate without vehicles until adequate roads became available, further, to operate in depth and avoid dispersion." The regiment's last battalion would remain in reserve.[22]

In the historic hotel salon at Spa, Hodges saw the plan and gave it his imprimatur. In his modest Rott *gasthaus*, Cota frowned. It reminded him of the 9th Infantry Division's October scheme. His assistant division commander, George Davis, thought it smacked of pursuit rather than an assault on set defenses. Essentially, the division's three regiments would be launching separate operations—three solitary arms reaching in three different, lonely directions, with no support on their immediate flanks—and across difficult terrain that would negate American advantages in firepower and maneuver. Cota also feared that one regiment would not be enough for each attack. Worst of all, Cota's division would be making the only attack along the entire 170-mile stretch of the western front. Planners thought it imperative that Cota's attack precede Collins's, but that would also make it easier for the Germans to send reinforcements. Cota could not help but disapprove.[23]

Cota and Gerow met often as October passed, sometimes in Rott and other times at V Corps headquarters in Eupen. One such meeting consumed two hours on Halloween Day. Cota told Gerow he was worried. "Before this operation began, I did not think it would succeed," Cota said later, although he gave it a "gambler's chance." Gerow heard Cota out, but the orders stood. In truth, the Virginian developed a few reservations of his own. Babysitting Collins's flank had little appeal, but Gerow suspected that Joe Collins was Hodges's favorite and would always draw the plum assignments. At least the army had learned something from the 9th Division's debacle. Hodges and Gerow reinforced Cota with a tank battalion, two tank destroyer battalions, three combat engineer battalions, a chemical mortar battalion, and seven artillery batteries. Five fighter-bomber groups from Maj. Gen. Elwood R. "Pete" Quesada's Ninth Tactical Air Command also stood by to support, weather permitting. Yet events would prove that Cota still remained woefully understrength. "The job was just too big for one division," Gerow said later, while Davis figured the job was best suited for a corps.[24]

Capt. John S. Howe, a combat historian, visited the 28th Division CP on Halloween Day. He found a tense atmosphere. Lt. Col. Thomas E. Briggs, the division G-3, "stressed the difficult nature of the terrain, and the misgivings of both himself and the Commanding General, Maj. Gen. Norman D. Cota, over having to attack into territory which was dominated by enemy-held high ground to the east, south and north." Briggs also explained that the poor roads and thick woods would hinder the use of armor. "None of the officers to whom we talked regarding this operation was in the least bit optimistic," Howe wrote. "Many were almost certain that if the operation succeeded it would be a miracle." Cota joined the group and complained that he had been told where to put his troops, but that his objections had been overruled.[25]

Carl Peterson was worried too. A Rotarian since 1914, Peterson had a deep baritone voice that made him sound like a newsreel announcer. Before leaving their last post, with his clear voice Peterson briefed his regimental staff about the planned attack. When the meeting ended, Peterson asked Dr. Albert Berndt, his regimental surgeon, to stay behind.

"Doc, this Schmidt attack is an absolute suicide mission for us," Peterson told Berndt. The colonel explained how the division's regiments would attack in diverging routes, and predicted that the division would find itself in a precarious position. While he thought his regiment could capture Schmidt, he feared an enemy armor assault, and preferred to stop at Kommerscheidt. But there was little Peterson could do. A few days later, Peterson arrived in Germeter and established his command post in the attic of a house.[26]

Lt. Col. Carl L. Peterson
Source: William A. Snider Jr./The 112th Infantry MIA Recovery Project

As the clock ticked away, "Dutch" Cota found few reasons

for optimism. Weather forecasts predicted poor weather, dashing his hopes for air support. Cota still tried to meet with air corps pilots and discuss the operation, just in case, but the meeting was canceled. Cota also worried about his main supply route, a muddy, narrow path through the forest called the Kall Trail. The only thing he still had faith in was the fiber of his men. "It was a fine Division, as good as any that fought in World War II," he wrote. Still, Cota could not shake his feeling of foreboding. "The 28th Infantry Division had been given a mission that had slim chance of success," he wrote.[27]

—◡—

Pete Lynn thankfully knew nothing of the gloom at headquarters, but he and his comrades began to suspect that combat was near. "This is the third time we Have Ben in and out [of Germany]," he wrote as he arrived in the Hürtgen Forest. "But Darling Don't you worry your sweet Little Head about it Ether For I will Be coming Back to my three Little Carolina Sunshine girls one of these Days Be Fore Long to Build that Bunglo for Four." To mark his arrival in Germany, Pete sent five Reichsmarks home as a souvenir.[28]

For the next few days, the Keystoners remained in reserve near Rott. There was time for training, church services, and improving foxholes and shelters. Good food continued to flow from mobile kitchens; one company breakfasted on hot cakes. On October 27, the sun even poked out of the clouds for over an hour.[29] Pete's Company B picked up a transfer from Company C, but otherwise the men passed the time much as they had in Belgium. If the troops knew little of what lay ahead, that was not the case for the leadership. On October 27, Peterson held a meeting at 9:00 A.M. at his regimental command post for battalion and attachment commanders. The regiment—now at 3,189 strong—put out local security and observation posts and, as a clerk wrote, "sat tight waiting to start the attack."[30]

The next day, the men of the 28th Infantry Division awoke to the rare sight of a warm sun shining in a clear blue sky. It had been about forty days since these soldiers had last seen the sun at dawn. Officers took advantage of it by putting portions of the division through training exercises. Late that afternoon, the olive drab soldiers worshiped together.[31] Attack preparation also continued. Both Cota and Davis visited Peterson's CP and discussed intelligence reports that put enemy strength at ten companies of seventy men each with good weapons and artillery but low morale.[32]

Patrol actions that Saturday ensured that neither Cota's men nor the Germans forgot the war. Early in the morning, a six-man German patrol probed the junction between Company L and Pete's B Company. One man died in the ensuing exchange of gunfire, and one man from each side was captured. Patrolling continued in the afternoon. Around 1:15 P.M., Hazlett's battalion spotted another enemy patrol moving across the fronts of both L and B Company. Three hours later, Keystone patrols captured another enemy soldier and also found a half dozen German bodies in front of Company L. These may have been casualties from the morning skirmish. One of the bodies was booby-trapped.[33]

Otherwise, the men of Company B passed a noneventful day in the Rott assembly area. Captain Hackard had other worries; one of his most experienced officers, Lt. Freeman McDonald, had to be evacuated for unknown reasons. This would leave Hackard short of experienced leadership for the coming battle.[34]

If Pete noted McDonald's departure he did not record it, but he did enjoy a comparatively wonderful day. The arrival of six letters from Ruth was enough to make him smile, but the news they bore made him positively giddy: Ruth was expecting! Nothing could snuff out his excitement, not even the skirmish or the eerie green flare that popped overhead around 8:30 P.M., hung in air for a few seconds, and went out. Pete happily replied to Ruth. After joking about some new long underwear he had received—"You out to see Me in the Long Johns. . . I Look Like a circus performer Ha Ha"—he focused on Ruth's big announcement. "Darling I wasn't very surprised at the news of the new arrival I Figgered that all along," he wrote. "Darling Please Rite me and Let me no how you get along and Don't tell me any Fibs either." Pete stepped away to enjoy supper from the company mobile kitchen, and then went back to his letter. "I am just Like you, I would Like to Have a Sun when I come Back if it is a Boy I Don't know whether Kings Mountain will Hold me or not Ha Ha," he told Ruth. Now, Pete had to plan on room for five in the little bungalow he and Ruth dreamed about. There was one more thing: if their boy ever decided to join the army, Pete would shoot him! With that, he closed the letter and went to work on his tent.[35]

October 29 brought more lovely weather except for a few passing afternoon showers. German and American soldiers continued to eye each other from their respective positions but no one made an offensive move. The only things that broke the silence were patrols and a loud explosion when a 2nd Battalion jeep hit a mine near Peterson's CP. Fortunately, the two riders were not seriously hurt. Meanwhile, thanks to observation and patrol reports, the locations of enemy roadblocks, mines, and bunkers awaiting them were becoming clearer. Intelligence identified minefields behind some barbed wire entanglements on either side of the Germeter-Vossenack road, but not on the road itself. Of particular interest to Hazlett was a report of two enemy machine gun positions about fifty meters to the right of the main road. It was the area his battalion was scheduled to hit. He decided to send a patrol to investigate the spot the next day.[36]

The day was mostly bearable for the troops. Over in Company K, the men enjoyed a breakfast of French Toast and endured a few more hours of training. During their free time, soldiers attended church services or took in a movie, but spirits were dampened when word came that the regiment was moving the next day.[37] In Company B's bivouac, nine replacements arrived and five men left for a new assignment with Headquarters Company. The shuffling brought Company B's roster to 187 enlisted men and officers present. Comings and goings aside, Pete still had a chance to read the latest issue of the *Invader*. Beneath the main headline, "Critical Scheldt Battle Rages as Armies Link Up," the lead article described how Allied armies were fighting to open the port at Antwerp. Other stories told of a thousand planes bombing Cologne, Russian forces clearing the Adriatic coast, and combat in the Philippines and Italy.[38]

Pete also satisfied a longstanding itch. He had always wanted to go deer hunting. Back home, his plan had been to visit Pisgah National Forest, a 500,000-acre mountain preserve about one hundred miles northwest of Kings Mountain. He never made it to Pisgah, but when the 28th arrived in the Hürtgen Forest, a few intrepid souls, Pete among them, went deer hunting. "Just sitting Hear Beside a trail waiting For a Deer," he wrote home on October 29. He and his fellow soldiers spent that entire Sunday hunting and bagged a half dozen. Pete only saw one big deer but he could not get a clear shot. Another Company B soldier took down a fine ten pointer that Pete thought resembled a cow. "Maby I will have Better [luck] this afternoon I have a good spot here," he told Ruth. The outing reminded him of his own "dear," so while he sat in the woods and waited for quarry he jotted a quick note to ask Ruth what the doctor thought about their unborn child. He also promised to suggest some names for the baby.[39]

Monday morning saw the return of gray, misty weather. It was almost as if the heavens knew that battle was near, as indeed it was; on this day, the Iron Division moved up to the line of departure. The soldiers struck their tents, made their bedrolls, had chow, and then marched about six miles deeper into Germany. It was late in the day when they arrived at their new position in the splintered woods immediately west of the tiny, battered village of Germeter, as well as in Germeter itself. Some men moved into the 9th Division's old foxholes, log-roofed pits, and command posts, while other soldiers dug new shelters and pitched tents. Then, they gathered around a company clerk to receive their pay for October. Ominously, it came in the form of German invasion marks, but it did not matter because there was no place to spend it. Battle detritus and fly-blown enemy corpses surrounded the soldiers and the paymaster. It was unnerving, and the gathering darkness made it worse. The night became so inky black that you could not see your finger in front of your nose. Occasionally, tiny lights pierced the void. "They were spooky," a soldier said. The night was cold, damp, and quiet, save for the occasional report of a rifle or machine gun or the burst of a mortar or artillery shell. "Words can't really describe the eerie, damp feeling of the forest," a soldier wrote, and the fact that the front was at hand added more tension. The new arrivals kept hand grenades and rifle clips handy, and shivered.[40]

Darkness aside, there was work to be done. Around Peterson's regiment, the 109th Infantry took position to the left and the 110th to the right. At battalion level, Hazlett set up a new command post and held a meeting with his special unit and battalion commanders. Meanwhile, there was plenty of activity to be seen and heard from Pete's position in the woods near Germeter. Division artillery fired a few rounds at reported road blocks in the area. In the distance a German plane fell from the sky, and a parachute popped open.[41] Hackard dispatched a patrol from the right side of the company sector to verify the report of two machine guns to the right of the main road. Departing at 6:30 P.M., the patrol carefully and quietly picked its way forward into the trees, crossed a stream, and struck a road parallel to the stream. From here, the men spotted an enemy roadblock made of logs. The soldiers threw some grenades in the general direction of the enemy position and withdrew. Hackard's men would return to that spot all too soon.[42]

Pete Lynn woke early on Halloween day. Clambering out of his tent, he queued up with Spaans, Hardaway, Gregorio, Sprinkle, and the rest of his buddies and trudged to the company's mobile kitchen. A big, hot breakfast awaited, its steam hovering over the food. If Pete was nervous about the coming attack, it did not curb his appetite. He feasted on seven hot cakes and syrup, eggs, potatoes, sausage, and prunes. Then, he went back for seconds. Meanwhile, planners delayed the forthcoming attack until Thursday, November 2. Rain was forecasted, and sure enough it showered hard enough during the afternoon to underscore the wisdom of the postponement. Thanks to this reprieve, the soldiers merely spent the day trying to stay dry. If Company K's experience is indicative of Company B's, Pete also enjoyed a hot meal for lunch and supper and topped off supper with cake and whipped cream.[43]

The war stayed close. Now that they were deeper into Germany, it was clear that this was not the quiet sector Cota's men held in October. Seven or eight rounds of 81mm mortar fire crashed in the Able Company area at 8:10 A.M. Other artillery and mortar rounds fell sporadically along the lines, and occasionally machine gun and rifle fire chattered in the distance. Somebody even detected chipping and sawing sounds nearby. Patrols continued, and one of them ran into sniper fire at 8:40 A.M. Later that morning, a V-1 bomb flew over, its engine cutting out shortly after it passed. At 11:45 A.M., someone in the regimental CP spotted smoke curling up from two houses in Vossenack but they could not see any enemy soldiers. Against this backdrop, the brass came and went. Visitors to Peterson's command post included Cota, assistant division commander Davis, and Gerow. The men in the ranks could not miss all of these preparations. Clearly, something was up. At last, officers at the company and platoon levels explained the plan. By now everybody knew what had happened to the 9th Division, but officers tried to be optimistic. "The Divisions had been shot up before them but this time it would work out," a clerk explained.[44]

Company B reports said Hackard's men had good morale that day, but Pete's outlook grew iffy now that he knew what lay in store.[45] That night, he wrote a letter to one of his sisters and also two separate letters to Ruth. "Well sis I Had Better Sine of I Have Ben Ritting all Evening I Don't know When I will get another Chance," he wrote.[46] He revealed more to Ruth, and clearly the fun of Sunday's hunt was forgotten. "Darling I Hope this letter finds you and the Kids well and Happy," he wrote. "[A]s For my self I am well But not Happy and want Be till this war is over and I get started back to you and Bob and Mick and Junior Ha Ha," he wrote. There was no hint of a real laugh.[47]

In a second letter, Pete offered his thanks for a gift Macedonia Church had sent. That got him thinking about his uxorial shopping list since Ruth's birthday fell on November 6 and Christmas was around the corner. He mailed Ruth $60 and told her to pick out something for herself and the kids. "Have a Hapy Birthday Dear," he wrote, "and Rember I will always Love you till the Day I Die."[48]

⸻

Across from Pete and the men of Company B waited a resilient, unbeaten foe.

FM Karl Rudolf Gerd von Rundstedt commanded the western front for the Third Reich. Born December 12, 1875, Rundstedt had been around soldiering every single one of his sixty-eight years. The first son of a hussar officer, Rundstedt was trained in the Prussian tradition, schooled at the German War Academy, and served in World War I. In the current war, he had led Nazi armies in the invasions of Poland, France, and the Soviet Union, and was promoted to field marshal for his service. Hitler appointed Rundstedt as western commander in chief in March 1942, relieved him as the fighting in Normandy went against the Germans, and then recalled him in September 1944. "Field-Marshal, I would like to place the Western Front in your hands again," Hitler told him. The fusty Rundstedt, proudly wearing the Oak Leaves to the Knight's Cross of the Iron Cross and a clipped mustache reminiscent of Hitler's, jumped at the chance. "My Führer, whatever you order, I shall do to my last breath," he replied.[49]

Rundstedt's immediate subordinate, FM Walter Model, was directly responsible for the Hürtgen Forest. Model was born on January 24, 1891, in a middle-class Lutheran family of teachers and innkeepers. He attended the *Kriegsschule* in Neisse, fought with distinction in World War I, and remained in the army through the turbulent interwar years. During World War II, on the bloody eastern front, Model rose from colonel to field marshal. Admirers dubbed him the Führer's *Feuerwehrmann* (fireman) as he tackled one trouble spot after another. Model embraced the role. Once, when asked what he had brought with him to restore a tricky situation, Model answered, "Myself." Ambitious, tactless, a stickler for duty, an independent thinker, and a Christian, Model was as unique a German as ever wore a monocle. He feared no man, including Hitler, who called Model his best field marshal but added, "I wouldn't want to serve under him." In July 1944, Model had assumed command in the west and also took over Army Group B. When von Rundstedt returned to duty, Model gladly relinquished overall command but kept Army Group B.[50]

Army Group B's zone of responsibility stretched from the English Channel to Bittburg, Germany. One of Army Group B's components was the Seventh Army, which in turn contained the LXXIV Corps. Commanded by Gen. der Infanterie Eric Straube, the LXXIV Corps guarded the Hürtgen Forest. Organized in August 1943, the corps had fought in Normandy and, in Straube's words, had just barely escaped behind the West Wall. Rather than stout fortifications, the Germans found the wall had only shelters bereft of weapons since they had been removed for use elsewhere. The Germans had no choice but to build new fortifications and to fill them with men who were sick, injured, old, untrained, and without experienced leaders. Seventh Army chief of staff Gen. Rudolf-Christoph von Gersdorff shared Straube's concerns. He also added others, including a shortage of cold-weather clothing, artillery shells, and antitank weapons. Yet the Germans made do, and prepared to fight. The sounds of men digging foxholes, stringing wire, laying mines, and building roadblocks rang against the pine trees.[51]

The LXXIV Corps contained two infantry divisions, the 89th and the 275th. The latter was the unit toiling on the forest defenses directly in front of Pete and the Bloody Bucket. Commanded by the robust, steady Gen. Hans Schmidt, the 275th's origins dated to December 1943 when it was formed from convalescent soldiers and recruits. D-Day found the nascent unit training and building fortifications in Brittany, whereupon it shipped to Normandy to bolster German defenses. The 275th stood manfully in the hedgerows for six weeks before Allied forces finally dislodged it during Operation COBRA. The division suffered mightily during the retreat to the German border. In September, German authorities pulled the unit out of the line; men from thirty-seven different units, including Navy and Luftwaffe formations, transferred in. When all was said and done, the division's component elements—the 983rd Infantry Regiment, 984th Infantry Regiment, and the 275th Fusilier Battalion—contained a grab bag of men. "There was much variance in age, training, experience, and physical condition," wrote one analyst. Schmidt could count on thirteen 105mm howitzers, one 210mm howitzer, six assault guns, and an antiaircraft regiment to support him. Thus bolstered, the division reentered the front lines in the Hürtgen Forest. It fought the 9th Infantry Division to a standstill but lost nearly half of its men in the process. Now its remnants prepared to face the 28th Infantry Division.[52]

The Germans expected an attack soon.[53] Having learned much from fighting the American 9th Infantry Division among the trees, the Seventh Army ordered Straube and Schmidt to hold the Forest as far west as possible. Military needs required it; the Germans had to protect the high ground and the dams, and they also had to mask Hitler's planned Ardennes offensive. There were also many benefits for defending such terrain, even though the Forest would hamper communications and observation. "We realized that here in the Hürtgen forest the superiority the Americans possessed in the air, in tanks, and in artillery could not be employed as effectively against the German forces as would be possible in open terrain," von Gersdorff wrote. The Germans also counted on the pillboxes of the West Wall, which ran through the Forest and commanded key roads and firebreaks. Even the weather promised to benefit the Nazis, as winter rains began to turn the soil into a muddy mess that would make movement difficult.[54]

Wednesday, November 1, dawned cloudy and foggy around Germeter, Germany. Along with the tiny adjacent village of Richelskaul to the south, Germeter sat on the Lammersdorf-Hürtgen highway, the last major north-south road west of the Roer River. From here, it was hard to see more than a couple of miles to the east, but the neighboring village of Vossenack was in plain sight. So were the menacing ridges in the distance. The clouds and fog lingered most of the day, and scattered light drizzle arrived in the afternoon.[55]

This dreary weather punctuated the final day of preparation for the 3,124 men of the 112th Infantry. At 9:25 A.M., battalion commanders met with Peterson at his command post, and then at 11:00 A.M. Cota arrived and the meeting continued. Battalion commanders met again in the early afternoon to iron out final details. Matters of the soul were not overlooked; Capt. Alan P. J. Madden, a Catholic priest and the senior chaplain of the 112th Infantry, conducted a worship service. Madden claimed the regiment as his own. Born November 11, 1905, in Butler, Pennsylvania, Madden studied at seminaries in Pennsylvania before being ordained at the National Shrine of the Immaculate Conception. He had been with the regiment since 1940, marrying and baptizing many soldiers along the way. In his opinion, the regiment was the best outfit in the army. Chaplain Ralph E. Maness, a Baptist minister from Missouri, assisted. With heads bowed, men murmured prayers that were likely more fervent than usual. "We knew that we were going to push off and that we would have tough fighting ahead of us," Madden wrote. Pete was almost certainly among them. Maness, who usually conducted the regiment's protestant services, later assured Ruth that the name "Pete" sounded familiar to him.[56]

Meanwhile, the 28th Infantry Division moved into position with the 109th on the left, the 112th in the center, and 110th on the right. In Peterson's regiment, the 3rd Battalion remained in reserve and the 2nd Battalion took position at the edge of Germeter. In Pete's 1st Battalion, Company A relieved L Company, 110th Infantry, and dug in at the junction of the Lammersdorf-Hürtgen road in front of Richelskaul. The rest of the battalion, Pete's Company B included, went into an assembly area a few hundred yards west of Richelskaul. The men of Company C were formed into three assault teams and were told, "If A or B Companies ran into fortifications, we were to be used to knock them out." B Company was likely formed in the same manner.[57]

Thus arrayed, the 3,214 men of the 112th Infantry faced the enemy. In the process, the regiment lost one man wounded and eleven for mostly unknown reasons. One of them was Sgt. Edward L. Zagar, a member of Pete's Company B, who was reported absent without leave (AWOL). A Company, in its new position before Richelskaul, had the busiest day of all, and Pete Lynn had a ringside seat in the woods to the rear. At one point, Company A opened fire on a suspected patrol. Around noon, battalion mortars set off some mines to the front, and then late in the day an American patrol chased off a ten-man enemy patrol with small arms and mortar fire. A Company soldiers also spotted an enemy antitank gun around Vossenack and forced it to withdraw by firing mortars in its direction. A Company even captured a German soldier who had wandered away from his company's position on the outskirts of Vossenack and gotten lost.[58]

Back in the wooded assembly area, the final alert for the assault arrived in the afternoon. H hour would be 9:00 A.M. The men cleaned their equipment and packed; according to orders one company received, the soldiers should carry a blanket and their overcoat in a horseshoe roll on their pack, and enough rations for four meals. Company clerks issued ammunition and weapons. Hot chow arrived, another sure sign that H hour was near. Company commanders assembled platoon leaders and briefed them, while other company officers and noncoms went up to the line of departure for a detailed reconnaissance. Company commanders met with Peterson too.[59]

The army's senior leadership also made ready. It was just twenty miles from MASTER headquarters to Cota's command post. After lunching together, Hodges and Gerow rode together to Cota's *gasthaus* to confer with their subordinate. It was the first time Cota and Hodges had seen each other since the 28th marched through Paris, but it was no friendly reunion. The army commander spent most of the visit chatting with General Davis, who had once served on Hodges's staff. Perhaps Cota and Hodges avoided each other because their relationship was tense. Cota did not mention his concerns about the planned assault, and the pall hanging over the room went undetected. On the contrary, Hodges "found the division in fine fettle, rarin' to go, and optimistic over their chances of giving the Boche a fine drubbing," recalled his aide, Maj. William C. Sylvan. Hodges also said that the plan was "excellent," while Sylvan noted that Davis "had never looked in better shape." Someone also pointed out that two groups of fighter-bombers were standing by, while two more waited on alert. Weather reports for the next day remained uncertain, but Hodges had waited long enough. He confirmed that the attack would begin the next day.[60]

Pete did not see much of the brass or their flag-flying vehicles. Seated in the woods nearby, his preparations finished, he stole a few minutes to write home. He had planned to write both Ruth and his parents, but when he discovered that he only had one envelope he prioritized and wrote Ruth. The soldier from Kings Mountain then took up his pen, and his frustration spilled onto the paper. There was so much Pete wanted to say, but he could only repeat himself due to censorship restrictions. "Darling we are expecting to move again so if you Don't Here from me for a Few Days Don't worry Darling," he wrote, and then added a joke: "If it ant a Boy I ant coming Home Ha Ha." He closed the letter when chow was ready but asked Ruth to send him some Sunday School literature.[61]

By now, Peterson's men had eaten and finished their preparations. They settled in for the long night, and it turned out to be a long one indeed. Twice before midnight some Germans passed near Hazlett's command post, drawing a flurry of machine gun and mortar fire. At 11:00 P.M., the stillness was shattered again: in front of Pete, A Company soldiers spotted a ten-man enemy patrol. The Americans opened fire with rifles, machine guns, and mortars and drove the Germans away, but that did not end it. In the wee hours of the morning, Company A soldiers again heard movement in their front and opened fire. The only enemy response came from a German machine gun in Vossenack. Meanwhile, Company C of the 103rd Engineers carefully cleared paths through American mine fields, and aerial photos arrived at the command post.[62] All the while, Vossenack burned: several houses in the village were in flames, and German soldiers could be seen scurrying about, trying to put the fires out, while overhead flares and illuminating mortar fire occasionally leaped into the sky. Mines exploded randomly, set off by American mortar fire. Dante would have approved of this backdrop for battle.[63]

The men of the 28th Infantry Division were as ready as they ever would be. Pete Lynn left no record of how he passed the night, but we do know he was about to experience his first major battle. We also know it was a noisy night that did not allow much sleep. It is easy to imagine him wide awake, nervous and shivering in his cold foxhole, and wondering what the next day would bring.

———

A light rain fell in the early morning darkness of November 2, 1944. Like an amanuensis, a soupy mist settled on trees, buildings, and foxholes. The dampness made it feel colder than it actually was, though the temperature was already near freezing. "It was pretty miserable outside," a German *landser* recalled.[64]

Gradually it grew light enough to see, but the sun stayed veiled behind clouds the color of dirty cotton. Soldiers stirred. Those selected to attack first rose first. Other companies, like Pete's Company B, would not jump off until later so they slept a little longer. It was 7:30 A.M. before these men shimmied groggily out of their blankets and sleeping bags. After eating a hot breakfast, the soldiers nervously finished packing and checked their equipment.[65]

Colonel Peterson woke early in his Germeter attic. His first task of the day was to establish a sandbagged observation post for General Davis. "I was to meet him at a specified point west of Germeter at a specified time on the morning of the attack to lead him to his CP," Peterson later wrote. It was not a task Peterson relished; the men called Davis "Stinky" because he had an abrasive personality. Dutifully, Peterson went to the appointed spot. When Davis did not appear, Peterson "deemed it necessary to get on with problems coincident with the attack." He made the right call, but Davis later chewed Peterson out for missing their rendezvous. It was an inauspicious start to the operation.[66]

At 8:00 A.M., American guns shattered the morning stillness. For the next hour, the massed artillery of the V and VII Corps fired 4,000 preparatory rounds while the 28th Infantry Division loosed 7,313 of its own shells toward known and suspected enemy positions. Cota described it as a "fierce concentration of fire" that increased in volume because the artillery shifted to nearer targets at 8:45 A.M. From the woods west of Germeter, the 112th's heavy guns—from the 707th Tank Battalion's

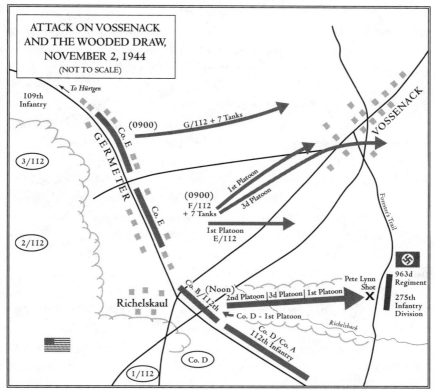

ATTACK ON VOSSENACK
AND THE WOODED DRAW,
NOVEMBER 2, 1944
(NOT TO SCALE)

Source: MacDonald, Three Battles

Assault Gun Platoon, Company B, 630th Tank Destroyer Battalion, the 112th's Antitank Company, and Company B, 86th Chemical Mortar Battalion—added their steel voices. Lt. Gunther Schmidt, a member of the German 272nd Volksgrenadier Division, endured the bombardment in the village of Schmidt. "There was a lot of confusion in the street, horses reared; we heard screams from the men that were hit," he wrote.[67]

Colonel Peterson and his artillery officers watched the bombardment from Peterson's headquarters. His regiment now contained 3,239 soldiers thanks to the arrival of replacements. In the street and among the houses and barns of Germeter below, the men of his 2nd Battalion waited nervously. This was the line of departure. At 8:45 A.M., tanks from the 707th Tank Battalion rolled up behind the soldiers and idled their engines.[68] The eastward view from the attic and street was normally good: open fields, marked by shell craters and the occasional fence, stretched between Germeter and Vossenack. Distant ridges framed the scene, but the shelling obstructed the view. "Schmidt, in the valley ahead, was hardly visible for the smoke of its burning houses and the thick white dust that lingered over each air-blast and shell-burst," wrote *New York Times* reporter Harold Denny. "What one could see at Schmidt was only broken walls and naked chimneys and in the foreground the hulks of two burned-out German tanks." Looking left, toward Hürtgen, Denny saw more "tall chimneys, about all that is left of towns and other hamlets."[69]

At 9:00 A.M., the attack began. At that moment, it was the only Allied assault along the entire western front. Two battalions from Strickler's 109th Infantry pushed north. Nicknamed the Old Gray Mare regiment after a popular song from World War I, the unit waded through blood and mud. One battalion reached the woods line west of the main road by early afternoon, but the other battalion, marching along the main road, stumbled into a minefield. The Germans called the field *Wilde Sau*, or Wild Pig, and the fiendish devices created havoc. Still, the regiment somehow managed to reached its objective in some woods overlooking the village of Hürtgen. On the division right, the 110th Infantry launched its separate assault. One battalion aimed for Simonskall and the other for Raffelsbrand. Concrete pillboxes and German small arms fire brought both battalions to a bloody halt almost immediately.[70]

Yet these moves were gambits. Peterson's 112th Infantry would make the main effort, starting at H hour with Lt. Col. Theodore Hatzfield's 2nd Battalion, and then at noon with Pete's 1st Battalion. In Germeter, tanks from the 707th Tank Battalion revved their engines and lurched forward; the soldiers of Companies F and G, their trench coats dampened by the frosty mist, rose reluctantly and followed. After carefully navigating through the paths in the minefield the engineers had cleared, the Americans emerged into open fields. They marched in two columns; Company F followed seven tanks in column of twos and angled slightly north of town, while Company G fell in behind a group of three tanks and headed a little farther north of Vossenack. Some wondered what was so important about the village ahead. "Not only had they never heard of it before, they didn't know how to pronounce its German name, Vossenack," a soldier recalled. As American artillery shifted to more distant targets, German artillery screamed down. Shells struck the line of departure and men fell, but it was not enough to halt the advance. The soldiers pushed on, carefully walking in tank tracks as a precaution against mines.[71]

The olive drab tanks started pumping shells into the tall steeple of Vossenack's church, which rose like a lighthouse on a distant shore. German soldiers replied with small arms and mortar fire. One of the defenders, a sniper, drove some American infantrymen into water-filled ditches, but the Americans soon realized he was a poor shot. Iron Division soldiers advanced and took him out, only to discover that the sniper was a woman. In front of Company G, a tank strayed and struck a mine, blowing its track off. Then another tank got mired in the mud. The infantry took casualties too. Two platoon leaders went down within the first 400 yards, while some machine gunners from Company H, which had been attached to Company G, blundered into a minefield. They set off multiple explosions that injured or killed a dozen men.[72]

On the right, the tanks leading Company F rolled along against little resistance save mortar fire. At first, the column maneuvered crabwise to avoid the wooded draw to the south and its suspected enemy positions. Some infantrymen peeled off toward the town, while the tanks moved to skirt the village. It did no good. Suddenly, a German soldier popped out of the wooded draw, lifted a panzerfaust to his shoulder, and fired. The missile knocked out a tank and sent black smoke curling into the misty sky. The remaining tanks turned their guns on the woodline but kept rolling, and the infantry followed. Their objective was Vossenack; the 1st Battalion would handle the wooded draw.[73]

In minutes, the first attackers reached their objective. They discovered that Vossenack was just a tiny mountain village. Only a block wide and 2,000 yards long, it consisted of a few dozen houses, a grocery store, and a post office along the main road. A German youth barracks was the only visible Nazi presence. As the tanks rolled into Vossenack, a German fired a burp gun from a house overlooking the street. Two 75mm tank rounds and an infantry charge solved that problem. A burst of machine gun fire from another building nearly wiped out a squad from Company F, and it took American grenades and an assault from two other squads to end that threat. The Americans lost a couple more tanks from mines and maintenance issues, but other green monsters rumbled down main street, firing into each structure. A squad of infantry followed on each side of the street. Soldiers stopped at each house, men sprayed the door with lead, tossed a grenade inside, and then dashed after it. The tanks also blew several new holes in the church. More Bloody Bucket men fell as the attack continued through town. Soon Company E and some additional tanks arrived to mop up, and the German defenders started to surrender or melt away. By early afternoon, the Americans had cleared Vossenack.[74]

Their mission accomplished, Hatzfield's battalion dug into the bald ridge beyond Vossenack and realized that they had just been part of a textbook attack. "The coordination between tanks and infantry was beautiful," the tankers reported.[75] Despite the 109th and 110th's struggles, General Cota could not help but be pleased. "Things went well," he wrote. Now it was time for the 1st Battalion's assault.[76]

Back in Germeter, Pete heard the fighting and could see some activity around Vossenack, but he could not tell what was happening. All he knew was that his turn was next.

Some 50 kilometers away, at Castle Schlenderhan west of Cologne, German officers wearing field gray tunics and Iron Crosses peered at maps tacked to ancient walls. Field Marshal Model was the ranking officer present. Seventh Army commander Gen. der Panzertruppen Erich Brandenberger stood nearby, along with his chief of staff, von Gersdorff. Also in the group were the commanders of the 89th, 275th, and 116th Panzer Divisions, plus myriad other officers from army, corps, and division levels. These men had gathered to war game the defense of the Hürtgen Forest, until a phone call turned their practice session into the real thing: the Americans had attacked! Now, instead of making moves on paper, they contemplated the real thing. Although some officers hurried back to headquarters, those who remained were able to move men and machines in a faster and more coordinated manner than if they had been separated. The 272nd Volksgrenadier Division was already on its way to relieve the 89th Division, but now the 89th would stay. The vaunted 116th Panzer Division, a veteran of the eastern front and Normandy, also received orders to move against the American threat. Adding these units to the 275th would give the Germans roughly four divisions to pit against Cota's one.[77]

— —

H hour + 3 nears. Along the 1st Battalion's line of departure a few men gripe or banter with each other, but most say little. Some soldiers play craps or a last hand of poker. Others cadge cigarettes or stomp their feet against the chill. Nobody writes letters, because just now home seems a distant dream. "Only the world of battle stays real," explained reporter Iris Carpenter, who witnessed many assaults. As the minutes tick away all talking stops, and the only sound is the gunfire emanating from Vossenack. Mechanically, men check and recheck their rifles, ammunition belts, and hand grenades. Some push their helmets down to make them more snug and tighten their chin straps. Time checks get more frequent, heartbeats quicken, and mouths go dry. The mood is tense, the wait interminable, and fear of the unknown is palpable. It has been said that before a battle every soldier thinks some other guy will get killed, but according to Carpenter one look at the face of such men disproves that idea. They know this is the last time some of them will be together, but there is nothing they can do about it. There is a job to do—a job that for some men would "shut out all the tomorrows."[78]

Pete Lynn was about to experience real combat for the first time.

We do not know what was going on in Pete Lynn's head, but one can easily surmise that he was frightened and wanted desperately to be back in the Best Little City in the World. In our mind's eye, one can still see him: huddled in his overcoat, with his breath puffing in the cold. His blue eyes, peering from beneath his damp helmet, glanced from his friends, to his officers, to Vossenack, to Germeter and Richelskaul, and finally to the wooded draw in the Hürtgen Forest. Maybe he saw eternity.

Then watch hands pointed to noon, November 2, 1944. Maj. Hazlett gave the order, and the men of Company B, 112th Infantry, thirty-four-year-old Felmer Lonzo Lynn among them, shouldered their equipment and stepped off.[79]

This main advance—indeed, the main effort of the entire First Army, not just the corps or division—was ambitious, to say the least. Planners wanted this column to pass south of Vossenack, cross the Kall River, ascend the next ridge, and capture Kommerscheidt. There A Company would set up a blocking position on the road leading to the southwest, B Company would pass through town and defend the exit to the southeast, while C Company guarded the northeastern and northwestern approaches. The 3rd Battalion would follow, bypass Kommerscheidt, and take Schmidt atop the next ridge. With this prize in hand, the division would be poised for further offensive action.[80]

Oddly, Hazlett's PBIs–Poor Bloody Infantrymen[81]—advanced in column with little support. Battalion attacks in column were common in the European theater, but they worked best with combined arms. That meant using everything at the Allies' disposal, including armor, smoke, maneuver, and air power (weather permitting) to tilt the odds in their favor. Yet no armor rolled with Hazlett's battalion, no shells fell ahead of it, no planes flew above, and the only smoke to be seen trailed skyward from contested Vossenack. The soldiers who captured Vossenack could have supported the 1st Battalion's advance, but they did not. This column's only friend was the terrain. The route led downhill into a deep, forested, and narrow vale. Here the Americans would be shielded from German guns frowning down from the Brandenberg-Bergstein Ridge, which the soldiers called the B&B Ridge for short. The column would also be invisible to any remaining Germans in Vossenack, which stood closer to the left. With nothing but open fields to the right, Hazlett's battalion would only have to worry about Germans in the wooded vale. But that was the problem: the Americans knew the wooded vale was defended. Patrols and a smoldering Sherman tank below Vossenack were the witnesses.[82]

Company D provided Hazlett's main support. Its 1st Platoon, machine gunners all, marched with Company B. Its 2nd Platoon, in foxholes next to Company A, started firing their .30-inch heavy machine guns toward the wooded draw. Meanwhile, in the woods about 900 yards to the rear, Company D's mortar men set up their half dozen 81mm tubes and prepared to fire high-explosive projectiles at any target within their 3,200-yard range. These were the largest weapons in Hazlett's control.[83] That was it: there would be no other help. Planners at army, corps, and division should have known better.

So it began. Below Germeter, Company B stepped off. Pete and his fellow soldiers, weighed down by packs and weapons, picked their way past A Company's Richelskaul foxholes. Once aligned in a column of companies, Hackard's troopers wound their way toward the wooded draw. The 1st Platoon was in front; evidently, Pete's squad was near the front of the column, if not in the lead. Next in line came the 3rd Platoon, the 2nd Platoon, and the machine gunners of the weapons platoon. Company C prepared to follow, while Company A remained in its foxholes and expected to bring up the rear.[84]

Except for a thin line of trees reaching east, a snatch of open ground stretched between the Lammersdorf-Hürtgen road and the first trees in the wooded draw. To the left, the men could make out Vossenack. By now, the little village surely looked like other fought-over towns in Europe, which a reporter described as "house frames slumped, grotesque, incongruous skeletons." Beneath them, the shell-pocked ground "looked as if a giant had been digging it."[85] The column pushed quickly ahead, with equipment clanking and soldiers muttering, and passed downhill into the pines. The arboreal surroundings gradually hid Vossenack and the distant ridges. Nearby, a little creek called the Richelsbach gurgled and pointed the way east to the Kall River. One hundred yards, two hundred yards, and on the soldiers groped forward. Phase lines had been selected to help the battalion measure progress, and the first one was a forester's trail about 400 yards east of Richelskaul. The north-south path connected Vossenack and the Simonskall road.[86]

The forester's trail was within reach when the little vale erupted in a heart-stopping diapason of noise. The column had stumbled onto a contingent of German soldiers—probably members of Oberst Alexius von Schmitz's 983rd Regiment of the 275th Infantry Division—who were dug in deeply near the trail. These Nazis opened fire with small arms, mortars, and artillery. Ear-shattering explosions, screams and shouts, the staccato chatter of machine guns, and the measured crack of rifles now echoed through the Forest. Smoke trailed upward while flames licked at dead leaves.[87]

Men who have experienced such an ambush will tell you that the sudden, "incessant, unrelenting noise" is deafening and the earth almost shakes as pieces of dirt, metal, and wood whine past. The air fills with the tangy smell of burnt powder, while soldiers scream and curse. Fighting back, a man is cognizant of enemy fire pouring at him, of his "rifle jerking with every shot," and of the thought that "at any instant, a bullet might smash into me." He is also aware of his emotions, which can be a farrago ranging from detachment to "stark, cold fear."[88]

During World War II, there was a less than one in ten chance that a member of the army would become a casualty. The chances of being killed in action were about one in one hundred, although the likelihood was higher for infantrymen, for obvious reasons. At this moment, the odds were quite poor for the men leading Hazlett's column.[89]

As the 1st Platoon leader, Lt. Ralph Spaans was near the front of Company B. He may have been the point man, although one after-action interview reported that Spaans was "taking his plat[oon] to the forward nose on the regimental right flank." Whatever his location, the man from New Jersey took the brunt of the ambush; German machine gun fire raked him from head to toe. "He was dead before he hit the ground," a soldier recalled. Germans in coal-scuttle helmets next turned their weapons—probably MG-42 machine guns and Mauser K-98 bolt-action rifles, or possibly MP-44 assault rifles—on the rest of the American column. Bullets tore past the fir trees and into the men, and some of them hit Spaans's sprawled body again and again.[90]

It was around 1:00 P.M., and Company B was in trouble. Confusion reigned. Men hid, crawled, yelled for help, and died. About eight or ten men, including Pete Lynn, Johnny Gregorio, and Guy Hardaway, were on or near the forester's trail and exposed to the same hail of gunfire that killed Spaans. Fellow Tar Heel Clyde Sprinkle was nearby and horrified. Captain Hackard, who had been close to Spaans when the first shots rang out, lost contact with the lieutenant as well as Lynn, Gregorio, and Hardaway. The rest of the company took cover.[91]

Hackard tried desperately to help Spaans's exposed platoon. He ordered the 3rd Platoon to move up. Platoon commander Jerry M. Burrill answered the call, but it was a forlorn hope. Burrill and his soldiers ran into a wall of enemy fire, and Burrill went down with a broken leg. Burrell painfully dragged himself across pine needles, rolled into a hole, tuned in his SCR 536 radio, and called for mortar fire. In the woods behind

Germeter, Company D's mortar men started feeding shells into their tubes, and in short order shells rained down, but it was not enough to stop the German fire. Pinned down, the 3rd Platoon could do no more.[92]

Now, both the 1st and 3rd Platoons were in trouble and out on a limb. German artillery and mortar fire continued to rain down while bullets whipped through the trees, clipping off twigs, churning up dirt and pine needles, and chewing up men. Any returned American fire was ineffective. The forest filled with the acrid effluvia of gunpowder and death. It was easy to feel hopeless.[93]

Hackard had more cards to play. About 1:30 P.M., he ordered his last platoon, the 2nd, to move up. One squad made it just past the trail, but German fire stopped these troopers cold too. There was some hope that Company D's 81mm mortars could break the impasse, and their shells continued falling with the guidance of Lieutenant Burrill, but there was no perceptible change to the situation. Hackard also requested artillery support, and at 3:10 P.M. the 229th Field Artillery Battalion fired a belated salvo of twenty-four rounds. According to a forward observer, the shells struck the German position "along the trail just south of Company B's attack route." The observer added that the results were "excellent," but the Germans did not budge and their fire continued unabated. Unaccountably, no other artillery fire was forthcoming. Company B was stuck, and there was nothing else Hackard could do.[94]

Not so Hazlett. Air support was unavailable due to the poor weather; only one mission flew over the battlefield the entire day.[95] Yet both Company C and Company A remained uncommitted. Hazlett could have brought up either or both companies to outflank the enemy position, but neither apparently moved an inch, possibly because the enemy fire was too heavy.[96] Instead, soon after the fight started, Hazlett scurried back to Germeter to confer with his boss. He arrived at Peterson's attic command post at 3:00 P.M., where the two men decided only to hold as much of the 1st Battalion's limited gains as possible. With the capture of Vossenack, Peterson had another avenue of advance open and preferred to reinforce success rather than failure. Hazlett returned to his embattled battalion about dusk and found that Company B was "stuck so far out front" that it could not stay where it was. He gave Hackard permission to withdraw. It was now about 5:00 P.M. Darkness was now descending, and in the gathering gloom the Americans fell back with mixed success. According to the army's official historian, 2nd Platoon soldiers set up in "a small patch of woods 200 to 250 yards in front of the line of departure," which apparently was nearly where it was when the attack started, just past the trail. A medic and another soldier evacuated Burrill on a litter. Somehow, the remnants of the 1st Platoon withdrew as well.[97]

Spaans, Gregorio, Hardaway, and Lynn were not among them. After being separated from their comrades and under enemy fire for four long hours, they did not make it out of the wooded draw. Their fate was unknown.

—◦—

This afternoon action in the draw, just like the entire Battle of the Hürtgen Forest, was not one of the U.S. Army's finest moments. "It is a curious fact," observed Raymond Fleig, one of the tankers on the field that day, "that a division attack became a regimental attack; which became a battalion attack, which became a company attack, which became a platoon attack, which was lead by a squad of riflemen preceded by two or more scouts. Several other questions remain unanswered," Fleig went on. "Why were the heavy machine guns of Company D never employed; why were there no requests for more artillery fire, why were no tanks committed in this main effort when both Company A and B, 707th Tank Battalion, were available?"[98]

Later, someone asked Colonel Peterson why Company B's attack was not reinforced with tanks, artillery, or more infantry. "Every battalion CO had an artillery liaison officer, and they were always excellent," he replied. "If artillery was not used, I do not know why. I do not recall that this was supposed to be a major attack. It seems that the original plans called for the major attack for Schmidt to go through Vossenack. If not, why would I have the 3rd battalion, 112th, fall in behind the 2nd battalion? The answer would seem to be that I planned to send them through the 2nd."[99]

Peterson's memory was simply incorrect. As we have seen, the original plan called for the 1st Battalion's assault to be the primary one. Peterson also had forgotten or was unaware that artillery had been employed that afternoon, but clearly it was underutilized. Finally, Hazlett and Peterson did not send more infantry or tanks to help Company B and chose instead to reinforce the successful capture of Vossenack. Although it made military sense to do that, it left the 1st Battalion with little to show for its effort, with the possible exception (in the opinion of historian Edward G. Miller) of relieving some pressure on the Vossenack attack.[100]

The only thing left for Hackard to do was pick up the pieces. As the smoke cleared, Company B stumbled back to the line of departure where, grimly, the survivors rallied. They dug in near Company A, which had not budged.[101]

Hackard and his surviving platoon commanders started counting noses. In the evening or early-morning darkness of November 2–3, casualties from the 3rd Platoon went on the company's reports first. In addition to Burill, a company clerk listed eleven men as wounded, one seriously. All were sent to various field hospitals such as the 1st Battalion's aid station in the woods west of Vossenack. Capt. Paschal Linguiti, the surgeon in charge, cared for these men and also checked five other men who had been evacuated with combat exhaustion.[102]

Accounting for every member of Company B proved to be no easy task. According to one estimate, only 55 of the company's 186 men made it back.[103] Pete's 1st Platoon was particularly hard hit, for the obvious reason that it had been in front and taken the brunt of the ambush. Multiple sources confirm that only fourteen men from the 1st Platoon—less than half its normal complement—returned to friendly lines unscathed that day.[104]

The tabulations of November 2 continued into November 3, another intemperate day. The red line on thermometers again hovered near freezing, while a cold drizzle fell out of the heavy mist that still shrouded the Forest. The wet weather made moving about unpleasant; mud clung to soldiers' leggings and shoes as they splashed through watery shell holes.[105] Except for a modest demonstration toward the enemy, Hackard's B Company sat still near Richelskaul along the Lammersdorf-Hürtgen highway, ostensibly "to guard the flank."[106] Meanwhile, at Company B's makeshift headquarters, four more wounded men, one of them serious, were added the tally, while another four soldiers were evacuated with combat exhaustion. This was reported to the regimental CP in Germeter where reports listed 6 killed, 91 wounded, 22 nonbattle casualties, and 113 evacuated for the entire regiment on November 2.[107]

Meanwhile, the rest of the 112th Infantry continued the war. Now Peterson bypassed the wooded draw and sent the rest of the regiment in the footsteps of the 2nd Battalion. Marching in column of battalions, the soldiers passed through muddy, ruined Vossenack, crossed the bald ridge, and entered the Forest. This time it was surprisingly easy; the soldiers traversed the Kall River gorge and captured Kommerscheidt. Hazlett's battalion (minus Company B) remained while the 3rd Battalion pushed on to the sixteenth-century village of Schmidt and surprised Germans eating lunch, riding bicycles, and drinking schnapps. It was a day of dizzying success. "A believing man with imagination," wrote historian Rick Atkinson, "could almost see the end of the war." Yet the day closed on ominous notes. As Peterson's men dug in, the tired soldiers sent out no patrols and carelessly tossed out sixty mines without camouflaging them. They also failed to guard the Kall Trail that led back through the trees to Vossenack. Meanwhile, the 707th Tank Battalion tried to reinforce, but several of its tanks got stuck or broke down on the narrow and muddy trail.[108]

The next morning found Company B still at the original line of departure. Some enemy soldiers counterattacked, probably from the wooded draw, but the company managed to repulse the assault. Heavy German artillery fire then came roaring in from the distant ridges and continued all day. A sniper took occasional potshots at the company with little result, but the shelling was a different story. It cost the life of PFC James L. Knight. A twenty-year-old sales clerk turned bazooka man from Anderson County, South Carolina—a town only a hundred miles from Kings Mountain—Knight died when a white phosphorus shell exploded nearby.[109] Word also arrived that Vernon D. Bowers, who had been evacuated on November 2, had died from his wounds. Pete's friend from Maryland could not overcome the shell fragment wound that had slammed into his chest. The only good news was that Pvt. Norris C. O'Neal, who had gone to the rear the same day with combat exhaustion, returned from the hospital.[110]

Finally, on Sunday, November 5, Spaans, Gregorio, Howard, and Lynn were listed as missing in action since none of them had been seen since the first violent minutes of the fight. Two other men, Pvts. Harold L. Jackson and Gino A. Bono, were listed as present but lightly injured. The impact of the battle was evident when six more men were evacuated with combat exhaustion, including Clyde Sprinkle. Losing a friend in combat is a terrible thing, and Sprinkle's evacuation to the 103rd Medical Clearing station suggests that he felt the loss of Pete and the other men deeply. The memory of those days plagued him for the rest of his life. (Sprinkle rarely talked about the war, but it would come rushing back at night. He would shout out in his sleep, "Get down in the hole, don't raise your head!") Total casualties for Company B now stood at thirty-three men, including sixteen wounded (one of whom died from his wounds), four missing in action, and twelve with combat exhaustion. Of the 186 men present on November 1, this represented a casualty rate of almost 18 percent.[111]

On November 5, Company B ended its vigil outside Richelskaul. Peterson summoned the company to reinforce the rest of the regiment in Kommerscheidt, but they did not follow the bloody path of November 2. "We went along the side of the draw," a trooper later wrote, which meant that the company went through Vossenack, picked up the Kall Trail, and marched into the forest. On the way, the column passed a dugout where medical personnel had set up an aid station, crossed the Kall River, and then "went straight up the hill, across the road, and into Kommerscheidt," a trooper wrote. It was nearly dark when Hackard's troopers arrived.[112]

As they entered the embattled village, Hackard dispatched his 2nd Platoon to the right to reinforce L Company. The other platoons angled to the left to help A company. It went smoothly, until the 2nd Platoon neared a burning building. "Every move silhouetted us, against this blaze," a trooper wrote. When German observers saw the moving soldiers, they sent artillery shells crashing down. Some of Hackard's men scattered. Others frantically started digging in. One soldier, platoon leader Sgt. Bruce Pitman, was not fast enough. He died in the shelling. The Forest had claimed another victim from Company B. He would not be the last.[113]

Meanwhile, four American soldiers, including one tall, skinny, blue-eyed, thirty-four-year-old man from Kings Mountain, were still missing, somewhere in the wooded vale. Having bypassed the spot where he disappeared, American troops would not return there for months. As the 28th Infantry Division continued its fight in the Hürtgen Forest, casualty news began to wind its slow way to America.

I will always Love you till the Day I Die.

CHAPTER 9

Bottom Fell Out

BACK HOME, THE UBIQUITOUS PINNACLE WAS NOW ARRAYED IN VIVID fall colors, but in the shadow of the monadnock, Ruth Lynn felt uneasy.

Maybe pregnancy had something to do with it. Her second trimester began in early November, and the baby inside her pushed and kicked until Ruth turned green. She hoped some company would improve her spirits, so on November's first day brother Joe brought their mother over for dinner and then he spent the night with her. When she felt no better the next morning, she sent the kids to Hazel's and took the day off from work.

Remarks from unthinking people did nothing for her mood. At one point, somebody kidded her that Pete had met a French gal. She grinned and bore it. "I'll just keep holding my tater and I[']ll hear from my sweet heart soon," she wrote.[1] Then a disrespectful jackanapes told Ruth that a good husband would not leave his wife in the lurch to serve. "What I said was a mouth full, you know me when I get mad," Ruth told Pete. "I said I guessed it was much my fault as yours & it wasn't costing her any thing so I didn't see why it was worrying her." Privately, Ruth admitted that it would have been so much easier had Pete not gone to war, but she promised to "carry on & remember you said you'd love me always and try to keep my chin up & be a good soldier like my sweetheart."[2]

There was also small comfort in the extra $10 checks that now showed up in her mailbox regularly. The money was for things that made Ruth fret: Pete's combat duty and overseas service. "I think & wonder if you stay warm [in] this cool weather," she wrote. "Dearest heart, you probably think I[']m talking through my hat, but I[']d gladly swap places with you if I could. It hurts a lot thinking about the one you love being so far away and probably cold & hungry."[3]

Ruth felt well enough to return to work on Friday, November 3, but could not shake her gloom. A V-mail letter from Pete arrived, but only his name and address were written on it. Otherwise, her mailbox remained ominously empty. She went to the doctor for her monthly checkup. He gave her a good report and prescribed medicine for a cold.[4]

That Saturday was Ruth's twenty-ninth birthday. Mae was away for the weekend, so Ruth did not have anything special planned. Three birthday cards arrived in the mail, including one from her parents with a dollar inside. After work, she took the girls to town and stopped by the drug store. "I told them we were having a birthday party for me," she joked. At one store, Ruth bought Bob a bonnet. "She looked like a doll, everybody looked at her & she laughed & cut up all over town," she wrote. Strolling along the sidewalk, Ruth thought about their third child. "I always think of our new baby as a son it may be a girl but I[']m hoping, keep your fingers crossed," she wrote Pete.[5]

Late that night, the feeling hit hardest. Waking up with a start, Ruth heard the sound of whistling coming from the porch, as if Pete was bounding up the front steps on his way home from the mill. She jumped out of bed and hurried to the front door, but there was no one there: the porch was empty, and the road in front of their little house dark and deserted. The sound was gone now, but she could have sworn the whistling had been real. Unable to shake the sensation, she sat up the rest of the night. "My birthday—Had bad dream nite of 4th," she wrote. "Afraid something happened to our Dady."[6]

The following days brought no news from Pete. The sun rose and set, Park Yarn's looms hummed, and Ruth tried to chase the bad dream from her mind. It was hard. Back from her trip, Mae gave Ruth a dress for her birthday, but that only made Ruth wish Pete could see it. There were distractions: Tuesday, November 7, was Election Day. Voters tramped to the polls to vote for either Roosevelt or his challenger, Republican Thomas E. Dewey. "We've had a time in the mill fussing about who to vote for," Ruth wrote. "None of us voted though."[7]

Although Park Yarn was not well represented in the ballot box, the *Kings Mountain Herald* dutifully published the final tally. President Roosevelt was reelected for an unprecedented fourth term. But if Ruth lingered over anything in the newspaper it was war news, not politics. In the same edition, the *Herald* announced the death of two Kings Mountain soldiers in France. That was worrisome enough, but if she had seen the *New York Times* she would have read about fighting in a small German town called Vossenack. "Yanks and Jerries both in church—and not getting married," a platoon leader reported. Ruth could only wonder about her soldier.[8]

A few good days followed her birthday scare as close friends and relatives came to the rescue. "If you were here you[']d sure think we were crazy," she wrote Pete. "Mae and . . . Nell has been out here awhile and we laughed at our selves about how silly we were to cry over our men." Bad dreams aside, Ruth also admitted that she was slowly getting accustomed to Pete's absence. "I don't take many crying fits any more, I found out it don't help a bit and I have plenty to do to keep busy & wait on the kids," she wrote. "They sure are sweet and so full of fun they can't be still."[9]

Her gloom completely vanished on November 9. Friends and relatives said they had received mail from Pete, and then the mailman delivered a letter just for her. On the outside, she saw that her soldier had identified himself as a private first class: "I was tickled and I bet you were too," she said. "I knew you wouldn't stay a Pvt. Always." Inside, she found a letter dated October 24, Mickie's birthday, in which Pete said that his unit had pulled back from the front! The mere thought of Pete being out of harm's way made her giddy. "I was so happy I acted silly as usual," she replied, and then chattered happily away about family news. A day like that would not come along again for a long time. (This was actually Pete's letter of October 25 telling Ruth that his unit was moving and that they could use the extra money from his promotion to buy ice cream.)[10]

The next day, an empty mailbox deflated her a little, but not much. "I'm still happy cause you're still safe & well," she wrote. "Sweet I[']ve talked about you all day—has your ears burned? I do love you darling so much you're always on my mind and in my heart. Do I make you sick talking love so much. I recon you've known me long enough to know you're my whole life and always will be. Since you're so far away it seems I love you more."[11]

And so Park Yarn's looms rolled on during those gray days. Ruth tramped from home to the mill and back again, oblivious to events in the Hürtgen Forest 4,000 miles away. November 12 was a rainy Sunday at

Park Yarn. Ruth and the girls put on their dresses and walked down the hill to Macedonia for Sunday School and the 11:00 A.M. worship service. "Church was full," she wrote. That afternoon, as Ruth sat down to write Pete a letter, the girls started singing "London Bridge" at the top of their lungs. Mae sang with them. Ruth laughed and wrote to Pete how much she appreciated her sister. Mae was a great help with the girls and also great company from morning to night. The women even had to share a bed since the tiny house had no other place to sleep.[12]

Ruth started worrying again a few days later. A letter from Pete arrived on Tuesday, November 14—this was Pete's letter of November 1—but it said little compared to the one Pete sent his dad. From what Charlie Lynn told Ruth, Pete's letter announced that he had been in Germany three times already. Rather than dwell on these ill tidings, Ruth preoccupied herself with something else. One night, after the kids went to bed, the sisters had a long talk about the future. It would not involve Park Yarn or Margrace; instead, the Lynns and Smiths would leave the mill behind. The menfolk would open a store, the ladies would open a lunchroom, and the girls would work as the waitresses. Ruth even gave her unborn baby a job as the curb service boy![13]

Thursday, November 16, dawned. It was a warm day with a trace of rain, but in truth it was the first of many black days to come for Ruth Lynn. If Kings Mountain was like most small towns, there would have been a small Western Union office somewhere in town, probably in the drug store. At 8:20 A.M., the teletype machine in the office came to life and clacked out a new message. A clerk arranged delivery, by messenger or taxi, and the telegram found Ruth at 10:00 A.M. Too soon, too soon. She tore open the envelope and saw these dreaded words in big blue letters:

THE SECRETARY OF WAR DESIRES ME TO EXPRESS HIS DEEP REGRET THAT YOUR HUSBAND PRIVATE FIRST CLASS FELMER L LYNN HAS BEEN REPORTED MISSING IN ACTION SINCE TWO NOVEMBER IN GERMANY.

As a tidal wave of grief and fear washed over her, Ruth grabbed a Bible. She flipped to Psalm 91 and searched its sixteen verses for something, anything, to comfort her. "I will say of the Lord, he is my refuge and my fortress: my God; in him will I trust."[14]

She couldn't work on Friday. Saturday passed and tears flowed in the little gray house. There was an outpouring of love and kindness. Family and friends came over, but nobody really knew what to say. All they could do was hope and pray, so on Sunday Macedonia church held a special prayer service for Pete. Prayers went up from a neighboring church too.

"Bottom fell out," Ruth wrote. "Pete said the last thing Keep your chin up hon!"[15]

—❦—

After Pete Lynn disappeared, the bottom fell out for the 28th Infantry Division.

The situation looked promising the day Company B marched into Kommerscheidt. The 112th had seized its main objectives of Kommerscheidt and Schmidt and Peterson moved his command post up. At Cota's stone-walled headquarters in Rott, officers buzzed with equal shares of relief and excitement while messages of congratulations arrived. Hodges pronounced himself "extremely satisfied," and Cota felt like a little Napoleon.[16] Yet for those with open eyes, warning signals flashed bright red. The rain, fog, and near-freezing temperatures persisted, so Quesada's airplanes remained grounded. The muddy, narrow Kall Trail begrudged the passing of tanks. A few made it through but others got stuck, broke down, or hit mines. The division's attacks to the north and south remained in bloody stalemate. Meanwhile, Peterson's battalions on the main objectives of Schmidt and Kommerscheidt hung alone, like a buffeted flag atop a tall thin pole.[17]

That's when the war gaming German officers at Castle Schlenderhan brought the hammer down. The 89th and 116th Panzer moved against the 112th, while the 275th resisted the rest of the division. German soldiers in coal-scuttle helmets, supported by hulking gray panzers, flung the Americans out of Schmidt. They also converged on the Kall Trail, which was defended by only a handful of engineers. German artillerymen along the Brandenberg-Bergstein ridge, with a press box view of the battlefield, zeroed in on exposed American positions and blew soldiers "right out of their foxholes."[18]

Suddenly, Cota was no Napoleon. He and his staff hunkered down in Rott and lost control of the battle. As German forces advanced, Cota scraped up reinforcements and sent them into the forest twice, but both Task Force Ripple and Task Force Davis failed. Everywhere Germans squeezed against the 112th's little salient. Meanwhile, back on the scene of November 2's fighting, soldiers dug in on Vossenack ridge could not stand the pinpoint shelling from the Brandenberg-Bergstein ridge. As German artillery plowed up the bald ridge, those poor soldiers finally broke. Shell-shocked, they ran from their foxholes, halting only beneath the torn steeple of Vossenack's church. "It was the saddest sight I have ever seen," a soldier wrote.[19]

Germans attacked Kommerscheidt next. Bolstered by American artillery, some tanks, a few of Schmidt's routed defenders, and occasional air support, the American position hung on. Pete's company was in the thick of it. Captain Hackard, though injured, grabbed a bazooka and knocked out a German tank. Cowed, two other panzers withdrew. The captain also gunned down a German machine gun crew. It was "unusual heroism" that earned him a Distinguished Service Cross, but it was not enough. Panzers and German troops broke through, waded among the American foxholes, and forced the Bloody Bucket men to fall back to the woods. Hazlett's entire staff was killed or captured, while clerks had to destroy most of the regiment's records. Only fifty-five Company B men made it out.[20]

Due to some miscommunication, Carl Peterson was not there. Thinking he had been summoned to Rott, he went to Cota's command post. He arrived on a stretcher after a harrowing trip through the enemy-infested woods. Having sent no such summons to Peterson, Cota thought that the colonel had abandoned his troops and relieved him; Col. Gustin M. Nelson, a forty-five-year-old West Pointer, stepped in. It was too much for Cota. Stress, worry, the weather, and the onset of diabetes, which was not discovered until later, flooded in and the general fainted dead away.[21]

Coming to his senses, Cota requested permission to withdraw behind the Kall. Gerow and Hodges grudgingly approved. When the bad news reached Eisenhower, he and Bradley went to Rott to see for themselves, star-studded flags flying from their vehicles. Standing outside Cota's stone *gasthaus*, Ike clucked. "Well, Dutch," he said, "it looks like you've

Eisenhower and Cota in Rott
Source: U.S. Army Heritage and Education Center

got a bloody nose." After Bradley and Eisenhower left, Hodges chewed out the division commander and considered firing him.[22]

With that the 28th Infantry Division pulled behind the Kall, although it remained in action for a few more days. Patrols crept through the trees to search for missing soldiers.[23] When it was finally relieved, the men gladly left that Death Valley for a quiet sector in the Ardennes Forest. German radio announced that its soldiers had completely annihilated the division. It was a boast not far off the mark. The 28th had suffered 6,184 casualties. The 112th fared worst of all, losing 2,093 men, including 167 killed, 719 wounded, and 431 missing—or 64 percent of its assigned strength. In Pete's first battalion, only 364 of 871 men survived. There was just one officer among them, and all of its mortars, most of its machine guns, and the entire battalion headquarters with its maps, orders, and staff journals were captured. Meanwhile, sixteen of the 893rd Tank Destroyer Battalion's twenty-four tank destroyers and thirty-one of the 707th Tank Battalion's fifty medium tanks were lost, along with numerous bulldozers, trucks, antitank guns, weasels, and small weapons.[24] It was the worst defeat experienced by the U.S. Army during World War II. In fact, only at Tarawa did another single division experience that kind of casualties.[25]

Yet the Hürtgen Forest was not finished with the U.S. Army. After Cota's division departed for the quiet Ardennes, other olive drab units marched into the evergreen meat grinder. By mid-December, six infantry divisions plus sundry other units had fought in the Hürtgen, largely aiming toward the dams. Each failed against fanatical resistance, losing 33,000 more casualties in the process. The air force even tried to breach the dams with air strikes, but to no avail.[26]

Each attacking unit found the battlefield littered with the effluvia of the fighting: equipment, torn trees, and corpses. "As for their dead," recalled a man from the 8th Infantry Division, "we were collecting them for days." A German soldier echoed that. "Everywhere we found a lot of equipment that the Americans left—weatherproof sleeping bags, little tents, cans with rations, little cookers, coffee, tea and cigarettes," he wrote. Wild dogs wandered amid the trees, feasting on phosphorus-burned corpses.[27]

Another battle ended the Hürtgen fighting. On December 16, 1944, Adolf Hitler launched a surprise counteroffensive in the Ardennes. The German attack rolled straight into Cota's resting division. Though outnumbered, pushed back, and bloodied, the 28th fought valiantly and contributed to the ultimate American victory in the Battle of the Bulge. In a different place, it was a different unit.

Meanwhile, the whereabouts of Pete Lynn remained a question mark.

In denial, Ruth groped for hope. A few days after she heard the bad news from Europe, she read a copy of *True Confessions*, a popular women's magazine. Her eye caught a poem by Alice E. Meany called "Wishing on a Star." It reminded her of better days, when Pete used to sing to her beneath a Carolina moon. She clipped the entire passage and underlined the last words:

> *Last night when all the world was still*
> *I stood upon our favorite hill,*
> *The grass, like velvet on the ground*
> *A magic carpet all around.*

Tall trees on guard, and way up high,
A silver moon to rule the sky,
In regal splendor shedding light
To part the curtains of the night.

And then I found one tiny star
The brightest of them all by far.
I made my wish and said this prayer,
"God keep you, darling, 'over there' ".[28]

When the smiles did not come, Ruth could only plod on with life. She desperately wanted news, but part of her was afraid of what that news might be. The holiday season, her first without Pete, soon arrived and only highlighted his absence, yet she determined that the kids would have a normal Christmas. On December 25, with the mills quiet in observance of the holiday, Mickie and Bobbie found plenty of presents waiting on them under the tree, including two dolls, a doll bed, alphabet blocks, and some books. After a three-day closure, the mills roared to life again. "New Year's Day was just another day of work altho I did manage to hear the last 6 minutes of the Sugar Bowl football game," the *Old Mountaineer* reported.[29]

Among the modest gifts Ruth received for Christmas was a new diary from Mae. She rarely wrote much, but what she did write spoke volumes. "Monday—No Mail," she jotted on New Year's Day 1945. "Hope I get good news from my sweetheart soon." Twenty-four hours later brought more of the same to mind. "2 months today since gov[ernment] said Pete was missing," she pointed out. "Still waiting, hoping & praying Read stories to Mick & Bob."[30]

The winter days that followed brought nothing to improve her state of mind. On January 4, a chilly and damp Thursday, a bundle of twenty letters she had written to Pete that fall showed up in her mailbox. Every letter was unopened, and the bundle was marked "missing." Seventeen more letters showed up on January 6 and twenty-one on January 8. Again, all were unopened, with the ominous word "missing" written on the outside.[31] Ruth bundled up all of these returned letters, marked them "Mail never received from me & kids," and set them aside, still unopened, because she could not bear to look at them. Then, a couple of weeks later, the boxes she had sent Pete for Christmas were returned. The mailman delivered them just as she heard another Kings Mountain man had been killed.[32]

Frightened but still in disbelief, Ruth soldiered on. "Wish the mail man would bring some word from our dady Pete—just to know he's well & not hungry or cold," she wrote. Later she added, "Bob, Mick & I sleep together & talk about Dady Pete & wonder where he is."[33]

She looked at the newspaper every day; maybe she would see an article or a photo with something, anything, about her husband's unit. One January day, she unfolded the newspaper and finally spotted a story about Col. Gustin Nelson leading the 112th Infantry in a bayonet charge across 250 yards of open Belgian ground while waving a cane. For Ruth, it was good to see news of her husband's division and its leaders, but it worried her to see that the unit was in heavy combat. She wondered if Pete was there.[34]

A column by Elsie Robinson in the January 12 *Charlotte Observer* also struck a chord because Ruth kept it. In her article, Robinson reminded readers of Jesus in the Garden of Gethsemane. Knowing that crucifixion was near, Jesus cried out to God. Robinson compared Jesus's sorrow with the wartime sorrows many readers faced. "And now you've come to your Gethsemane," the columnist wrote. "Now, all alone, in darkness, you pray, 'God, stay Your hand! I cannot bear this thing!'" Ruth had exactly those feelings, so she read carefully what the columnist had to say next. "For there are tests which no soul may evade," Robinson wrote. "He who made you still will see you through." Ruth scribbled in the margin, "and we cry & feel sorry for ourselves—Can almost hear Pete say Keep your chin up no matter what happens."[35]

So Ruth tried to keep her chin up. After Christmas, she gave up her job as planned, but the mills kept on churning without her. "Here at the plant it is Duck and more Duck," the *Old Mountaineer* wrote of Margrace Mill pouring out its goods. Ruth turned her attention to baby preparations, which included shopping for clothes and getting a crib ready.[36]

But that did not fill all of her time, so Ruth decided to learn something about Pete's whereabouts on her own. In late January, she wrote letters to four "boys" in Pete's company to ask if they could tell her anything. "Hope I hear something soon from them," she said, and to be certain of delivery she also sent the men a V-mail.[37] When she could think of nothing else to do, Ruth sought encouragement from more dubious sources. One February night, she joined some friends around a Ouija board. When her turn came, Ruth naturally asked about Pete. The board said that Pete was a prisoner of war (POW) in Germany and would be home in April 1945. "Wouldn't that be heaven," she wrote.[38] Ruth chased rumors too. One day she heard that Pete had been seen in Belgium with four other men, so she telephoned everybody she could think of, only to hit dead end after dead end. Then another acquaintance called and said a buddy had met a man named Lynn in a German POW camp. "Don't know whether it was Pete or not," Ruth moaned helplessly.[39]

Day after day, more questions rose in her mind, but zero answers came. Valentine's Day 1945 was especially hard on her. "Wonder if Bud worm is thinking about what day it is our 11th anniversary," she told her diary. "Thought of him & our life together—It just can't be over." Meanwhile, the unopened letters kept coming—three more on February 27—while Mickie talked "about her & dady seeing the band on Halloween 1943."[40]

———

In Europe, the Allies looked up from the newly won Bulge battlefields and remembered the damn dams. Before Ike's combat divisions could resume marching east, they had to wrestle the dams from German hands.

Gee Gerow had been promoted to lead the new Fifteenth U.S. Army. In his stead, Maj. Gen. Clarence R. Huebner took command of the V Corps, which still stood in front of the dams. Between Huebner and the dams lay unconquered stretches of the Hürtgen Forest, including the old battlefields around Schmidt. Ghosts wandered there. "The very name of the town of Schmidt had become a kind of bugaboo among American soldiers," army historian MacDonald wrote, but it had to be seized. On February 5, the 78th Infantry Division attacked through the torn, fought-over forest. Two days later, these men wearing distinctive lightning bolt patches reached Kommerscheidt and Schmidt. With the help of tanks and tank destroyers, the 78th slogged past pillboxes and minefields and braved small arms, mortar, and artillery fire to conquer the villages for the last time. Pushing on, the 78th Division finally captured Schwammenauel

Dam on February 9, but not before German engineers blew critical discharge valves. A steady flow of water rushed downstream and delayed the Allies for almost a fortnight.[41]

Enter the 82nd Airborne Division, a part of the XVIII Airborne Corps. These crack paratroopers had fought in the Sicily, Normandy, Market-Garden, and Ardennes campaigns. Their leader, Maj. Gen. James M. "Jumpin' Jim" Gavin—handsome, dashing, and the paramour of a string of women from WACs to Marlene Dietrich—was the army's youngest division commander. His orders were to move into the Kall River Valley to relieve some 78th Division units and also cut enemy escape routes. On February 8, Gavin set up his command post in Rott, where Dutch Cota had once commanded inside the stone *gasthouse* across from the church of St. Antonius.[42]

For Gavin, this would be a mission unlike any other. "We had been hearing a great deal about the Huertgen Forest and the horrors of it," he wrote. When patrols brought word that the Germans had now withdrawn behind the Roer River, it was enough to make a man praise the heavens, but it did not change what lay in store for these Americans. The forest, Gavin wrote, "proved to be a monster, an ice-coated moloch, with an insatiable capacity for humans."[43]

From Vossenack, Gavin and his men walked down the Kall River Trail. Splintered and broken trees crowded around them. Underfoot, only a few patches of winter snow lingered, laying bare the forest's pine needle floor that now glistened damp and muddy. Gavin saw discarded equipment and wrecked tanks, some deep in the gorge where they had been shoved. Another sight stirred him more: "All along the sides of the trail there were many, many dead bodies, cadavers that had just emerged from the winter snow," he wrote. "Their gangrenous, broken, and torn bodies were rigid and grotesque, some of them with arms skyward, seemingly in supplication." Most of the dead wore the blood red Keystone badge of the 28th Infantry Division. When the sun began to set, the urge to leave this place seized Gavin: "it was an eerie scene, like something from the lower levels of Dante's *Inferno*."[44]

As Gavin's paratroopers reclaimed the forest, graves registration soldiers followed. Their job was a grim one: to collect, identify, and sort the dead. Somewhere in the forest, soldiers discovered some temporary graves containing American soldiers. The ebb and flow of combat had prevented burial of the corpses Gavin saw, but in the case of these Americans, German soldiers had hastily put them in the ground. Each man was probably buried in typical orderly German fashion, with a rifle stuck in the ground at the head of the grave by its bayonet, the deceased's dog tags hanging from the stock, and his helmet atop the rifle butt.[45]

At one of these makeshift graves, searchers found a dog tag hanging from a rifle that read, "Felmer Lonzo Lynn, serial number 34963373." The sound of shovels slicing into the ground rang against the trees. From the muck emerged a cold body, which graves registration men loaded onto a truck.[46]

Carrying its sad payload, the truck rumbled eastward. Its destination was a new American cemetery across the border in Belgium. On September 12, 1944, the 1st Infantry Division had liberated a spot a few miles east of Liege that officials thought ideal for a First Army burial ground: the flat, 57-acre spot crowned a low ridge overlooking a pastoral swath of Belgian countryside. On September 28, Henri-Chapelle opened as a temporary facility, but quickly became permanent as casualties from the Hürtgen Forest and the Bulge made it the largest American cemetery in Europe. The smell of death hung about the place.[47]

The truck carrying Pete's body was just one of dozens that arrived at Henri-Chapelle that winter, each loaded with stacks of corpses. When the truck rolled to a halt, workers moved the bodies to a receiving platform. Sometimes the bodies were frozen stiff. Other times, they were wet. It made for gruesome work as attendants from the 607th Quartermaster Graves Registration Company, which managed the cemetery, rifled through pockets, bags, and gear in search of ammunition and ordnance. Identification came next: a dog tag was the easiest way, but officials could also use the man's pay book, ID bracelet, immunization register, or theater ID card. When all other means failed, they checked fingerprints or compared teeth against dental records.[48] Clerks also prepared a Burial Report for each corpse. On its sterile form went a full description of the remains such as hair color, race, weight, height, clothing, and equipment. The form even had a place for cataloging missing body parts. If the clerk could determine it, he listed the cause of death.[49]

An attendant had no trouble identifying the body of Felmer Lonzo Lynn. His dog tags were present, along with a ring, watch, and a few other articles. Inside his mouth, they found a full upper and lower denture, which had been fashioned at Camp Fannin by a U.S. Army dentist. On the Burial Report, the clerk listed the cause of death as "GSW left side," and also noted that Lynn's left femur was broken.[50]

After removing overshoes for reuse and personal effects for return to the family, the body was ready for burial. Out in the cemetery, men wielded pneumatic jackhammers and drove backhoes to dig hundreds of graves in the frozen soil. Each grave was 5 feet deep, 2 feet wide, and 6½ feet long. One was prepared for Pete.[51]

At 2:00 P.M. on February 24, 1945, someone put Pete's dog tag in his mouth (the standard method of attaching tags to the body), wrapped him in a mattress cover, and lowered him into Plot Number SSS, Row Number 10, Grave Number 190. Another dog tag went on his marker. Twelve inches to his right they interred Charles W. Bradshaw; 12 inches to his left they buried Harry G. Menefee Jr. Pete had known neither of them, but he was not entirely among strangers. More than 600 Bloody

Pete's grave at Henri-Chapelle.
Source: Lynn Collection

Bucket men, including 202 from the 112th Infantry Regiment, eventually filled Henri-Chapelle's ranks. No other cemetery held more of Cota's soldiers.[52]

On March 14, after receiving an updated report from Europe, the War Department officially changed Pete's missing in action status to killed in action, and his date of death was listed as November 2, 1944. Then a typist in Washington composed a telegram addressed to a young wife in a little house in the shadow of a mill.[53]

While the terrible news wound its way from Europe to Washington, the third and final trimester of Ruth's pregnancy arrived. Ruth experienced the normal trials of carrying a baby at this stage, but her doctor declared the baby was healthy. Thus assured, Ruth occupied herself with Bobbie and Mickie and trying to find out something about Pete's whereabouts. On March 6, she heard from David Eubanks, the Cleveland County boy who had been with Pete in New Jersey. Eubanks had made it home safely, but he could only tell Ruth about their brief time together at Camp Kilmer. She also learned that Pete's regimental chaplain was in a German POW camp, so no information would be forthcoming from him. It was small comfort. "Nerves shot again didn't sleep any last nite," she wrote. "Its so hard to hear from other boys and not my own. Take care of him Lord wherever he is."[54]

A week later, the hard truth arrived. March 14, 1945, was a Wednesday. Just a year had passed since Pete had packed up and left for Fort Bragg and basic training at Camp Fannin. Now, with thermometers edging past 60 degrees and no rain to be seen, downtown Kings Mountain bustled with people going about their daily business. At the Western Union office, at 2:46 P.M., the telegram machine clacked again.[55]

A little after 4:00 P.M., a deliveryman left the Western Union office. He drove a short distance down Highway 29. Not far from the Southern Railway tracks, where Pete and Ruth had once strolled hand in hand, he turned left into Park Yarn village. The deliveryman then drove past Ted Wier's store, and past the mill where machinery whirred. Finally, the man parked in front of the Lynns'. He stepped onto the silent porch and knocked. It was around 4:30 P.M. When Ruth opened the door, she saw, for the second time in four months, a man on her doorstep with an official-looking telegram in hand. With a tip of his cap, he handed over the telegram and departed, and Ruth at last held in her hands exactly what she wanted, and the last thing she wanted: news about Pete. Heart pounding, she opened the envelope and read:

THE SECRETARY OF WAR DESIRES ME TO EXPRESS HIS DEEP REGRET THAT YOUR HUSBAND PFC LYNN FELMER L WAS KILLED IN ACTION IN GERMANY 02 NOV 44 HE HAD PREVIOUSLY BEEN REPORTED MISSING IN ACTION CONFIRMING LETTER FOLLOWS.[56]

Ruth was crushed. "Can't believe it," she wrote later that day. "It seems my world has really stopped now that I can't look for him back."[57]

The days that followed were a blur of tears, denial, visitors, letters, telegrams, and more tears. On March 19, a cloudy day that brought some light rain, the confirming letter from the War Department arrived but it offered nothing new. "Cried all morning," she wrote. "Mick & Bob are all that keep me going." Letters of sympathy from North Carolina senator Josiah W. Bailey and New York mayor William O'Dwyer appeared in her mailbox, but they were not very consoling.[58] She also heard from Gen. George C. Marshall, U.S. Army chief of staff, indirectly. "General Marshall extends his deep sympathy in your bereavement," the letter said. "Your husband fought valiantly in a supreme hour of his country's need. His memory will live in the grateful heart of a nation." It was a form letter, but she kept it.[59]

Local tributes came too, and she was moved by it. "Dear Editor, I think the Lions Club deserves all the publicity you can give them in the *Herald* for the beautiful floral tribute presented the families in memory of the boys killed for service," she wrote. "I know they didn't do it for any praise but it was a very wonderful thing to do and every family like myself and children can't express our thanks. And I know the other boys overseas will be glad to know of the fine things their friends are doing for the bereaved families of their buddies lost in action. Yours truly, Mrs. 'Pete' Lynn, Route 2, Kings Mountain."[60]

Given the outpouring of support, she also sent a thank-you note to the newspaper. "Words cannot express our appreciation for the many expressions of sympathy we have received since the news of the death of our husband and daddy in Germany," she wrote. "May God's greatest blessings rest on everyone. Mrs. F.L. (Pete) Lynn and children."[61]

Of more interest was a note from Col. Gustin Nelson, who Ruth remembered from the newspaper. He only had words of small comfort to offer. "Felmer was interred with full military honors in an American military cemetery in Belgium with the Protestant Chaplain officiating," he wrote. Nelson suggested Ruth write to the quartermaster general in Washington to ask the exact location of Pete's grave, and then closed with condolences. "I desire to extend to you my sincerest sympathy together with that of the officers and men of this organization in your hour of bereavement," he wrote. "Your husband served with distinction and was a credit to his family, the service, and the United States. He was a splendid soldier and was held in high regard by all members of this command. His loss is deeply felt by his many friends." Gustin did not add that he never knew Pete personally since he took command after Pete went missing in action.[62]

Seven long days later, Ruth felt no better. "Been 1 week since telegram came, <u>seems I['ve lived a year</u>. Everything seems so empty & useless," she wrote.[63] On March 22, Ruth received an answer to the letter and also a V-mail she had sent to Pete's company back when she only knew he was missing. Cpl. Albert J. Pesek, a clerk from Chicago, had served with Pete in Company B. He wrote his letter on March 8 from somewhere in Germany. "I was unable to answer the first letter as we over here were involved in quite a battle so I referred it to our personnel section where such matters are taken care of. Really I'm at a loss to say what did happen to Lynn only that he is missing," Pesek wrote. He either did not know the truth or was loath to say. "We were in the battle for <u>Schmidt</u> at the time and up until now I have received no other word of him. I trust that everything will turn out for the best though and that you will hear something of Lynn soon." In closing, Pesek added, "May God bless the two little girls and to you—thanks for bringing me the opportunity to answer your letter. Keep your chin up."[64] Ruth thought Al's letter was sweet, but it told her nothing. She distracted herself by making Easter dresses for the girls.[65]

There was one person who really understood what Ruth was going through. Next door, Nell Moss was deep in mourning herself. Lester had been killed in Germany on January 4 while fighting with the 44th Infantry Division. Those proud sunny days with camera in hand and Pete and Lester smiling now seemed so long ago. The two women naturally gravitated to each other in their grief and helped each other heal. "Nell came & we talked bout Less & Pete," Ruth told her diary. They also sought God's comfort and attended church together during Easter Week.[66]

All of this helped a little, but nothing could truly relax the grip of grief except for pushing through it. That was harder than anything Ruth ever did. "Sun shining today don't seem to be any sunshine for me any more—Petes name in casualty list in paper yesterday," she wrote on April 4. She found little solace in the proceeds of Pete's $10,000 life insurance policy, which arrived the same month. "Saturday went to town to have insurance check cashed," she wrote. "Wish I could give it all back and Pete come home." Soon after, she mailed her Social Security survivor's claim so she could start to draw those benefits too. In the back of her mind, she could probably still hear Pete saying, "If I Do get Bunked Off you will Have enuff to Do you and the Kids a while."[67]

If Ruth ever managed to get Pete out of her mind, reminders in the form of official correspondence would show up in her mailbox. Several came in April. "Got letter telling Pete was buried in Belgium," she wrote on April 3. "Seems Ill have to give up hope[.] Doesn't seem much use in going on." Yet go on she did, and followed Colonel Nelson's suggestion and wrote for details on the cemetery.[68]

Later that spring, Pete's Purple Heart arrived. It came with some certificates that were rolled up inside a tube addressed to Mrs. Evelyn R. H. Lynn, Route #2, Kings Mountain, North Carolina. One of the certificates was emblazoned with the seal of the United States and signed by the president himself. "He stands in the unbroken line of patriots who have dared to die that freedom might live, and grow, and increase its blessings," it read. "Freedom lives, and through it, he lives—in a way that humbles the undertakings of most men." Neither the beribboned medal nor the certificates impressed her. She stuffed all of it in an overseas bag and tossed it into a closet.[69]

Indeed, everything about the war held little interest now, but she could not ignore the sudden death of President Roosevelt. On April 12, the president died of a massive cerebral hemorrhage at his Warm Springs, Georgia retreat. The news shocked the country. Since 1933, Roosevelt had been as much a fixture in Washington as its monuments, but now he was gone. It was a sad event. "Thursday—no sleep again—felt bad all day—made trip to Dr. Bill everything O.K. so far—wt 152," she wrote that fateful day. "Pres. Roosevelt died today—about 4:30." Five hours later, the train bearing Roosevelt's coffin to Washington chugged slowly through Kings Mountain along the same tracks that had ferried Pete to war. Ignoring her now protruding belly, Ruth took the kids to see it. "Big Crowd," was her only comment.[70]

One event did staunch the tears, if only for a time. It was May 6, 1945, and new life was in the air. Rising at 5:30 A.M., Ruth began to feel something going on inside her. The time had come. When contractions started rolling, Ruth called for help. She wished desperately for Pete but had to make do with an aunt. The steadfast Dr. Bill Ramseur, assisted by a nurse named Daisy Heavner, came to Ruth's bedside as well. Everything went quickly and smoothly. At 11:15 A.M. a baby girl popped out, and Ruth was ready with a name. She had been thinking about it for months. Boy's names had come easily; after briefly considering William "Buddy" Charles after Pete's grandfather, she decided to name him after his "daddy Pete." Her intentions did not change when a girl appeared, and another girl certainly would not have disappointed Pete despite his joke the day before he died. Ruth named the baby Felma Ruth, or Petie for short. Friends and family converged on the house to welcome little Petie, and all agreed that the name was perfect and the baby was a beautiful blessing.[71]

Two days later, Germany surrendered. "V day in Germany," Ruth told her diary. It was hard to miss the irony: Pete's namesake arrived when the European war ended.[72]

It took a couple of weeks for Ruth to recover physically from her third delivery. A little emotional healing transpired too, thanks to little Petie. Ruth cast her love on the little girl and, as visitors streamed to the little house and cards from well-wishers arrived, Ruth slowly started to pick up the pieces of her life. Soon she felt good enough to bake a cake, do a little house work, and take Petie to Macedonia church. "Sure looked sweet in pink cap, sweater & booties to match," she wrote. "Had a house full of company after dinner." At times life almost felt normal, although Pete's death still hovered in the darkest recesses of her mind. Ruth and Nell talked about their plight often, sometimes for hours. Other times, when it was quiet, the memories crowded in. "Have had Pete on my mind so much think Ill go crazy," she wrote. "If he could just come home."[73]

Despite the progress, many hard days lay ahead. In the Pacific, the war still raged and reminded her of her own sacrifice. So did the white service flag that hung limply on their mill house. The flag now displayed a gold star instead of a blue one to signify a bereaved family. She had so many unanswered questions. "Just another day of thoughts of my soldier," she wrote. "Maybe sometime somewhere we'll understand & be together again."[74]

As summer's heat and humidity lowered on King's Mountain, Ruth began to lose weight, which prompted her doctor to write a prescription for her. If the medicine stabilized her weight, it did nothing to help her rest. On many nights she found herself tossing, turning, and staring wide-eyed at the ceiling as she endlessly hoped her soldier would come home. "Didn't sleep till about 3," she wrote one night. "Kept listening for someone's footsteps."[75]

Tough decisions also kept Ruth awake. She worried about being a single parent. "Hope I can raise all three of my girls," she wrote. She had to decide where to live. Typically mills did not provide housing for singles, but Park Yarn made an exception for the bereaved Lynn family. Mill officials told Ruth that she could stay as long as she wanted. It was a gracious offer, but too many memories stalked the little mill house. Ruth knew it would not do, so she started to consider alternatives. Maybe she could even manage to buy the house she and Pete had always dreamed about.[76]

Whether she was planning for the future or just puttering around the house, Ruth could not forget. Her own plight aside, Pete's fate bothered her more than anything. How did he die? Did he suffer? Where did it happen, and why? It was a mystery that haunted her, so she decided to find out everything she could. It would be a difficult quest. Neither her responsibilities nor her bank account would allow her to do more than rely on the U.S. Postal Service, but she knew she had to try, if only for the comfort it might bring. Her search started with Colonel Nelson. On April 15, Ruth wrote him another letter, but in this one she asked for details about Pete's death. Nelson replied quickly. "The company was then engaged in the vicinity of Kommerscheidt, Germany in the Hurtgen Forest," he explained. "A counter-attack of the enemy drove the Americans back and a checkup showed your husband missing. The ground was not retaken until about the 24th of February 1945 and by another unit of the First Army. At that time your husband's body was found in a temporary grave placed there by the Germans. Identification tags were found on the body as was a ring, watch, and various other articles which have been forwarded to you." Nelson went on to tell Ruth about his death. "An examination of your husband's body indicated that he had been instantly killed by a bullet which penetrated his left side."[77]

The letter provided some answers at least. "Got letter with details of my darling's death & burial," she wrote. "Don't know how but I have to keep up for the kids." Later that summer, Ruth finally received a response from Washington about Pete's burial spot. The quartermaster general confirmed that Pete was interred in U.S. Military Cemetery #1, Henri-Chapelle, Belgium.[78]

Ruth hurt more when she saw war veterans come home that summer and fall while her own soldier did not. The July 20 return to the states of the 44th Infantry Division made her especially melancholy because they arrived in New York harbor aboard the *Queen Elizabeth*. "This is one my soldier went over on—wish he were back on it," she wrote. "Ole Park Yarn wouldn't hold me." Nell Moss certainly shared those feelings since the 44th was Lester's old unit.[79] Meanwhile, local servicemen came home too. Among them was Mae's husband Smitty, who arrived in September 1945 after mustering out of the navy. In his case, Ruth and the whole family was glad to see him safe and sound.[80]

The unkindest cut of all came in a nondescript package. It appeared in Ruth's mailbox on August 13, a year and two days since a train had whisked Pete away. On the outside of the box was the return address of the Army Effects Bureau: 601 Hardesty Avenue, Kansas City, Missouri. Within that twelve-story concrete monolith, 900 miles away from Kings Mountain, workers sorted the effects of the war dead. A conveyer belt carried containers from floor to floor and station to station, where inspectors removed classified documents, pornography, ammunition, and anything else that "you would not want returned to your family if *you* were the soldier." Sometimes the job required grinding stones and dentist drills to remove corrosion and blood stains from helmets and clothing. At the end of the assembly line, each container was labeled with an inventory and then typists sent as many as 70,000 letters a month to the next of kin.[81]

Ruth was expecting the package because she had received one of those letters. Her husband's property, "consisting of a few small items," was on its way, it read. "I regret the circumstances prompting this letter," the typist added, "and wish to express my sympathy in the loss of your husband."[82] Advance notice did not make it any easier when she opened the package and saw the few things Pete had left behind: a ring, the Remington wristwatch Bill had given him (minus the band), the New Testament he had received in Luxembourg, and a billfold. Nothing else.[83]

On closer examination, Ruth realized that the billfold was not Pete's. For one thing, she had Pete's personal wallet—a brown leather billfold that bore in gold letters the words "Felmer Lynn"—in her possession. She also found some information in the returned wallet that proved it was not Pete's, and gathered from a photo and other information that it was the property of Pvt. Ernest Potts, a black man from Alabama. She put the billfold back in the box and returned it to Hardesty Avenue, and asked "if by some chance the billfolds were mixed and I got the wrong one." Later, the army assured her that they had nothing else.[84]

So her quest went on, but hit several dead ends. On November 22, she wrote First Army headquarters and asked for the addresses of men who had served with Pete. Lt. J. L. Closson explained that the 28th Infantry Division was at Camp Shelby, Mississippi, so he forwarded her letter there. A staff officer at Camp Shelby then informed her that the 112th Infantry had already been deactivated and its records had been sent to Washington, DC.[85]

Undeterred, Ruth tried a different tack. She sent a letter to the 28th Infantry Division seeking information about the Hürtgen Forest battles. Although the division was about to deactivate, a personnel department sergeant replied. He warned, "I am afraid that I will be of very little use to you in this matter" because he had not been with Company B at the time and added, a bit insensitively, that "all the men of B Co. who were with the Co. at the time are all happy civilians now." All he could offer were some details from Company B's morning report for November 2 and a booklet on the division. He also suggested that she write the commanding general and request a copy of *Historical and Pictorial Review of the 28th Infantry Division in World War II*, but Ruth had to wait until it was published the following year.[86]

Try as she might, Ruth could learn no more, and the terrible year of 1945 drew to a close. "Sat up alone and wondered what the new year held for us," she wrote on New Year's Eve. "Very lonely, heart awfully heavy to think I have to face it alone."[87]

Bottom fell out.

CHAPTER 10

Home Before Thanksgiving

ON NEW YEAR'S DAY, 1946, RUTH LYNN OPENED HER DIARY AND TOOK a pen in her hand. "All hope gone!" she wrote, but in truth there was some hope budding. An old dream had returned, a dream that gave her something to cling to. "What a way to start a new year. I[']ll sure need help to keep from being bitter sure hope I find a house soon."[1]

Bobbie, Petie, and Mickie, about 1947
Source: Lynn Collection

Dreams of home ownership aside, her desire to find out more about Pete's death was still undiminished. Looking for any clues, she clipped articles that mentioned fallen soldiers from neighboring communities who had served in Pete's regiment or had trained at Camp Fannin. Fresh inspiration came when she saw photos of Pete's grave. A friend's son, Blaine Eaker, was in the service and drove ninety miles out of his way to Henri-Chapelle to snap some pictures before he came home.[2] The sight of Pete's cross, surrounded by row after row of graves on a bleak plain, was at once comforting and dismaying. "Dreamed of my soldier last night again, he's on my mind always, keep wishing & praying I'd hear from him," she wrote.[3]

Ruth fired off yet another letter to Washington. The adjutant general's department replied that it had no further information about Pete's death, but did supply the emergency addresses for three men in Pete's company as well as for Colonel Nelson and Capt. Alan Madden.[4] Since she had already connected with Colonel Nelson twice, Ruth tried the regimental chaplain. Her first letter to Captain Madden, written on Valentine's Day 1946, was opened by Mrs. Mary Madden, Madden's mother and his emergency contact, in a quiet residential section of Pittsburgh not far from the Monongahela River.[5]

In Mary Madden, Ruth found both a counselor and someone to emulate. Mary's husband had died when she was forty-three. In the three decades since, Mrs. Madden had not dated anyone. Her only goal, she told Ruth, had been "to be a good mother to his children and mine and to look forward to the day when he and I would be reunited in a happy Eternity where all our faults and short comings would be obliterated and only love would remain," she wrote. By all accounts she had accomplished her goal, as her five sons and one daughter had grown into successful adults. Mrs. Madden was sure that Ruth could follow that same formula. "Now my dear, dear Ruth my heart goes out to you on this the 12th anniversary of your wedding," she wrote. "So it will be with you, my dear, with God's help."[6]

These words resonated with Ruth. So began an on-again off-again correspondence between Ruth and seventy-two-year-old Mary Madden. Mrs. Madden also passed along her son's contact information, and told

Ruth what to expect. "You understand he has received hundreds of letters similar to yours; those seeking news of their loved ones," she wrote. "He told me he always writes if he can recall anything about the soldier that would interest their loved ones." Mrs. Madden also encouraged Ruth to take better care of herself since Ruth had admitted she was not eating much. "'You can't make the car go without gas,'" she cajoled. It would not be the last time that "Mother Madden" offered Ruth advice.[7]

Ruth meanwhile wrote and mailed a letter to the chaplain and, as Mary predicted, her son answered in short order. Forty-year-old Father Alan P. J. Madden had seen a lot since November 1944. Wounded and captured during the Battle of the Bulge, he persuaded some Germans to allow a convoy of wounded troops pass to safety before escaping himself. His freedom did not last long, however. Madden was recaptured and spent Christmas traveling east in a boxcar. After a stint in a German prisoner of war (POW) camp, he emerged to receive a Purple Heart, Bronze Star, and Silver Star, but his experiences in the Hürtgen and the Bulge haunted him for the rest of his life. As he later put it, frequent, close contact with death was not easy to take. Sometimes, in the dark of night, he would pray the rosary aloud in his sleep, as if a dying soldier lay beside him. Other times, he would wake up screaming.[8]

Father Madden gave Ruth the most detailed glimpse of the Hürtgen Forest she ever got. It was a snapshot of hell. His story began when the 1st Battalion's aid station, which Madden accompanied, moved up from Germeter. (This was after Company B hit German defenses in the wooded draw near Vossenack.) "As we passed through forests and captured pillboxes, we had some casualties from enemy artillery," he wrote. After pausing in Vossenack on November 4, Madden and the medics "continued to push cross-country. It was heavily wooded and hilly country," he explained, so rough that Weasels could not follow. Eventually, the men reached Kommerscheidt, which Madden described as "a cluster of houses on top of a steep hill," and "the town of Schmidt was in full view."[9]

In Kommerscheidt, the aid men cared for a flood of casualties and suffered some of their own as German artillery exploded about them. Only two of the 1st Battalion's thirty-three medics would eventually make it out of the forest. Forced to relocate as the battle worsened, the aid station moved "to a heavily wooded ravine between Kommerscheidt and Vossenack," where it joined forces with 3rd Battalion medics. Here, alongside the Kall Trail, Madden watched helplessly as wounded men died and German forces surrounded them. "The next few days I wish I could forget," he told Ruth. "The Germans controlled the road to our rear and would not permit us to evacuate our wounded. Aside from this one point, the Germans I saw and talked to were good soldiers, very considerate of our wounded. They directed our wounded to our Aid Station and several times carried our men there." Eventually, the Germans allowed the Americans to evacuate their wounded and all medical personnel except for two medical officers, a Protestant Chaplain, and Madden, although a few days later the four men escaped. (Madden's Silver Star was awarded for his fearlessness while ministering to and evacuating the wounded in the midst of heavy enemy fire.)[10]

Madden could only speculate on Pete's fate. "In your letter, Mrs. Lynn, you state that Felmer was reported missing 2 November. The situation was so confused that he might well have been fighting several days after that date," he mused. "Since his grave was found near Kommerschied I think that is what happened." Madden added that the area was not recaptured from the enemy for several months. "This explains why your husband was buried by the Germans," he wrote.[11]

Madden then reverted to his ministerial persona. "As a consoling thought, Mrs. Lynn, I would say that our men in combat lived good lives—even holy lives," he assured Ruth. "The men of the Infantry knew their life expectancy was short, and they lived good lives. Felmer, I am sure, was well prepared to meet God. Tell your little girls to hold their heads high for their father was a good man. His outfit was the best in the Army." He closed with words of encouragement. "For yourself, Mrs. Lynn, I know that the fighting of life's battles without the aid, comfort, and companionship of your husband is hard. I know that the Blessed Mother and her Divine Son will help you carry the heavy burden placed on your shoulders."[12]

For Ruth, this was the most welcome letter yet. It brought her closer to the truth, even though Madden probably did not know Pete. She also noticed that Madden mentioned a protestant chaplain; maybe he did know Pete, so she wrote Madden back to ask about him. Madden identified the protestant chaplain as Rev. Ralph E. Maness. Madden and Maness were close, having endured a German POW camp together until their liberation on April 6. "I saw Ralph last about a week later," Madden wrote. "He was seated in a truck waiting to be driven to the ship. I was staying behind for I was trying to return to the Regiment. I said to Ralph as we shook hands: 'We have been through a lot together.' He said, 'We certainly have, Father.' I have not seen him since."[13]

Ruth wasted no time tracking down Reverend Maness. She found him serving as interim pastor of First Baptist Church in Springfield, Missouri. Now thirty-seven-years-old and a father to three daughters, Maness was a graduate of both Bolivar College and Central Baptist Theological Seminary. After serving at Baptist churches in Missouri, he had traded his three-piece suit for fatigues. Maness answered Ruth's letter with sympathy. "As you already know I was with the 112th Infantry during their first five months of combat and preached a number of times to the fellows of the First Battalion though they were not my primary responsibility as I worked most of the time with the Third Battalion," he replied. "I did conduct nearly all of their Protestant services during those five months of combat and the name 'Pete' sounds quite familiar to me." Maness also assured Ruth, "The fellows attended church in a fine fashion during those months and a great many of them made profession of faith in Christ; in fact I think nearly all of them did who had not already done so." Ruth could be confident, Maness assured her, that Pete died a Christian.[14]

Washington had new information too. About the same time, Ruth received a letter from a Colonel Carle in the adjutant general's office who explained how Lynn "and other members of his organization departed on a mission to Kommerscheid, Germany, to set up road blocks." Ruth never learned that Carle's statement was inaccurate, but Carle did write truthfully when he added that these soldiers encountered enemy forces near Vossenack, Germany, after which Lynn was reported missing. "A later report received from the same source stated that he was killed in action, the same day he was previously reported missing," the colonel wrote. "Additional information has now been received which confirms these reports and shows he was killed by enemy small arms fire."[15]

These new details about her husband's life and fate, however sparse and incorrect, brought a sense of closure. She finally thought she knew enough. Satisfied, she tucked Pete's letters and memorabilia in his overseas bag and put it in a closet. Time helped too. As 1946 passed, the days got just a little easier, the grief a little more distant. Between work and caring for the girls, her days filled with activity and thoughts of the future began to crowd out pangs of the past. "I wonder what the year holds," she told her diary on New Year's Day, 1947. Her dream of home ownership now burned brighter than ever, although it still seemed no closer. She was still living at her dad's farm, where she had been since vacating Park Yarn the previous spring, but she continued to see that arrangement as temporary. "I'm praying that this year will mean a home for us," she wrote.[16]

❦

As it turned out Ruth did not get a new home in 1947, but something that helped her heal did happen: Pete Lynn came home.

Already Pete had been the subject of some action at Henri-Chapelle. In December 1946, someone noticed that his marker was incorrect and updated it to reflect his proper rank of private first class.[17] Once the marker was fixed, officials sent Ruth a photo of Pete's grave, thus adding to the photographic record Blaine Eaker had started. "It is my sincere hope that you may gain some solace from this view of the surroundings in which your loved one rests," wrote Brig. Gen. George A. Horkan. "As you can see, this is a piece of simple dignity, neat and well cared for." Horkan added that Henri-Chapelle was still considered a temporary resting place for Pete until final disposition was arranged.[18]

Horkan was right. The U.S. government had long envisioned that its war dead would be buried permanently in a place their next of kin selected, whether overseas or in the United States. Ruth knew this too after reading and clipping a February 1945 newspaper article about a bill before Congress. According to the bill, relatives could choose the final disposition of their loved one. The bill passed in 1946. The approved program would ultimately take six years and see more than 170,000 bodies returned to the United States at a cost of $200 million.[19]

After reading the article, Ruth heard little else about the program until March 14, 1947, when a letter from quartermaster general Maj. Gen. Thomas B. Larkin arrived in her mailbox. It was just one of the form letters mailed to the next of kin of all men buried overseas. "The people of the United States," Larkin wrote, "through the Congress have authorized the disinterment and final burial of the heroic dead of World War II." Quartermaster Form 345, "Request for Disposition of Remains," accompanied the letter. It gave Ruth the choice of leaving Pete in a permanent American military cemetery overseas, bringing him to the states for burial in a national cemetery, or bringing him home for burial in a private cemetery. For Ruth, it was an easy choice. It took her barely a week to fill out the form, have it notarized, and mail it back: she wanted Pete laid to rest in Mountain Rest Cemetery in Kings Mountain.[20]

It took the U.S. government a while to follow Ruth's instructions due to a series of unfortunate delays. Red tape was part of the problem; with the peacetime reduction of the military complex, there were not enough clerks to expedite paperwork. Meanwhile, a shortage of steel for caskets developed. A postwar boom in consumer demand for things like refrigerators and automobiles was partially at fault, along with strikes in steel mills and coal fields. The summer passed before anyone took action on Ruth's directive.[21]

But events were moving, and Ruth knew it: officials planned to start shipping the dead home from European cemeteries, and the process would start in July at Henri-Chapelle. The day arrived, and afterward Ruth read an article that described nearly 5,000 Belgian citizens descending on the cemetery by bus, bicycle, and foot. Dignitaries came to mark the day too, including representatives of the Belgian government, the American ambassador to Belgium, and Lt. Gen. Clarence R. Huebner, deputy commander in chief, Europe. Bands played and a picked honor guard from the U.S. Army, the Belgian army, and the mounted Belgian police stood at silent attention as disinterments began.[22]

On September 8, the sound of shovels slicing into damp sod rang across the flat landscape of Henri-Chapelle. One turned dirt from Grave 190, Row 10, Plot Number SSS, where diggers gently removed the remains of Felmer Lonzo Lynn by hand. A worker named Harris D. Nelson took charge, starting with the marker at the head of the grave. He copied its inscription on a form, removed the ID tag, and then discarded the marker for burning. Turning to the remains, he found Pete still in his uniform and wrapped in a mattress cover. He verified Pete's identity by his dog tag and his full upper and lower denture, noted that Pete's left femur was fractured, and then escorted the remains to the cemetery's morgue. There the body underwent further preparation; his clothing was removed and burned, and deodorants and embalming chemicals were sprayed on the decomposing corpse. Next, Nelson wrapped Pete in a new blanket, covered him with a sheet, and placed him carefully in a brand new, 200-pound metal casket lined with rayon satin. Nelson pinned one of Pete's dog tags to the blanket, wired the other to the end of the casket, verified the shipping address, and sealed the casket. A clerk named Charles E. Heckler took it from there. He put the casket in a shipping container and stenciled on the outside Pete's name, serial number, rank, company, and unit along with Ruth's name and address.[23]

With that, Pete Lynn was ready to start for home. He departed Henri-Chappelle the same way he had arrived: the next day, workers loaded the casket onto a truck, which Sgt. Lupe J. Velenzuela drove to Antwerp by way of Liege. Five days later, the truck rolled to a stop at Port Pier 140 on the Barge Fluviale. There the casket sat dockside for a month as more bodies were collected in warehouses throughout Europe at ports like Cherbourg and Cardiff.[24]

At last, all was ready. Sailing day was set for October 4, and it would be marked by a solemn ceremony. That morning, the rising sun revealed Antwerp draped with flags and 5,000 Belgians crowding into the city's 400-year-old Grand Plaza. In the center of the square sat a single, flag-draped casket holding an unidentified GI who had died defending Belgium. Chaplains of different faiths offered prayers, and then speakers paid homage to the dead.

We see around us a troubled world. We have not yet found the lasting peace for which we fought for and for which these men died in their youth.

The bells of Notre-Dame Cathedral pealed. As speakers quieted and laid wreaths at the foot of the catafalque, an infantry squad fired three volleys and a bugler sounded "Taps." With precise movements and clicking heels, military pallbearers lifted the single casket onto a caisson. Flanked by an American and Belgian guard of honor and trailed by officials of the two countries, the caisson slowly made its way to a pier on the Scheldt. Bands played the national anthems of America and Belgium while overhead twenty-four American Thunderbolts roared past.[25]

The procession halted at the dock where the USAT *Joseph V. Connolly* was tied up. Named for the late president of King Features Syndicate and the International News Service, the *Connolly* was a Liberty ship that displaced 7,176 tons. With its hull freshly painted in white and purple and its decks blanketed from stem to stern with flowers, the *Connolly* shone in the autumn sun. Her ensign fluttered at half-staff.[26]

By the thousands, people packed onto the pier while others lined the banks of the Scheldt. They watched silently as a crane lowered the honored casket into the ship's holds. It joined 5,598 other caskets, 202 of which held North Carolinians, including Pete Lynn. Then the *Joseph V. Connolly* gathered steam and slipped its moors. With the push and pull of a few tug boats and the destroyer *USS Vesole* riding escort, the Liberty ship sailed down the estuary. Burdened with its sad cargo, the ghost ship disappeared into the Atlantic.[27]

———

At 8:25 P.M. on Saturday, October 24, the *Joseph V. Connolly* reappeared off Lightship *Ambrose*. New York Harbor's main shipping channel was at hand.[28] Six hundred additional caskets, picked up in Newfoundland, now rode in the *Connolly*'s holds. Following army tradition, each dead man was listed on the ship's manifest as a passenger, but the word "Deceased" appeared after each name, including Pete's.[29]

The next morning, the ghost ship began its run into port under a cloudless sky. A reporter watched as the ship "broke through the haze outside the Narrows at 9 A.M., a shadowy hulk all gray and tank, with a funeral wreath at her forepeak." On the *Connolly*'s deck waited a single flag-draped coffin flanked by a knot of men. Two flower-laden destroyers, the *USS Bristol* and *USS Beatty*, and the Coast Guard cutter *Spencer*, all "gleaming white" in the sunshine, rode alongside. Fireboats and sundry other vessels skittered about. Just beyond West Bank Light, the formation stopped on the glittering waters. Sailors aboard the destroyers lined the rails at rapt attention. At 9:15 A.M. the *Connolly*, its ensign still at half mast, started at a deliberate ten knots.[30]

Her screws churning the brackish harbor waters, the *Connolly* followed the same path Pete had sailed three years before, but in reverse: through the Narrows, past the Statue of Liberty, between Governor's Island and Ellis Island, and up the Hudson. More ships joined the procession, including the mighty battleship *USS Missouri*. It thundered a 16-inch gun salute whose sounds echoed off the tall gray towers of the city. A flight of fighter planes roared overhead and then banked away. When the "Sabbath stillness" returned, a man on the *Bristol*'s fantail raised his bugle and played "Church Call."[31]

The *Connolly* tied up at Pier 61, at the mouth of West Twenty-first Street in Chelsea, just short of where Pete had boarded the *Queen Elizabeth*. Thousands of GIs had departed for the war from this very pier. Now thousands returned. With the tall towers of Manhattan looming in the background, clergy from multiple faiths offered prayers. A bugler played "Taps." Somebody read the Twenty-Third Psalm. Onlookers stood silently, bareheaded, heads bowed. On the pier, a sailor spotted some fading and painted-over signs. "Welcome Home" and "Well Done," the signs read. The sailor nodded at the dead. "They came in too late," he said. "There's something ironic in that."[32]

The autumn day warmed. As the heat increased, a summer-like haze wimpled the city. At 12:45 P.M., workers unloaded the lone casket from the deck of the *Connolly*. Inside lay the remains of an unnamed Medal of Honor recipient killed in the Battle of the Bulge. He would represent Pete and the rest of the fallen. Pallbearers from each branch of the military placed the heavy casket on a caisson hitched to an armored car. A bugle sounded, and 6,000 city officials, veterans, and military personnel—General Eisenhower among them—fell in behind the car. Slowly they marched. Mounted police led the column east to the intersection of West Twenty-third Street and Fifth Avenue. Here they paused while Pete's erstwhile army commander, Courtney Hodges, who was also marching, placed a wreath at the Eternal Light Monument in Madison Square Park. Erected in 1923, the monument commemorated the return of American troops from World

War I. The parade lurched into motion again, and snaked up Fifth Avenue. The Victory Parade marking the end of World War II had followed this exact route, but the cheers and ticker tape were long gone. Now there were just muffled drums beating a slow cadence. From the sidewalks, more than 400,000 New Yorkers watched quietly. Many cried.[33]

The parade stopped at Central Park, where another 150,000 people spilled across the grass. They descended on the Sheep Meadow. There were two minutes of silence. Then, artillery from West Point fired a salute, a military band played a dirge called "Dolore," eight pallbearers set the coffin on a catafalque draped in purple and black, and the band played the national anthem. Prayers and tributes followed, from chaplains, priests and clerics, and from the mayor, the governor, the American Legion, and the secretary of the army. A firing squad loosed one last volley, a drummer beat a slow roll, a bugler blew "Taps," dignitaries placed wreaths, and then the coffin was escorted back to the *Connolly*.[34]

The next day, the ghost ship dropped down the Hudson and docked at the Brooklyn Army Terminal, the country's largest military supply base. After another short service, hatless longshoremen in blue dungarees scurried aboard the *Connolly* and began offloading each walnut-stained coffin. While MPs on the pier stood ramrod straight, the longshoremen wrestled the caskets onto a special sling, two at a time. As a crane lifted the caskets from the ship to the dock, and workers sorted and stacked them in large storage sheds, handlers took special care to leave the American flags draped on each casket undisturbed. Workers then loaded the caskets on mortuary cars, each with windows shaded against prying eyes, doors chained shut, and the words UNITED STATES ARMY TRANSPORTATION CORPS stenciled on the side. Under the protective gaze of more MPs, locomotives pulled the cars through rail yards to the adjacent Bush Terminal, a huge warehouse and shipping complex. Here more stevedores rolled the mortuary cars onto tracked car floats, which little tugboats, their American flags snapping in the wind, pushed across New York Harbor, throwing a wake of white spume. The floats tied up at a Pennsylvania Railroad hub in Greenville, New Jersey, where the cars were sorted for trips to army distribution centers across the country.[35]

The train carrying Pete Lynn departed in a din of blowing whistles and creaking wheels. From Jersey, the cars swayed south past Baltimore, Washington, Richmond, Raleigh, and a dozen other places Pete had once seen from a train window.[36] People noticed as these funeral cars filled America's railways. Full fare had been paid for each casualty, and their names appeared on each train's passenger manifest. Here and there, civilians saw the cars and removed their hats. In one midwestern town, civilians saw a casket and wondered if the project was too expensive for taxpayers, or if the homecoming would be too hard on the families. "Why bring him home?" they said.[37]

At 11:30 A.M. on Sunday, November 2, 1947, a locomotive pulling six Pullman funeral cars slowed to a halt at the Charlotte railroad depot.[38]

Exactly three years had passed since Pete Lynn disappeared in the Hürtgen Forest.

Stevedores emerged from the depot, which for all the world looked like a Spanish mission. They wrestled the caskets off the train and then transported them to the Charlotte Quartermaster Depot, a massive facility with six warehouses sprawled across 72 acres just north of downtown. At its peak, the depot had employed 2,500 civilians and 80 army officers who worked night and day to supply army posts in the Carolinas, Virginia, and West Virginia with everything from toothpicks to uniforms. Now that peace had returned the demands on the depot had abated, but with the arriving cargo a new task was about to claim the depot's 1 million square feet of storage space. A detachment of the Graves Registration Division, the Quartermaster Corps unit responsible for this grim work, placed Pete's casket and the others alongside those just in from the Pacific. Flag-covered and neatly arranged, the caskets now awaited paperwork and transportation.[39] "We hope to have them all home before Thanksgiving," said Lt. Col. Frederic W. Dennis, the depot's commanding officer.[40]

Ruth expected it. A week before, she received a telegram from the Quartermaster Depot asking her to confirm where Pete's remains should be delivered. (The telegram also advised her to contact a local "patriotic or veterans organization" if she wanted military honors for the funeral.) She answered that Pete's remains should be delivered to Sisk Funeral Home at 309 East King St, Kings Mountain.[41] She also knew, after reading the *Charlotte Observer*, roughly when Pete's remains would arrive. The *Observer* covered the *Joseph V. Connolly*'s arrival in New York City, and announced that the remains of the men on board were expected to arrive in Charlotte the following Sunday. The paper explained that another two weeks would pass before the bodies reached their final destinations. The *Observer* also published a list of the men on the ship, and there was Felmer Lonzo Lynn.[42]

Patience was not a virtue Ruth Lynn possessed in abundance. She pushed to get the wheels turning, probably with a visit or call to Sisk Funeral Home. Funeral home owner Sisk sprung into action. Late on the afternoon of November 10, he picked up the phone and called Colonel Dennis to ask about the status of Pete Lynn's remains. After checking his files, Dennis told Sisk that the body was scheduled to leave the depot on Thursday. An escort would accompany the casket. Dennis promised to send Sisk a telegram with the train's schedule.[43]

Colonel Dennis was an administrator who knew his business. Around 10:00 A.M. on November 13, workers loaded Pete's remains onto a westbound train. An hour later, the train sidled into the little Kings Mountain station, where Bill Lynn had given Pete a watch and Charlie and Ruth had blinked away tears. Now the station was quiet, devoid of tantaras. Pete Lynn's casket was loaded into a government car and driven away from the station.[44]

A uniformed, bemedaled escort wearing a black arm band rode with the casket, and looked out the car window at the Best Little City in the World. He was authorized to stay with the body for up to seventy-two hours, and he was supposed to be a man from the same branch, race, religion, and rank as the deceased.[45] Indeed, army S/Sgt. Linwood P. Comer did have much in common with Pete Lynn. He was white, a Christian, and hailed from nearby Tennessee. A veteran, he was even about the same age as Pete. Comer also had a tender heart, and escorting remains home affected him deeply. Echoes of those days found its way into poetry he wrote later in life. "My tears . . . they fell like rain!" he wrote. If only he could have told Ruth then what he learned later. "What can I say to you,

My Friend!" he would write one day. "As, now, I watch you weep; that you may Know and Understand . . . This Hour means Not defeat! . . . Your Cup will fill again!"[46]

It was a short drive from the station to the funeral home: right on Battleground, left on King. Ruth met the casket at the funeral home. The sight of that cold box was enough to remind Ruth of the life she used to have, of everything she had endured in the last three years: the draft notice. The letters back and forth to Camp Fannin. Pete's last leave home, a joyous time of love and laughter and smiles. Then he got back on the train, and the letters started flowing again, this time to and from Europe, and then the letters stopped. Finally, the dreaded telegrams announced that he was missing and then he was gone. Ever since, her life had been a slow beat of uncertainty, searing grief, and wondering how she could go on. But she had, and she had managed, somehow, to move on, but now suddenly Pete was here. "Met casket at funeral home. S/Sgt. Comer came along, Bronze casket nice as could be," she told her diary, as if the metal somehow made it better.[47]

Ruth and Sisk discussed plans for the funeral. When they finished, Ruth hesitated. She did not want to leave Pete's side, and if Sisk had allowed it she would have strapped the casket across her back and took it home. Her thoughts flittered to the home she dreamed of; "If I had a home so I could at least have the casket near one day," she said. It was all so unreal, and painful. "Everything seems so useless," she wrote. "All seems a dream making plans to rebury Pete's body. Words don't help a bit theres just an empty hurt." Charlie Lynn felt it too. He refused to believe that his son was inside that accursed box, and when the casket arrived he resolved to go to the funeral home and look inside. Nobody thought that was a good idea. Fortunately a sudden storm washed out his plans, and Charlie never did look.[48]

Two days later, everything was ready. November 16 was a Sunday, so the sharp-teethed machinery of Park Yarn and Margrace sat in silence while millhands and their families packed into Macedonia Baptist Church. Pete's casket, which funeral home attendants positioned beneath the pulpit, arrived an hour early so everyone could pay their last respects. At 3:00 P.M., the church doors swung open and Pete's family entered the

Pete's funeral tent
Source: Lynn Collection

sanctuary. Everyone stood as Ruth, Mickie, Bobbie, Petie, Pete's parents, brother, and sisters and Ruth's parents shuffled down the aisle. A galaxy of clergy, Bibles in hand, waited at the front of the church. There was Macedonia's pastor, the Rev. C. B. Bobbitt. He was flanked by four other local pastors. Pallbearers from Otis D. Green Post 155 of the American Legion in their Legion caps stood by.[49]

The service began. Sniffles and sobs sounded from the congregation. Thernodies rose from the choir loft: "Abide with Me," "Rock of Ages," and "Sometime, Somewhere We'll Understand." After one of the preachers said a prayer, a second minister read a Bible passage. On Reverend Bobbitt devolved the honor of delivering the eulogy.[50]

Once the service concluded, a line of cars with their headlights burning left the church and drove the short two miles to Mountain Rest Cemetery.

Other drivers pulled over as the procession passed. Arriving at the cemetery, they parked on the flatter, northern side and everyone gathered around a freshly dug hole. A tent had been erected to protect the family, and an abundance of flower arrangements surrounding a photo of Pete in uniform almost filled it whole. Clergymen said their final remarks. Sergeant Comer gave Ruth the American flag that had lain on Pete's casket. Just 20 feet away was the grave of Lester Moss.[51] Afterward came hugs, handshakes, and expressions of sympathy. Among the well-wishers were Blaine Eaker, the serviceman who had sent Ruth photos of Pete's grave.[52]

Afterward, Ruth thought the service was perfect. "Everything just right," she wrote. "Sgt. Comer as nice as could be." PFC Felmer Lonzo Lynn, Serial Number 34963373, Co. B, 112th Infantry Regiment, 28th Infantry Division, father, husband, friend, and Park Yarn card hand, was home at last.[53]

Epilogue

Wishing on a Star

Grandma Ruth died on September 23, 1993, without really knowing the truth about her husband's death.

For its part, the U.S. Army was satisfied that Pete died on November 2, 1944, in the wooded draw below Vossenack. Multiple reports in his Individual Deceased Personnel File, held by the army's Human Resource Command, underscore this. According to one of those reports, Pete was originally listed as missing in action from November 2, 1944, but then on March 14, 1945, "evidence considered sufficient to establish the fact of death" on November 2 was received "from a Commander in the European area." In 1946, Colonel Carle explained this to Ruth. "A later report received from the same source stated that he was killed in action, the same day he was previously reported missing," he wrote. "Additional information has now been received which confirms these reports and shows he was killed by enemy small arms fire."[1]

Ruth refused to believe any of this. She always suspected that the moment of Pete's death came when she had that terrible dream on the night of November 4 in Kings Mountain, which would have been early on November 5 in Germany. Daughter Petie Lynn Bass, who has spent a lifetime searching for information about the battle, agreed with her mother, especially since one report stated that her father's body was found near Kommerscheidt. "My search has been painful at times, as I have read of the horrors of the fighting in the Forest and knowing that my father died there," she said. "Many questions about my father's death will go unanswered."[2]

In many ways, Petie is right; it is impossible to say conclusively what happened that day. However, a close examination of the evidence still points to November 2 as the date of Pete Lynn's death. After-action interviews make it clear that Ralph Spaans died in the initial burst of enemy gunfire that sad day. Most likely, either the volley that struck Spaans or subsequent volleys were responsible for the demise of Lynn as well as Gregorio and Hardaway. However, in the confusion that followed, they were separated from the rest of the company. Nobody was sure what happened to those men. As a result, a company clerk simply listed them all as missing in action.[3] (According to one source, Spaans's body was found on the evening of November 2 at 6:30 P.M., but this information cannot be reconciled with contemporary reports.[4])

An absence of survivors from that action makes reconstructing that morning difficult. "No one is left to tell much about what happened there," said one combat historian.[5] Fortunately, we do know more about Pete's death. According to official reports, a bullet smashed into his left side and killed him instantly. The instant death diagnosis is questionable. The records do not state exactly where in his side the bullet lodged. They also do not state how the examiner arrived at this conclusion, but unless the bullet struck a vital spot immediate death was unlikely. During World War II, only one in four bullet wounds proved fatal, with wounds to the abdomen being the most dangerous. It is just as likely, if not more so, that Pete bled to death; exsanguination was very common on World War II battlefields. We also know that Pete suffered a broken left femur, but we do not know why. Many things could have caused it, either before or after he died, but if it occurred while he still lived the added trauma surely contributed to his death.[6]

If Pete did not die instantly, and if Pete was not wounded in the first volley, he surely froze in fear; after all, the high cyclic rate of a German machine gun, which sounded like a sheet being torn in two, was enough to make anybody freeze. The MG-42 fired 1,500 rounds a minute, and its impact was palpable. "It scared the holy hell out of us," one veteran recalled. "It was a vicious, wicked gun." Yet freezing was the worst thing a man could do. "Actually," one European Theater veteran once mused, "it's suicidal to stay in place where enemy fire can seek you out; the only real safety is in getting ahead and driving off the enemy." World War II statistics show that most men got hit while crouching, kneeling, or laying down instead of moving. So if Pete did indeed stop as gunfire exploded around him, flying shrapnel and bullets surely found him during the four-hour-long battle.[7]

Ruth at Pete's grave
Source: Lynn Collection

Is it possible that Pete Lynn lived through that frightening fire-fight? Perhaps. It is quite clear from contemporary reports that Pete never returned to his company, even though he had ample opportunity to do so since his comrades withdrew the short distance to Germeter and stayed there until November 5. Pete could have survived in the vale for minutes, hours, or even days, but was so desperately wounded or so close to German lines that he could not get away. It is also remotely possible that a confused Pete somehow made it to another American position, such as the 2nd Battalion's lodgment in Vossenack, but there is no record that Pete, Gregorio, or Hardaway reported to any other American unit. If these men did somehow manage that, they were surely swallowed up in the debacle that soon engulfed the 28th Infantry Division.

The most compelling evidence of all can be found in the timing of their burials at Henri-Chapelle. Again, the record shows conclusively that Spaans died on November 2. If Lynn, Hardaway, and Gregorio were buried on different days or in different places at Henri-Chapelle, then their bodies likely arrived at the cemetery in different trucks and different times than Spaans. That means their bodies would have come from different places on the battlefield, which suggests that they somehow managed to get away from where Spaans died. On the other hand, if they were buried close together at Henri-Chapelle, then it follows that they were found close together on the same battlefield, buried by German soldiers in the same place, collected by American forces at the same time, transported in the same truck, and arrived at Henri-Chapelle at the same time.

As it turns out, all four men were buried at Henri-Chapelle on the same day and in the same area of the cemetery. Ralph W. Spaans was buried there on February 24, 1945, in Plot SSS, Row 10, Grave 199. Johnny Gregorio died from a shell fragment wound to his head and was buried the same day right next to Spaans, in Grave 200. Guy Hardaway also died from a shell fragment striking his head and was also buried on February 24. His plot, RRR, was not quite as close as the others but he was in Grave 161, Row 9 and thus still in the vicinity. And Pete Lynn, as described earlier, was buried on the same day, in Plot SSS, and on the same row, in Grave 190.[8]

So, the most likely scenario is that thirty-four-year-old PFC Felmer Lonzo Lynn, serial number 34963373, died on November 2 before the German guns in the wooded draw below Vossenack, Germany. He also probably died alone, separated from his comrades, not far from where a German statue stands today that bears the inscription, *Soldiers Never Die Alone.*[9]

Whatever the exact date, he died in a battle that had been nothing short of a disaster. "In retrospect it was a battle that should not have been fought," wrote one American general. The 28th Division's role in the battle was the most suspect of all; it remained the army's worst division defeat of the entire war. Historians also roundly damn the battle. Carlo D'Este is one; he has called it "the most ineptly fought series of battles of the war in the West."[10]

After the bottom fell out, Ruth Lynn went on to live a good life.

Granted, it wasn't easy for her, especially in those days immediately after the war. She watched sadly as other men came home—the Allman twins, who survived a German prisoner of war (POW) camp, and Rob Pearson, who served in the navy, and Bill Shytle, who left for the war the same time Pete did. Seeing so many men return safely made her dream of Pete constantly and wish things were different. Sometimes, it seemed that remembering was all that was left, and for a long time she felt a hole in her heart. "The days stretch out in an endless emptiness, nothing to look forward too or care for but the babies," she wrote.[11]

Like Mrs. Madden, she never remarried. "There was never another man in her life," Petie Bass explained. "She said there was never anybody who could take his place. She never dated, never. She stayed with us. She was totally devoted to him and he to her."[12] Fortunately, Ruth was not entirely alone. There were other women dealing with the loss of their husbands. One was Nell Moss, whose husband Lester lies close to Pete. However, Nell chose a different path. She remarried in 1958, and by all accounts rebuilt her life successfully.[13]

With the closure Ruth found when Pete came home in 1947, she devoted herself to starting anew. In February 1948, she bought a house at 122 Dixon School Road. It was the house she and Pete had dreamed about. Although less than a mile from Park Yarn, it felt miles away from mill life. A modest 1,144 square feet in size, the house had a large covered porch in front and a big yard where the kids could play. She paid about $5,000 for the property, so she was able to use part of the proceeds of Pete's $10,000 life insurance policy to cover the cost.[14]

In that home of her dreams, Ruth focused entirely on her children. She made sure they never forgot their father. As the oldest child, Mickie had some memory of her father, but her recollections were vague. Bobbie had no recollection, and Petie of course never met him. That did not deter Ruth. She told her daughters about their father often. They remembered him in other ways too; on Father's Day, Ruth bought red, white, and blue flowers in his memory. There was even a constant reminder at Macedonia church, for after the war the church dedicated a mural in memory of Pete and the congregation's other veterans. Ruth also kept all of Pete's letters, memorabilia, and the correspondence from her research.[15]

Ruth Lynn
Source: Author's Collection

If the girls never got the chance to really know their father, they certainly knew the void he left behind. "We weren't the only ones," Petie Bass said. "I know of two other girls right off whose father was also killed. Of course, in school, there was always the question of my mother's name, father's name. My response was always, 'He was killed in the war.' Everyone was very nice about it. It was just difficult because you saw all the other kids in the neighborhood doing things with Dad, so it made it very difficult because you wondered what that would be like."[16]

Ruth worked hard to make ends meet. "Having to raise three children under 5 years old on her own without advanced education like we get now, she did the best she could," Petie wrote.[17] She worked in the mills for a few years after Pete's death, and then took a job in the cafeteria of Park Grace school. When it closed, she transferred to the Kings Mountain High School cafeteria. She spent the rest of her working years there, serving meals to young people.

Ruth's best turned out to be very good. Somehow, although she never made much money, she managed to give her kids everything they needed. At one point, she bought an old upright piano so the girls could learn to play. In a time when family vacations were not the norm, especially in a poor mill town, Ruth also arranged a few summer road trips. A 1954 vacation to visit Hazel and Vic, who were living in Florida at the time, was a particularly memorable event. Ruth also saw to it that her children were reared in church. She also kept close ties to Macedonia Baptist Church, which had supported her and Pete so well. When she briefly moved to another congregation while she lived at the farm with her parents, Ruth usually sent flowers to the church on Father's Day. After buying her house, she resumed regular attendance at Macedonia and remained a member until her death.[18]

Thanks to Ruth's hard work, her daughters went on to be successful. All three graduated from college. Petie Lynn, who became a pharmacist, married Norman Bass. Bobbie, who had a successful career as a nurse, married Steve Blake, whose father had been killed in the Philippines during the war. Mickie, who worked as both a teacher and a homemaker, married another Kings Mountain native, Buddy W. Connor. They had two children together, Chris and Laurie, before Mickie was stricken with bone cancer and died on August 19, 1977, at the age of thirty-six.

After Mickie's death, Grandma Ruth helped Buddy raise Chris and Laurie. She spent many hours with them during weekends and summer vacations. Ruth and Laurie were especially close, as Ruth became in many ways a second mother to Laurie. Sometimes at night, they would study the nighttime sky together. Ruth would tell Laurie that Mickie and Daddy Pete were the stars looking down on them, just as Alice Meaney had written in her poem, "Wishing on a Star."

As time passed, Kings Mountain changed before Ruth's eyes. Increasing competition in the textile industry, especially from overseas, gutted Kings Mountain's mills. Neisler Mills Inc. remained in operation until 1955, when the family sold out to another company. The following year, Neisler sold the village's houses to its occupants, including Pete's parents. Production at Margrace continued until the late 1970s. In 1984, the boarded-up facility was sold for salvage. Today, the mill's buildings are mostly gone, but fortunately many of the mill houses remain to mark the site. It is a place, a historian reported, that offers an "extraordinary survival of the village streetscape and the strong character of sameness and repetition that defined its original appearance and which retains its power in setting the Margrace village apart today." The story of Park Yarn is the same. That business was sold to other companies but ultimately failed as well. None of its houses have survived, including Pete and Ruth's little house, and little of the factory itself remains. Even Macedonia Baptist Church has not escaped change. The sanctuary was replaced in 1956, on a spot farther back from the road than the original building.[19]

In 1990, Ruth moved into a senior living village with the unfortunate name of Battle Forest. She lived there until her death, but passed almost every day with a smile on her face despite the hard times she had endured. "My mother had every reason in the world to be very bitter. She was never bitter," Petie later observed. "She never acted as though she thought it was wrong. She thought [Pete] did his duty. She was proud of him and believed in the cause of the war." The only thing that bothered her was seeing the country build memorials for the soldiers of Vietnam and Korea before a memorial was built to honor World War II servicemen.[20]

Through it all, there was one constant that had been present at the beginning around the little house, the mill, the mill village, and the town. That one thing was still there in the end. Pete Lynn loved his family and loved his country, and gave his all for both. Though the very bottom fell out of her world, Ruth carried on and loved her family each and every day. She planted seeds of love that remain in her family today. Among the clippings in Ruth's papers is an Elsie Robinson column about a grieving widow. "No matter what it costs, love's worth the price," Robinson wrote. "Only love heals the hurt that love can give. Only more love can fill love's empty place."[21]

Pete and Ruth Lynn paid a steep price, but filled the empty place with love and sacrifice. They were two of millions who helped change the world.

Notes

Introduction

1   Erna Risch and Charles L. Kieffer, *The Quartermaster Corps : Organization, Supply, and Services*. Vol. 2. *U.S. Army in World War II* (Washington, DC: Center of Military History, 1995), 402, 404; Ronald H. Bailey, *The Home Front : U.S.A.* (Alexandria, VA: Time-Life Books, 1997), 42. According to the National World War II Museum, 418,500 Americans died in the war. The war in Europe, in which Pete Lynn fought, cost the United States 586,628 casualties, including 135,576 dead. Weigley, *Eisenhower's Lieutenants : The Campaign of France and Germany, 1944–1945* (Bloomington and Indianapolis: Indiana University Press, 1981), 727; Rick Atkinson, *Guns at Last Light : The War in Western Europe, 1944–1945* (New York: Henry Holt and Company, 2013), 637.

2   Hugh Talmage Lefler and Albert Ray Newsome, *North Carolina : The History of a Southern State* (Chapel Hill: University of North Carolina Press, 1954), 623; Anita Price Davis and James M. Walker, *Images of America: Cleveland County in World War II* (Charleston, SC: Arcadia, 2005), 2, 4; Spencer Bidwell King, Jr., *Selective Service in North Carolina in World War II* (Chapel Hill: University of North Carolina Press, 1949), 321; *Kings Mountain Herald*, August 23, 1945. Only eight North Carolina counties contributed more men to the service than Cleveland County, which sent 6,500 men. About 11 percent of its population served.

3   David Stahel, *Operation Barbarossa and Germany's Defeat in the East* (Cambridge, MA: Cambridge University Press, 2009), 149 n. 54.

Chapter 1: I Love You Best of All

1   Mrs. Bobbie Blake, interview with the author, July 6, 2013; Mr. Robert C. Pearson, Interview with the author, November 15, 2015.

2   Mrs. Bobbie Blake, interview with the author, July 6, 2013. Bobbie Blake, Pete's daughter, remembers her father whistling to this day, although she remembers little else about her father. The Pinnacle was one of two peaks overlooking King's Mountain and the only one visible from the Lynns' house. The other peak is Crowder's Mountain.

3   U.S. Census for 1940, Kings Mountain, North Carolina ED 23-16A, http://1940census.archives.gov. The exact house number is in question. The number reported in the 1940 U.S. Census was number 57; the house number listed in Petie Lynn's 1945 baby book was number 16.

4   Pete Lynn to "Hi toots," May 28, 1944, Lynn Collection.

5   Jacquelyn Dowd Hall, James Leloudis, Robert Korstad, Mary Murphy, Lu Ann Jones, and Christopher B. Daly, *Like a Family: The Making of a Southern Cotton Mill World* (Chapel Hill and London: The University of North Carolina Press, 1987), 255.

6   Betty Hoyle Interview, May 20, 2012.

7   Mrs. Cornelia Moss Davis, telephone interview with the author, March 30, 2014. Mrs. Davis remarked on Ruth's sweet and caring personality.

8   Memories Scrapbook, Lynn Collection; *Alleghany News*, March 24, 2005.

9   Davyd Foard Hood, "Margrace Mill Village Historic District," National Register of Historic Places Nomination, North Carolina State Historic Preservation Office,

May 6, 2009 23–24; Davyd Foard Hood, "Southern Railway Overhead Bridge," National Register of Historic Places Nomination, North Carolina State Historic Preservation Office, April 19, 2007, 4. The rail line became part of the Southern Railway Company around the turn of the century. The line was double-tracked in 1919 between Charlotte and Spartanburg, South Carolina.

10   Tommy Tomlinson, "Kings Mountain," http://www.ourstate.com/articles/kings-mountain; Dave Baity, *Tracks Through Time: A History of the City of Kings Mountain, 1874–2005* (Charlotte, NC: Josten Books, for the Kings Mountain Historical Museum Foundation, 2005), 1–4, 6; Hood, "Margrace Mill Village Historic District," 23–24, 25. The town was called White Plains initially.

11   J. T. Anderson, *Industrial Directory and Reference Book of the State of North Carolina* (Durham, NC: Christian Printing Company, 1938), 769, 323. The town's first mill, the Kings Mountain Manufacturing Company, became known as "The Old Mill." *Kings Mountain Herald*, February 21, 1935.

12   Quoted in Hall et al., *Like a Family*, 144.

13   Mildred Gwin Barnwell, *Faces We See* (Gastonia, NC: Southern Combine Yarn Spinners Association, 1939), 11.

14   Tom Shytle, *Carolina Roots: From Whence I Came* (Privately published, 2008), 13, 41–42; Brent D. Glass, *The Textile Industry in North Carolina: A History* (Raleigh, NC: North Carolina Division of Archives and History, 1992), 30, 74; Hall et al., *Like a Family*, xvii, 31–32, 44.

15   *Kings Mountain Herald*, February 21, 1935.

16   Hall et al., *Like a Family*, 48; Hood, "Margrace Mill Village Historic District," 2, 3; Mr. Robert C. Pearson, Interview with the author, November 15, 2015.

17   Hall et al., *Like a Family*, 117.

18   Mr. Robert C. Pearson, Interview with the author, November 15, 2015.

19   Shytle, *Carolina Roots*, 62; George G. Suggs, Jr., *"My World Is Gone": Memories of Life in a Southern Cotton Mill Town* (Detroit, MI: Wayne State University Press, 2002), 47.

20   Hood, "Margrace Mill Village Historic District," 42; *Tracings: Schools and Schooling: A History of Black Schools and Cleveland County, Kings Mountain District, and Shelby City School Systems, 1800-1970*, vol. 1, series 4 (Shelby, NC: Westmoreland Printers, Inc., 2009), 37–38. The building closed in 1969 but the school system continued using it for several years, mostly as a maintenance facility.

21   Shytle, *Carolina Roots*, 60; Information from Petie Bass, February 5, 2011; and U.S. Census for 1940, Kings Mountain, North Carolina ED 23-16A, http://1940census.archives.gov.

22   Hall et al., *Like a Family*, 127. Park Grace did eventually become part of the Cleveland County School System and after 1962 the Kings Mountain School System.

23   Betty Hoyle Interview, May 20, 2012; Hall et al., *Like a Family*, 128–29; "How Textile Mills Worked," at http://www.historians.org/tl/LessonPlans/nc/Leloudis/factory.html.

24   Memories Scrapbook, Lynn Collection.

25   Hood, "Margrace Mill Village Historic District," 1, 22–27; Betty Hoyle Interview, May 20, 2012; *Kings Mountain Herald*, February 21, 1935; "Raising the Curtain on Neisler," reprinted from *Esso Oilways*, February 1945, in Letters to Service Men, Mauney Memorial

Library; Mildred Gwin Andrews, *The Men and the Mills: A History of the Southern Textile Industry* (Macon, GA: Mercer University Press, 1987), 268–70. The Margrace Mill Village Historical District is today on the National Register of Historic Places. Sources disagree on the date of completion but Hayne Neisler confirmed the year was 1919 in an e-mail to the author on June 5, 2013. The Patricia was built in 1920 and the Pauline around 1910. About 60 percent of the company's output was in upholstery and drapery fabrics, and the rest was in tablecloth, napkins, bedspreads, and some clothing material.

26 Betty Hoyle Interview, May 20, 2012; Hood, "Margrace Mill Village Historic District," 6, 13; Barnwell, *Faces We See*, 17.

27 Memories Scrapbook, Lynn Collection; "Johnston Mill," http://www.cmhpf.org/surveys&rjohnstonmill.htm; Gary Mock to the author, January 26, 2011, via e-mail; Record of Incorporations, Cleveland County, NC, 1888–1950, vol. 3, 85–86, North Carolina State Archives, Raleigh, NC; *Clark's Directory of Southern Textile Mills*, 19th ed. (Charlotte, NC: Clark Publishing Company, January 1, 1921); Anderson, *Industrial Directory and Reference Book of the State of North Carolina*, 323; Baity, *Tracks Through Time*, 8; *Kings Mountain Herald*, February 21, 1935; Hayne Neisler, e-mail to the author, June 5, 2013; Mr. Robert C. Pearson, Interview with the author, November 15, 2015. When Johnston (1861–1941) died, he ran thirteen mills in the Carolinas. Hayne Neisler stated that Park Yarn spun fine count cotton yarns.

28 Floor Plan, December 1926; "Specifications of Electric Wiring for Park Yarn Mills, Kings Mountain, NC, March 4, 1927," Gilman Paint & Varnish Co. to Mr. George Weber, January 7, 1927; R. C. Biberstein to R. H. Johnston, October 2, 1926; all in Biberstein, Bowles, Meacham & Reed Records, Special Collections, Atkins Library, UNC-Charlotte.

29 "How Textile Mills Worked," at http://www.historians.org/tl/LessonPlans/nc/Leloudis/factory.html; exhibit at North Carolina Museum of History, May 2012.

30 Floor Plan, December 1926; "Specifications of Electric Wiring for Park Yarn Mills, Kings Mountain, NC, March 4, 1927," Gilman Paint & Varnish Co. to Mr. George Weber, January 7, 1927 and R. C. Biberstein to R. H. Johnston, October 2, 1926, both in Biberstein, Bowles, Meacham & Reed Records, Special Collections, Atkins Library, UNC-Charlotte.

31 Mr. Robert C. Pearson, Interview with the author, November 15, 2015; Pete Lynn to "Hello Darling," September 29, 1944, Lynn Collection; U.S. Census for 1940, Kings Mountain, North Carolina ED 23-16A, http://1940.archives.gov; Hall et al., *Like a Family*, 69.

32 Quoted in Hall et al., *Like a Family*, 81–82.

33 Quoted in Hall et al., *Like a Family*, 82.

34 Mr. Robert C. Pearson, Interview with the author, November 15, 2015. Later, Pearson's family moved to a larger house near the church. A veteran of the U.S. Army Air Force, Pearson was drafted in 1944 but rejected when doctors at Fort Jackson, SC, diagnosed him with a perforated eardrum. "That perforated ear drum might have saved my life," he said.

35 "How Textile Mills Worked," at http://www.historians.org/tl/LessonPlans/nc/Leloudis/factory.html; Mr. Robert C. Pearson, Interview with the author, November 15, 2015.

36 Suggs, *My World Is Gone*, 47.

37 Quoted in Hall et al., *Like a Family*, 53.

38 David M. Kennedy, *Freedom from Fear: The American People in Depression and War, 1929–1945* (New York and Oxford: Oxford University Press, 1999), 40–41, 66–67.

39 Kennedy, *Freedom from Fear*, 89, 91.

40 Kennedy, *Freedom from Fear*, 163–64.

41 Kennedy, *Freedom from Fear*, 139–40.

42 Hall et al., *Like a Family*, 56, 77, 80, 195, 289–90; "How Textile Mills Worked," at http://www.historians.org/tl/LessonPlans/nc/Leloudis/factory.html.

43 Hall et al., *Like a Family*, 195, 77, 56, 80, 290; "How Textile Mills Worked," at http://www.historians.org/tl/LessonPlans/nc/Leloudis/factory.html; Kennedy, *Freedom from Fear*, 151, 181–82, 185, 215.

44 U.S. Census for 1940, Kings Mountain, North Carolina ED 23-16A, http://1940census.archives.gov.

45 Hall et al., *Like a Family*, 79, 298–99, 301; "How Textile Mills Worked," at http://www.historians.org/tl/LessonPlans/nc/Leloudis/factory.html.

46 Draft Registration Card of Felmer Lonzo Lynn, October 16, 1940, NA; U.S. Census for 1940, Kings Mountain, North Carolina ED 23-16A, http://1940census.archives.gov; Kennedy, *Freedom from Fear*, 321. Keller and his wife Julia lived at Park Yarn. He was sixty-five in 1940.

47 Hall et al., *Like a Family*, 302–3, 310.

48 The bedroom suit is still owned by the family.

49 Kennedy, *Freedom from Fear*, 276, 282.

50 Amity Shlaes, *The Forgotten Man: A New History of the Great Depression* (New York: Harper Perennial, 2007), 9.

51 Suggs, *My World Is Gone*, 47.

52 Kennedy, *Freedom from Fear*, 181–82, 185, 215, 295–96; Hall et al., *Like a Family*, 183, 299–300; Liston Pope, *Millhands and Preachers: A Study of Gastonia* (New Haven, CT: Yale University Press, 1942), 3.

53 Pete Lynn to "Hello Darling," July 7, 1944, Lynn Collection.

54 Quoted in Hall et al., *Like a Family*, 140.

55 Hall et al., *Like a Family*, 141–42.

56 Lake Junaluska Souvenir Folder, 1931, Lynn Collection.

57 Hall et al., *Like a Family*, 142–43, 255.

58 Ruth's sister Betty recalls that the Lynns owned a car. Betty Hoyle Interview, May 20, 2012. Daughter Petie Bass, however, states that the Lynns did not own a car until Bobbie turned sixteen. The Lynns relied on taxis or buses for transportation. The confusion likely is around timing.

59 Pete Lynn to "Hello Darling," April 21, 1944, Lynn Collection.

60 1932 Christmas Card, Lynn Collection.

61 Pete Lynn to "Hello Darling," April 21 and May 3, 1944, both in the Lynn Collection.

62 Pete Lynn to "My Dearst Darling," May 9, 1944, Lynn Collection.

63 Pete Lynn to "Hi toots," May 28, 1944, Lynn Collection.

64 Kennedy, *Freedom from Fear*, 165.

65   Memories Scrapbook, Lynn Collection; Cleveland County Marriage Register, 1870–1945, North Carolina State Archives, Raleigh, NC. Hotel details from the Sanborn Insurance Map of Kings Mountain, NC, for May 1919, http://web.lib.unc.edu/nc-maps/sanborn.php.

66   Hall et al., *Like a Family*, 143; Betty Hoyle Interview, May 20, 2012.

67   Pete Lynn to "Hi toots," May 28, 1944, Lynn Collection.

68   *Alleghany News*, March 24, 2005.

69   Hood, "Margrace Mill Village Historic District," 39; Glass, *Textile Industry in North Carolina*, 40, 42; Hall et al., *Like a Family*, 126. Mr. Robert C. Pearson provided the number of houses in the Park Yarn village, during an interview with the author, November 15, 2015.

70   Glass, *Textile Industry in North Carolina*, 40–42; Hood, "Margrace Mill Village Historic District," 2–3; Mrs. Cornelia Moss Davis, telephone interview with the author, March 30, 2014. The reference to plain weatherboard siding is based on the construction of houses at Margrace, which were likely similar.

71   Kennedy, *Freedom from Fear*, 160–62; Richard Lowitt and Maurine Beasley, *One Third of a Nation: Lorena Hickok Reports on the Great Depression* (Urbana and Chicago: University of Illinois Press, 1981), 176. Hickok added, "The best of the workers live in the mill villages, on company property. The mills feel a sense of responsibility toward them. They are the last to be laid off. And if the mills really want a workman, on full time, they will make room for him in the mill villages."

72   Pete Lynn to "My Dearst Wife and Babys," July 23, 1944, Lynn Collection; Mr. Robert C. Pearson, Interview with the author, November 15, 2015.

73   U.S. Census for 1940, Kings Mountain, North Carolina ED 23-16A, http://1940census.archives.gov.

74   Pete Lynn to "Hello Dear[e]st," April 9, 1944; Hood, "Margrace Mill Village Historic District," 39; Glass, *Textile Industry in North Carolina*, 40–42; Shytle, *Carolina Roots*, 21–22, 47, 50; Mr. Robert C. Pearson, Interview with the author, November 15, 2015; Mrs. Cornelia Moss Davis, telephone interview with the author, March 30, 2014. Detail on the telephone from the Betty Hoyle Interview, May 20, 2012, and Draft Registration Card of Felmer Lonzo Lynn, October 16, 1940, NA. Margrace mill homes did have bathrooms. See Hood, "Margrace Mill Village Historic District," 43.

75   Pete Lynn to "My Dearst Wife and Babys," April [May] 2, 1944, Lynn Collection. Ruth was indeed cold-natured, and Pete often teased her about it: "You know me, you always said I froze in the summer," she wrote. See Ruth Lynn to "Hi Hon," November 12, 1944, Lynn Collection.

76   Jennings J. Rhyne, *Some Southern Cotton Mill Workers and Their Villages* (Chapel Hill: The University of North Carolina Press, 1930), 16–17.

77   Shytle, *Carolina Roots*, 49; Mr. Robert C. Pearson, Interview with the author, November 15, 2015. Pearson differs with Shytle and recalled electricity only being available at night. It is likely that both men were right and just recalling different time periods.

78   Hall et al., *Like a Family*, 252, 258, 261; Pete Lynn to "Hello Dear," July 24 [2], 1944, Lynn Collection; http://www.lib.unc.edu/blogs/morton/index.php/2008/10/the-legendary-grady-cole/; *The State*, December 2, 1944; May 13, 1950. Cole was also on the air every weekday morning at 5:00 A.M.

79 Quoted in Hall et al., *Like a Family*, 146.

80 U.S. Census for 1940, Kings Mountain, North Carolina ED 23-15, http://1940census.archives.gov; Hall et al., *Like a Family*, 225.

81 Betty Hoyle Interview, May 20, 2012.

82 Betty Hoyle Interview, May 20, 2012; Hood, "Margrace Mill Village Historic District," 6, 13.

83 U.S. Census for 1940, Kings Mountain, North Carolina ED 23-15, http://1940census.archives.gov; Bill Lynn Interview, April 3, 2011. Ada was listed in the census as Flossie, but according to Petie Bass she always went by Ada.

84 *Kings Mountain Herald*, December 1, 1938.

85 Pete Lynn to "Hi Kid Sis," June 11, 1944, Lynn Collection; http://www.southcarolinaparks.com/kingsmountain.

86 Bill Lynn Interview, April 3, 2011; U.S. Census for 1940, Kings Mountain, North Carolina ED 23-15, http://1940census.archives.gov; Mr. Robert C. Pearson, Interview with the author, November 15, 2015. According to Pearson, one of the water towers held drinking water and the other was for the fire system. As for Pete's sisters, their married names were Lillian Lynn Mitchem, Eva Lynn Barrett, and Marene Lynn Stroupe.

87 Pete Lynn to "Hello Sweet Hart and Babys," April 28, 1944, Lynn Collection.

88 Betty Hoyle Interview, May 20, 2012.

89 Pete Lynn to "Hell[o] Dear," April? 1944, Lynn Collection.

90 Pete Lynn to "Hello Honey," June 2, 1944, Lynn Collection.

91 Betty Hoyle Interview, May 20, 2012; Mrs. Bobbie Blake, interview with the author, July 6, 2013.

92 Bill Lynn Interview, April 3, 2011; Ruth Lynn to "Dearest Love," September 15, 1944, Lynn Collection.

93 *Kings Mountain Herald*, February 28, 1935; Hood, "Margrace Mill Village Historic District," 42, 2, 4. The original Macedonia Baptist Church building was replaced in 1956.

94 Hall et al., *Like a Family*, 124–25; "How Textile Mills Worked," at http://www.historians.org/tl/LessonPlans/nc/Leloudis/factory.html.

95 Betty Hoyle Interview, May 20, 2012.

96 *Kings Mountain Herald*, March 21, 1935; March 28, 1935; July 25, 1935; February 20, 1936; February 11, 1937.

97 Hall et al., *Like a Family*, 129–30.

98 Suggs, *My World Is Gone*, 134.

99 Mrs. Cornelia Moss Davis, telephone interview with the author, March 30, 2014; Shytle, *Carolina Roots*, 21, 45–46, 59; Norma Hamrick Drewery to the author, February 23, 2011; Hood, "Margrace Mill Village Historic District," 42; Memories Scrapbook, Lynn Collection; U.S. Census for 1940, Kings Mountain, North Carolina ED 23-16A, http://1940census.archives.gov; Hall et al., *Like a Family*, 164; Mr. Robert C. Pearson, Interview with the author, November 15, 2015. According to the 1940 Census, Ware had an annual income of, $1,140.

100 Mrs. Bobbie Blake, interview with the author, July 6, 2013. Weir gave Steve Blake, Bobbie's future husband, his stamp of approval.

101 *Kings Mountain Herald*, January 17, 1935.

102 *Kings Mountain Herald*, March 21, 1935.

103 *Kings Mountain Herald*, October 31, 1935.
104 Barnwell, *Faces We See*, 11. This book was published by the Southern Combed Yarns Spinners' Association, of which Park Yarn was a part. See p. 111.
105 *Kings Mountain Herald*, May 7, 1936; Suggs, *My World Is Gone*, 109.
106 *Kings Mountain Herald*, March 21, 1935; November 28, 1935.
107 *Kings Mountain Herald*, September 19, 1935.
108 *Kings Mountain Herald*, October 31, 1935.
109 *Kings Mountain Herald*, March 14, 1935; March 21, 1938.
110 *Kings Mountain Herald*, January 19, 1935; January 17, March 7, and December 12, 1935; June 11, 1936.
111 *Kings Mountain Herald*, February 18, 1937; September 15, 1938.
112 *Kings Mountain Herald*, September 13 and 17, 1936.
113 *Kings Mountain Herald*, November 5, 1936.
114 Kennedy, *Freedom from Fear*, 281.

Chapter 2: *You Have Now Been Selected*

1 Hayne Neisler, e-mail to the author, June 5, 2013; Mr. Robert C. Pearson, Interview with the author, November 15, 2015.
2 Mrs. Bobbie Blake, interview with the author, July 6, 2013; Mr. Robert C. Pearson, Interview with the author, November 15, 2015. Neisler also related that Margrace did not have a whistle, but many in the area did.
3 Mildred Gwin Barnwell, *Faces We See* (Gastonia, NC: Southern Combine Yarn Spinners Association, 1939), 16–17.
4 *Kings Mountain Herald*, July 11, 1940; David M. Kennedy, *Freedom from Fear: The American People in Depression and War, 1929–1945* (New York and Oxford: Oxford University Press, 1999), 402, 427; Amity Shlaes, *The Forgotten Man: A New History of the Great Depression* (New York: Harper Perennial, 2007), 353.
5 *Kings Mountain Herald*, August 15, September 21, and September 28, 1940, and February 20, 1941.
6 Edward R. Murrow in *London after Dark*, August 24, 1940 broadcast, http://www.otr.com/ra/news/londonafterdark_082440.mp3; Conrad Black, *Franklin Delano Roosevelt: Champion of Freedom* (New York: Public Affairs, 2003), 580, 582.
7 Spencer Bidwell King Jr., *Selective Service in North Carolina in World War II*. (Chapel Hill: University of North Carolina Press, 1949), 81; *London Can Take It*, http://www.youtube.com/watch?v=bLgfSDtHFt8.
8 Russell F. Weigley, *Eisenhower's Lieutenants: The Campaign of France and Germany, 1944–1945* (Bloomington and Indianapolis: Indiana University Press, 1981), 12; Kennedy, *Freedom from Fear*, 487; Ronald H. Bailey, *The Home Front: U.S.A.* (Alexandria, VA: Time-Life Books, 1997), 43; King, *Selective Service in North Carolina*, 17, 21; Lee Kennett, *G.I.: The American Soldier in World War II* (Norman: University of Oklahoma Press, 1987), 3–4.
9 King, *Selective Service in North Carolina*, 78, 80–81; Edward A. Fitzpatrick, ed., *Selective Service in Wartime: Second Report of the Director of Selective Service, 1941–1942* (Washington, DC: Government Printing Office, 1943), 97; Kennett, *G.I.*, 6.

10 Author's Collection; Arthur Jones to "Dear Sis," February 17, 1919, Lynn Collection. The letter to Jones's sister mentions "Little Ruth." Jones served in Company D.

11 Bailey, *The Home Front*, 43–44.

12 *Kings Mountain Herald*, October 10, 1940 and October 17, 1940; King, *Selective Service in North Carolina*, 84; Sarah McCulloh Lemmon, *North Carolina's Role in World War II* (Raleigh: Division of Archives and History, North Carolina Department of Cultural Resources), 11; Fitzpatrick, *Selective Service in Wartime*, 97. Over 3.5 million people lived in the state in 1940 (Lefler and Newsome, *North Carolina*, 620). By June 1945, North Carolina draft boards registered 1.1 million men (Hugh Talmage Lefler and Albert Ray Newsome, *North Carolina: The History of a Southern State* [Chapel Hill: University of North Carolina Press, 1954], 620, 622). Kings Mountain's draft board expanded in February 1941 with the addition of O. O. Jackson of the Cleveland Motor Company, D. R. Hamrick of Bridges and Hamrick, C. H. McDaniel of Fulton's Mortuary, and J. E. Keeter of Keeter's Department Store (*Kings Mountain Herald*, February 6, 1941).

13 *Kings Mountain Herald*, October 10, 1940 and October 17, 1940; King, *Selective Service in North Carolina*, 84; Lemmon, *North Carolina's Role*, 11.

14 Draft Registration Card of Felmer Lonzo Lynn, October 16, 1940, National Archives, hereafter cited as NA; Fitzpatrick, *Selective Service in Wartime*, 95; Kennett, *G.I.*, 7.

15 *Kings Mountain Herald*, October 10 and October 29, 1940; Bailey, *The Home Front*, 43; Fitzpatrick, *Selective Service in Wartime*, 149; Mr. Robert C. Pearson, Interview with the author, November 15, 2015. Mitchell Ann rarely went by her full name. Pete shortened it to either Mick or Micky with a y, while most other family members spelled it Mickie. The latter convention is used in the text while Pete's spelling is preserved in direct quotes.

16 Kennedy, *Freedom from Fear*, 468–69, 627.

17 Black, *Franklin Delano Roosevelt*, 662–63.

18 *Kings Mountain Herald*, June 26, 1941.

19 *Kings Mountain Herald*, December 11, 1940; Radio broadcasts, http://www.otr.com/r-a-i-new_pearl.shtml.

20 Bailey, *The Home Front*, 42.

21 Tom Shytle, *Carolina Roots: From Whence I Came* (privately published, 2008), 59.

22 Memories Scrapbook, Lynn Collection; Bill Lynn Interview, April 3, 2011; The *Alleghany News*, March 24, 2005.

23 Pete Lynn to "Hello Darling," September 29, 1944, Lynn Collection; Pete Lynn to "My Dearst Darling," May 9, 1944, Lynn Collection. Among the parenting challenges Pete and Ruth faced in these days was a problem with the development of Mickie's feet. She had to wear corrective braces for a period of time.

24 Pete Lynn to "Hi toots," May 28, 1944, Lynn Collection; Pete Lynn to "Hello Dear," October 5, 1944, Lynn Collection.

25 Pete Lynn to "Hell[o] Dear," April[?] 1944, Lynn Collection; Pete Lynn to "Hello Sweet Hart and Babys," April 28, 1944, Lynn Collection.

26 Pete Lynn to "Hell[o] My Dearest Wife," April 22, 1944, Lynn Collection.

27 Pete Lynn to "Hello Darling," May 5, 1944, Lynn Collection; Pete Lynn to "Hello Dear," October 5, 1944, Lynn Collection.

28   Lemmon, *North Carolina's Role in World War II*, 20–21.

29   Shytle, *Carolina Roots*, 59; Mary Best, ed., *North Carolina's Shining Hour: Images and Voices from World War II* (Winston-Salem, NC: Our State Books, 2005), 50; Lefler and Newsome, *North Carolina*, 623; Lemmon, *North Carolina's Role in World War II*, 25, 27.

30   Verona Jones to "Dear Ruth," April 24, 1944, Lynn Collection; Ruth Lynn to "Dearest One," September 17, 1944, Lynn Collection.

31   *Old Mountaineer*, July 30, 1942, Letters to Service Men, Mauney Memorial Library.

32   Lemmon, *North Carolina's Role in World War II*, 28, 30; Bailey, *The Home Front*, 107–8.

33   Bailey, *The Home Front*, 103, 114; Lemmon, *North Carolina's Role in World War II*, 32, 34; Shytle, *Carolina Roots*, 60.

34   Best, *North Carolina's Shining Hour*, 125; Bailey, *The Home Front*, 108.

35   *Old Mountaineer*, April 29, 1943, Letters to Service Men, Mauney Memorial Library.

36   Lemmon, *North Carolina's Role in World War II*, 30; Best, *North Carolina's Shining Hour*, 126; Lefler and Newsome, *North Carolina*, 623; Bailey, *The Home Front*, 108; Kennedy, *Freedom from Fear*, 623–24.

37   *Old Mountaineer*, January 30, 1943, April 29, 1943, and February 29, 1944, Letters to Service Men, Mauney Memorial Library; Newspaper clipping inserted into the *Old Mountaineer*, June 29, 1943, Letters to Service Men, Mauney Memorial Library.

38   Lemmon, *North Carolina's Role in World War II*, 30–31; Bailey, *The Home Front*, 104–5; *Kings Mountain Herald*, January 13, 1944. Air-raid preparations declined after November 1943 as it became more apparent that air raids in any part of the United States were unlikely.

39   Quoted in Lemmon, *North Carolina's Role in World War II*, 35–36.

40   *Old Mountaineer*, January 30, 1943, Letters to Service Men, Mauney Memorial Library.

41   *Old Mountaineer*, April 29, 1943, Letters to Service Men, Mauney Memorial Library.

42   *Old Mountaineer*, January 30, 1943, Letters to Service Men, Mauney Memorial Library.

43   Bailey, *The Home Front*, 117.

44   Pete Lynn to "My Dearest Wife and Babys," April 8, 1944 [?], Lynn Collection.

45   Betty Hoyle Interview, May 20, 2012; *Kings Mountain Herald*, March 29, 1941.

46   Pete Lynn to "Hello Dear[e]st," April 9, 1944, both in Lynn Collection.

47   Enlistment Record for J. C. Lynn, NA; J. C. Lynn Personnel Record, National Personnel Records Center, St. Louis; Bill Lynn Interview, April 3, 2011; *Old Mountaineer*, October 30 [?], 1942 and January 30, 1943, Letters to Service Men, Mauney Memorial Library. After the war, Bill became a plumber. He died on January 12, 2012, at age ninety-two, survived by his wife of seventy years, two daughters and a son, plus numerous grandchildren and great grandchildren.

48   George Clarence Smith Personnel Record, National Personnel Records Center, St. Louis. Ruth Lynn to "Dearest Dady Pete," November 9, 1944, Lynn Collection. Smitty, who lived with Mae at 706 N. Piedmont Avenue in Kings Mountain, enlisted in Raleigh on April 26, 1942.

49   Fitzpatrick, *Selective Service in Wartime*, 127, 13; Bailey, *The Home Front*, 44–45; Kennedy, *Freedom from Fear*, 634; Kennett, *G.I.*, 13; *Old Mountaineer*, January 30, 1943,

Letters to Service Men, Mauney Memorial Library; Leonard L. Lerwill, *The Personnel Replacement System in the United States Army* (Washington, DC: Department of the Army, 1954), 271–72.

50 Rick Atkinson, *The Guns at Last Light: The War in Western Europe, 1944–1945* (New York: Henry Holt and Company, 2013), 408; Fitzpatrick, *Selective Service in Wartime*, 35, 113–14, 133–34, 159, 165; Kennedy, *Freedom from Fear*, 632.

51 Fitzpatrick, *Selective Service in Wartime*, 136–37, 147; King, *Selective Service in North Carolina*, 197.

52 *Time*, August 16, 1943; Robert R. Palmer, Bell I. Wiley, and William R. Keast, *The Procurement and Training of Ground Combat Troops*. In *U.S. Army in World War II* (Washington, DC: Center of Military History, 1948), 28, 193–95, 203–4, 207; Weigley, *Eisenhower's Lieutenants*, 14, 374; *Time*, January 24, 1944, 21; Kennett, *G.I.*, 22; Lerwill, *Personnel Replacement System*, 270–74.

53 *Old Mountaineer*, January 30, 1943, Letters to Service Men, Mauney Memorial Library.

54 Atkinson, *Guns at Last Light*, 408; Kennedy, *Freedom from Fear*, 634.

55 *Old Mountaineer*, January 31, 1944, Letters to Service Men, Mauney Memorial Library.

56 Letters to Service Men, Mauney Memorial Library.

57 *Kings Mountain Herald*, February 16, 1944.

58 Certificate of Fitness, February 1944, Lynn Collection; *Kings Mountain Herald*, February 16, 1944; *Old Mountaineer*, January 31, 1944, and February 29, 1944, both in Letters to Service Men, Mauney Memorial Library. Another 104 fathers went for preinduction physicals in March.

59 *Old Mountaineer*, January 31, 1944, Letters to Service Men, Mauney Memorial Library; Camp Croft History, http://www.schistory.net/campcroft/history.html.

60 Fitzpatrick, *Selective Service in Wartime*, 44, 46, 595; Bailey, *The Home Front*, 45; Kennett, *G.I.*, 18; Certificate of Fitness, February 1944, Lynn Collection; *Old Mountaineer*, March 31, 1944, Letters to Service Men, Mauney Memorial Library.

61 Charles M. Wiltse, ed., *Physical Standards in World War II* (Washington, DC: Office of the Surgeon General, Department of the Army, 1967), 21–23; Fitzpatrick, *Selective Service in Wartime*, 44, 46, 595; Bailey, *The Home Front*, 45; Atkinson, *Guns at Last Light*, 19; Certificate of Fitness, February 1944, Lynn Collection.

62 Bailey, *The Home Front*, 43–44; *Old Mountaineer*, January 31, 1944, Letters to Service Men, Mauney Memorial Library.

63 Kennett, *G.I.*, 24.

64 *Old Mountaineer*, February 29, 1944, Letters to Service Men, Mauney Memorial Library.

65 Order to Report for Induction, March 4, 1944, Lynn Collection.

66 Fitzpatrick, *Selective Service in Wartime*, 39–43.

67 Betty Hoyle Interview, May 20, 2012; Ruth Lynn to "Darling," and Pete Lynn to "Hello My Dearst," both dated September 13, 1944, Lynn Collection. Ballard's identity is elusive, but he may have been thirty-eight-year-old James McDowell Ballard, who is listed in the 1940 Census for Kings Mountain as a textile operator. No other Ballards listed in the census are old enough to have had enough sway to help Pete avoid the draft.

68   *Kings Mountain Herald*, March 14, 1944; Kennett, *G.I.*, 24–25.

69   Ruth Lynn Diary, March 14, 1944, Lynn Collection; Pete Lynn to "Hello My Dear[e]st," April 23, 1944, Lynn Collection. The evidence in the diary suggests that Ruth did not even receive this diary until Christmas 1944; it appears that she went back and made entries for memorable days earlier that year.

70   Ruth Lynn Diary, March 15, 1944, both in Pete Lynn to "Hello Darling," May 14, 1944 [2], Lynn Collection; Note in "Handbook of Information: Infantry Replacement Training Center, Camp Fannin, Texas."

71   Kennett, *G.I.*, 24–25, 31–32; Lefler and Newsome, *North Carolina*, 622; Fayetteville History, http://www.visitfayettevillenc.com/community/history.html.

72   Fitzpatrick, *Selective Service in Wartime*, 48–49, 52–53, 51–53; Kennett, *G.I.*, 24–26, 30, 32, 34; Robert Sterling Rush, *Hell in Hürtgen Forest* (Lawrence, KS: University Press of Kansas, 2001), 69–70; Enlistment Record for Felmer L. Lynn, NA; Ruth Lynn Diary, March 17, 1944, Lynn Collection.

73   Kennett, *G.I.*, 28–29, 34–35; Fitzpatrick, *Selective Service in Wartime*, 48–49, 52–53, 51–53; Rush, *Hell in Hürtgen Forest*, 70–71; Lerwill, *Personnel Replacement System*, 348–49; Enlistment Record for Felmer L. Lynn, NA; Ruth Lynn Diary, March 17, 1944, Lynn Collection. Typically, the thorough physical took place at the Induction Center and swearing in took place at the Reception Center; in Pete's case, there is no record that he went to a separate facility. For Pete, the entire process seems to have taken place at Bragg over the course of a few days, as he was sworn in on either March 15 or 17 (the sources are unclear) and signed the insurance policy on March 20.

74   Ruth Lynn Diary, March 17, 1944, Lynn Collection; "Memorial Album," Lynn Collection; Memories Scrapbook, Lynn Collection; Application for National Service Life Insurance, Lynn Collection; Pete Lynn to "Hello Dear[e]st," April 9, 1944.

75   Kennett, *G.I.*, 34; Rush, *Hell in Hürtgen Forest*, 69–70.

76   Enlistment Record for Felmer L. Lynn, NA; Ruth Lynn Diary, March 17, 1944, Lynn Collection.

77   Kennett, *G.I.*, 30; Rush, *Hell in Hürtgen Forest*, 69–70; Lerwill, *Personnel Replacement System*, 348; Ruth Lynn Diary, March 17, 1944, Lynn Collection. Typically, men were given the oath at the induction center and then given a furlough.

Chapter 3: This Sandy Place They Call Texas

1   *Old Mountaineer*, March 31, 1944, Letters to Service Men, Mauney Memorial Library.

2   Note in "Handbook of Information: Infantry Replacement Training Center, Camp Fannin, Texas," Ruth Lynn Diary, March 24, 1945, Lynn Collection.

3   Robert R. Palmer, Bell I. Wiley, and William R. Keast. *The Procurement and Training of Ground Combat Troops*. In *U.S. Army in World War II* (Washington, DC: Center of Military History, 1948), 177.

4   http://www.texasescapes.com/DEPARTMENTS/Guest_Columnists/East_Texas_all_things_historical/McDonald_Camp_Fannin_91000.htm; *Handbook of Information: Infantry Replacement Training Center, Camp Fannin, Texas*, Lynn Collection; Easter Sunrise Service Order of Service, Camp Fannin, Texas, April 9, 1944, Lynn Collection; "CAMP FANNIN," *Handbook of Texas Online* (http://www.tshaonline.org/

handbook/online/articles/qbc11); Leslie Stewart Ellis Collection, Veterans History Project, American Folklife Center, Library of Congress. Brammel took command in August 1943.

5 Palmer et al., *Procurement and Training*, 375–76.

6 *Handbook of Information: Infantry Replacement Training Center, Camp Fannin, Texas*, 8, Lynn Collection.

7 *Handbook of Information: Infantry Replacement Training Center, Camp Fannin, Texas*, 6, Lynn Collection.

8 Leonard L. Lerwill, *The Personnel Replacement System in the United States Army* (Washington, DC: Department of the Army, 1954), 364.

9 Lee Kennett, *G.I.: The American Soldier in World War II* (Norman: University of Oklahoma Press, 1987), 45; Guyowen Howard Sr., retrieved from http://www.campfannin.com/members/alphabetical/GH/Howard_sr_,_guyowen.htm (no longer available); Lacy A. Sciame Collection, Veterans History Project, American Folklife Center, Library of Congress.

10 Ruth Lynn Diary, March 1944.

11 "Dear Sweetheart & Daddy," March 2223, 1944, and Ruth Lynn to "My Own Dearest Soldier," March 28, 1944, Lynn Collection.

12 Ruth Lynn to "Dearest Daddy & Sweeetheart," March 30, 1944, Lynn Collection.

13 Ruth Lynn to "My Own Dearest Love," not dated [1944], Lynn Collection. This letter was postmarked March 30, 1944.

14 Ruth Lynn to "My Own Dearest Love," not dated [1944]; Ruth Lynn to "Dearest Darling," April 10, 1944, Lynn Collection.

15 Joe W. Hawkins to "Dearest Big Sis," May 22, 1944; Joe W. Hawkins to "My Dearest Sis," April 18, 1944, both in Lynn Collection.

16 Ruth Lynn to "Dearest Darling," April 10, 1944; Ruth Lynn to "Dearest Daddy & Sweeetheart," March 30, 1944; Ruth Lynn to "Dearest Love," March 25[?], 1944; BS Pete Lynn to "My Dearest wife," June 3, 1944, all in the Lynn Collection. The March 25 letter's date is inferred based on a postmark of March 31 and the words "Saturday nite" written on the letter.

17 Ruth Lynn to "Dearest Darling," April 10, 1944, Lynn Collection.

18 Ruth Lynn to "Dearest Daddy & Sweeetheart," March 30, 1944; Ruth Lynn to "Dearest Love," March 25[?], 1944; BS Pete Lynn to "My Dearest wife," June 3, 1944, all in the Lynn Collection.

19 "Dear Sweetheart & Daddy," March 22–23, 1944, Lynn Collection; *Alleghany News*, March 24, 2005; Ronald H. Bailey, *The Home Front: U.S.A.* (Alexandria, VA): Time-Life Books, 1997), 103.

20 Ruth Lynn to "Dearest Love," March 25[?], 1944, Lynn Collection; Ruth Lynn to "Dearest soldier," March 24[?], 1944, Lynn Collection.

21 Ruth Lynn to "Dearest Darling," April 10, 1944, Lynn Collection.

22 Ruth Lynn to "Dearest soldier," March 24[?], 1944, Lynn Collection.

23 *Old Mountaineer*, May 3, 1944, Letters to Service Men, Mauney Memorial Library.

24 *Old Mountaineer*, June 10, 1944, Letters to Service Men, Mauney Memorial Library.

25 Ruth Lynn to "My Dear Husband," April 3, 1944, Lynn Collection.

26 Pete Lynn to "Hello Darling," May 8, 1944, Lynn Collection.

27 Kennett, *G.I.*, 42, 45.

28   Bailey, *The Home Front*, 47; Palmer et al., *Procurement and Training*, 387.

29   Ova Ratliff to "Dearest Hazel and Kiddies," April 11 and April 16, 1944, in Thomas G. Ratliff, *I Can Hear the Guns Now: A World War II Story of Love and Sacrifice* (Carlisle, OH: Thomas G. Ratliff, 1999), 76–77, 84.

30   Palmer et al., *Procurement and Training*, 2–3; Robert Sterling Rush, *Hell in Hürtgen Forest* (Lawrence: University Press of Kansas, 2001), 89; Kennett, *G.I.*, 47, 55; David M. Kennedy, *Freedom from Fear: The American People in Depression and War, 1929–1945* (New York and Oxford: Oxford University Press, 1999), 711.

31   "Dear Sweetheart & Daddy," March 22–23, 1944, Lynn Collection; Lacy A. Sciame Collection, Veterans History Project, American Folklife Center, Library of Congress; Kennett, *G.I.*, 53; Kennedy, *Freedom from Fear*, 711.

32   Lacy A. Sciame Collection, Veterans History Project, American Folklife Center, Library of Congress; Pete Lynn to "Hello Darling," April 21, 1944; Pete Lynn to "My Dearest Wife," April 12 and April 13[?], 1944, both in Lynn Collection. Pete sent his watch to Ruth to get it repaired.

33   Pete Lynn to "My Dearest Wife," April 12, 1944, Lynn Collection.

34   Pete Lynn to "My Dearest Wife and Babys," April 14, 1944, Lynn Collection.

35   Pete Lynn to "Hello My Dear[e]st," April 23, 1944, Lynn Collection.

36   Pete Lynn to "Hello Darling," May 15, 1944, Lynn Collection.

37   Pete Lynn to "My Dear Wife and Babys," April [May] 2, 1944; Pete Lynn to "Hello Dear," April 10, 1944; Pete Lynn to "My Dearest Wife," April 12, 1944, all in Lynn Collection. Pete was right, as the Garand weighed 9.5 lbs.

38   Pete Lynn to "Hello Dear," April 24, 1944, and Pete Lynn to "Hello My Dear," April 27, 1944, both in Lynn Collection.

39   Pete Lynn to "Hello Sweet Hart and Babys," April 28, 1944; Pete Lynn to Hello Dear, April 28 (30), 1944; Pete Lynn to "Hello My Dearst Wife," April 28 (29), 1944, all in Lynn Collection. Lynn dates the last letter "Sat nite April 28"; Saturday was April 29, and he had already written on April 27, so April 29 is the likely date of the letter.

40   Pete Lynn to "Hello My Dear Sister," Sunday evening [April 30, 1944], Lynn Collection.

41   Pete Lynn to "Hello Darling Wife," May 2, 1944, Lynn Collection.

42   Pete Lynn to "Hello Darling," May 5, 1944, Lynn Collection.

43   Pete Lynn to Hello Dear, April 28 (30), 1944, Lynn Collection.

44   Pete Lynn to "My Dearest Wife and Babys," April 8, 1944 [?], Lynn Collection.

45   Paul William Johanningmeier Collection, Veterans History Project, American Folklife Center, Library of Congress; Pete Lynn to "My Dearest Wife," April 13[?], 1944, Lynn Collection; Kennett, *G.I.*, 48.

46   Pete Lynn to "Hello Darling," May 5, 1944, Lynn Collection.

47   Pete Lynn to "Hello Dear and Babies," May 7, 1944; Pete Lynn to "Hello Darling," May 14, 1944; Pete Lynn to "Hell[o] My Dearst Darling," May 20, 1944; Pete Lynn to "My Dearst Darling," May 9, 1944, all in the Lynn Collection. Pete was also right about the BAR's rate of fire. Depending on the model, the weapon could fire between 500 and 650 rounds per minute.

48   Ova Ratliff to "Dearest Family," May 21, 1944, in Ratliff, *I Can Hear the Guns Now*, 127.

49 Pete Lynn to "Hell[o] My Dearest Wife," April 22, 1944; Pete Lynn to "Hi Kid Sis," June 11, 1944; Pete Lynn to "Hello Darling," May 5, 1944, Lynn Collection.

50 Palmer et al., *Procurement and Training*, 390; Pete Lynn to "Hello Honey," June 2, 1944, Lynn Collection.

51 Pete Lynn to "Hello My Sugar," June [July] 3, 1944, Lynn Collection.

52 Pete Lynn to "Hell[o] my Dearst Darling," May 20, 1944, and Pete Lynn to "Hello Baby Sister," May 21, 1944, both in Lynn Collection.

53 Kennett, *G.I.*, 52; Kennedy, *Freedom from Fear*, 711.

54 Pete Lynn to "Hello Sugar," May 27, 1944, Lynn Collection.

55 Pete Lynn to "Hello Darling," May 14, 1944 [2], Lynn Collection.

56 Pete Lynn to "Hello My Dears wife," May 24, 1944, Lynn Collection.

57 Pete Lynn to "Hell Dear," April[?] 1944, Lynn Collection; Kennedy, *Freedom from Fear*, 710; Rick Atkinson, *The Guns at Last Light: The War in Western Europe, 1944–1945* (New York: Henry Holt and Company, 2013), 19; Kennett, *G.I.*, 22–23.

58 Kennedy, *Freedom from Fear*, 710; Atkinson, *Guns at Last Light*, 19; Kennett, *G.I.*, 22–23.

59 Pete Lynn to "Hello My Dearst Wife and Babys," May 11, 1944, Lynn Collection.

60 Pete Lynn to "Hello Dear," April 10, 1944, Lynn Collection.

61 Pete Lynn to "My Dearest Wife and Babys," April 14, 1944, Lynn Collection.

62 Pete Lynn to "My Dearst Darling," May 9, 1944, Lynn Collection.

63 Pete Lynn to "Hello Sugar Foot," May 3, 1944, Lynn Collection. *Springtime in the Rockies* was also the name of a popular 1942 movie starring Betty Grable.

64 Pete Lynn to "Hello Darling," July 7, 1944, Lynn Collection.

65 Pete Lynn to "Hell[o] My Dearst Darling," May 20, 1944, Lynn Collection.

66 Pete Lynn to "Hello My Dears wife," May 24, 1944, Lynn Collection. For another toilet reference, see Pete Lynn to "Hello Sweet Hart and Babys," April 28, 1944, Lynn Collection.

67 Pete Lynn to "Hi Darling," July 20, 1944, Lynn Collection.

68 Pete Lynn to "Hello Dear[e]st," April 9, 1944, Lynn Collection.

69 Pete Lynn to "Hello Dear," April[?] 1944, Lynn Collection.

70 Pete Lynn to "Hello My Dear[e]st," April 23, 1944, Lynn Collection.

71 Pete Lynn to "Hell[o] My Dearest Wife," April 22, 1944, Lynn Collection.

72 Pete Lynn to "Hello My Dear[e]st," April 23, 1944, Lynn Collection.

73 Pete Lynn to "Hello Darling," May 8, 1944; Pete Lynn to "My Dearest Wife and Babys," April 14, 1944; Pete Lynn to "Hello Dear[e]st," April 4, 1944; Pete Lynn to "My Dear Wife and Babys," April [May] 2, 1944, all in the Lynn Collection. Lynn misdated the latter letter to April, as the postmark on the letter clarifies.

74 http://en.wikipedia.org/wiki/Curt_Teich.

75 Pete Lynn to his girls, postcards not dated, Lynn Collection.

76 Bailey, *The Home Front*, 84.

77 Bailey, *The Home Front*, 86, 90; Mary Best, ed., *North Carolina's Shining Hour: Images and Voices from World War II* (Winston-Salem, NC: Our State Books, 2005), 50.

78 Ruth Lynn Diary, June 1, 1944; Ruth Lynn to "Dearest Love," September 3, 1944, both in Lynn Collection.

79   *Old Mountaineer*, June 10, 1944, Letters to Service Men, Mauney Memorial Library.

80   Bailey, *The Home Front*, 80, 83; Ruth Lynn to "Dearest One," September 17, 1944, Lynn Collection.

81   *Kings Mountain Herald*, June 6, 1944.

82   Ruth Lynn to "Dearest Daddy & Sweeetheart," March 30, 1944, Lynn Collection.

83   Pete Lynn to "My Dearest Wife," April 12, 1944, Lynn Collection.

84   Charles M. Wiltse, ed., *Physical Standards in World War II* (Washington, DC: Office of the Surgeon General, Department of the Army, 1967), 24; Kennett, *G.I.*, 17; Kennedy, *Freedom from Fear*, 710.

85   Pete Lynn to "Hello Darling," April 21, 1944, Lynn Collection.

86   Pete Lynn to "Hello Darling," April 21, 1944, and Pete Lynn to "Hell[o] My Dearest Wife," April 22, 1944, Lynn Collection.

87   Pete Lynn to "Hello Darling Wife," May 2, 1944, Lynn Collection.

88   Pete Lynn to "Hello My Dearst Sweet Heart," May 9, 1944, and Pete Lynn to "Hello Darling," May 30, 1944, Lynn Collection.

89   Pete Lynn to "Hello My Dearst Wife and Babys," May 11, 1944, Lynn Collection.

90   Pete Lynn to "Hell[o] My Dearst Darling," May 20, 1944, Lynn Collection.

91   Pete Lynn to "Hello My Sugar," June [July] 3, 1944; Pete Lynn to "Hello My Sweet Heart," July 10, 1944; Pete Lynn to "Hello Darling," July 7, 1944, all in the Lynn Collection.

92   Wiltse, *Physical Standards in World War II*, 23–24; Kennett, *G.I.*, 17; Kennedy, *Freedom from Fear*, 710.

93   Pete Lynn to "Hello Dear," April 19, 1944, Lynn Collection.

94   Pete Lynn to "Hello Dear," April 24, 1944, Lynn Collection.

95   Pete Lynn to "Hello Dear," April 26, 1944, Lynn Collection.

96   Pete Lynn to "Hello Darling," May 8, 1944, Lynn Collection.

97   Pete Lynn to "Hell[o] My Dearst Darling," May 20, 1944; Pete Lynn to "Hello Sweet Hart and Babys," April 28, 1944; Pete Lynn to "Hell[o] Dear," April[?] 1944; Pete Lynn to "Hello Dear," May 23, 1944, all in Lynn Collection. For bayonet training at the camp, see Paul William Johanningmeier Collection, Veterans History Project, American Folklife Center, Library of Congress.

98   Pete Lynn to "Hello Dear[e]st," April 4, 1944, Lynn Collection.

99   Pete Lynn to "Hi Darling," July 20, 1944, Lynn Collection.

100   Pete Lynn to "Hello Darling," July 20, 1944, Lynn Collection.

101   Pete Lynn to "My Dear Wife and Babys," April [May] 2, 1944; Pete Lynn to "My Dearest wife," June 3, 1944, both in Lynn Collection.

102   Pete Lynn to "My Darling," May 10, 1944, Lynn Collection.

103   Pete Lynn to "Well Dear," July 23, 1944, Lynn Collection.

104   Pete Lynn to "Hello Dear[e]st," April 9, 1944; Pete Lynn to "Hi Kid Sis," June 11, 1944; Pete Lynn to "Hello Dear," April 28 (30), 1944, all in Lynn Collection.

105   Pete Lynn to "My Dearest Wife and Babys," April 8, 1944 [?], Lynn Collection.

106   Pete Lynn to "Hell[o] My Dearst Darling," May 20, 1944, Lynn Collection. At times, the severe weather of Texas caused casualties. During a week of heavy storms and flooding in early May 1944, two soldiers were killed and seventeen hurt by a cyclone.

Ova Ratliff to "Dearest Hazel and Children," May 7, 1944, in Ratliff, *I Can Hear the Guns Now*, 100.

107 Pete Lynn to "Hi Dearst Love," May 29, 1944, Lynn Collection; Pete Lynn to "Hi Sis," June 2, 1944, Lynn Collection; Kennett, *G.I.*, 44.

108 Pete Lynn to "My Dearest Wife and Babys," April 8, 1944 [?], Lynn Collection; Pete Lynn to "Hello My Dearst Wife and Babys," May 11, 1944, Lynn Collection.

109 Pete Lynn to "Hello My Dear[e]st," April 23, 1944, Lynn Collection.

110 Palmer et al., *Procurement and Training*, 485; Pete Lynn to "My Dearest Wife," April 13[?], 1944, Lynn Collection.

111 Ruth Lynn to "Dearest Daddy & Sweeetheart," March 30, 1944, Lynn Collection.

112 Pete Lynn to "My Dearest Wife and Babys," April 8, 1944 [?]; Pete Lynn to "Hello My Dearst Wife," April 28 (29), 1944; Pete Lynn to "Hello Sweet Hart and Babys," April 28, 1944; Pete Lynn to "Hello Dear," April 28 (30), 1944, all in Lynn Collection. The letters cited here are a bit garbled on dating.

113 Pete Lynn to "My Dearest Wife," April 13[?], 1944, Lynn Collection; Pete Lynn to "Hello Honey," June 2, 1944, Lynn Collection; Pete Lynn to "Hello Dear," April 28 (30), 1944, Lynn Collection; Pete Lynn to "Hello My Sugar," June [July] 3, 1944, Lynn Collection. For the guard duty system, see Paul William Johanningmeier Collection, Veterans History Project, American Folklife Center, Library of Congress.

114 Pete Lynn to "Hi Kid Sis," June 11, 1944, Lynn Collection.

115 Pete Lynn to "Hell Dear," April[?] 1944; Pete Lynn to "Hello Dear[e]st," April 9, 1944; Pete Lynn to "Good Morning Darling," May 28, 1944, Pete Lynn to "My Dearst Sweet Heart," May 4, 1944, all in the Lynn Collection.

116 Pete Lynn to "Hello Dearst," July 20, 1944, Lynn Collection; Pete Lynn to "My Dearest Wife," April 13[?], 1944, Lynn Collection; Pete Lynn to "Hi toots," May 28, 1944, Lynn Collection.

117 "Camp Fannin Religious Services," April 23, 1944; Pete Lynn to "Good Morning Darling," May 28, 1944; Pete Lynn to "Hello My Sugar," June [July] 3, 1944, all in Lynn Collection.

118 Easter Sunrise Service Order of Service, Camp Fannin, Texas, April 9, 1944; Pete Lynn to "Hello Dear[e]st," April 9, 1944, both in Lynn Collection. In his April 9 letter, Pete wrote that he heard someone singing "If I Could Hear My Mother Pray Again," and to Pete "it seemed as tho I could just here mother praying and I believe she was."

119 Pete Lynn to "My Dearest Wife and Babys," April 23, 1944, Lynn Collection.

120 *Handbook of Information: Infantry Replacement Training Center, Camp Fannin, Texas*; Pete Lynn to "Hello Darling," April 21, 1944; Pete Lynn to "My Dearest Wife," April 12, 1944; Pete Lynn to "Hello Dear and Babies," May 7, 1944; Pete Lynn to "Hello Dear[e]st," April 9, 1944, all in Lynn Collection.

121 Pete Lynn to "Hello Dear and Babies," May 7, 1944; Pete Lynn to "Hello My Dear[e]st," April 23, 1944; Pete Lynn to "My Dearest Wife and Babys," April 23, 1944, all in Lynn Collection. The photo Pete had taken was enclosed with his letter of April 23.

122 Pete Lynn to "Hello Darling," May 14, 1944; Pete Lynn to "My Dearest wife," June 3, 1944, Pete Lynn to "Hell[o] My Dearest Wife," April 22, 1944; Pete Lynn to "Hi toots," May 28, 1944; Pete Lynn to "My Darling," May 10, 1944, all in Lynn Collection.

123 Pete Lynn to "My Dearest Wife and Babys," April 23, 1944, Lynn Collection.
124 *Handbook of Information: Infantry Replacement Training Center, Camp Fannin, Texas*, 40, Lynn Collection.
125 Pete Lynn to "Hello My Sweet Heart," July 10, 1944, Lynn Collection; Kennett, *G.I.*, 57.
126 Pete Lynn to "My Dearst Wife and Babys," July 23, 1944, Lynn Collection.
127 Pete Lynn to "My Dearest wife," June 3, 1944; Pete Lynn to "Well Dear," July 23, 1944, both in Lynn Collection.
128 Pete Lynn to "Good Morning Dear," June 4, 1944, Lynn Collection.
129 Pete Lynn to "Hello Dear[e]st," April 4, 1944.
130 Pete Lynn to "Hi Darling," July 20, 1944; Pete Lynn to "Hello Sugar Foot," May 3, 1944; Pete Lynn to "Well Dear," July 23, 1944, all in the Lynn Collection; Archie P. McDonald, "Camp Fannin," http://texasescapes.com/departments/guest_columnists/east_texas_all_things_historical/McDonald) Camp_Fannin_91000.htm.
131 *Handbook of Information: Infantry Replacement Training Center, Camp Fannin, Texas*, 42, Lynn Collection.
132 Pete Lynn to "Hello Dear[e]st," April 4, 1944, Lynn Collection.
133 Pete Lynn to "My Dearest Wife and Babys," April 14, 1944, Lynn Collection; Kennett, *G.I.*, 57.
134 *Camp Fannin Guidon*, May 4, 1944 and May 25, 1944; Pete Lynn to "Hello Dear," July 24 [2], 1944, Lynn Collection.
135 Pete Lynn to "Hello Dear and Babies," May 7, 1944; Pete Lynn to "Hello Darling," May 14, 1944, both in Lynn Collection.
136 Pete Lynn to "Hello My Dearst Wife and Babys," May 11, 1944, and Pete Lynn to "My Darling," May 10, 1944, both in Lynn Collection.
137 Pete Lynn to "My Dear Wife and Babys," April [May] 2, 1944, Lynn Collection.

Chapter 4: The Best Little City in the World
1 Pete Lynn to "Hello Sweet Hart and Babys," April 28, 1944; Pete Lynn to "Hello Darling," April 21, 1944; Pete Lynn to "Hi toots," May 28, 1944, all in Lynn Collection.
2 Pete Lynn to "Hell[o] My Dearest Wife," April 22, 1944, Lynn Collection.
3 Pete Lynn to "Hello Dear," April 26, 1944, Lynn Collection.
4 Pete Lynn to "Hello Darling," May 30, 1944, Lynn Collection.
5 Pete Lynn to "Here I Am Again Dear," May 28, 1944, and Pete Lynn to "Hell[o] My Dearest Wife," April 22, 1944, Lynn Collection. For another example of his attitude, in Pete Lynn to "Hello my Dearst Wife and Babys," May 11, 1944, Lynn Collection, he wrote, "Darling you Don't Have to worry about me ever going across the Pond for I will never get that Far I am to old and gray. But if I shuld go I wouldn't be gone Long for I would go thro them Japs Like a Dose of salts Ha Ha." Ova Ratliff said that he heard on the radio that pre–Pearl Harbor fathers would not have to face combat unless the war worsened. Ova Ratliff to "Dearest Hazel and Kiddies," April 16, 1944, in Thomas G. Ratliff, *I Can Hear the Guns Now: A World War II Story of Love and Sacrifice* (Carlisle, OH: Thomas G. Ratliff, 1999), 84

6   Ova Ratliff to "Dearest Hazel," May 27, 1944, in Ratliff, *I Can Hear the Guns Now*, 135. For even more rumors, see Ova Ratliff to "Dearest Hazel and Children," June 29 and July 2, 1944, in Ratliff, *I Can Hear the Guns Now*, 179.

7   Pete Lynn to "Hello Dear," May 22, 1944, Lynn Collection.

8   Pete Lynn to "Hello Dearst," July 20, 1944, and Pete Lynn to "Hello my Sweet Heart," July 10, 1944, Lynn Collection.

9   Pete Lynn to "Hello My Sugar," June [July] 3, 1944, Lynn Collection.

10   Pete Lynn to "Hi Darling," July 22, 1944, Lynn Collection.

11   Pete Lynn to "Hello Darling," July 24, 1944; Pete Lynn to "Hello Dear," July 24, 1944; Pete Lynn to "Hello Dear," July 24 [2], 1944, Lynn Collection.

12   Pete Lynn to "Hello Dear," July 24 [2], 1944, Lynn Collection.

13   Pete Lynn to "My Dearst Wife," July 27, 1944, Lynn Collection.

14   Ruth Lynn Diary, July 29, 1944, Lynn Collection.

15   Ruth Lynn Diary, July 30, 1944, and note under July 31, 1944, Lynn Collection. The note on July 31 is lightly "x'd" out and has an arrow pointed to July 30. According to a note in "Handbook of Information: Infantry Replacement Training Center, Camp Fannin, Texas," the time of Pete's arrival on July 30 was 9:00 P.M.

16   Ruth Lynn to "Hi Bud Worm," August 30, 1944, and Pete Lynn to "Hello Darling," August 13, 1944, Lynn Collection.

17   Note in "Handbook of Information: Infantry Replacement Training Center, Camp Fannin, Texas."

18   Ruth Lynn Diary, August 1, 1944, Lynn Collection.

19   Leonard L. Lerwill, *The Personnel Replacement System in the United States Army* (Washington, DC: Department of the Army, 1954), 379.

20   Ruth Lynn Diary, August 3–5, 1944, and Ruth Lynn to "Dearest Bud Worm," August 29, 1944, Lynn Collection.

21   Ruth Lynn Diary, August 2, 1944; Ruth Lynn to "Dearest," September 6, 1944; Ruth Lynn to "Hi Bud Worm," August 30, 1944, all in the Lynn Collection; Ronald H. Bailey, *The Home Front: U.S.A.* (Alexandria, VA: Time-Life Books, 1997), 147. The U.S. birth rate soared as men prepared to head overseas.

22   Pete Lynn to "Hello My Dearst," August 26, 1944, and Pete Lynn to "Hi Darling Wife," September 16, 1944, Lynn Collection.

23   U.S. Census for 1940, Kings Mountain, North Carolina ED 23-16A, http://1940census.archives.gov on April 4, 2012; *Kings Mountain Herald*, August 3, 1944; Mrs. Bobbie Blake, interview with the author, July 6, 2013; http://www.harrisfunerals.com/fh/print.cfm?type=obituary&co_id+1245279&fh?id+12915; Mrs. Cornelia Moss Davis, telephone interview with the author, March 30, 2014. Unlike Pete, Moss volunteered, enlisting on June 14, 1941 (Enlistment Record for Lester P. Moss).

24   U.S. Census for 1940, Kings Mountain, North Carolina ED 23-16A, http://1940census.archives.gov on April 4, 2012; *Kings Mountain Herald*, August 3, 1944; Mrs. Bobbie Blake, interview with the author, July 6, 2013; Mrs. Cornelia Moss Davis, telephone interview with the author, March 30, 2014. Nell's brother would also be killed in 1944; see chapter 5.

25   *Kings Mountain Herald*, August 24, 1944.

26 Ruth Lynn Diary, August 8, 1944, Lynn Collection.

27 *Kings Mountain Herald*, August 10, 1944.

28 *Kings Mountain Herald*, August 3, 1944; Lynn Diary, August 6, 1944, Lynn Collection. This diary entry is actually listed under August 7 but a note above the entry states that it belongs with the previous day, a Sunday.

29 Ruth Lynn Diary, August 9, 1944, Lynn Collection.

30 Ruth Lynn Diary, August 10, 1944, Lynn Collection.

31 Betty Hoyle Interview, May 20, 2012.

32 Note in "Handbook of Information: Infantry Replacement Training Center, Camp Fannin, Texas."

33 *Kings Mountain Herald*, August 24, 1944; "Final Rites for Felmer Lynn, War Casualty, to Be Held Sunday at 3," Unprovenienced Newspaper Article, Lynn Collection.

34 Ruth Lynn to "Hi Hon," November 6, 1944, Lynn Collection.

35 Hood, "Southern Railway Overhead Bridge," 4. According to the Memories Scrapbook, Lynn Collection, Pete's leave lasted from July 30 to August 10, but Ruth's diary is clear that he left on August 11.

36 Bill Lynn Interview, April 3, 2011.

37 Pete Lynn to "My Dearst Wife and Babies," August 25, 1944, Lynn Collection.

38 Ruth Lynn Diary, August 11, 1944, and August 11, 1945, Lynn Collection.

39 Pete Lynn to "Hello Dear," August 22, 1944, Lynn Collection.

40 Pete Lynn to "Hello Darling Wife," September 10, 1944, Lynn Collection.

41 Pete Lynn to "My Dearest Little Wife," August 12, 1944; Ruth Lynn Diary, August 12, 1944; Pete Lynn to "Hi Darling and Babys," August 18[?], 1944, all in Lynn Collection.

42 Robert R. Palmer, Bell I. Wiley, and William R. Keast. *The Procurement and Training of Ground Combat Troops*. In *U.S. Army in World War II* (Washington, DC: Center of Military History, 1948), 187; http://www.ftmeade.army.mil/pages/history/history.html; Lerwill, *Personnel Replacement System*, 383, 384; Emily George, "Fort George G. Meade, Maryland," *On Point: The Journal of Army History* 21 (Summer 2015): 46. The average stay is that of Ford Ord, California, which played the same role as Meade. Today Fort Meade is the home of several Defense Department agencies, including the National Security Agency.

43 Lerwill, *Personnel Replacement System*, 382, 380.

44 Pete Lynn to "My Dearest Little Wife," August 12, 1944; Ruth Lynn Diary, August 12, 1944; Pete Lynn to "Hi Darling and Babys," August 18[?], 1944, all in Lynn Collection.

45 Pete Lynn to "My Dearest Little Wife," August 12, 1944; Pete Lynn to "Hello Darling," August 13, 1944, both in Lynn Collection.

46 Ova Ratliff to "My Dearest Hazel & Kiddies," August 24, 1944, and Ova Ratliff to "Dearest Hazel, H.E. & O.W.," August 25, 1944, both in Ratliff, *I Can Hear the Guns Now*, 240–41.

47 William Bradford Huie, *The Execution of Private Slovik* (Yardley, PA: Westholme, 1954), 100. Slovik was at Meade in late July 1944.

48   Pete Lynn to "Hello Darling," August 13, 1944, Lynn Collection.

49   Pete Lynn to "Hello Darling," August 13, 1944, Lynn Collection.

50   Pete Lynn to "Hello Dearst," August 14, 1944, Lynn Collection.

51   Pete Lynn to "Hello Dearst," August 18, 1944, Lynn Collection.

52   Pete Lynn to "Hello Darling," August 13, 1944; Pete Lynn to "Hi Darling and Babys," August 18[?], 1944; Pete Lynn to "Hello Dearst," August 14, 1944; Pete Lynn to "Hi Darling and Babys," August 18[?], 1944, all in Lynn Collection.

53   Lerwill, *Personnel Replacement System*, 380, 383.

54   Pete Lynn to "Hi Darling," August 15, 1944; Pete Lynn to "Hello Dearst," August 14, 1944, both in Lynn Collection; Lerwill, *Personnel Replacement System*, 380; "Human Logistics: The Supplying of Men," Ground Forces Enforcement Command Replacement Study, Entry UD 578, Container 3946, Adm 571 J, RG 498, NA, 3; Rick Atkinson, *The Guns at Last Light: The War in Western Europe, 1944–1945* (New York: Henry Holt and Company, 2013), 19; Huie, *Execution of Private Slovik*, 168. Before deductions, privates typically earned $50 a month and staff sergeants $96. As for the rifle, weapons shortages had developed in Europe, so the army found it easier to have men carry their own rifles rather than ship them separately.

55   Pete Lynn to "Hello Darling," August 16, 1944, and Pete Lynn to "Hi Darling," August 15, 1944, Lynn Collection.

56   Pete Lynn to "Hello Darling," August 13, 1944, Lynn Collection.

57   Pete Lynn to "Hello Dearst," August 18, 1944, with postscript dated August 19, and Pete Lynn to "My Dearest Little Wife," August 12, 1944, Lynn Collection.

58   Pete Lynn to "Hello Darling," August 16, 1944, Lynn Collection.

59   Pete Lynn to "Hello Dearst," August 18, 1944, Lynn Collection; it includes a postscript dated August 19.

60   Huie, *Execution of Private Slovik*, 100, 123; Lee Kennett, *G.I.: The American Soldier in World War II* (Norman: University of Oklahoma Press, 1987), 113–14.

61   "Human Logistics: The Supplying of Men," Ground Forces Enforcement Command Replacement Study, Entry UD 578, Container 3946, Adm 571 J, RG 498, NA, 3; Pete Lynn to "Hi Darling," August 20, 1944, Lynn Collection.

62   Pete Lynn to "Hello My Dearst," August 23, 1944, Lynn Collection. According to a notation in the "Memorial Album," Lynn Collection, Pete left for overseas on August 19, but that was actually the date of his posting to Camp Kilmer, as other evidence shows.

63   Hayne Neisler, e-mail to the author, June 5, 2013; *Old Mountaineer*, May 3, 1944, Letters to Service Men, Mauney Memorial Library.

64   Pete Lynn to "Hello my Dearst," August 26, 1944, and Pete Lynn to "Hello My Dearst," August 23, 1944, Lynn Collection.

65   Kennett, *G.I.*, 113–14; Myrtle Ledbetter to "Dear Mrs. Lynn," June 20, [?], Lynn Collection; Ruth Lynn Diary, March 6, 1945, Lynn Collection; World War II Enlistment Record for David P. Eubanks, RG 64, NA "David P. Eubanks," www.findagrave.com; U.S. Census for 1940, Kings Mountain, North Carolina ED 23-16A, http://1940census.archives.gov; Daniel Allen Butler, *Warrior Queens: The Queen Mary and Queen Elizabeth in World War II* (Mechanicsburg, PA: Stackpole, 2002), 128–29, xiv, 86; http://www.nyc.com/visitor_guide/cruise_terminals.966323/editorial_review.aspx. They were probably either at Pier 90 or 92.

66   Butler, *Warrior Queens*, xiv, 20, 37–39, 43, 46, 54, 85, 175.

67   Lerwill, *Personnel Replacement System*, 381; 4th Replacement Battalion History, RG 407, WWII Operations Reports, 1941–1948, Replacements, Box 18185, Entry 427, REBN 4-0.1, NARA; Butler, *Warrior Queens*, 128–29; Kennett, *G.I.*, 94, 114.

68   World War II Troop Ships website, http://www.ww2troopships.com/crossings/1944b.htm; Myrtle Ledbetter to "Dear Mrs. Lynn," June 20, [?], Lynn Collection; Butler, *Warrior Queens*, 92, 129. According to the WW2Troopships website, all passenger lists, manifests, logs of vessels, and troop movement files of U.S. Army transports for World War II were destroyed in 1951.

69   4th Replacement Battalion History, RG 407, WWII Operations Reports, 1941–1948, Replacements, Box 18185, Entry 427, REBN 4-0.1, NARA; Huie, *Execution of Private Slovik*, 124; Charles A. Haug Collection, AFC 2001/001/35134, Veterans History Project, American Folklife Center, Library of Congress. Planning for each journey took place in the Allied Combined Shipping Operations Office, which was located in the former German consulate in New York. Butler, *Warrior Queens*, 126.

70   Butler, *Warrior Queens*, 87, 129–30, 85, 90; Atkinson, *Guns at Last Light*, 18.

71   Butler, *Warrior Queens*, 39, 129–30, 124; Kennett, *G.I.*, 115; William F. Meller, e-mail to the author, February 12, 2013.

72   Butler, *Warrior Queens*, 128–30; 4th Replacement Battalion History, RG 407, WWII Operations Reports, 1941–1948, Replacements, Box 18185, Entry 427, REBN 4-0.1, NARA; Kennett, *G.I.*, 114–15.

73   Kennett, *G.I.*, 115; 4th Replacement Battalion History, RG 407, WWII Operations Reports, 1941–1948, Replacements, Box 18185, Entry 427, REBN 4-0.1, NARA; Butler, *Warrior Queens*, 132–36; Roy Nix Collection, AFC 2001/001/53460, American Folklife Center, Veterans History Project, Library of Congress.

74   Charles A. Haug Collection, AFC 2001/001/35134, Veterans History Project, American Folklife Center, Library of Congress; Butler, *Warrior Queens*, 87, 130–33; Kennett, *G.I.*, 115; 4th Replacement Battalion History, RG 407, WWII Operations Reports, 1941–1948, Replacements, Box 18185, Entry 427, REBN 4-0.1, NARA.

75   "The 'Queens' Moved 1,250,000 Troops," *Saturday Evening Post*, August 4, 1945; H. C. Sumner, "North Atlantic Hurricanes and Tropical Disturbances of 1944," *Monthly Weather Review* 72 (December 1944): 238; Butler, *Warrior Queens*, 135–36.

76   Myrtle Ledbetter to "Dear Mrs. Lynn," June 20, [?], Lynn Collection. There is some discrepancy on the actual arrival date; according to the World War II Troop Ships website, http://www.ww2troopships.com/crossings/1944b.htm, the ship arrived on September 2. The contemporary source is followed in the text, which seems likelier as the shorter journey seems too short, even for the Cunard liner.

77   Butler, *Warrior Queens*, 87.

78   Butler, *Warrior Queens*, 134; William F. Meller, e-mail to the author, February 12, 2013.

79   Butler, *Warrior Queens*, 86.

80   World War II Troop Ships website, http://www.ww2troopships.com/crossings/1944b.htm; Butler, *Warrior Queens*, 86, 134; Atkinson, *Guns at Last Light*, 19. Ernie Pyle, the famous journalist, decided he needed a break from the war and sailed home on the *Queen Elizabeth* just after Pete vacated it. Atkinson, *Guns at Last Light*, 183.

81   Myrtle Ledbetter to "Dear Mrs. Lynn," June 20, [?], Lynn Collection.

82   Atkinson, *Guns at Last Light*, 19; Butler, *Warrior Queens*, 125; William F. Meller, e-mail to the author, February 12, 2013; Lerwill, *Personnel Replacement System*, 452–53; "Human Logistics: The Supplying of Men," Ground Forces Enforcement Command Replacement Study, Entry UD 578, Container 3946, Adm 571 J, RG 498, NA, 3–4. According to both Lerwill and the Ground Forces Enforcement Command study, American troops arrived usually at Glasgow, Bristol, or Liverpool. Small lighters often took men from the ships to the wharves to conserve dock space. Such was not the case with the *Queens*.

83   Myrtle Ledbetter to "Dear Mrs. Lynn," June 20, [?], Lynn Collection; Lerwill, *Personnel Replacement System*, 452–53; Dorothy Chernitsky, *Voices from the Foxholes: By the Men of the 110th Infantry, World War II* (Uniontown, PA: Dorothy Chernitsky, 1991), 260–61; William F. Meller, e-mail to the author, February 12, 2013; "Human Logistics: The Supplying of Men," Ground Forces Enforcement Command Replacement Study, Entry UD 578, Container 3946, Adm 571 J, RG 498, NA, 3–4.

84   Clarence Blakeslee, *A Personal Account of WWII by Draftee #36887149* (Rockford, MI: The Rockford Squire, 1998), 22; William F. Meller, e-mail to the author, February 12, 2013.

Chapter 5: I Wish the Ole Army Would Be Over

1   Ruth Lynn Diary, August 14, 1944, Lynn Collection.

2   Ruth Lynn to "Dearest," August 27, 1944; Ruth Lynn to "Hi Hon!" August 28, 1944, both in Lynn Collection.

3   *Kings Mountain Herald*, August 24, 1943. The board was dedicated on August 26, 1943.

4   Hayne Neisler, e-mail to the author, June 5, 2013; Letters to Service Men, Mauney Memorial Library; *Old Mountaineer*, July 30, 1942, September 30, 1943, and February 29, 1945, Letters to Service Men, Mauney Memorial Library. According to the newsletter, which began in the summer of 1942, the V stood in front of mills other than Margrace. Some 275 copies of the publication were mailed each month.

5   "Dear Sweetheart & Daddy," March 22–23, 1944, Lynn Collection; *Alleghany News*, March 24, 2005; Hayne Neisler, e-mail to the author, June 5, 2013; "Raising the Curtain on Neisler," Reprinted from *Esso Oilways*, February 1945, in Letters to Service Men, Mauney Memorial Library. The patriotism at Margrace was palpable. When officials asked for volunteers to pull a shift on a wartime Christmas Day, nearly 95 percent of employees raised their hands.

6   Ruth Lynn to "Dearest," August 25, 1944, Lynn Collection.

7   Ruth Lynn to "Hi Soldier," August 26, 1944, Lynn Collection.

8   Ruth Lynn to "Dearest Soldier," October 1, 1944; Ruth Lynn to "Dearest Love," September 3, 1944; Ruth Lynn to "So Sweet," October 8, 1944; Ruth Lynn to "Hi Soldier," August 26, 1944; Ruth Lynn to "Darling," September 22, 1944, all in Lynn Collection.

9   Ruth Lynn to "Dearest One," September 17, 1944, Lynn Collection.

10   Ruth Lynn to "Dearest," August 27, 1944, Lynn Collection.

11   Ruth Lynn to "Dearest Love," September 15, 1944; Ruth Lynn to "Darling," September 13, 1944, Lynn Collection.

12   Ruth Lynn to "Dearest," September 6, 1944; Ruth Lynn to "Daniel Boone," November 15, 1944; Ruth Lynn to "Darling," September 13, 1944, all in Lynn Collection.

13   Ruth Lynn to "Dearest Soldier," September 30, 1944, Lynn Collection; Sarah McCulloh Lemmon, *North Carolina's Role in World War II* (Raleigh: Division of Archives and History, North Carolina Department of Cultural Resources, 1964), 38–39, 46–47.

14   *Old Mountaineer*, September 29, 1944, Letters to Service Men, Mauney Memorial Library.

15   Tom Shytle, *Carolina Roots: From Whence I Came* (Privately published, 2008), 93.

16   *Old Mountaineer*, September 29, 1944, and November 30, 1944, Letters to Service Men, Mauney Memorial Library.

17   Ruth Lynn to "Dear Bed Worm," October 9, 1944; Ruth Lynn to "Dearest," September 6, 1944, Lynn Collection.

18   Ruth Lynn to "Dearest Bud Worm," September 7, 1944; Ruth Lynn to "Dearest Sweetheart," August 31, 1944; Pete Lynn to "Hi Darling Wife," September 16, 1944, Lynn Collection.

19   Ruth Lynn to "Darling," September 22, 1944, Lynn Collection.

20   Ruth Lynn to "Dearest Soldier," September 5, 1944; Ruth Lynn to "My Darling Husband," October 29, 1944, Lynn Collection.

21   Ruth Lynn to "Dearest," August 4, 1944; Ruth Lynn to "Dearest," September 6, 1944, Lynn Collection.

22   Ruth Lynn to "Dearest Soldier," September 5, 1944, Lynn Collection.

23   Ruth Lynn to "Hi Darling," November 10, 1944; Ruth Lynn to "Well Soldier," October 22, 1944; Ruth Lynn to "Dearest Sweetheart," September 29, 1944, Lynn Collection.

24   Ruth Lynn to "Dearest One," September 17, 1944, Lynn Collection.

25   Mrs. Cornelia Moss Davis, telephone interview with the author, March 30, 2014; Ruth Lynn to "Hi Bud Worm," October 3, 1944, Lynn Collection.

26   Ruth Lynn to "My Darling," October 25, 1944, Lynn Collection.

27   Ruth Lynn to "Dearest One," September 17, 1944; Ruth Lynn to "My Dearest Soldier," September 11, 1944; Ruth Lyn to "Hi Old Deer Hunter," November 13, 1944, Lynn Collection.

28   Ruth Lynn to "Dear Bed Worm," October 9, 1944, Lynn Collection.

29   Ruth Lynn to "Hi Darling," September 10, 1944, Lynn Collection. She expected to receive $100 a month.

30   Ruth Lynn to "Hi Darling," September 10, 1944; Ruth Lynn to "Dearest Love," September 3, 1944; Ruth Lynn to "Hi Darling," November 10, 1944, all in Lynn Collection.

31   Ruth Lynn to "Hi Bud Worm," October 3, 1944; Ruth Lynn to "Dearest One," September 17, 1944, Lynn Collection.

32   Ruth Lynn to "Daniel Boone," November 15, 1944, Lynn Collection.

33   Ruth Lynn to "Dearest Love," October 31, 1944; Ruth Lynn to "My Dearest," October 22, 1944, Lynn Collection.

34 Ruth Lynn to "Hello Dearest," September 26, 1944, Lynn Collection.
35 Ruth Lynn to "My Darling Husband," October 29, 1944; Ruth Lynn to "Dearest Bud Worm," September 24, 1944, Lynn Collection.
36 Ruth Lynn to "Hi Darling," September 10, 1944; Ruth Lynn to "Hello Dearest," October 8, 1944, Lynn Collection.
37 Ruth Lynn to "Dearest Soldier," October 1, 1944; Ruth Lynn to "Dearest," September 6, 1944; Ruth Lynn to "Dearest Sweetheart," September 29, 1944, Lynn Collection; http://www.postalmuseum.si.edu/VictoryMail/.
38 Ruth Lynn to "Hi Soldier," October 5, 1944; Ruth Lynn to "So Sweet," October 8, 1944, Lynn Collection.
39 Ruth Lynn to "Dearest Bud Worm," September 7, 1944; Ruth Lynn to "Dearest Bud Worm," October 26, 1944, Lynn Collection.
40 Ruth Lynn to "Dearest Sweetheart," October 26, 1944, Lynn Collection.
41 Ruth Lynn to "Hi Bud Worm," October 3, 1944, Lynn Collection.

Chapter 6: Here I Lay in My Pup Tent Many Many Miles from You

1 Ruth Lynn Diary, September 4–5, 1944, Lynn Collection; Leonard L. Lerwill, *The Personnel Replacement System in the United States Army* (Washington, DC: Department of the Army, 1954), 452–53. Although most sources point to Southampton as the most used port of transit to the front, Pete could also have left from Plymouth or Portsmouth.
2 Dorothy Chernitsky, *Voices from the Foxholes: By the Men of the 110th Infantry, World War II* (Uniontown, PA: Dorothy Chernitsky, 1991), 232–33, 260–61; Lerwill, *Personnel Replacement System*, 452–53; Donald D. Hogzett, *Recollections of an Infantry Lieutenant, WWII* (published by Donald D. Hogzett, 1996); Clarence Blakeslee, *A Personal Account of WWII by Draftee #36887149* (Rockford, MI: The Rockford Squire, 1998), 23–24; William F. Meller, e-mail to the author, February 12, 2013; Elzo Newton Dickerson Collection, AFC 2001/001/11237, Veterans History Project, American Folklife Center, Library of Congress.
3 Lerwill, *Personnel Replacement System*, 452–53; "Human Logistics: The Supplying of Men," Ground Forces Enforcement Command Replacement Study, Entry UD 578, Container 3946, Adm 571 J, RG 498, NA, 5; Chernitsky, *Voices from the Foxholes*, 260–61. This system of landing on the D-Day beaches would remain in place until the port at Le Havre was captured and opened in November.
4 Hogzett, *Recollections of an Infantry Lieutenant*; Charles A. Haug Collection, AFC 2001/001/35134, American Folklife Center, Veterans History Project, Library of Congress.
5 Chernitsky, *Voices from the Foxholes*, 232–33; William F. Meller, e-mail to the author, February 12, 2013; Blakeslee, *A Personal Account*, 23–24.
6 Elzo Newton Dickerson Collection, AFC 2001/001/11237, Veterans History Project, American Folklife Center, Library of Congress.
7 "Human Logistics: The Supplying of Men," Ground Forces Enforcement Command Replacement Study, Entry UD 578, Container 3946, Adm 571 J, RG 498, NA, 7–8; Lerwill, *Personnel Replacement System*, 453; Blakeslee, *A Personal Account*, 26.
8 Leroy Schaller, e-mail to the author, February 16, 2013.

9 Hogzett, *Recollections of an Infantry Lieutenant*; Blakeslee, *A Personal Account*, 24; Charles A. Haug Collection, AFC 2001/001/35134, American Folklife Center, Veterans History Project, Library of Congress; William F. Meller, e-mail to the author, February 12, 2013.

10 William Bradford Huie, *The Execution of Private Slovik* (Yardley, PA: Westholme, 1954), 126; William F. Meller, e-mail to the author, February 12, 2013; "Human Logistics: The Supplying of Men," Ground Forces Enforcement Command Replacement Study, Entry UD 578, Container 3946, Adm 571 J, RG 498, NA, 9–14.

11 Robert L. Smith, *"Medic!": A WWII Combat Medic Remembers* (Berkeley, CA: Creative Arts Book, 2001), 4; Blakeslee, *A Personal Account*, 25.

12 Chernitsky, *Voices from the Foxholes*, 260–61.

13 William F. Meller, e-mail to the author, February 12, 2013; "Human Logistics: The Supplying of Men," Ground Forces Enforcement Command Replacement Study, Entry UD 578, Container 3946, Adm 571 J, RG 498, NA, 13–14.

14 Myrtle Ledbetter to "Dear Mrs. Lynn," June 20, [?], Lynn Collection.

15 William F. Meller, e-mail to the author, February 12, 2013; Blakeslee, *A Personal Account*, 24; Alexander H. Hadden, *Not Me! The World War II Memoir of a Reluctant Rifleman* (Bennington, VT: World War II Historical Society, 1997), 31; Charles A. Haug Collection, AFC 2001/001/35134, American Folklife Center, Veterans History Project, Library of Congress; "Human Logistics: The Supplying of Men," Ground Forces Enforcement Command Replacement Study, Entry UD 578, Container 3946, Adm 571 J, RG 498, NA, 15; Huie, *Execution of Private Slovik*, 127. For an example of a soldier riding in an open deuce-and-a-half, cold weather or not, see Blakeslee, *A Personal Account*, 38.

16 "Human Logistics: The Supplying of Men," Ground Forces Enforcement Command Replacement Study, Entry UD 578, Container 3946, Adm 571 J, RG 498, NA, 10; Stephen E. Ambrose, *Citizen Soldiers: The U.S. Army from the Normandy Beaches to the Bulge to the Surrender of Germany, June 7, 1944–May 7, 1945* (New York: Simon & Schuster, 1997), 276.

17 William F. Meller, *Bloody Roads to Germany: At Huertgen Forest and the Bulge – an American Soldier's Courageous Story of World War II* (New York: Berkley Caliber, 201), 65.

18 Lerwill, *Personnel Replacement System*, 443, 447. Records state that the facility moved to Paris on September 6, but a man who followed the same trail as Pete still went through LeMans.

19 "Human Logistics: The Supplying of Men," Ground Forces Enforcement Command Replacement Study, Entry UD 578, Container 3946, Adm 571 J, RG 498, NA, 10, 25–31; Lerwill, *Personnel Replacement System*, 394, 454.

20 Joseph Balkoski, *From Brittany to the Reich: The 29th Infantry Division in Germany, September–November 1944* (Mechanicsburg, PA: Stackpole, 2012), 291; Oral History of David Sive, Oral History Archives, Rutgers University, http://oralhistory.rutgers.edu/component/content/article/30-interviewees/interview-html-text/191-sive-david-part-1; Meller, *Bloody Roads to Germany*, 65; Huie, *Execution of Private Slovik*, 126.

21 "Human Logistics: The Supplying of Men," Ground Forces Enforcement Command Replacement Study, Entry UD 578, Container 3946, Adm 571 J, RG 498, NA, 23.

22   William F. Meller, e-mail to the author, February 12, 2013; Hadden, *Not Me!*, 31; Huie, *Execution of Private Slovik*, 126.

23   Pete Lynn to "Hello My Dearst," September 9, 1944, Lynn Collection.

24   Pete Lynn to "Hello Darling Wife," September 10, 1944; Pete Lynn to "Hello My Dearst," September 13, 1944; Pete Lynn to "Hi Darling Wife," September 16, 1944, all in Lynn Collection.

25   "Human Logistics: The Supplying of Men," Ground Forces Enforcement Command Replacement Study, Entry UD 578, Container 3946, Adm 571 J, RG 498, NA, 28–30; Pete Lynn to "Hello My Dearst," September 13, 1944; Pete Lynn to "Hi Darling," September 15, 1944; Pete Lynn to "Hello Darling Wife," September 10, 1944, all in Lynn Collection.

26   Pete Lynn to "Hi Darling Wife," September 16, 1944, Lynn Collection.

27   "Human Logistics: The Supplying of Men," Ground Forces Enforcement Command Replacement Study, Entry UD 578, Container 3946, Adm 571 J, RG 498, NA, 73; Lerwill, *Personnel Replacement System*, 265, 268.

28   Russell F. Weigley, *Eisenhower's Lieutenants: The Campaign of France and Germany, 1944–1945* (Bloomington and Indianapolis: Indiana University Press, 1981), 372.

29   Weigley, *Eisenhower's Lieutenants*, 372–73.

30   Huie, *Execution of Private Slovik*, 245–46; Thomas Bradbeer, "General Cota and the Battle of the Hürtgen Forest," *Army History* 75 (Spring 2010), 23.

31   Quoted in Rick Atkinson, *The Guns at Last Light: The War in Western Europe, 1944–1945* (New York: Henry Holt and Company, 2013), 410.

32   Huie, *Execution of Private Slovik*, 59.

33   Hadden, *Not Me!*, 35.

34   Balkoski, *From Brittany to the Reich*, 291; Lerwill, *Personnel Replacement System*, 467.

35   William P. Shaw, *Fellowship of Dust: The WWII Journey of Sergeant Frank Shaw*, National World War II Museum, 69.

36   "Human Logistics: The Supplying of Men," Ground Forces Enforcement Command Replacement Study, Entry UD 578, Container 3946, Adm 571 J, RG 498, NA, 52–53.

37   Forrest C. Pogue, *Pogue's War: Diaries of a WWII Combat Historian* (Lexington: University Press of Kentucky), 2001, 110.

38   Huie, *Execution of Private Slovik*, 139; Lee Kennett, *G.I.: The American Soldier in World War II* (Norman: University of Oklahoma Press, 1987), 146.

39   Hadden, *Not Me!*, 31; Balkoski, *From Brittany to the Reich*, 27. Pete Lynn left no account of his route to the front. The most likely scenario is presented in the text, although there were soldiers who rode trucks from Normandy toward Belgium. One man recalled seeing Paris, Rheims, and Liege from the back of a truck as he stopped at various replacement depots along the way. See Chernitsky, *Voices from the Foxholes*, 232–33. The infamous Private Eddie Slovik, the only soldier shot during the war for desertion, also traveled to the front by truck, although he allegedly deserted during the trip. See Huie, *Execution of Private Slovik*, 119.

40   Hadden, *Not Me!*, 31; Battle of the Bulge/Hurtgen Forest Recollection of Alexander "Sparky" Kisse, at www.youtube.com/watch?v=PTE9BPmi2No.

41   Pete Lynn to "Hello My Dearst Wife and Babys," September 21, 1944, Lynn Collection.

42   Charles A. Haug Collection, AFC 2001/001/35134, American Folklife Center, Veterans History Project, Library of Congress.

43   Lerwill, *Personnel Replacement System*, 394, 444–45, 454; Ambrose, *Citizen Soldiers*, 276; "Human Logistics: The Supplying of Men," Ground Forces Enforcement Command Replacement Study, Entry UD 578, Container 3946, Adm 571 J, RG 498, NA, 10, 38. These depots shifted often as the front moved. The Third Replacement Depot was at Mortain about two weeks before Pete arrived. Other forward depots were located at Namur in western Belgium and Verviers in eastern Belgium. See Huie, *Execution of Private Slovik*, 126; Blakeslee, *A Personal Account*, 37; Atkinson, *Guns at Last Light*, 411.

44   "Human Logistics: The Supplying of Men," Ground Forces Enforcement Command Replacement Study, Entry UD 578, Container 3946, Adm 571 J, RG 498, NA, 38, 39–40, 42, 43.

45   "Human Logistics: The Supplying of Men," Ground Forces Enforcement Command Replacement Study, Entry UD 578, Container 3946, Adm 571 J, RG 498, NA, 34–35; Lerwill, *Personnel Replacement System*, 457–58.

46   Charles A. Haug Collection, AFC 2001/001/35134, American Folklife Center, Veterans History Project, Library of Congress.

47   Hadden, *Not Me!*, 32.

48   Blakeslee, *A Personal Account*, 37.

49   Charles A. Haug Collection, AFC 2001/001/35134, American Folklife Center, Veterans History Project, Library of Congress. Haug, who was assigned to Pete's company just after Pete's death, was met by a handful of Hürtgen Forest veterans whose "clothes were all caked with mud" and "their faces were all dirt and grease. The veterans would not speak to the new arrivals. "They just sat and stared," he wrote. "Occasionally, one would drop his head between his knees and sob like a baby. They had had enough. They didn't want us to replace their buddies whom they had just seen fall, because this meant they would have to go up into it again."

50   John B. Allard, "A Replacement in the 'Bloody Bucket,'" in Ray Merriam, ed., *True Tales of World War II: "We Were There"* (Bennington, VT: Merriam Press, 2011), 5.

51   Meller, *Bloody Roads to Germany*, 95–96; William F. Meller, e-mail to the author, February 12, 2013.

52   Charles A. Haug Collection, AFC 2001/001/35134, American Folklife Center, Veterans History Project, Library of Congress.

53   Pete Lynn to "Hello My Dearst Wife and Babys," September 21, 1944, Lynn Collection.

54   Pete Lynn to "Hello Dearst Wife and Babys," September 22, 1944, Lynn Collection.

55   Morning Reports, Company B, 112th Infantry Regiment, 28th Infantry Division, September 24, 1944, National Personnel Records Center, St. Louis.

56   Morning Reports, Company B, 112th Infantry Regiment, 28th Infantry Division, September 24, 1944, National Personnel Records Center, St. Louis; World War II Enlistment Records for the men of Company B, 112th Infantry Regiment, 28th Infantry Division, RG 64, NA.

57   Karl Baedeker, *Belgium and Holland, including the Grand-Duchy of Luxembourg: Handbook for Travellers* (Leipzig: Karl Baedeker, 1910), 285; Bedford M. Davis, *Frozen Rainbows: The World War II Adventures of a Combat Medical Officer* (Elk River, MN: Meadowlark, 2003), 174; Pete Lynn to "Hello Dearst Wife and Babys," September 22, 1944, Lynn Collection.

58   "History of 1st Battalion, 21 Aug.–25 Sept. 1944," RG 407, NA; Davis, *Frozen Rainbows*, 177. Headquarters had just moved to Rippig from Bettendorf. The journey of these replacements is reconstructed based on extant records.

59   Pete Lynn to Hello Dearst Wife and Babys," September 23[?], 1944, Lynn Collection.

60   Hadden, *Not Me!*, 36, 40. Like Charles Haug, Hadden was assigned to Company B shortly after Pete Lynn's death. He recalled that the company had been reduced from its normal complement of 190 men to just 30 men and no officers.

61   Hadden, *Not Me!*, 36, 40; Morning Reports, Company B, 112th Infantry Regiment, 28th Infantry Division, September 24, 1944, National Personnel Records Center, St. Louis.

62   New Testament Bible, Lynn Collection.

63   Pete Lynn to "Hi Dearst," September 25, 1944, Lynn Collection.

64   Pete Lynn to "Hello Darling," September 29, 1944, Lynn Collection.

Chapter 7: Gentlemen from Hell

1   *Daily Courier*, February 24, 1945; *Invader*, November 16, 1944 and other copies, Pennsylvania National Guard Museum.

2   *Invader*, November 16, 1944 and other copies, Pennsylvania National Guard Museum. The earliest copies of the *Invader* did not include the phrase; it was evidently added later in the war.

3   "Human Logistics: The Supplying of Men," Ground Forces Enforcement Command Replacement Study, Entry UD 578, Container 3946, Adm 571 J, RG 498, NA, 1–3.

4   Russell F. Weigley, *Eisenhower's Lieutenants: The Campaign of France and Germany, 1944–1945* (Bloomington and Indianapolis: Indiana University Press, 1981), 356; Robert A. Miller, *Division Commander: A Biography of Major General Norman D. Cota* (Spartanburg, SC: The Reprint Company, 1989), 94–95. This was the largest U.S. ground combat force ever created, with four field armies and twelve corps. Maj. Daniel P. Bolger, "Zero Defects: Command Climate in First US Army, 1944–1945," *Military Review* LXXI (May 1991): 61.

5   Robert Grant Crist, ed., *The First Century: A History of the 28th Infantry Division* (Harrisburg, PA: 28th Infantry Division, 1979), 20–21, 33, 39, 41–42, 45, 48, 59, 93–95; *Historical and Pictorial Review of the 28th Infantry Division in World War II* (Indiantown Gap, PA: 28th Infantry Division, 1946); William Bradford Huie, *Execution of Private Slovik* (Yardley, PA: Westholme, 1954), 104–6; Cecil B. Currey, *Follow Me and Die: The Destruction of an American Division in World War II* (New York: Stein and Day, 1984), 52; Miller, *Division Commander*, 94–95; Jack Goldbaugh, *The Bloody Patch: A True Story of the Daring 28th Infantry Division* (New York, Washington, Hollywood: Vantage Press, 1973), xii.

6   Crist, *The First Century*, 20–21, 33, 39, 41–42, 45, 48, 59, 93–95, 132; *Historical and Pictorial Review of the 28th Infantry Division in World War II*; Huie, *Execution of Private Slovik*, 104–6; Unit History, Headquarters Company, 1st Battalion, 112th Infantry, Box 8617, RG 407, NA; *112th Infantry Regiment: "Strive Obey Endure,"* www.bloodybucket.be/112thlRengl.htm; Currey, *Follow Me and Die*, 53.

7   "Brief History of Commanding Officers of the 1st Battalion, 112th Infantry," File 328 Inf (112) 7-0.1, Entry 427, RG 407, NA; *112th Infantry Regiment: "Strive Obey Endure,"* www.bloodybucket.be/112thlRengl.htm; Huie, *Execution of Private Slovik*, 109–10; Currey, *Follow Me and Die*, 53, 55; Miller, *Division Commander*, 94–95.

8   "Brief History of Commanding Officers of the 1st Battalion, 112th Infantry," File 328 Inf (112) 7-0.1, Entry 427, RG 407, NA; *112th Infantry Regiment: "Strive Obey Endure,"* www.bloodybucket.be/112thlRengl.htm; Huie, *Execution of Private Slovik*, 109–10; Rick Atkinson, *The Guns at Last Light: The War in Western Europe, 1944–1945* (New York: Henry Holt and Company, 2013), 153; Michael E. Weaver, *Guard Wars: The 28th Infantry Division in World War II* (Bloomington and Indianapolis: Indiana University Press), 2010, 170; Currey, *Follow Me and Die*, 55; Miller, *Division Commander*, 94–95.

9   "With the 28th Infantry Division at the Port of Embarktion," Press Release, Historical File, 28th Division—Personal Stories, Pennsylvania National Guard Museum; Gordon Frederick Smith Jr. Collection, AFC 2001/001/10027, American Folklife Center, Veterans History Project, Library of Congress.

10   *Invader*, August 30, 1944, Pennsylvania National Guard Museum; Crist, *The First Century*, 165; Atkinson, *Guns at Last Light*, 184–85; Miller, *Division Commander*, 100. Among the generals and leaders present were Charles DeGaulle, Omar Bradley, George Patton, Courtney Hodges, and Leonard Gerow.

11   Individual Deceased Personnel File, Johnny Gregorio, U.S. Army Human Resources Command, Alexandria, VA. Gregorio's address was 6038 North Phillips St.

12   World War II Enlistment Record for Albert J. Pesek, RG 64, NA.

13   Individual Deceased Personnel File, Vernon D. Bowers, U.S. Army Human Resources Command, Alexandria, VA; World War II Enlistment Record for Vernon Davis Bowers, RG 64, NA; "Vernon Davis Bowers," www.findagrave.com.

14   Maj. Gen. Edward F. Witsell to Mrs. Ruth Lynn, February 13, 1946, Lynn Collection; *Orlando Sentinel*, February 26, 2012; obituary at www.newcomertitusville. com. When he enlisted, his address was 5 Edwards Street in Sane Souci. Floyd survived the war, earning a Presidential Citation and two Bronze Stars in the process. After the war, he enlisted in the U.S. Air Force and later worked with the Department of Defense. His family remembered him as loving husband, dad, brother, and friend. He died in February 2012 and is buried in the National Cemetery in Bushnell, FL.

15   Morning Reports, Company B, 112th Infantry, 28th Infantry Division, September 24, 1944, National Personnel Records Center, St. Louis; Interview with Clydene Sprinkle Sparks, August 3, 2015.

16   World War II Enlistment Record for Ralph W. Spaans, RG 64, NA; http://www. in-honored-glory.info/html/stories/ifspaans.htm; Reconstructed Personnel File for Ralph W. Spaans, National Personnel Records Center, St. Louis, copy in possession of the author. The latter file also suggests that Spaans may have been as old as twenty-seven at the time of his death but enlistment records confirm his age.

17 Glover S. Johns, *The Clay Pigeons of St. Lo* (Mechanicsburg, PA: Stackpole, 2002), 253; Morning Reports, Company B, 112th Infantry, 28th Infantry Division, September–October 1944, National Personnel Records Center, St. Louis. I am indebted to historian Robert S. Rush for translating the officer's service numbers of Lt. Wayne T. Welch (0-1319806) and Lt. Ralph Spaans (0-1319233) to determine their OCS training and commissioning dates, as the numbering system indicates that information. According to Rush, the authorized strength for rifle companies during this period was 193 men.

18 Johns, *Clay Pigeons of St. Lo*, 253; Charles B. MacDonald and Sidney T. Matthews, *United States Army in World War II. Three Battles: Arnaville, Altuzzo, and Schmidt* (Washington, DC: United States Army Center of Military History, 1952. Reprint, 1999), 284; Albert L. Berndt, MD, *Comments on "Objective: Schmidt"*, Background Files, Study, *Three Battles: Arnaville, Altuzzo, and Schmidt*, Box 1, Entry P-39, RG 319, NA. The leader of Company B's heavy weapons platoon at this time is unknown.

19 "Biography of Maj. Gen. Cota," Press Release, Historical File, 28th Division—Personal Stories, Pennsylvania National Guard Museum; "Norman Daniel Cota," Press Release, Historical File, 28th Division—Personal Stories, Pennsylvania National Guard Museum; "With the 28th Infantry Division at the Port of Embarktion," Press Release, Historical File, 28th Division—Personal Stories, Pennsylvania National Guard Museum; Huie, *Execution of Private Slovik*, 113–14. Other members of Cota's West Point class included future generals Joe Collins, Matt Ridgeway, and Mark Clark.

20 "Biography of Maj. Gen. Cota," Press Release, Historical File, 28th Division—Personal Stories, Pennsylvania National Guard Museum; "Norman Daniel Cota," Press Release, Historical File, 28th Division—Personal Stories, Pennsylvania National Guard Museum; "With the 28th Infantry Division at the Port of Embarktion," Press Release, Historical File, 28th Division—Personal Stories, Pennsylvania National Guard Museum; Huie, *Execution of Private Slovik*, 113–14.

21 "Biography of Maj. Gen. Cota," Press Release, Historical File, 28th Division—Personal Stories, Pennsylvania National Guard Museum; "Norman Daniel Cota," Press Release, Historical File, 28th Division—Personal Stories, Pennsylvania National Guard Museum; "With the 28th Infantry Division at the Port of Embarktion," Press Release, Historical File, 28th Division—Personal Stories, Pennsylvania National Guard Museum; Huie, *Execution of Private Slovik*, 113–14; Charles H. Corlett to Dwight D. Eisenhower, August 30, 1944, Norman D. Cota Papers, DDE.

22 "Norman Daniel Cota," Press Release, Historical File, 28th Division—Personal Stories, Pennsylvania National Guard Museum; "With the 28th Infantry Division at the Port of Embarktion," Press Release, Historical File, 28th Division—Personal Stories, Pennsylvania National Guard Museum; "Biography of Maj. Gen. Cota," Press Release, Historical File, 28th Division—Personal Stories, Pennsylvania National Guard Museum.

23 J. T. Shea, "Account of the Actions Taken by Brig. Gen. Norman D. Cota on June 6, 1944," June 16, 1944, Norman D. Cota Papers, DDE; Weaver, *Guard Wars*, 173; Huie, *Execution of Private Slovik*, 114–15; Forrest C. Pogue, *Pogue's War: Diaries of a WWII Combat Historian* (Lexington: University Press of Kentucky, 2001), 53. According to some sources, it was Cota who said the famous words, "Two kinds of people are staying on the beach, the dead and those about to die. Now let's get the hell out of here!" Historian John C. McManus, in his book *The Dead and Those about to Die*, convincingly argues that the words actually originated with Col. George Taylor.

24   Pogue, *Pogue's War*, 53; J. T. Shea to Colonel Mason, June 16, 1944, Norman D. Cota Papers, DDE; Atkinson, *Guns at Last Light*, 185; Thomas Bradbeer, "General Cota and the Battle of the Hürtgen Forest," *Army History* 75 (Spring 2010): 22; "With the 28th Infantry Division at the Port of Embarktion," Press Release, Historical File, 28th Division—Personal Stories, Pennsylvania National Guard Museum; Michael D. Doubler, *Closing with the Enemy: How GIs Fought the War in Europe, 1944–1945* (Lawrence: University Press of Kansas, 1994), 49; Charles H. Corlett to Dwight D. Eisenhower, August 30, 1944, Norman D. Cota Papers, DDE; Huie, *Execution of Private Slovik*, 115; Charles H. Corlett to Dwight D. Eisenhower, August 30, 1944, Norman D. Cota Papers, DDE.

25   Omar N. Bradley to Samuel Edelman, September 24, 1948, Norman D. Cota Papers, DDE; "With the 28th Infantry Division at the Port of Embarktion," Press Release, Historical File, 28th Division—Personal Stories, Pennsylvania National Guard Museum; Cleaves Jones to Mrs. Norman D. Cota, May 17, 1944, Norman D. Cota Papers, DDE; William F. Meller, *Bloody Roads to Germany: At Huertgen Forest and the Bulge—an American Soldier's Courageous Story of World War II* (New York: Berkley Caliber, 2012), 35.

26   "Norman Daniel Cota," Press Release, Historical File, 28th Division—Personal Stories, Pennsylvania National Guard Museum; "Award of the Silver Star," June 20, 1944, "Award of the Distinguished Service Cross," June 29, 1944, "Citation for Distinguished Service Cross," and Distinguished Service Order Certificate, all in Norman D. Cota Papers, DDE; "Biography of Maj. Gen. Cota," Press Release, Historical File, 28th Division—Personal Stories, Pennsylvania National Guard Museum; Miller, *Division Commander*, 90.

27   Pogue, *Pogue's War*, 53; J. T. Shea to Colonel Mason, June 16, 1944, Norman D. Cota Papers, DDE; Atkinson, *Guns at Last Light*, 185; Bradbeer, "General Cota and the Battle of the Hürtgen Forest," 22; "With the 28th Infantry Division at the Port of Embarktion," Press Release, Historical File, 28th Division—Personal Stories, Pennsylvania National Guard Museum; Charles H. Corlett to Dwight D. Eisenhower, August 30, 1944, Norman D. Cota Papers, DDE.

28   Charles H. Corlett to Dwight D. Eisenhower, August 30, 1944, Norman D. Cota Papers, DDE; "With the 28th Infantry Division at the Port of Embarktion," Press Release, Historical File, 28th Division—Personal Stories, Pennsylvania National Guard Museum; "Biography of Maj. Gen. Cota," Press Release, Historical File, 28th Division—Personal Stories, Pennsylvania National Guard Museum; Miller, *Division Commander*, 92–93, 95; Huie, *Execution of Private Slovik*, 113–16; Charles H. Corlett to Dwight D. Eisenhower, August 30, 1944, Norman D. Cota Papers, DDE.

29   James M. Gavin, "Bloody Huertgen," *American Heritage*, December 1979, accessed at http://www.americanheritage.com/content/bloody-huertgen-battle-should-never-have-been-fought, 9; Stephen E. Ambrose, *Citizen Soldiers: The U.S. Army from the Normandy Beaches to the Bulge to the Surrender of Germany, June 7, 1944–May 7,*

1945 (New York: Simon & Schuster, 1997), 107, 110; David M. Kennedy, *Freedom from Fear: The American People in Depression and War, 1929–1945* (New York and Oxford: Oxford University Press, 1999), 732–33, 737; John C. McManus, *September Hope: the American Side of a Bridge Too Far* (New York: NAL Caliber, 2012), 1.

30   *Historical and Pictorial Review of the 28th Infantry Division in World War II*; Postwar Interview with Truman C. Thorson, Background Files, *The Siegfried Line Campaign*, Box 10, Entry P-35, Folder 4, RG 319, NA; James M. Gavin, "Bloody Huertgen," *American Heritage*, December 1979, accessed at http://www.americanheritage.com/content/bloody-huertgen-battle-should-never-have-been-fought, 4; Kennedy, *Freedom from Fear*, 732–33, 737; Ambrose, *Citizen Soldiers*, 107; Charles B. MacDonald and Sidney T. Matthews, *United States Army in World War II. The European Theater of Operations: The Siegfried Line Campaign.* (Washington, DC: Office of the Chief of Military History, Department of the Army, 1963), 3–4.

31   *V Corps Operations in the ETO: 6 January 1942–9 May* 1945 (Washington, DC: U.S. Army, 1945); Crist, *The First Century*, 165–66; Robert L. Smith, *"Medic!": A WWII Combat Medic Remembers* (Berkeley, CA: Creative Arts Book, 2001), 62; Pogue, *Pogue's War*, 215; "With the 28th Infantry Division at the Port of Embarktion," Press Release, Historical File, 28th Division—Personal Stories, Pennsylvania National Guard Museum; MacDonald and Matthews, *Siegfried Line Campaign*, 39–40, 44; Currey, *Follow Me and Die*, 56; After Action Report, 112th Infantry, 28th Infantry Division, September 1944, Entry 427, RG 407, NA; Bradbeer, "General Cota and the Battle of the Hürtgen Forest," 25; Miller, *Division Commander*, 100; Lt. Col. Carl Peterson Papers. Some sources say Peterson took command on September 11, but the contemporary regimental after action report confirms the date.

32   Charles H. Corlett to Dwight D. Eisenhower, August 30, 1944, Norman D. Cota Papers, DDE.

33   *V Corps Operations in the ETO: 6 January 1942–9 May 1945*, 242, 247, 248, 250, 254, 256, 258, 262; MacDonald and Matthews, *Siegfried Line Campaign*, 39–40, 44, 56–65; Morning Reports, Company B, 112th Infantry Regiment, 28th Infantry Division, September 14–15, 1944, National Personnel Records Center, St. Louis; Crist, *The First Century*, 165–66; Smith, *"Medic!"*, 62; Pogue, *Pogue's War*, 215; "With the 28th Infantry Division at the Port of Embarktion," Press Release, Historical File, 28th Division—Personal Stories, Pennsylvania National Guard Museum; Currey, *Follow Me and Die*, 56; After Action Report, 112th Infantry, 28th Infantry Division, September 1944, Entry 427, RG 407, NA; Bradbeer, "General Cota and the Battle of the Hürtgen Forest," 25; Miller, *Division Commander*, 100.

34   *V Corps Operations in the ETO: 6 January 1942–9 May* 1945, 260.

35   Bradbeer, "General Cota and the Battle of the Hürtgen Forest," 23; Weigley, *Eisenhower's Lieutenants*, 48, 79; MacDonald and Matthews, *Siegfried Line Campaign*, 20–23; Edward G. Miller, *A Dark and Bloody Ground: The Hurtgen Forest and the Roer River Dams, 1944–1945* (College Station: Texas A&M University Press, 1995), 13; Gavin, "Bloody Huertgen," *American Heritage*, December 1979, accessed at http://www.americanheritage.com/content/bloody-huertgen-battle-should-never-have-been-fought, 4; Bolger, "Zero Defects," 61, 62–63, 65, 68, 70; Miller, *Division Commander*, 132; David W. Hogan Jr., *A Command Post at War: First Army Headquarters in Europe, 1943–45*

(Honolulu, HI: University Press of the Pacific, 2006), 170; Major Jade E. Hinman, *When the Japanese Bombed the Huertgen Forest: How the Army's Investigation of Pearl Harbor Influenced the Outcome of the Huertgen Forest, Major General Leonard T. Gerow and His Command of V Corps 1943–1945* (Fort Leavenworth, KS: School of Advanced Military Studies, United States Army Command and General Staff College, 2011), 1–2, 5–6, 17; Postwar Interview with Truman C. Thorson, Background Files, *The Siegfried Line Campaign*, Box 10, Entry P-35, Folder 4, RG 319, NA; David Irving, *The War between the Generals: Inside the Allied High Command* (New York: Congdon & Weed, 1981), 311. In the words of Rick Atkinson, in *Guns at Last Light*, 310–11, "First Army was the largest American fighting force in Europe, and Hodges was the wrong general to command it."

36   MacDonald and Matthews, *Siegfried Line Campaign*, 65; Bradbeer, "General Cota and the Battle of the Hürtgen Forest," 23.

37   Bradbeer, "General Cota and the Battle of the Hürtgen Forest," 23; Miller, *Division Commander*, 1–6; M. Bedford Davis, MD, *Frozen Rainbows: The World War II Adventures of a Combat Medical Officer* (Elk River, MN: Meadowlark, 2003), 187; *Invader*, August 30, 1944, Pennsylvania National Guard Museum.

38   *V Corps Operations in the ETO: 6 January 1942–9 May 1945*, 261; History, September 1944, 2nd Battalion, 112th Infantry Regiment, Entry 427, RG 407, NA; History, 1st Battalion, 112th Infantry, 328 Inf (112) 0.1, Entry 427, RG 407, NA; After Action Report, September 25, 1944, 112th Infantry Regt, 28th Inf Div, 328 Inf (112) 0.1, Entry 427, RG 407, NA. Company B's Morning Reports (Morning Reports, Company B, 112th Infantry, 28th Infantry Division, September 29, 1944, National Personnel Records Center, St. Louis) are confusing from this period and often report the company as being located in a separate location than other records state. In this case, the records continue to put the company at Doennange, a small town about forty miles northeast of Beidweiler, but all other records, including those cited here, are clear about the company's actual position. This confusion likely stems from the fact that company clerks often stayed with the personnel section and the company records at division rear echelon headquarters, away from the main body of their company (James A. Huston, *Biography of a Battalion: The Life and Times of an Infantry Battalion in Europe in World War II* [Mechanicsburg, PA: Stackpole, 2003], 11).

39   S-2 Journals and Daily Summary for the 112th Infantry Regiment, September 24, 1944, in World War II Operations Records for the 112th Infantry Regiment, S-2 and S-3 Journals, Field Orders, Overlays, and Daily Summaries, September 16–30, 1944, Entry 427, Box 7470, RG 407, NA.

40   After Action Report, September 25, 1944, 112th Infantry Regiment, 28th Infantry Division, 328 Inf (112) 0.1, Entry 427, RG 407, NA; Daily Summary for the 112th Infantry Regiment, September 25, 1944, in World War II Operations Records for the 112th Infantry Regiment, S-2 and S-3 Journals, Field Orders, Overlays, and Daily Summaries, September 16–30, 1944, Entry 427, Box 7470, RG 407, NA; *V Corps Operations in the ETO: 6 January 1942–9 May 1945*, 261; History, September 1944, 2nd Battalion, 112th Infantry Regiment, Entry 427, RG 407, NA; History, 1st Battalion, 112th Infantry, 328 Inf (112) 0.1, Entry 427, RG 407, NA; Historical and Pictorial Review of the 28th Infantry Division in World War II; Change #1 to Defense Plan,

Luxembourg, September 24, 1944, World War II Operations Records for the 112th Infantry Regiment, S-2 and S-3 Journals, Field Orders, Overlays, and Daily Summaries, September 16–30, 1944, Entry 427, Box 7470, RG 407, NA.

41 S-3 Journals, September 26, 1944; Daily Summary for the 112th Infantry Regiment, September 26, 1944; Secret, RCT 112, Beidweiler, September 25, 1944; Route Overlay Change 2 to Annex 2, RCT 112, Beidweiler, September 26, 1944; March Table for RCT 112, September 25, 1944; Secret, RCT 112, March Table for 112th Infantry Regiment, September 26, 1944; Route Overlay, September 25, 1944, all in World War II Operations Records for the 112th Infantry Regiment, S-2 and S-3 Journals, Field Orders, Overlays, and Daily Summaries, September 16–30, 1944, Entry 427, Box 7470, RG 407, NA; History, September 1944, 2nd Battalion, 112th Infantry Regiment; History, Headquarters, 2nd Battalion, 112th Infantry, 328 Inf (112) 0.1; After Action Report, September 26, 1944, 112th Infantry Regt, 28th Inf Div, 328 Inf (112) 0.1, all in Entry 427, RG 407, NA; *Headquarters, 28th Infantry Division*, September 26, 1944, Pennsylvania National Guard Museum; *Historical and Pictorial Review of the 28th Infantry Division in World War II*. The regiment suffered four nonbattle casualties during the move.

42 Maj. Richard A. Dana, Memoranda to All Units, September 27, 1944, in World War II Operations Records for the 112th Infantry Regiment, S-2 and S-3 Journals, Field Orders, Overlays, and Daily Summaries, September 16–30, 1944, Entry 427, Box 7470, RG 407, NA; After Action Report, September 27, 1944, 112th Infantry Regiment, 28th Infantry Division, 328 Inf (112) 0.1, Entry 427, RG 407, NA; History, Headquarters, 2nd Battalion, 112th Infantry, 328 Inf (112) 0.1, Entry 427, RG 407, NA; *Headquarters, 28th Infantry Division*, September 27, 1944, Pennsylvania National Guard Museum; S-2 Journal, S-3 Journal and Daily Summary, September 27, 1944, in World War II Operations Records for the 112th Infantry Regiment, S-2 and S-3 Journals, Field Orders, Overlays, and Daily Summaries, September 16–30, 1944, Entry 427, Box 7470, RG 407, NA; *Historical and Pictorial Review of the 28th Infantry Division in World War II*.

43 S-2 Journal, S-3 Journal and Daily Summary, September 27–28, 1944, in World War II Operations Records for the 112th Infantry Regiment, S-2 and S-3 Journals, Field Orders, Overlays, and Daily Summaries, September 16–30, 1944, Entry 427, Box 7470, RG 407, NA; After Action Report, September 28, 1944, 112th Infantry Regiment, 28th Infantry Division, 328 Inf (112) 0.1, Entry 427, RG 407, NA; History, Headquarters, 2nd Battalion, 112th Infantry, 328 Inf (112) 0.1, Entry 427, RG 407, NA; History, September 1944, 2nd Battalion, 112th Infantry Regiment, Entry 427, RG 407, NA; *Headquarters, 28th Infantry Division*, September 28, 1944, Pennsylvania National Guard Museum. Company B's rear area outpost also moved on September 29 from Doennage to Buchet, where it would remain until October 3. Morning Reports, Company B, 112th Infantry, 28th Infantry Division, September 29–October 3 1944, National Personnel Records Center, St. Louis. The 28th yielded its position to soldiers of the 2nd and 4th Infantry Divisions. See Crist, *The First Century*, 167–68; *Historical and Pictorial Review of the 28th Infantry Division in World War II*.

44 *Headquarters, 28th Infantry Division*, September 29, 1944, Pennsylvania National Guard Museum; S-2 Journal and Daily Summary for the 112th Infantry Regiment,

September 29, 1944, in World War II Operations Records for the 112th Infantry Regiment, S-2 and S-3 Journals, Field Orders, Overlays, and Daily Summaries, September 16–30, 1944, Entry 427, Box 7470, RG 407, NA.

45 Pete Lynn to "Darling," September 29, 1944, Lynn Collection.

46 S-2 Journal and Daily Summary for the 112th Infantry Regiment, September 29, 1944, in World War II Operations Records for the 112th Infantry Regiment, S-2 and S-3 Journals, Field Orders, Overlays, and Daily Summaries, September 16–30, 1944, Entry 427, Box 7470, RG 407, NA; After Action Report, September 30, 1944, 112th Infantry Regiment, 28th Infantry Division, 328 Inf (112) 0.1, Entry 427, RG 407, NA.

47 Morning Reports, Company B, 112th Infantry Regiment, 28th Infantry Division, September 25 and 28, 1944, National Personnel Records Center, St. Louis.

48 *Headquarters, 28th Infantry Division*, September 30, 1944, Pennsylvania National Guard Museum; History, Co. F, 112th Infantry Regiment, Entry 427, RG 407, NA; History, Headquarters, 2nd Battalion, 112th Infantry, 328 Inf (112) 0.1, Entry 427, RG 407, NA; History, September 1944, 2nd Battalion, 112th Infantry Regiment, Entry 427, RG 407, NA; After Action Report, September 30, 1944, 112th Infantry Regt, 28th Infantry Division, 328 Inf (112) 0.1, Entry 427, RG 407, NA; S-2 and S-3 Journals and Daily Summary, September 30, 1944, in World War II Operations Records for the 112th Infantry Regiment, S-2 and S-3 Journals, Field Orders, Overlays, and Daily Summaries, September 16–30, 1944, Entry 427, Box 7470, RG 407, NA.

49 History, Headquarters, 2nd Battalion, 112th Infantry, 328 Inf (112) 0.1, Entry 427, RG 407, NA; History, Co. F, 112th Infantry Regiment, Entry 427, RG 407, NA. According to History, Headquarters, 2nd Battalion, 112th Infantry, 328 Inf (112) 0.1, Entry 427, RG 407, NA. The hill in question was two miles southeast of Burg-Reuland.

50 Postwar Interview with Truman C. Thorson, Background Files, *The Siegfried Line Campaign*, Box 10, Entry P-35, Folder 4, RG 319, NA.

51 Omar N. Bradley and Clay Blair, *A General's Life: An Autobiography by General of the Army Omar N. Bradley* (New York: Simon & Schuster, 1983), 337.

52 Edward G. Miller and David T. Zabecki, "Tank Battle in Kommerscheidt," *World War II* 15, no. 4 (November 2000): 43.

53 Patrol Activity Local Security Plan, Horseshoe Red, October 2, 1944, in World War II Operations Records for the 112th Infantry, S-2 and S-3 Journals, Field Orders, Overlays, and Daily Summaries, October 1–15, 1944, Entry 427, Box 7470, RG 407, NA.

54 S-2 and S-3 Journals and Daily Summary, October 2, 1944, in S-2 and S-3 Journals and Daily Summary for the 112th Infantry, September 30, 1944, in World War II Operations Records for the 112th Infantry, S-2 and S-3 Journals, Field Orders, Overlays, and Daily Summaries, October 1–15, 1944, Entry 427, Box 7470, RG 407, NA.

55 S-2 and S-3 Journals and Daily Summary, October 2, 1944, in S-2 and S-3 Journals and Daily Summary for the 112th Infantry, September 30, 1944, in World War II Operations Records for the 112th Infantry, S-2 and S-3 Journals, Field Orders, Overlays, and Daily Summaries, October 1–15, 1944, Entry 427, Box 7470, RG 407, NA.

56 Paul Boesch, *Road to Huertgen: Forest in Hell* (Houston, TX: Gulf, 1962), 154.

57   Morning Reports, Company B, 112th Infantry, 28th Infantry Division, October 1–4, 1944, National Personnel Records Center, St. Louis. The reports for October 4 also note that the company left Buchet, traveled approximately thirty-two miles, and arrived at a place near Berg, Belgium, but as previously noted this apparently concerned the company's rear elements and not the main body.

58   MacDonald and Matthews, *Siegfried Line Campaign*, 4, 251; CG 28th Infantry Division to CO 112th Infantry, October 2, 1944, and FO 20, October 2, 1944, in World War II Operations Records for the 112th Infantry, S-2 and S-3 Journals, Field Orders, Overlays, and Daily Summaries, October 1–15, 1944, Entry 427, Box 7470, RG 407, NA. According to Crist, *The First Century*, 167–68, the 28th Infantry Division went into corps reserve at this point to train, rest, and refit, but the evidence presented in the text suggests otherwise as it continued manning a position along the front, albeit a quiet one.

59   FO 19, 28th Infantry Division, October 2, 1944, and Transport Office, 28th Infantry Division, to Commanding Officer, 112th Infantry, October 2, 1944, in World War II Operations Records for the 112th Infantry, S-2 and S-3 Journals, Field Orders, Overlays, and Daily Summaries, October 1–15, 1944, Entry 427, Box 7470, RG 407, NA; Divisional Truck Company Instructions and Route for Division Movement, in World War II Operations Records for the 112th Infantry, S-2 and S-3 Journals, Field Orders, Overlays, and Daily Summaries, October 1–15, 1944, Entry 427, Box 7470, RG 407, NA; Daily Summary for the 112th Infantry, October 3, 1944, in World War II Operations Records for the 112th Infantry, S-2 and S-3 Journals, Field Orders, Overlays, and Daily Summaries, October 1–15, 1944, Entry 427, Box 7470, RG 407, NA; Annex 1 to FO 25, March Table, and Position Overlay of RCT 112, October 4, 1944, in World War II Operations Records for the 112th Infantry, S-2 and S-3 Journals, Field Orders, Overlays, and Daily Summaries, October 1–15, 1944, Entry 427, Box 7470, RG 407, NA.

60   *Headquarters, 28th Infantry Division*, October 4, 1944, Pennsylvania National Guard Museum.

61   Morning Reports, Company B, 112th Infantry, 28th Infantry Division, October 5, 1944, National Personnel Records Center, St. Louis; History, Headquarters, 2nd Battalion, 112th Infantry, 328 Inf (112) 0.1, Entry 427, RG 407, NA.

62   Pete Lynn to "Hello Dear," October 5, 1944, Lynn Collection.

63   S-2 Journal for the 112th Infantry, October 6, 1944, in World War II Operations Records for the 112th Infantry, S-2 and S-3 Journals, Field Orders, Overlays, and Daily Summaries, October 1–15, 1944, Entry 427, Box 7470, RG 407, NA.

64   Positions Overlay, RCT 112, Krinkelt, October 6, 1944, and Horseshoe Red Positions, October 6, 1944, both in World War II Operations Records for the 112th Infantry, S-2 and S-3 Journals, Field Orders, Overlays, and Daily Summaries, October 1–15, 1944, Entry 427, Box 7470, RG 407, NA; Operations Overlay, RCT 112, Krinkelt, October 6, 1944, in World War II Operations Records for the 112th Infantry, S-2 and S-3 Journals, Field Orders, Overlays, and Daily Summaries, October 1–15, 1944, Entry 427, Box 7470, RG 407, NA.

65   *Historical and Pictorial Review of the 28th Infantry Division in World War II*; Annex #1 to FO #26, RCT 112, October 5, 1944, in World War II Operations Records for the 112th Infantry, S-2 and S-3 Journals, Field Orders, Overlays, and Daily Summaries,

October 1-15, 1944, Entry 427, Box 7470, RG 407, NA; History, Headquarters, 2nd
Battalion, 112th Infantry, 328 Inf (112) 0.1, Entry 427, RG 407, NA; *Headquarters,
28th Infantry Division*, October 6, 1944, Pennsylvania National Guard Museum;
Headquarters, 28th Infantry Division, Co K, October 6, Pennsylvania National Guard
Museum; History, Headquarters, 2nd Battalion, 112th Infantry, 328 Inf (112) 0.1, Entry
427, RG 407, NA.

66   Morning Reports, Company B, 112th Infantry, 28th Infantry Division, October 6,
1944, National Personnel Records Center, St. Louis.

67   Pete Lynn to "Hello My Dearst," October 6[?], 1944, Lynn Collection.

68   History, Headquarters, 2nd Battalion, 112th Infantry, 328 Inf (112) 0.1,
Entry 427, RG 407, NA; *Headquarters, 28th Infantry Division*, October 6–7, 1944,
Pennsylvania National Guard Museum; *Headquarters, 28th Infantry Division*, Co K,
October 6, Pennsylvania National Guard Museum; Annex #1 to FO #26, RCT 112,
October 5, 1944; FO 27, RCT 112, Krinkelt, October 6, 1944; S-2 and S-3 Journals and
Daily Summary for the 112th Infantry, October 7, 1944, all in World War II Operations
Records for the 112th Infantry, S-2 and S-3 Journals, Field Orders, Overlays, and Daily
Summaries, October 1–15, 1944, Entry 427, Box 7470, RG 407, NA.

69   Morning Reports, Company B, 112th Infantry, 28th Infantry Division, October
7, 1944, National Personnel Records Center, St. Louis; "Guy Hinton Hardaway," www.
findagrave.com, accessed September 27, 1944; World War II Enlistment Record for Guy
H. Hardaway, RG 64, NA; *Augusta Chronicle*, December 18, 1947, and March 17, 1945;
Author's Correspondence with Cliff and Julie Hardaway, October–November, 2014.
"Company [B] moved by foot to new assembly area from Berg, Belgium . . . marched 4
1/2 miles," a clerk recorded in the company's morning reports for October 7.

70   Ruth Lynn Diary, October 7, 1944, Lynn Collection; Pete Lynn to "Hello My
Darling," October 7, 1944, Lynn Collection.

71   Alex Kershaw, *The Longest Winter: The Battle of the Bulge and the Epic Story of World
War II's Most Decorated Platoon* (New York: Da Capo Press, 2004), 44.

72   *Headquarters, 28th Infantry Division*, October 8, 1944, Pennsylvania National
Guard Museum; S-2 and S-3 Journals and Daily Summary for the 112th Infantry,
October 8, 1944, in World War II Operations Records for the 112th Infantry, S-2 and
S-3 Journals, Field Orders, Overlays, and Daily Summaries, October 1–15, 1944, Entry
427, Box 7470, RG 407, NA.

73   Morning Reports, Company B, 112th Infantry, 28th Infantry Division, October 8,
1944, National Personnel Records Center, St. Louis; *Historical and Pictorial Review of the
28th Infantry Division in World War II*.

74   Pete Lynn to "Hello My Dearst wife and Babys," October 8, 1944, Lynn
Collection.

75   Daily Summary for the 112th Infantry and Overlay, RCT 112, October 9, 1944,
in World War II Operations Records for the 112th Infantry, S-2 and S-3 Journals,
Field Orders, Overlays, and Daily Summaries, October 1–15, 1944, Entry 427, Box
7470, RG 407, NA; *Headquarters, 28th Infantry Division*, October 9, 1944, Pennsylvania
National Guard Museum; S-3 Journal and Daily Summary for the 112th Infantry,
October 10, 1944, in World War II Operations Records for the 112th Infantry, S-2 and
S-3 Journals, Field Orders, Overlays, and Daily Summaries, October 1–15, 1944, Entry

427, Box 7470, RG 407, NA; *Headquarters, 28th Infantry Division*, October 10, 1944, Pennsylvania National Guard Museum.

76 Morning Reports, Company B, 112th Infantry, 28th Infantry Division, October 9, 1944, National Personnel Records Center, St. Louis.

77 Daily Summary for the 112th Infantry, October 11, 1944, in World War II Operations Records for the 112th Infantry, S-2 and S-3 Journals, Field Orders, Overlays, and Daily Summaries, October 1–15, 1944, Entry 427, Box 7470, RG 407, NA; *Headquarters, 28th Infantry Division*, October 11, 1944, Pennsylvania National Guard Museum.

78 *Headquarters, 28th Infantry Division*, Co K, October 11, Pennsylvania National Guard Museum.

79 *Historical and Pictorial Review of the 28th Infantry Division in World War II*; Joseph Balkoski, *From Brittany to the Reich: The 29th Infantry Division in Germany, September–November 1944* (Mechanicsburg, PA: Stackpole, 2012) 155–56; *Invader*, October 12, 1944, Pennsylvania National Guard Museum; Forrest C. Pogue, *George C. Marshall: Organizer of Victory, 1943–1945* (New York: Viking Press, 1973), 54; Bradley and Blair, *A General's Life*, 337–38; Crist, *The First Century*, 167–68. Marshall visited five armies, eight corps, and twenty-four divisions during his tour.

80 S-3 Journal and Daily Summary for the 112th Infantry, October 12, 1944, in World War II Operations Records for the 112th Infantry, S-2 and S-3 Journals, Field Orders, Overlays, and Daily Summaries, October 1–15, 1944, Entry 427, Box 7470, RG 407, NA.

81 *Invader*, October 12, 1944, Pennsylvania National Guard Museum.

82 S-2 and S-3 Journal and Daily Summary for the 112th Infantry, October 13, 1944, in World War II Operations Records for the 112th Infantry, S-2 and S-3 Journals, Field Orders, Overlays, and Daily Summaries, October 1–15, 1944, Entry 427, Box 7470, RG 407, NA.

83 Morning Reports, Company B, 112th Infantry, 28th Infantry Division, October 13, 1944, National Personnel Records Center, St. Louis; *Austin-American Statesman*, March 3–4, 2015, quoted in the entry for Clifford Thorne Hackard, www.findagrave. com. Again, my thanks to Rob Rush for deciphering Hackard's officer's service number, 0-1296023.

84 S-2 and S-3 Journals and Daily Summary, October 14, 1944, in World War II Operations Records for the 112th Infantry, S-2 and S-3 Journals, Field Orders, Overlays, and Daily Summaries, October 1–15, 1944, Entry 427, Box 7470, RG 407, NA.

85 S-2 and S-3 Journals, Daily Summary, and Intelligence Summary for the 112th Infantry, in World War II Operations Records for the 112th Infantry, S-2 and S-3 Journals, Field Orders, Overlays, and Daily Summaries, October 1–15, 1944, Entry 427, Box 7470, RG 407, NA. Peterson's command post was in Krinkelt according to map grids recorded in the regiment's records (vK977043); *Headquarters, 28th Infantry Division*, October 15, 1944, Pennsylvania National Guard Museum. The patrol action took place at wF037058. The defending Germans were identified as members of the 412th Ersatz Battalion.

86 Historical and Pictorial Review of the 28th Infantry Division in World War II; Lt. Col. Carl Peterson Papers. Peterson was 6 feet tall and weighed about 170 pounds.

87   Training Memorandum, October 17, 1944, in World War II Operations Records for the 112th Infantry, S-2 and S-3 Journals, Field Orders, Overlays, and Daily Summaries, October 16–31, 1944, Entry 427, Box 7470, RG 407, NA.

88   S-3 Journal, Daily Summary, and Intelligence Summary, October 21, 1944, World War II Operations Records for the 112th Infantry, S-2 and S-3 Journals, Field Orders, Overlays, and Daily Summaries, October 16–31, 1944, Entry 427, Box 7470, RG 407, NA.

89   History, Headquarters, 2nd Battalion, 112th Infantry, 328 Inf (112) 0.1, Entry 427, RG 407, NA; Harold Denny, "Life on the West Front," *New York Times Magazine*, November 5, 1944; Jeffrey J. Clarke and Robert Ross Smith, *Riviera to the Rhine*. Part of the *United States Army in World War II* series. Reprint (Atlanta, GA: Whitman, 2012), 566–67; Meller, *Bloody Roads to Germany*, 71; Iris Carpenter, *No Woman's World* (Boston, MA: Houghton Mifflin, 1946), 33.

90   History, Headquarters, 2nd Battalion, 112th Infantry, 328 Inf (112) 0.1, Entry 427, RG 407, NA; *Headquarters, 28th Infantry Division*, October 16, Pennsylvania National Guard Museum.

91   Denny, "Life on the West Front"; Maj. Jeffrey P. Holt, *Operational Performance of the U.S. 28th Infantry Division, September to December 1944* (Fort Leavenworth, KS: Master's Thesis, U.S. Army Command and General Staff College, June 1994), 115–17.

92   *Headquarters, 28th Infantry Division*, Oct 17–18, 1944, Pennsylvania National Guard Museum; S-3 Journal and Daily Summary, October 17, 1944, in World War II Operations Records for the 112th Infantry, S-2 and S-3 Journals, Field Orders, Overlays, and Daily Summaries, October 16–31, 1944, Entry 427, Box 7470, RG 407, NA.

93   *Headquarters, 28th Infantry Division*, October 5, 1944, Pennsylvania National Guard Museum; History, Headquarters, 2nd Battalion, 112th Infantry, 328 Inf (112) 0.1, Entry 427, RG 407, NA.

94   Lee Kennett, *G.I.: The American Soldier in World War II* (Norman: University of Oklahoma Press, 1987), 103; Denny, "Life on the West Front"; Clarke and Smith, *Riviera to the Rhine*, 565–67; Holt, *Operational Performance of the U.S. 28th Infantry Division, September to December 1944*, 115–17; Caddick-Adams, *Snow and Steel*, 341; *Headquarters, 28th Infantry Division*, October 19, Pennsylvania National Guard Museum. Most soldiers preferred the M-1943 Eisenhower field jacket, but it did not arrive in the field in great numbers until 1945. However, some replacements brought them to Europe in 1944.

95   Clarke and Smith, *Riviera to the Rhine*, 565–67; Holt, *Operational Performance of the U.S. 28th Infantry Division, September to December 1944*, 115–17; Caddick-Adams, *Snow and Steel*, 341; Kennett, *G.I.*, 103–4.

96   Kennett, *G.I.*, 104.

97   *Headquarters, 28th Infantry Division*, October 16, Pennsylvania National Guard Museum; History, Headquarters, 2nd Battalion, 112th Infantry, 328 Inf (112) 0.1, Entry 427, RG 407, NA.

98   Caddick-Adams, *Snow and Steel*, 295–97; Kennett, *G.I.*, 99-100; Johns, *Clay Pigeons of St. Lo*, 97–98; Pogue, *Pogue's War*, 78–79; Denny, "Life on the West Front."

99   History, Headquarters, 2nd Battalion, 112th Infantry, 328 Inf (112) 0.1; S-3 Journals, October 1, 1944, and Unit Report No. 4, 112th Infantry, November 1 for the period October 1–30, 1944; Lt. Col. Carl Peterson to G-3, 28th Infantry Division, October 20, 1944; all in World War II Operations Records for the 112th Infantry, S-2 and S-3 Journals, Field Orders, Overlays, and Daily Summaries, October 1–15, 1944 and October 16–31, 1944, Entry 427, Box 7470, RG 407, NA; *Headquarters, 28th Infantry Division*, October 1 and 3, October 13–14, 1944, and *Headquarters, 28th Infantry Division*, Co K, October 13, both in Pennsylvania National Guard Museum.

100   Pete Lynn to "My Darling wife," October 21, 1944, Lynn Collection.

101   History, Headquarters, 2nd Battalion, 112th Infantry, 328 Inf (112) 0.1, Entry 427, RG 407, NA; Lt. Col. Carl Peterson to G-3, 28th Infantry Division, October 20, 1944; in World War II Operations Records for the 112th Infantry, S-2 and S-3 Journals, Field Orders, Overlays, and Daily Summaries, October 16–31, 1944, Entry 427, Box 7470, RG 407, NA; *Headquarters, 28th Infantry Division*, October 13–14, 1944, and *Headquarters, 28th Infantry Division*, Co K, Oct 13, both in Pennsylvania National Guard Museum.

102   *Headquarters, 28th Infantry Division*, October 22, Pennsylvania National Guard Museum; Davis, *Frozen Rainbows*, 186; Albert L. Berndt, MD, *Comments on "Objective: Schmidt"*, Background Files, Study, *Three Battles: Arnaville, Altuzzo, and Schmidt*, Box 1, Entry P-39, RG 319, NA.

103   Memorandum of Lt. Col. Carl Peterson, October 14, 1944, in World War II Operations Records for the 112th Infantry, S-2 and S-3 Journals, Field Orders, Overlays, and Daily Summaries, October 1–15, 1944, Entry 427, Box 7470, RG 407, NA.

104   *Historical and Pictorial Review of the 28th Infantry Division in World War II*; Davis, *Frozen Rainbows*, 187; Training Memorandum, October 17, 1944, in World War II Operations Records for the 112th Infantry, S-2 and S-3 Journals, Field Orders, Overlays, and Daily Summaries, October 16–31, 1944, Entry 427, Box 7470, RG 407, NA.

105   Memorandum, October 19, 1944, World War II Operations Records for the 112th Infantry, S-2 and S-3 Journals, Field Orders, Overlays, and Daily Summaries, October 16–31, 1944, Entry 427, Box 7470, RG 407, NA; Memorandum, October 18, 1944, in World War II Operations Records for the 112th Infantry, S-2 and S-3 Journals, Field Orders, Overlays, and Daily Summaries, October 16–31, 1944, Entry 427, Box 7470, RG 407, NA; Lt. Col. Thomas E. Briggs to CO 109th, October 20, 1944, World War II Operations Records for the 112th Infantry, S-2 and S-3 Journals, Field Orders, Overlays, and Daily Summaries, October 16–31, 1944, Entry 427, Box 7470, RG 407, NA.

106   S-3 Journal and Daily Summary, October 16, 1944, in World War II Operations Records for the 112th Infantry, S-2 and S-3 Journals, Field Orders, Overlays, and Daily Summaries, October 16–31, 1944, Entry 427, Box 7470, RG 407, NA.

107   Morning Reports, Company B, 112th Infantry, 28th Infantry Division, October 17, 1944, National Personnel Records Center, St. Louis; *Headquarters, 28th Infantry Division*, October 16–20 1944, Pennsylvania National Guard Museum; History, Headquarters, 2nd Battalion, 112th Infantry, 328 Inf (112) 0.1, Entry 427, RG 407, NA. The sources state that the company moved to the intermediate position, which must have been Krinkelt.

108 Gen. Norman Cota to CO 112th Infantry, October 17, 1944, both in World War II Operations Records for the 112th Infantry, S-2 and S-3 Journals, Field Orders, Overlays, and Daily Summaries, October 16–31, 1944, Entry 427, Box 7470, RG 407, NA; S-3 Journal and Daily Summary, World War II Operations Records for the 112th Infantry, S-2 and S-3 Journals, Field Orders, Overlays, and Daily Summaries, October 16–31, 1944, Entry 427, Box 7470, RG 407, NA.

109 Memorandum, October 18, 1944, in World War II Operations Records for the 112th Infantry, S-2 and S-3 Journals, Field Orders, Overlays, and Daily Summaries, October 16–31, 1944, Entry 427, Box 7470, RG 407, NA.

110 E-mail, John Cope, North Carolina Division of Archives and History, to the author, May 13, 2015; Voris Weldon McBurnette, *The 108th Training Command: A History of Embracing Innovation and Shaping the Future, 1946–2010* (Charlotte, NC: Palette Communications, 2010), 7, 14; http://en.wikipedia.org/wiki/108th_Training_Command_(Initial_Entry_Training); http://www.thegriffon108.com; http://www.globalsecurity.org/military/agency/army/108d.htm. Today, the 108th Training Command still exists as one of the seven training divisions for the Army, Army Reserve, and National Guard. It is, ironically, based in Charlotte, not far from Kings Mountain.

111 Daily Summary, October 19, 1944, World War II Operations Records for the 112th Infantry, S-2 and S-3 Journals, Field Orders, Overlays, and Daily Summaries, October 16–31, 1944, Entry 427, Box 7470, RG 407, NA.

112 S-3 Journal and Daily Summary, October 20, 1944, in World War II Operations Records for the 112th Infantry, S-2 and S-3 Journals, Field Orders, Overlays, and Daily Summaries, October 16–31, 1944, Entry 427, Box 7470, RG 407, NA; Morning Reports, Company B, 112th Infantry, 28th Infantry Division, October 20, 1944, National Personnel Records Center, St. Louis.

113 S-3 Journal, Daily Summary, and Intelligence Summary, October 21, 1944, World War II Operations Records for the 112th Infantry, S-2 and S-3 Journals, Field Orders, Overlays, and Daily Summaries, October 16–31, 1944, Entry 427, Box 7470, RG 407, NA; *Headquarters, 28th Infantry Division*, Co. K, October 21, Pennsylvania National Guard Museum; *Headquarters, 28th Infantry Division*, October 21, 1944, Pennsylvania National Guard Museum.

114 Morning Reports, Company B, 112th Infantry, 28th Infantry Division, October 21, 1944, National Personnel Records Center, St. Louis.

115 S-2 and S-3 Journal and Daily Summary, October 22, 1944, World War II Operations Records for the 112th Infantry, S-2 and S-3 Journals, Field Orders, Overlays, and Daily Summaries, October 16–31, 1944, Entry 427, Box 7470, RG 407, NA.

116 History, Headquarters, 2nd Battalion, 112th Infantry, 328 Inf (112) 0.1, Entry 427, RG 407, NA.

117 Morning Reports, Company B, 112th Infantry, 28th Infantry Division, October 23, 1944, National Personnel Records Center, St. Louis.

118 S-2 and S-3 Journal and Daily Summary, October 23, 1944, World War II Operations Records for the 112th Infantry, S-2 and S-3 Journals, Field Orders, Overlays, and Daily Summaries, October 16–31, 1944, Entry 427, Box 7470, RG 407, NA.

119 Pete Lynn to "My Darling wife," October 23, 1944, Lynn Collection.

120 Maj. Richard A. Dana to All Battalion and Special Unit Commanders, October 23, 1944, World War II Operations Records for the 112th Infantry, S-2 and S-3 Journals, Field Orders, Overlays, and Daily Summaries, October 16–31, 1944, Entry 427, Box 7470, RG 407, NA.

121 Maj. Richard A. Dana to All Battalion and Special Unit Commanders, October 23, 1944, World War II Operations Records for the 112th Infantry, S-2 and S-3 Journals, Field Orders, Overlays, and Daily Summaries, October 16–31, 1944, Entry 427, Box 7470, RG 407, NA; *Headquarters, 28th Infantry Division*, Oct 24, Pennsylvania National Guard Museum; History, Headquarters, 2nd Battalion, 112th Infantry, 328 Inf (112) 0.1, Entry 427, RG 407, NA; *Headquarters, 28th Infantry Division*, October 24–25, 1944, Pennsylvania National Guard Museum: Morning Reports, Company B, 112th Infantry, 28th Infantry Division, October 24, 1944, National Personnel Records Center, St. Louis; S-2 Journal and Daily Summary, October 24, 1944, World War II Operations Records for the 112th Infantry, S-2 and S-3 Journals, Field Orders, Overlays, and Daily Summaries, October 16–31, 1944, Entry 427, Box 7470, RG 407, NA; Pete Lynn to "Hello My Darling wife and Babys," October 25, 1944, Lynn Collection; Company Orders Number 18, October 9, 1944, in Morning Reports, Company B, 112th Infantry, 28th Infantry Division, National Personnel Records Center, St. Louis. The order promoting Pete was dated October 9, but it is clear from Pete's letter that he only learned the news on October 24.

122 Daily Summary, October 25, 1944, World War II Operations Records for the 112th Infantry, S-2 and S-3 Journals, Field Orders, Overlays, and Daily Summaries, October 16–31, 1944, Entry 427, Box 7470, RG 407, NA; *Headquarters, 28th Infantry Division*, Oct 25, Pennsylvania National Guard Museum.

123 Morning Reports, Company B, 112th Infantry, 28th Infantry Division, October 25, 1944, National Personnel Records Center, St. Louis; Pete Lynn to "Hello My Darling wife and Babys," October 25, 1944, Lynn Collection.

Chapter 8: I Will Always Love You till the Day I Die

1 M. Bedford Davis, MD, *Frozen Rainbows: The World War II Adventures of a Combat Medical Officer* (Elk River, MN: Meadowlark, 2003), 193; Paul Boesch, *Road to Huertgen: Forest in Hell* (Houston, TX: Gulf, 1962), 150; *Philadelphia Inquirer*, November 18, 1944; Mack Morris, "War in the Huertgen Forest," *Reporting World War II* 2 (1995): 562; Rick Atkinson, *The Guns at Last Light: The War in Western Europe, 1944–1945* (New York: Henry Holt and Company, 2013), 313; Postwar Interview with Carl L. Peterson, Background Files, Study, *Three Battles: Arnaville, Altuzzo, and Schmidt*, Box 1, Interviews Folder, RG 319, NA; Lt. Col. Raymond E. Fleig, *707th Tank Battalion in World War II* (Springfield, OH: Raymond E. Fleig, 1993). The Markham poem was called "The Man with a Hoe."

2 Charles B. MacDonald and Sidney T. Matthews, *The Battle of the Huertgen Forest* (New York: Jove, 1963), 3, 5, 68; Davis, *Frozen Rainbows*, 182; Robert A. Miller, *Division Commander: A Biography of Major General Norman D. Cota* (Spartanburg, SC: The Reprint Company, 1989), 116; Russell F. Weigley, *Eisenhower's Lieutenants: The Campaign of France and Germany, 1944–1945* (Bloomington and Indianapolis: Indiana

University Press, 1981), 365; Edward G. Miller, *A Dark and Bloody Ground: The Hurtgen Forest and the Roer River Dams, 1944–1945* (College Station: Texas A&M University Press, 1995), 12–13; Atkinson, *Guns at Last Light*, 312–13; Robert Sterling Rush, *Hell in Hurtgen Forest* (Lawrence: University Press of Kansas, 2001), 17, 19, 22; Boesch, *Road to Huertgen*, 1; Michael D. Doubler, *Closing with the Enemy: How GIs Fought the War in Europe, 1944–1945* (Lawrence: University Press of Kansas, 1994), 174.

3 Charles B. MacDonald and Sidney T. Matthews, *United States Army in World War II. The European Theater of Operations: The Siegfried Line Campaign.* (Washington, DC: Office of the Chief of Military History, Department of the Army, 1963), 6–8, 11; Miller, *A Dark and Bloody Ground*, 9–10; Omar N. Bradley and Clay Blair, *A Soldier's Story* (New York: Modern Library), 407.

4 MacDonald and Matthews, *Siegfried Line Campaign*, 36–38; Bradley and Clair, *A Soldier's Story*, 411; Miller, *A Dark and Bloody Ground*, 10–11; David W. Hogan Jr., *A Command Post at War: First Army Headquarters in Europe, 1943–45* (Honolulu, HI: University Press of the Pacific, 2006), 160; Thomas Bradbeer, "General Cota and the Battle of the Hurtgen Forest," *Army History* 75 (Spring 2010): 24. One of Hodges's corps, the XIX, was actually closer to the British flank than the V or VII Corps, but it would receive the lowest priority of supply because Hodges needed to close a gap on his army's right.

5 MacDonald and Matthews, *Siegfried Line Campaign*, 36–38; Miller, *A Dark and Bloody Ground*, 11–12. For the 28th Infantry Division's attack, see chapter 7.

6 MacDonald and Matthews, *Siegfried Line Campaign*, 323–24; MacDonald and Matthews, *Battle of the Huertgen Forest*, 61–62; Weigley, *Eisenhower's Lieutenants*, 366; Miller, *Division Commander*, 111–13; James M. Gavin, "Bloody Huertgen," *American Heritage*, December 1979, accessed at http://www.americanheritage.com/content/ bloody-huertgen-battle-should-never-have-been-fought, 6; Gary Wade, transcriber, *Conversations with General J. Lawton Collins* (Fort Leavenworth, KS: Combat Studies Institute Press, 1983), 2, 9, 10; Hogan, *A Command Post at War*, 32, 161–62; Atkinson, *Guns at Last Light*, 313–14; Bradbeer, "General Cota and the Battle of the Hurtgen Forest," 24.

7 Miller, *Division Commander*, 111–13; *G-2 Journal: Algiers to the Elbe*, Benjamin A. Dickson Papers, USAMHI; Wade, *Conversations with General J. Lawton Collins*, 10; Iris Carpenter, *No Woman's World* (Boston, MA: Houghton Mifflin, 1946), 177, 188–89; Atkinson, *Guns at Last Light*, 314–15; MacDonald and Matthews, *Siegfried Line Campaign*, 324–28; Hogan, *A Command Post at War*, 179, 181.

8 Weigley, *Eisenhower's Lieutenants*, 365–66; MacDonald and Matthews, *Siegfried Line Campaign*, 66–67, 84–85, 92–95, 328–40; Miller, *A Dark and Bloody Ground*, 14–16; Bradbeer, "General Cota and the Battle of the Hurtgen Forest," 24; MacDonald and Matthews, *The Battle of the Huertgen Forest*, 28; Atkinson, *Guns at Last Light*, 313; Edward G. Miller and David T. Zabecki, "Tank Battle in Kommerscheidt," *World War II* 15, no. 4 (November 2000): 43; Carpenter, *No Woman's World*, 178–80; Gavin, "Bloody Huertgen," 7. German leaders later praised the 9th Division; see Lucian Heichler, *The First Battle of the Huertgen Forest*, Background Files, *The Siegfried Line Campaign*, R-Series #42, RG 319, NA, 20.

9 MacDonald and Matthews, *Siegfried Line Campaign*, 90–95.

10   Atkinson, *Guns at Last Light*, 300–1.

11   Hogan, *A Command Post at War*, 181–82; Bradley and Blair, *A Soldier's Story*, 433–38; MacDonald and Matthews, *Battle of the Huertgen Forest*, 87–88; Atkinson, *Guns at Last Light*, 312; Forrest C. Pogue, *The Supreme Command*. Part of the *United States Army in World War II* (Washington, DC: Center of Military History, United States Army, 1989), 310; Jeffrey J. Clarke and Robert Ross Smith, *Riviera to the Rhine*. Part of the *United States Army in World War II* series. Reprint (Atlanta, GA: Whitman, 2012), 351–53; Miller, *Division Commander*, 109–11.

12   Hogan, *A Command Post at War*, 170–71; Major William C. Sylvan and Captain Francis G. Smith, *Normandy to Victory: The War Diary of General Courtney H. Hodges and the First U.S. Army*, edited by John T. Greenwood (Lexington: University Press of Kentucky, 2008), 151, 153, 155; Dwight D. Eisenhower, *Crusade in Europe* (Baltimore and London: Johns Hopkins University Press, 1948), 328; *G-2 Journal: Algiers to the Elbe*, Benjamin A. Dickson Papers, USAMHI; Forrest C. Pogue, *Pogue's War: Diaries of a WWII Combat Historian* (Lexington: University Press of Kentucky, 2001), 251; Bradley and Blair, *A Soldier's Story*, 362, 439, 440; Atkinson, *Guns at Last Light*, 309–11.

13   MacDonald and Matthews, *Siegfried Line Campaign*, 340–41; MacDonald and Matthews, *Battle of the Huertgen Forest*, 88–89; Miller, *Division Commander*, 113; Norman Cota to Commanding General, V Corps, Summary of the Operations of the 28th Infantry Division for the period November 2–8, 1944, November 18, 1944, copy in Lynn Collection; Atkinson, *Guns at Last Light*, 312.

14   Albert L. Berndt, MD, *Comments on "Objective: Schmidt"*, Background Files, Study, *Three Battles: Arnaville, Altuzzo, and Schmidt*, Box 1, Entry P-39, RG 319, NA. According to Berndt, the 112th received the attack orders a week or ten days before their October 25 move date, but that is unlikely since the orders were certainly not cut until after Eisenhower's October 18 conference.

15   MacDonald and Matthews, *Siegfried Line Campaign*, 72–73; Hogan, *A Command Post at War*, 181–82.

16   Miller, *Division Commander*, 80–81; Fleig, *707th Tank Battalion in World War II*; Atkinson, *Guns at Last Light*, 317.

17   *Historical and Pictorial Review of the 28th Infantry Division in World War II* (Indiantown Gap, PA: 28th Infantry Division, 1946); S-2 Journal and Daily Summary, October 26, 1944, World War II Operations Records for the 112th Infantry, S-2 and S-3 Journals, Field Orders, Overlays, and Daily Summaries, October 16–31, 1944, Entry 427, Box 7470, RG 407, NA; George Wilson, *If You Survive: From Normandy to the Battle of the Bulge to the End of World War II, One American Officer's Riveting True Story* (New York: Ivy Books, Random House Publishing Group, Kindle Edition, 1987), 187.

18   *Headquarters, 28th Infantry Division*, October 26, 1944, Pennsylvania National Guard Museum; History, Headquarters, 2nd Battalion, 112th Infantry, 328 Inf (112) 0.1, Entry 427, RG 407, NA; *Headquarters, 28th Infantry Division*, Co. K, October 26, Pennsylvania National Guard Museum; *Historical and Pictorial Review of the 28th Infantry Division in World War II*; Morning Reports, Company B, 112th Infantry, 28th Infantry Division, October 26, 1944, National Personnel Records Center, St. Louis.

19   Miller, *Division Commander*, 114; Hogan, *A Command Post at War*, 182. There is some debate over who planned the attack. Charles B. MacDonald and Sidney

T. Matthews, *Three Battles: Arnaville, Altuzzo, and Schmidt* (Washington, DC: United States Army Center of Military History, 1952. Reprint, 1999), 253, and Miller, *A Dark and Bloody Ground*, 51, state that Gerow's corps staff planned the attack. Doubler, *Closing With the Enemy*, 180–81, noted "excessive control" at both army and corps. Hodges's aide said that the 28th Division's assistant commander planned it (Sylvan and Smith, *Normandy to Victory*, 161), but Davis himself does not claim that and even criticizes the plan. The safest analysis is that both corps and army staffers had something to do with the plan.

20   Major Jade E. Hinman, *When the Japanese Bombed the Huertgen Forest: How the Army's Investigation of Pearl Harbor Influenced the Outcome of the Huertgen Forest, Major General Leonard T. Gerow and His Command of V Corps 1943–1945* (Fort Leavenworth, KS: School of Advanced Military Studies, United States Army Command and General Staff College, 2011), 14, 16–17, 25–28, 30, 32, 34. According to Hinman, Gerow relinquished command of the V Corps to Maj. Gen. Edward Broocks on September 15. After testifying in Washington, he returned to Europe and resumed command on October 5.

21   MacDonald and Matthews, *Three Battles: Arnaville, Altuzzo, and Schmidt*, 254; Miller, *Division Commander*, 116–17; Postwar Interview with Carl L. Peterson, Background Files, Study, *Three Battles: Arnaville, Altuzzo, and Schmidt*, Box 1, Interviews Folder, RG 319, NA; Combat Interview, Maj. Richard S. Dana, File 328 Inf (112) 0.1, Entry 427, RG407, NA; copy in Lynn Collection; Norman Cota to Commanding General, V Corps, Summary of the Operations of the 28th Infantry Division for the period November 2–8, 1944, November 18, 1944, copy in Lynn Collection.

22   MacDonald and Matthews, *Three Battles: Arnaville, Altuzzo, and Schmidt*, 253–54; Miller, *Division Commander*, 116; Bradbeer, "General Cota and the Battle of the Hurtgen Forest," 25, 40 n. 25; Norman Cota to Commanding General, V Corps, Summary of the Operations of the 28th Infantry Division for the period November 2-8, 1944, November 18, 1944, copy in Lynn Collection; Doubler, *Closing with the Enemy*, 180–81.

23   Bradbeer, "General Cota and the Battle of the Hurtgen Forest," 25; Miller, *Division Commander*, 113–14, 116; Hogan, *A Command Post at War*, 32, 161–62, 182, 184; Brig. Gen. George A. Davis to Maj. Gen. Orlando Ward, Background Files, Study, *Three Battles: Arnaville, Altuzzo, and Schmidt*, Box 1, Entry P-39, RG 319, NA; Sylvan and Smith, *Normandy to Victory*, 161; Atkinson, *Guns at Last Light*, 313–14, 317; "Vossenack-Kommerscheidt-Schmidt, 28th Infantry Division—November 2–8, 1944, Interviews with Maj. Gen. Norman D. Cota and Brig. Gen. George A. Davis," Combat Interviews, 328 Inf (112) 0.1, Entry 427, RG 407, NA; Miller and Zabecki, "Tank Battle in Kommerscheidt," 44.

24   Interview with Maj. Gen. (Ret.) Norman D. Cota, not dated; Maj. Gen. (Ret.) Norman D. Cota to Major H. P. Halsell, March 14, 1948; Brig. Gen. George A. Davis to Maj. Gen. Orlando Ward, not dated; and Let. Gen. Leonard T. Gerow to General Malony, November 8, 1948, all in Background Files, Study, *Three Battles: Arnaville, Altuzzo, and Schmidt*, Box 1, Entry P-39, RG 319, NA; Bradbeer, "General Cota and the Battle of the Hurtgen Forest," 25; Miller, *Division Commander*, 113–14, 117; Hogan, *A Command Post at War*, 182, 184; Cecil B. Currey, *Follow Me and Die: The Destruction of* *an American Division in World War II* (New York: Stein and Day, 1984), 59–60. Gerow was not alone in his belief that Collins was Hodges favorite. See Hogan, *A Command Post at War*, 170.

25   "Hurtgen Forest Campaign, First U.S. Army (V Corps Sector)," Combat Interviews, 328 Inf (112) 0.1, Entry 427, RG 407, NA. This document summarizes the activities of combat historians Capt. John S. Howe, Capt. William J. Fox, 1st Lt. Harry Tackson, and T/3 Jose M. Topete to chronicle the campaign.

26   Albert L. Berndt, MD, *Comments on "Objective: Schmidt"*, Background Files, Study, *Three Battles: Arnaville, Altuzzo, and Schmidt*, Box 1, Entry P-39, RG 319, NA; www.youtube.com/watch?v=_MrkkRtgN4I; Postwar Interview with Carl L. Peterson, Background Files, Study, *Three Battles: Arnaville, Altuzzo, and Schmidt*, Box 1, Interviews Folder, RG 319, NA; Postwar Interview with Carl L. Peterson, Background Files, Study, *Three Battles: Arnaville, Altuzzo, and Schmidt*, Box 1, Interviews Folder, RG 319, NA. The YouTube file is a recording of Colonel Peterson addressing a 1949 Rotary Club meeting in Pennsylvania.

27   Maj. Gen. (Ret.) Norman D. Cota to Major H. P. Halsell, March 14, 1948, in Background Files, Study, *Three Battles: Arnaville, Altuzzo, and Schmidt*, Box 1, Entry P-39, RG 319, NA; Let. Gen. Leonard T. Gerow to General Malony, November 8, 1048, Background Files, Study, *Three Battles: Arnaville, Altuzzo, and Schmidt*, Box 1, Entry P-39, RG 319, NA; Lt. Col. Benjamin G. Taylor, "Operation Schmidt," *Military Review* 34 (August 1954): 32–33.

28   Pete Lynn to "Hello My Darling wife and Babys," October 25, 1944, Lynn Collection. Lynn started this letter on October 25 but finished it two days later.

29   *Headquarters, 28th Infantry Division*, October 27–29, 1944, Pennsylvania National Guard Museum.

30   S-3 Journal and Daily Summary, October 27, 1944, World War II Operations Records for the 112th Infantry, S-2 and S-3 Journals, Field Orders, Overlays, and Daily Summaries, October 16–31, 1944, Entry 427, Box 7470, RG 407, NA; Morning Reports, Company B, 112th Infantry, 28th Infantry Division, October 27, 1944, National Personnel Records Center, St. Louis.

31   Diary, October 28, 1944, Co. K, 112th Infantry, 328 Inf (112) 0.1, Entry 427, RG 407, NA; MacDonald and Matthews, *Three Battles: Arnaville, Altuzzo, and Schmidt*, 268. Similar records for Company B do not exist as they were lost in the battle that followed. However, the experiences of Company K were undoubtedly similar and are useful in reconstructing what Pete saw and did during these days.

32   S-2 and S-3 Journal and Daily Summary, October 28, 1944, World War II Operations Records for the 112th Infantry, S-2 and S-3 Journals, Field Orders, Overlays, and Daily Summaries, October 16–31, 1944, Entry 427, Box 7470, RG 407, NA.

33   S-2 and S-3 Journal and Daily Summary, October 28, 1944, World War II Operations Records for the 112th Infantry, S-2 and S-3 Journals, Field Orders, Overlays, and Daily Summaries, October 16–31, 1944, Entry 427, Box 7470, RG 407, NA.

34   Morning Reports, Company B, 112th Infantry, 28th Infantry Division, October 28, 1944, National Personnel Records Center, St. Louis.

35 S-2 and S-3 Journal and Daily Summary, October 28, 1944, World War II Operations Records for the 112th Infantry, S-2 and S-3 Journals, Field Orders, Overlays, and Daily Summaries, October 16–31, 1944, Entry 427, Box 7470, RG 407, NA; Pete Lynn to "Hello Dearst wife and Babys," October 28, 1944, Lynn Collection.
36 S-2 and S-3 Journal and Daily Summary, October 29, 1944, World War II Operations Records for the 112th Infantry, S-2 and S-3 Journals, Field Orders, Overlays, and Daily Summaries, October 16–31, 1944, Entry 427, Box 7470, RG 407, NA.
37 Diary, October 29, 1944, Co. K, 112th Infantry, 328 Inf (112) 0.1, Entry 427, RG 407, NA; *Headquarters, 28th Infantry Division*, October 29, Pennsylvania National Guard Museum.
38 Morning Reports, Company B, 112th Infantry, 28th Infantry Division, October 29, 1944, National Personnel Records Center, St. Louis; *Invader*, October 29, 1944, Pennsylvania National Guard Museum.
39 Pete Lynn to "Hello Darling," October 29, 1944, Lynn Collection. Pete's letter was postmarked on November 11.
40 Diary, October 30, 1944, Co. K, 112th Infantry, 328 Inf (112) 0.1, Entry 427, RG 407, NA; History, Headquarters, 2nd Battalion, 112th Infantry, 328 Inf (112) 0.1, Entry 427, RG 407, NA; Robert Grant Crist, ed., *The First Century: A History of the 28th Infantry Division* (Harrisburg, PA: 28th Infantry Division, 1979), 168; MacDonald and Matthews, *Three Battles: Arnaville, Altuzzo, and Schmidt*, 268; Hillard Morris, *A View from the High Point of Hell: Memoirs of S/Sgt. Hillard Morris, 81mm Mortar Observer, 196 Days Combat, Normandy to the Rhine River, July 1944–April 1945* (privately published, not dated), 66–67; William F. Meller, *Bloody Roads to Germany: At Huertgen Forest and the Bulge—an American Soldier's Courageous Story of World War II* (New York: Berkley Caliber, 2012), 56–57; Postwar Interview with Carl L. Peterson, Background Files, Study, *Three Battles: Arnaville, Altuzzo, and Schmidt*, Box 1, Interviews Folder, RG 319, NA; *Headquarters, 28th Infantry Division*, October 30, 1944, Pennsylvania National Guard Museum. According to Capt. William J. Fox, the 1st Battalion went into reserve west of Germeter "at the base of the CR at (C18324)." Combat Interview, Maj. Richard S. Dana, File 328 Inf (112) 0.1, Entry 427, RG407, NA; copy in Lynn Collection.
41 S-2 and S-3 Journal and Daily Summary, October 30, 1944, World War II Operations Records for the 112th Infantry, S-2 and S-3 Journals, Field Orders, Overlays, and Daily Summaries, October 16–31, 1944, Entry 427, Box 7470, RG 407, NA.
42 *Headquarters, 28th Infantry Division*, October 30, 1944, Pennsylvania National Guard Museum; S-2 and S-3 Journal and Daily Summary, October 30, 1944, World War II Operations Records for the 112th Infantry, S-2 and S-3 Journals, Field Orders, Overlays, and Daily Summaries, October 16–31, 1944, Entry 427, Box 7470, RG 407, NA.
43 Pete Lynn to "Hello Kid Sis," October 31, 1944, Lynn Collection; S-2 and S-3 Journal and Daily Summary, October 30, 1944, World War II Operations Records for the 112th Infantry, S-2 and S-3 Journals, Field Orders, Overlays, and Daily Summaries, October 16–31, 1944, Entry 427, Box 7470, RG 407, NA; Crist, *The First Century*, 169; Fleig, *707th Tank Battalion in World War II*; Sylvan and Smith, *Normandy to Victory*, 161; "Vossenack-Kommerscheidt-Schmidt, 28th Infantry Division—November 2–8, 1944,

Interviews with Maj. Gen. Norman D. Cota and Brig. Gen. George A. Davis," Combat Interviews, 328 Inf (112) 0.1, Entry 427, RG 407, NA. According to Cota and Davis, the attack had to go off by November 3; Diary, October 31, 1944, Co. K, 112th Infantry, 328 Inf (112) 0.1, Entry 427, RG 407, NA.

44 S-2 and S-3 Journal and Daily Summary, October 31, 1944, World War II Operations Records for the 112th Infantry, S-2 and S-3 Journals, Field Orders, Overlays, and Daily Summaries, October 16–31, 1944, Entry 427, Box 7470, RG 407, NA; *Headquarters, 28th Infantry Division*, October 31, Pennsylvania National Guard Museum; *Headquarters, 28th Infantry Division*, October 31, 1944, Pennsylvania National Guard Museum.

45 Morning Reports, Company B, 112th Infantry, 28th Infantry Division, October 31, 1944, National Personnel Records Center, St. Louis.

46 Pete Lynn to "Hello Kid Sis," October 31, 1944, Lynn Collection.

47 Pete Lynn to "Hi Darling," October 31, 1944, Lynn Collection. Pete's letter from this day was postmarked on November 12.

48 Pete Lynn to "Well Dear," October 31, 1944, Lynn Collection. This letter was postmarked November 3.

49 Earl F. Ziemke, "Rundstedt," in Correlli Barnett, ed., *Hitler's Generals: Authoritative Portraits of the Men Who Waged Hitler's War* (New York: Quill/William Morrow, 1989), 175–201.

50 Carlo D'Este, "Model," in Barnett, *Hitler's Generals*, 319–27.

51 Erich Straube, *LXXIV Corps from September to December 1944*, U.S. Army Military History Institute, 1–3; Rush, *Hell in Hurtgen Forest*, 49; Lucian Heichler, *The First Battle of the Huertgen Forest*, Background Files, *The Siegfried Line Campaign*, R-Series #42, RG 319, NA, 9; Rudolf-Christoph von Gersdorff, *The Battle of the Hurtgen Forest*, 5–6, USAMHI; *G-2 Journal: Algiers to the Elbe*, Benjamin A. Dickson Papers, USAMHI.

52 Rush, *Hell in Hurtgen Forest*, 52; MacDonald and Matthews, *The Battle of the Huertgen Forest*, 68; Lucian Heichler, *The First Battle of the Huertgen Forest*, Background Files, *The Siegfried Line Campaign*, R-Series #42, RG 319, NA, 1–2, 5–7, 8; *G-2 Journal: Algiers to the Elbe*, Benjamin A. Dickson Papers, USAMHI; Atkinson, *Guns at Last Light*, 313. The 275th Division had a strength of 6,500 men when the 9th attacked.

53 Rudolf-Christoph von Gersdorff, *The Battle of the Hurtgen Forest*, 2–3, 8, 14–15, USAMHI.

54 Rudolf-Christoph von Gersdorff, *The Battle of the Hurtgen Forest*, 7–11, USAMHI.

55 MacDonald and Matthews, *Battle of the Huertgen Forest*, 68; S-2 Journal, 112th Infantry, November 1, 1944, Entry 427, RG 407, NA.

56 Unit Report #5, 1 November 1944, 112th Infantry, 28th Infantry Division, RG 407, Box 8607, NA; S-2 and S-3 Journal and Daily Summary, November 1, 1944, World War II Operations Records for the 112th Infantry, S-2 and S-3 Journals, Field Orders, Overlays, and Daily Summaries, November 1–15, 1944, Entry 427, Box 7470, RG 407, NA; Ralph E. Maness to Mrs. Ruth H. Lynn, May 10, 1946, and Capt. Alan P. Madden to Ruth Lynn, April 13, 1946, both in the Lynn Collection; Press Release, Obituary of Fr. Alan Madden, February 1981, Copy courtesy of Fr. Francis Fugini, Archivist of the Capuchins; *The Pittsburgh Press*, February 3, 1981. Madden joined the National Guard in 1940 and was inducted into the U.S. Army on February 17, 1941.

57   MacDonald and Matthews, *Three Battles: Arnaville, Altuzzo, and Schmidt*, 268; Combat Interview, S/Sgt. Nathaniel Quentin, T/Sgt. George A. Lockwood, S/Sgt. Stephen J. Kertes, and Sgt. Travis C. Norton, A Company, December 7, 1944, Box 24032, Entry 427, RG 407, NA; "Vossenack-Kommerscheidt-Schmidt, 28th Infantry Division—November 2–8, 1944," Combat Interviews, 328 Inf (112) 0.1, Entry 427, RG 407, NA.

58   S-2 and S-3 Journal and Daily Summary, November 1, 1944, World War II Operations Records for the 112th Infantry, S-2 and S-3 Journals, Field Orders, Overlays, and Daily Summaries, November 1–15, 1944, Entry 427, Box 7470, RG 407, NA; Morning Reports, Company B, 112th Infantry, 28th Infantry Division, November 1, 1944, National Personnel Records Center, St. Louis. The German soldier said his company contained thirty men, had two bazookas and four machine guns, and other companies guarded its flanks.

59   Diary, November 1, 1944, Co. K, 112th Infantry, 328 Inf (112) 0.1, Entry 427, RG 407, NA; *Headquarters, 28th Infantry Division*, November 1, 1944, Pennsylvania National Guard Museum; History, Company F, 112th Infantry, 328 Inf (112) 0.1, Entry 427, RG 407, NA; S-2 and S-3 Journal and Daily Summary, November 1, 1944, World War II Operations Records for the 112th Infantry, S-2 and S-3 Journals, Field Orders, Overlays, and Daily Summaries, November 1–15, 1944, Entry 427, Box 7470, RG 407, NA.

60   Sylvan and Smith, *Normandy to Victory*, 161; Miller, *Division Commander*, 118–19; Bradbeer, "General Cota and the Battle of the Hurtgen Forest," *Army History* 75 (Spring 2010), 27; Atkinson, *Guns at Last Light*, 317. In apparent reference to the 109th's attack toward Hürtgen, the army commander also explained that "they are feinting to the north in hopes of fooling the Boche into the belief that this is the main effort" before "whacking him with everything in the direction of the town of Schmidt" with the 112th.

61   Pete Lynn to "Hi Darling Wife," November 1, 1944, Lynn Collection. The letter was postmarked November 3. It was the last letter to Ruth Pete ever wrote.

62   Fleig, *707th Tank Battalion in World War II*; Unit Report #5, November 1, 1944, 112th Infantry, 28th Infantry Division, RG 407, Box 8607, NA; Combat Interview, Maj. Richard S. Dana, File 328 Inf (112) 0.1, Entry 427, RG407, NA; copy in Lynn Collection; S-2 and S-3 Journal and Daily Summary, November 1, 1944, World War II Operations Records for the 112th Infantry, S-2 and S-3 Journals, Field Orders, Overlays, and Daily Summaries, November 1–15, 1944, Entry 427, Box 7470, RG 407, NA.

63   Morning Reports, Company B, 112th Infantry, 28th Infantry Division, November 1, 1944, National Personnel Records Center, St. Louis; S-2 and S-3 Journal and Daily Summary, November 1, 1944, World War II Operations Records for the 112th Infantry, S-2 and S-3 Journals, Field Orders, Overlays, and Daily Summaries, October 16–31, 1944, Entry 427, Box 7470, RG 407, NA.

64   S-2 Journal, 112th Infantry, November 2, 1944, Entry 427, RG 407, NA; Gunther Schmidt, "The 272 VGD in Action in the Eifel, 1944–1945," http://www.dererstezung.com/272ndInAction/272ndInAction(3).htm, accessed on July 27, 2013, 3; Atkinson, *Guns at Last Light*, 317; Fleig, *707th Tank Battalion in World War II*. The rain began at 3:00 A.M. according to the 112th Infantry's S-2 Journal.

65   *Headquarters, 28th Infantry Division*, November 2, 1944, Pennsylvania National Guard Museum.

66   Postwar Interview with Carl L. Peterson, Background Files, Study, *Three Battles: Arnaville, Altuzzo, and Schmidt*, Box 1, Interviews Folder, RG 319, NA. For Davis's nickname, see Harry M. Kemp, *The Regiment: Let the Citizens Bear Arms! A Narrative History of an American Infantry Regiment in World War II* (Austin, TX: Nortex Press, 1990), 120.

67   Combat Interview, Maj. Richard S. Dana, File 328 Inf (112) 0.1, Entry 427, RG407, NA; copy in Lynn Collection; Atkinson, *Guns at Last Light*, 317; MacDonald and Matthews, *Three Battles: Arnaville, Altuzzo, and Schmidt*, 259; Bradbeer, "General Cota and the Battle of the Hurtgen, 27; "Vossenack-Kommerscheidt-Schmidt, 28th Infantry Division—November 2–8, 1944, Interviews with Maj. Gen. Norman D. Cota and Brig. Gen. George A. Davis," Combat Interviews, 328 Inf (112) 0.1, Entry 427, RG 407, NA; Gavin, "Bloody Huertgen," 8; Schmidt, "The 272 VGD in Action in the Eifel, 1944–1945," 3; Fleig, *707th Tank Battalion in World War II*. Gavin listed the total shells fired by the 28th as 7,313.

68   History, Headquarters, 2nd Battalion, 112th Infantry, 328 Inf (112) 0.1, Entry 427, RG 407, NA; MacDonald and Matthews, *Three Battles: Arnaville, Altuzzo, and Schmidt*, 259; Unit Report, November 2, 1944, Entry 427, File 328 Inf (112) 0.9, RG 407, NA; History, Company F, 112th Infantry, 328 Inf (112) 0.1, Entry 427, RG 407, NA.

69   *New York Times*, November 6, 1944. Based on the dateline of the article, Denny may have been writing of action later in the battle but the vista was similar throughout.

70   "Vossenack-Kommerscheidt-Schmidt, 28th Infantry Division—November 2–8, 1944, Interviews with Maj. Gen. Norman D. Cota and Brig. Gen. George A. Davis," Combat Interviews, 328 Inf (112) 0.1, Entry 427, RG 407, NA; MacDonald and Matthews, *Three Battles: Arnaville, Altuzzo, and Schmidt*, 259, 271–72; Miller, *Dark and Bloody Ground*, 57–58; Fleig, *707th Tank Battalion in World War II*; Miller, *Division Commander*, 119; History, Headquarters, 2nd Battalion, 112th Infantry, 328 Inf (112) 0.1, Entry 427, RG 407, NA; Unit Report #5, November 2, 1944, 112th Infantry, 28th Infantry Division, RG 407, Box 8607, NA; Kemp, *The Regiment*, 26, 158–64. The 110th's attack started at noon.

71   *A Soldier Remembers: The 112th Infantry in the 20th Century*, 13–14; *28th Infantry (Keystone) Division (Mechanized): 125 Years of Service*, 126; Fleig, *707th Tank Battalion in World War II*; History, Company F, 112th Infantry, 328 Inf (112) 0.1, Entry 427, RG 407, NA; MacDonald and Matthews, *Three Battles: Arnaville, Altuzzo, and Schmidt*, 62; Miller, *Dark and Bloody Ground*, 60; Combat Interview, Maj. Richard S. Dana, File 328 Inf (112) 0.1, Entry 427, RG407, NA; copy in Lynn Collection.

72   *A Soldier Remembers: The 112th Infantry in the 20th Century* (Erie, PA: 112th Infantry Regiment Association, 2001), 13–14; *28th Infantry (Keystone) Division (Mechanized): 125 Years of Service* (Nashville, TN and Paducah, KY: Turner Publishing Company, 2005), 126; Fleig, *707th Tank Battalion in World War II*; MacDonald and Matthews, *Three Battles: Arnaville, Altuzzo, and Schmidt*, 259, 261, 262–63; Charles L. Crain Collection, AFC 2001/001/396, American Folklife Center, Veterans History Project, Library of Congress.

73   Unit Report #5, 2 November 1944, 112th Infantry, 28th Infantry Division, RG 407, Box 8607, NA; Fleig, *707th Tank Battalion in World War II*; "Vossenack-Kommerscheidt-Schmidt, 28th Infantry Division—November 2–8, 1944, Interviews with Maj. Gen. Norman D. Cota and Brig. Gen. George A. Davis," Combat Interviews, 328 Inf (112) 0.1, Entry 427, RG 407, NA; Crist, *The First Century*, 170; MacDonald and Matthews, *Three Battles: Arnaville, Altuzzo, and Schmidt*, 262–63.

74   Edward Brandt Hipp Collection, Veterans History Project, American Folklife Center, Library of Congress; Unit Report #5, November 2, 1944, 112th Infantry, 28th Infantry Division, RG 407, Box 8607, NA; Fleig, *707th Tank Battalion in World War II*; "Vossenack-Kommerscheidt-Schmidt, 28th Infantry Division—November 2–8, 1944, Interviews with Maj. Gen. Norman D. Cota and Brig. Gen. George A. Davis," Combat Interviews, 328 Inf (112) 0.1, Entry 427, RG 407, NA; Crist, *The First Century*, 170; MacDonald, *Three Battles: Arnaville, Altuzzo, and Schmidt*, 263–66; Bradbeer, "General Cota and the Battle of the Hurtgen Forest," 28; Combat Interview, Maj. Richard S. Dana, File 328 Inf (112) 0.1, Entry 427, RG407, NA; copy in Lynn Collection.

75   Unit Report #5, November 2, 1944, 112th Infantry, 28th Infantry Division, RG 407, Box 8607, NA; After Action Report, December 3, 1944, 707th Tank Battalion, October–December 1944, April 1945–May 6, 1945, Combined Arms Digital Research Library, http://cgsc.contentdm.oclc.org/cdm/singleitem/collection/p4013coll8/id/3454/rec/15, accessed November 5, 2012; History, Company F, 112th Infantry, 328 Inf (112) 0.1, Entry 427, RG 407, NA; MacDonald and Matthews, *Three Battles: Arnaville, Altuzzo, and Schmidt*, 261.

76   "Vossenack-Kommerscheidt-Schmidt, 28th Infantry Division—November 2–8, 1944, Interviews with Maj. Gen. Norman D. Cota and Brig. Gen. George A. Davis," Combat Interviews, 328 Inf (112) 0.1, Entry 427, RG 407, NA; Unit Report #5, November 2, 1944, 112th Infantry, 28th Infantry Division, RG 407, Box 8607, NA; After Action Report, December 3, 1944, 707th Tank Battalion, October–December 1944, April 1945– May 6, 1945, Combined Arms Digital Research Library, http://cgsc.contentdm.oclc.org/cdm/singleitem/collection/p4013coll8/id/3454/rec/15, accessed November 5, 2012; History, Company F, 112th Infantry, 328 Inf (112) 0.1, Entry 427, RG 407, NA.

77   Miller, *Division Commander*, 117–19; Rudolf-Christoph von Gersdorff, *The Battle of the Hurtgen Forest*, 14–17, USAMHI; Siegfried von Waldenberg, *Report on 116th Panzer Division*, USAMHI; Fleig, *707th Tank Battalion in World War II*; Atkinson, *Guns at Last Light*, 319; *G-2 Journal: Algiers to the Elbe*, Benjamin A. Dickson Papers, USAMHI; Doubler, *Closing with the Enemy*, 181.

78   Carpenter, *No Woman's World*, 249, 250–51; Clarke and Smith, *Riviera to the Rhine*, 565–66.

79   Fleig, *707th Tank Battalion in World War II*; History, Headquarters, 2nd Battalion, 112th Infantry, 328 Inf (112) 0.1, Entry 427, RG 407, NA; MacDonald and Matthews, *Three Battles: Arnaville, Altuzzo, and Schmidt*, 268–69; Morning Reports, Company B, 112th Infantry, 28th Infantry Division, November 2, 1944, National Personnel Records Center, St. Louis; Postwar Interview with Carl L. Peterson, Background Files, Study, *Three Battles: Arnaville, Altuzzo, and Schmidt*, Box 1, Interviews Folder, RG 319, NA;

Morning Reports, Company B, 112th Infantry, 28th Infantry Division, November 2, 1944; Sgt. Charlton R. Vincent to Mrs. Ruth Lynn, December 4, 1945, Lynn Collection.

80   Combat Interview, Capt. Richard Gooley, December 4, 1944, Box 24032, Entry 427, RG 407, NA; Fleig, *707th Tank Battalion in World War II*; MacDonald and Matthews, *Three Battles: Arnaville, Altuzzo, and Schmidt*, 268–69; Interview, Capt. Richard Cooley, December 4, 1944, copy in Lynn Collection.

81   Carpenter, *No Woman's World*, 179.

82   Maj. Gen. (Ret.) Norman D. Cota to Maj. H. P. Halsell, March 14, 1948, in Background Files, Study, *Three Battles: Arnaville, Altuzzo, and Schmidt*, Box 1, Entry P-39, RG 319, NA; MacDonald and Matthews, *Three Battles: Arnaville, Altuzzo, and Schmidt*, 263, 269; Fleig, *707th Tank Battalion in World War II*; Doubler, *Closing with the Enemy*, 104, 232; Kemp, *The Regiment*, 155. According to Doubler, *Closing with the Enemy*, 172–73, official U.S. Army doctrine called for soldiers to attack in column when fighting in forests, but did not specifically call for the employment of combined arms despite European war lessons to the contrary.

83   Peter Caddick-Adams, *Snow & Steel: The Battle of the Bulge, 1944–45* (New York: Oxford University Press, 2015); MacDonald and Matthews, *Three Battles: Arnaville, Altuzzo, and Schmidt*, 269.

84   Combat Interview, S/Sgt. Eugene Holden, December 6, 1944, Box 24032, Entry 427, RG 407, NA; Richelskaul, 268–69; Interview, Capt. Richard Cooley, December 4, 1944, copy in Lynn Collection; Fleig, *707th Tank Battalion in World War II*; Combat Interview, T/Sgt. Roy Littlehales and Sgt. Clarence J. Skains, File 328 Inf (112) 0.1, Entry 427, RG407, NA; copy also in Lynn Collection; MacDonald and Matthews, *Three Battles: Arnaville, Altuzzo, and Schmidt*, 269.

85   Carpenter, *No Woman's World*, 239.

86   Combat Interview, T/Sgt. Roy Littlehales and Sgt. Clarence J. Skains, File 328 Inf (112) 0.1, Entry 427, RG407, NA; copy also in Lynn Collection; MacDonald and Matthews, *Three Battles: Arnaville, Altuzzo, and Schmidt*, 269; Fleig, *707th Tank Battalion in World War II*; Rush, *Hell in Hurtgen Forest*, 53, 129, 131.

87   Combat Interview, T/Sgt. Roy Littlehales and Sgt. Clarence J. Skains, File 328 Inf (112) 0.1, Entry 427, RG407, NA; copy also in Lynn Collection; MacDonald and Matthews, *Three Battles: Arnaville, Altuzzo, and Schmidt*, 269; Fleig, *707th Tank Battalion in World War II*; Rush, *Hell in Hurtgen Forest*, 53, 129, 131. According to Littlehales and Skains, the column had covered about 700 yards, but the text follows MacDonald's account, which is based on broader evidence. Meanwhile, Rush writes that the German 983rd contained about 600 men.

88   Clarke and Smith, *Riviera to the Rhine*, 565–66.

89   Lee Kennett, *G.I.: The American Soldier in World War II* (Norman: University of Oklahoma Press, 1987), 173.

90   Combat Interview, T/Sgt. Roy Littlehales and Sgt. Clarence J. Skains, File 328 Inf (112) 0.1, Entry 427, RG407, NA; Combat Interview, S/Sgt. Eugene Holden, December 6, 1944, Box 24032, Entry 427, RG 407, NA; copy also in Lynn Collection; MacDonald and Matthews, *Three Battles: Arnaville, Altuzzo, and Schmidt*, 269; Caddick-Adams, *Snow and Steel*, 199.

91 Morning Reports, Company B, 112th Infantry, 28th Infantry Division, November 5, 1944, National Personnel Records Center, St. Louis; Combat Interview, S/Sgt. Eugene Holden, December 6, 1944, Box 24032, Entry 427, RG 407, NA; http://www.in-honored-glory.info/html/stories/ifspaans.htm, accessed December 31, 2013. Holden recalled that the column reached its farthest point about 1:30 P.M., while according to the cited online account Hackard lost contact with Spaans about 1 P.M. The morning reports tell the rest of the story. We know from multiple accounts that Spaans was in front and killed immediately. The other men mentioned in the text were listed right after Spaans on the morning report as missing in action or as having combat exhaustion. Clearly all of these men were caught in the same crossfire.

92 MacDonald and Matthews, *Three Battles: Arnaville, Altuzzo, and Schmidt*, 269; Combat Interview, T/Sgt. Roy Littlehales and Sgt. Clarence J. Skains, File 328 Inf (112) 0.1, Entry 427, RG407, NA; copy also in Lynn Collection; Morning Reports, Company B, 112th Infantry, 28th Infantry Division, November 2, 1944, National Personnel Records Center, St. Louis; Fleig, *707th Tank Battalion in World War II*; Sgt. Charlton R. Vincent to Mrs. Ruth Lynn, December 4, 1945, Lynn Collection.

93 Morning Reports, Company B, 112th Infantry, 28th Infantry Division, November 2, 1944; Sgt. Charlton R. Vincent to Mrs. Ruth Lynn, December 4, 1945, Lynn Collection; Combat Interview, Maj. Richard S. Dana, File 328 Inf (112) 0.1, Entry 427, RG407, NA; copy in Lynn Collection. For the sensations of a man in the midst of a similar attack, see Wilson, *If You Survive*, 144.

94 MacDonald and Matthews, *Three Battles: Arnaville, Altuzzo, and Schmidt*, 269; Morning Reports, Company B, 112th Infantry, 28th Infantry Division, November 2, 1944, National Personnel Records Center, St. Louis; Fleig, *707th Tank Battalion in World War II*.

95 Taylor, "Operation Schmidt," 32–33.

96 Combat Interview, S/Sgt. Eugene Holden, December 6, 1944, Box 24032, Entry 427, RG 407, NA. There is one extant report to the contrary. A regimental summary states that both Company A and B were pinned down by machine gun fire at Objective A and Company C was moving to the right flank. At 3:47 P.M., B was said to be on the right and Company A was on the left on Objective C. No other accounts support this version of events. See S-2 and S-3 Journal and Daily Summary, November 1, 1944, World War II Operations Records for the 112th Infantry, S-2 and S-3 Journals, Field Orders, Overlays, and Daily Summaries, November 1–15, 1944, Entry 427, Box 7470, RG 407, NA.

97 MacDonald and Matthews, *Three Battles: Arnaville, Altuzzo, and Schmidt*, 269, 271; Combat Interview, T/Sgt. Roy Littlehales and Sgt. Clarence J. Skains, File 328 Inf (112) 0.1, Entry 427, RG407, NA; copy also in Lynn Collection; Combat Interview, S/Sgt. Eugene Holden, December 6, 1944, Box 24032, Entry 427, RG 407, NA; Taylor, "Operation Schmidt," 31–32; Crist, *The First Century*, 170; Morning Reports, Company B, 112th Infantry, 28th Infantry Division, November 2, 1944, National Personnel Records Center, St. Louis; Fleig, *707th Tank Battalion in World War II*; Sgt. Charlton R. Vincent to Mrs. Ruth Lynn, December 4, 1945, Lynn Collection. Burrill was listed as seriously wounded in action on the morning reports for November 2.

98 Fleig, *707th Tank Battalion in World War II*.

99   Postwar Interview with Carl L. Peterson, Background Files, Study, *Three Battles: Arnaville, Altuzzo, and Schmidt*, Box 1, Interviews Folder, RG 319, NA.

100   Maj. E. G. Miller, "A Brief Account of B Company (Capt. Clifford T. Hackard), 1st Battalion (MAJ Robert T. Hazlett) 112th Infantry in the Hurtgen Forest," Lynn Collection.

101   Combat Interview, T/Sgt. Roy Littlehales and Sgt. Clarence J. Skains, File 328 Inf (112) 0.1, Entry 427, RG407, NA; copy also in Lynn Collection"; "Vossenack-Kommerscheidt-Schmidt, 28th Infantry Division—November 2–8, 1944," Combat Interviews, 328 Inf (112) 0.1, Entry 427, RG 407, NA; Interview, Capt. Richard Cooley, December 4, 1944, copy in Lynn Collection; Combat Interview, S/Sgt. Nathaniel Quentin, T/Sgt. George A. Lockwood, S/Sgt. Stephen J. Kertes, and Sgt. Travis C. Norton, A Company, December 7, 1944, Box 24032, Entry 427, RG 407, NA. These sources differ slightly as to Company B's destination. Littlehales and Skain claimed that the company settled into the "edge of the woods," while the second cited source placed the company near Company A. Company A's position, located along the main road through Vossenack, was not in a tree line.

102   Morning Reports, Company B, 112th Infantry, 28th Infantry Division, November 2, 1944, National Personnel Records Center, St. Louis: Linguiti, Paschal and Michael DeMarco. "Subject: Evacuation of Wounded from Vossenack Kommerscheidt and Schmidt Areas, November 2–11, 1944," http://history.armedd.army.mil/booksdocs/wwii/Schmidt/DemarcoLinguitiRept.htm, accessed March 20, 2010, courtesy Charlie Oelig. The phrase "Morning Report" is a misnomer because the recorded casualties were incurred in the afternoon of November 2. Also, it is not certain that all of the men on this day's report were from the 3rd Platoon, but it is likely since Burrill's name was included. One man, PFC Lowell Applegate, was also listed as sick on November 2.

103   Interview, Capt. Richard Cooley, December 4, 1944, copy in Lynn Collection.

104   Combat Interview, T/Sgt. Roy Littlehales and Sgt. Clarence J. Skains, File 328 Inf (112) 0.1, Entry 427, RG407, NA; copy also in Lynn Collection; "Vossenack-Kommerscheidt-Schmidt, 28th Infantry Division—November 2–8, 1944," Combat Interviews, 328 Inf (112) 0.1, Entry 427, RG 407, NA.

105   Fleig, *707th Tank Battalion in World War II.*

106   Combat Interview, S/Sgt. Eugene Holden, December 6, 1944, Box 24032, Entry 427, RG 407, NA; Combat Interview, Maj. Richard S. Dana, File 328 Inf (112) 0.1, Entry 427, RG407, NA; copy in Lynn Collection; Major E.G. Miller, "A Brief Account of B Company (Capt. Clifford T. Hackard), 1st Battalion (MAJ Robert T. Hazlett) 112th Infantry in the Hurtgen Forest," Lynn Collection.

107   Morning Reports, Company B, 112th Infantry, 28th Infantry Division, November 3, 1944, National Personnel Records Center, St. Louis; Unit Report #5, November 3, 1944, 112th Infantry, 28th Infantry Division, RG 407, Box 8607, NA. Four replacements also joined Company B on November 3.

108   Combat Interview, Maj. Richard S. Dana, File 328 Inf (112) 0.1, Entry 427, RG407, NA; copy in Lynn Collection; Combat Interview, S/Sgt. Eugene Holden, December 6, 1944, Box 24032, Entry 427, RG 407, NA; Norman Cota to Commanding General, V Corps, Summary of the Operations of the 28th Infantry Division for the period November 2–8, 1944, November 18, 1944, copy in Lynn Collection;

Headquarters, 28th Infantry Division, November 3, 1944, Pennsylvania National Guard Museum; Miller, *Division Commander,* 119; Fleig, *707th Tank Battalion in World War II;* Miller and Zabecki, "Tank Battle in Kommerscheidt," 45; Atkinson, *Guns at Last Light,* 318–19.

109 Combat Interview, T/Sgt. Roy Littlehales and Sgt. Clarence J. Skains, File 328 Inf (112) 0.1, Entry 427, RG407, NA; copy also in Lynn Collection; Morning Reports, Company B, 112th Infantry, 28th Infantry Division, November 4 and 6, 1944, National Personnel Records Center, St. Louis; World War II Enlistment Record for James L. Knight, RG 64, NA; "James Luther Knight," www.findagrave.com. Knight is buried in East View Cemetery in Honea Path, South Carolina.

110 Disinterment Directive for Vernon Bowers; Individual Deceased Personnel File, Vernon Bowers, U.S. Army Human Resources Command, Alexandria, VA; World War II Enlistment Record for Vernon Davis Bowers, RG 64, NA; "Vernon Davis Bowers," www.findagrave.com; Morning Reports, Company B, 112th Infantry, 28th Infantry Division, November 3, 1944, National Personnel Records Center, St. Louis. Bowers was wrapped in two blankets and a mattress cover and buried at Henri-Chapelle in Plot R, Row 10, Grave 199. His effects included coins in a coin purse, religious articles, photos, a pay book, and souvenir money. In 1947, he was exhumed, shipped home, and reburied in the Grantsville Cemetery in Grantsville, Maryland.

111 Morning Reports, Company B, 112th Infantry, 28th Infantry Division, November 1–5, 1944, National Personnel Records Center, St. Louis; Interview with Clydene Sparks, August 3, 2015. Clyde Sparks's daughter later remembered him as a "a quiet type man" who wore khaki pants all the time. He was known to drink too much home-made liquor, which turned him into an angry man. Searching for other outlets, Sprinkle hunted and also took to collecting antiques. He retired from RJ Reynolds Tobacco Company and died of congestive heart failure in 1994. Sparks's wife destroyed all the letters he wrote home during the war.

112 Morning Reports, Company B, 112th Infantry, 28th Infantry Division, November 5, 1944, National Personnel Records Center, St. Louis; Combat Interview, T/Sgt. Roy Littlehales and Sgt. Clarence J. Skains, File 328 Inf (112) 0.1, Entry 427, RG407, NA; copy also in Lynn Collection.

113 Morning Reports, Company B, 112th Infantry, 28th Infantry Division, November 5, 1944, National Personnel Records Center, St. Louis; Combat Interview, T/Sgt. Roy Littlehales and Sgt. Clarence J. Skains, File 328 Inf (112) 0.1, Entry 427, RG407, NA; copy also in Lynn Collection. Hackard, who received the Distinguished Service Cross for the Hürtgen as well as a purple heart thanks to a sniper's bullet, remained in the army after the war and served with the occupation army of Japan, in the Korean War, and as a military advisor in Indochina. Retiring from the army in 1962, Hackard and his wife, Lucille, settled in Austin, Texas. They had two more children, and he took a job with the Texas Employment Commission. Hackard kept hunting and became a firearms expert and collector. He was a fixture at gun shows in Texas and Oklahoma and kept shooting skeet until failing eyesight forced him to give it up in his ninety-first year. After Lucille died in 1968, Hackard remarried Lois Margery Good in 1970. He died on February 28, 2015, and is buried in Austin. *Austin-American Statesman,* March 3–4, 2015, quoted in the entry for Clifford Thorne Hackard, www.findagrave.com.

Chapter 9: Bottom Fell Out

1   Ruth Lynn to "Hello Dearest," November 2, 1944, Lynn Collection.
2   Ruth Lynn to "Dearest Soldier," November 5, 1944, Lynn Collection.
3   Ruth Lynn to "Hello Dearest," November 2, 1944, Lynn Collection.
4   Ruth Lynn to "Dearest Bud Worm," November 3, 1944, Lynn Collection.
5   Ruth Lynn to "Dearest Soldier," November 5, 1944, Lynn Collection.
6   *Alleghany News*, March 24, 2005; Ruth Lynn Diary, November 4, 1944, Lynn Collection.
7   Ruth Lynn to "Dearest Soldier," November 7, 1944, Lynn Collection.
8   *Kings Mountain Herald*, November 9, 1944; *New York Times*, November 8, 1944.
9   Ruth Lynn to "Hi Hon," November 6, 1944, Lynn Collection.
10   Ruth Lynn to "Dearest Dady Pete," November 9, 1944, Lynn Collection. For the letter Ruth refers to, see chapter 7.
11   Ruth Lynn to "Hi Darling," November 10, 1944, Lynn Collection.
12   Ruth Lynn to "Hi Hon," November 12, 1944, Lynn Collection; Ruth Lynn to "Dearest Dady Pete, November 9, 1944, Lynn Collection.
13   Ruth Lynn to "Hi Hon," November 14, 1944, Lynn Collection. Pete's last three letters home were dated October 29, October 31, and November 1, but his last letter was actually postmarked on November 3 while the other two were postmarked on November 11 and 12, respectively.
14   Ruth Lynn Diary, November 16, 1944, Lynn Collection; Battle Casualty Report for Lynn, Felmer L., Individual Deceased Personnel File for Felmer Lonzo Lynn, U.S. Army Human Resources Command, Alexandria, VA; Telegram, November 16, 1944, Lynn Collection; "Record of Climatological Observations," November 16, 1944, National Oceanic & Atmospheric Administration. The *Kings Mountain Herald* of November 23, 1944, confirmed that Mr. F. H. Lynn was reported missing "last Thursday." The time on the telegram is actually 8:25 P.M., but that late time is unlikely. It must have been an error for there is a handwritten notation that states, "8:20 A.M."
15   Ruth Lynn Diary, November 17–18, 1944, Lynn Collection.
16   Rick Atkinson, *The Guns at Last Light: The War in Western Europe, 1944–1945* (New York: Henry Holt, 2013), 318; Lucian Heichler, *The First Battle of the Huertgen Forest*, Background Files, *The Siegfried Line Campaign*, R-Series #42, RG 319, NA, 10; Robert A. Miller, *Division Commander: A Biography of Major General Norman D. Cota* (Spartanburg, SC: The Reprint Company, 1989), 122; Charles B. MacDonald and Sidney T. Matthews, *The Battle of the Huertgen Forest* (New York: Jove, 1963), 100–2.
17   Miller, *Division Commander*, 119–20.
18   Miller, *Division Commander*, 121, 123, 125–26; Clarence Blakeslee, *A Personal Account of WWII by Draftee #36887149* (Rockford, MI: The Rockford Squire, 1998), 40; Atkinson, *Guns at Last Light*, 319–26; MacDonald and Matthews, *Battle of the Huertgen Forest*, 102–5, 108; Charles L. Crain Collection, AFC 2001/001/396, American Folklife Center, Veterans History Project, Library of Congress.
19   Edward G. Miller and David T. Zabecki, "Tank Battle in Kommerscheidt," *World War II* 15, no. 4 (November 2000): 47; Miller, *Division Commander*, 124–27; Edward G. Miller, *A Dark and Bloody Ground: The Hurtgen Forest and the Roer River*

Dams, 1944–1945 (College Station: Texas A&M University Press, 1995), 74–75, 78–83; MacDonald and Matthews, *Battle of the Huertgen Forest*, 107, 111–13.
20 Citation for Distinguished Service Cross, Capt. Clifford T. Hackard, File 328 Inf (112) 0.1, Entry 427, RG407, NA; Miller, *Division Commander*, 121; Major E. G. Miller, "A Brief Account of B Company (Capt. Clifford T. Hackard), 1st Battalion (MAJ Robert T. Hazlett) 112th Infantry in the Hurtgen Forest," Lynn Collection; Maj. Ed Miller to Petie Bass, July 9, 1994, Lynn Collection; Combat Interview, Capt. Richard Gooley, December 4, 1944, Box 24032, Entry 427, RG 407, NA; Miller, *A Dark and Bloody Ground*, 73, 75; MacDonald and Matthews, *Battle of the Huertgen Forest*, 106–7, 117–18.
21 Postwar Interview with Carl L. Peterson, Background Files, Study, *Three Battles: Arnaville, Altuzzo, and Schmidt*, Box 1, Interviews Folder, RG 319, NA; Miller, *Division Commander*, 127–30; "Biographical Data, Gustin Mac A. Nelson," Press Release, Historical File, 28th Division—Personal Stories, Pennsylvania National Guard Museum; MacDonald and Matthews, *Battle of the Huertgen Forest*, 118.
22 Miller, *Division Commander*, 125, 128, 129; Miller, *A Dark and Bloody Ground*, 83; MacDonald and Matthews, *Battle of the Huertgen Forest*, 119–20.
23 Atkinson, *Guns at Last Light*, 324.
24 MacDonald and Matthews, *Battle of the Huertgen Forest*, 120; Charles B. MacDonald and Sidney T. Matthews, *Three Battles: Arnaville, Altuzzo, and Schmidt* (Washington, DC: United States Army Center of Military History, 1952. Reprint, 1999), 414–15; Robert L. Smith, *"Medic!": A WWII Combat Medic Remembers* (Berkeley, CA: Creative Arts Book Company, 2001), 71; Miller, *Division Commander*, 130; John Allard, "A Replacement in the Bloody Bucket," in Ray Merriam, ed., *True Tales of World War II: "We Were There"* (Bennington, VT: Merriam Press, 2011), 8; "Monthly Summary and Daily Summaries, 112th Infantry Regiment, 28th Infantry Division, Sep, Oct-Month of November 1944," RG 407, Box 8607, NA; Robert Grant Crist, ed., *The First Century: A History of the 28th Infantry Division* (Harrisburg, PA: 28th Infantry Division, 1979), 172; Miller and Zabecki, "Tank Battle in Kommerscheidt,", 88; Jack Goldbaugh, *The Bloody Patch: A True Story of the Daring 28th Infantry Division* (New York, Washington, Hollywood: Vantage Press, 1973), 83–84; Michael D. Doubler, *Closing with the Enemy: How GIs Fought the War in Europe, 1944–1945* (Lawrence: University Press of Kansas, 1994), 186–87. Peterson's own estimate was that the first battalion had only seventy-six men left after the battle. Lt. Col. Carl Peterson Papers.
25 Doubler, *Closing with the Enemy*, 193; *Saturday Evening Post*, September 28, 1946; Crist, *The First Century*, 172; Paul Boesch, *Road to Huertgen: Forest in Hell* (Houston, TX: Gulf, 1962), 1; Miller and Zabecki, "Tank Battle in Kommerscheidt,", 88. The First Army suffered heavier American losses per square mile here than in any other sector it assaulted.
26 Boesch, *Road to Huertgen*, 1; Atkinson, *Guns at Last Light*, 325; Charles B. MacDonald and Sidney T. Matthews, *The Last Offensive*. United States Army in World War II: The European Theater of Operations (Washington, DC: Office of the Chief of Military History, Department of the Army, 1993), 70.

27   Iris Carpenter, *No Woman's World* (Boston, MA: Houghton Mifflin, 1946), 181; Gunther Schmidt, "The 272 VGD in Action in the Eifel, 1944–1945," http://www. dererstezung.com/272ndInAction/272ndInAction(3).htm, accessed on July 27, 2013, 4; Atkinson, *Guns at Last Light*, 325.

28   "Poems for Remembrance," Lynn Collection. On the clipping she wrote, "While Pete was in France & Germany Sept to Nov.," and also the date "Nov. 20, 1944." She also cut out another poem, "Love Falls Like Rain," and underlined the words, "Revive, look up, and smile again."

29   Ruth Lynn to "Hi Hon," November 12, 1944, Lynn Collection; *Old Mountaineer*, February 3, 1945, Letters to Service Men, Mauney Memorial Library. Duke beat Alabama 29–26 in the game.

30   Ruth Lynn Diary, January 1–2, 1945, Lynn Collection. There are entries in the diary that predate Christmas 1944. Apparently, Ruth made some entries from memory for momentous dates for 1944.

31   Ruth Lynn Diary, January 4, 6, and 8, 1945, Lynn Collection.

32   Ruth Lynn Diary, February 5, 1945, Lynn Collection. Some of the letters were still unopened when this author examined them decades later.

33   Ruth Lynn Diary, January 11, 1945, Lynn Collection.

34   "Colonel with Cane Leads Yank Charge," Unprovenienced newspaper article, January 9, 1945.

35   *Charlotte Observer*, January 12, 1945, Lynn Collection.

36   *Old Mountaineer*, February 3, 1945, Letters to Service Men, Mauney Memorial Library; Ruth Lynn to "Dearest Dady Pete, November 9, 1944, Lynn Collection.

37   Ruth Lynn Diary, January 29, 1945, Lynn Collection.

38   Ruth Lynn Diary, February 13, 1945, Lynn Collection. See also Cpl. Al Pesek to "Dear Mrs. Lynn," March 8, 1945, Lynn Collection.

39   Ruth Lynn Diary, February 15–16, 1945, Lynn Collection.

40   Ruth Lynn Diary, February 24, 1945, and February 27, 1945, Lynn Collection.

41   MacDonald and Matthews, *The Last Offensive*, 71, 73, 74–83; *V Corps Operations in the ETO: 6 Jan. 1942–9 May 1945* (Washington, DC: U.S. Army, 1945), 368, 374–80; Atkinson, *Guns at Last Light*, 537.

42   MacDonald and Matthews, *The Last Offensive*, 80; Caddick-Adams, *Snow and Steel*, 398–99; James M. Gavin, "Bloody Huertgen," *American Heritage*, December 1979, accessed at www.americanheritage.com/print/53860?page+show, 1; James M. Gavin, *On to Berlin: Battles of an Airborne Commander, 1943–1946* (New York: Bantam, 1978), 288–90; Atkinson, *Guns at Last Light*, 537.

43   Gavin, *On to Berlin*, 284.

44   Gavin, *On to Berlin*, 290–92; James M. Gavin, "Bloody Huertgen," 3.

45   Atkinson, *Guns at Last Light*, 537; George Wilson, *If You Survive: From Normandy to the Battle of the Bulge to the End of World War II, One American Officer's Riveting True Story* (New York: Ivy Books, Random House Publishing Group, Kindle Edition, 1987), 30; Col. G. M. Nelson to Mrs. Evelyn L. Lynn, May 3, 1945, Lynn Collection.

46   Col. G. M. Nelson to Mrs. Evelyn L. Lynn, May 3, 1945, Lynn Collection.

47   *Henri-Chapelle American Cemetery and Memorial*, American Battle Monuments Commission, 5–6; Carpenter, *No Woman's World*, 187; Joseph T. Layne and Glenn

D. Barquest, *Margraten, U.S. Ninth Army Military Cemetery*, National World War II Museum, 5; *Charlotte Observer*, October 26, 1947; "Americans Gave Their Lives to Defeat the Nazis," *Washington Post*, May 26, 2015. About 17,000 graves were there originally. The cemetery and its memorial were completed in 1960, and 7,992 graves remain there today. The "smell of death" is based on another European cemetery, Margraten, but it was certainly characteristic of all.

48   Layne and Barquest, *Margraten, U.S. Ninth Army Military Cemetery*, 8-9; Joseph James Shomon, *Crosses in the Wind* (New York: Stratford House, 1947), 72–73, 97; https://www.med-dept.com/unit-histories/607th-quartermaster-graves-registration-company.

49   Layne and Barquest, *Margraten, U.S. Ninth Army Military Cemetery*, 8–9, 16; Atkinson, *Guns at Last Light*, 488; Shomon, *Crosses in the Wind*, 182.

50   Report of Burial, February 24, 1945, Felmer L. Lynn, Individual Deceased Personnel File, Felmer Lonzo Lynn, U.S. Army Human Resources Command, Alexandria, VA; Disinterment Directive, Individual Deceased Personnel File for Felmer Lonzo Lynn, U.S. Army Human Resources Command, Alexandria, VA; Col. G. M. Nelson to Mrs. Evelyn L. Lynn, May 3, 1945, Lynn Collection.

51   Layne and Barquest, *Margraten, U.S. Ninth Army Military Cemetery*, 7, 8–9, 16; Atkinson, *Guns at Last Light*, 488; https://www.med-dept.com/unit-histories/607th-quartermaster-graves-registration-company.

52   Report of Burial, February 24, 1945, Felmer L. Lynn, Individual Deceased Personnel File, Felmer Lonzo Lynn, U.S. Army Human Resources Command, Alexandria, VA; Disinterment Directive, Individual Deceased Personnel File for Felmer Lonzo Lynn, U.S. Army Human Resources Command, Alexandria, VA; Layne and Barquest, *Margraten, U.S. Ninth Army Military Cemetery*, 7–9; Hayne Neisler, e-mail to the author, June 5, 2013; Lt. Col. Earl M. Honaman, Chaplain, "Burials of Division Personnel in Military Cemeteries," to Norman D. Cota, June 25, 1945, Norman D. Cota Papers, DDE. The site of Pete's grave is outside the bounds of the modern Henri-Chapelle cemetery.

53   Report of Death, March 19, 1945, Individual Deceased Personnel File, Felmer Lonzo Lynn, U.S. Army Human Resources Command, Alexandria, VA.

54   Ruth Lynn Diary, March 6–8, 1945, Lynn Collection; World War II Enlistment Record for David P. Eubanks, RG 64, NA; "David P. Eubanks," www.findagrave.com; Ruth Lynn Diary, March 8, 1945, Lynn Collection. Eubanks later moved to Spartanburg, SC. He died on July 12, 1994, and is buried in Greenlaw Memorial Gardens in Spartanburg.

55   Telegram, [March] 14, 1944, Lynn Collection

56   Telegram, [March] 14, 1944, Lynn Collection.

57   Ruth Lynn Diary, March 14–15, 1945, Lynn Collection.

58   Ruth Lynn Diary, March 19, 1945, Lynn Collection; Josiah W. Bailey to Mrs. Evelyn R. H. Lynn, March 26, 1945, Lynn Collection; William O'Dwyer to Mrs. Evelyn R. H. Lynn, December 8, 1947, Lynn Collection.

59   Official Communication from George C. Marshall, March 15, 1945, Lynn Collection.

60   "Letter to Editor," Unprovenienced Newspaper Article, Lynn Collection.

61 "Card of Thanks," Unprovenienced Newspaper Article, Lynn Collection.

62 Col. G. M. Nelson to Mrs. Evelyn Lynn, March 6, 1945, Lynn Collection.

63 Ruth Lynn Diary, March 21, 1945, Lynn Collection.

64 Cpl. Al Pesek to "Dear Mrs. Lynn," March 8, 1945, Lynn Collection. According to Pesek, it reached him on March 8 and the V-mail "some time ago."

65 Ruth Lynn Diary, March 22, 1945, Lynn Collection; World War II Enlistment Record for Albert J. Pesek, RG 64, NA. Pesek died in 1964 and is buried in St. Adalbert Catholic Cemetery in Niles, Illinois.

66 Ruth Lynn Diary, March 26, March 31, April 2, 1945, Lynn Collection. Moss served in the 114th Infantry Regiment.

67 Ruth Lynn Diary, April 4, 1945, April 7, 1945, and April 27, 1945, Lynn Collection. For Pete's comment on insurance, see chapter 2. Ruth apparently opted to receive lifetime monthly payments of $37.10 starting November 2, 1944, rather than a lump sum settlement. Notice of Settlement, National Service Life Insurance, Lynn Collection.

68 Ruth Lynn Diary, April 3, 1945, Lynn Collection; *Alleghany News*, March 24, 2005. Ruth actually wrote two letters: Mrs. Evelyn R. Lynn to Quartermaster General's Office, April 1, 1945, and Mrs. Evelyn R. Lynn to "Dear Sir," April 9, 1945, both in Individual Deceased Personnel File for Felmer Lonzo Lynn, U.S. Army Human Resources Command, Alexandria, VA.

69 Henry L. Stimson to Mrs. Evelyn R. H. Lynn, April 9, 1945, Lynn Collection. To this day, the certificates, dated May 2, 1945, remain rolled up in the tube they arrived in.

70 Ruth Lynn Diary, April 12–13, 1945, Lynn Collection.

71 Ruth Lynn to "Dearest Dady Pete, November 9, 1944, Lynn Collection; Ruth Lynn Diary, May 6, 1945, Lynn Collection; *Alleghany News*, March 24, 2005; Memories Scrapbook, Lynn Collection; Mary Best, ed., *North Carolina's Shining Hour: Images and Voices from World War II* (Winston-Salem, NC: Our State Books, 2005), 172; Baby Book for Petie Lynn. Petie later marveled how her mother managed to have a child in May after learning of her husband's death in March.

72 Ruth Lynn Diary, May 6, 1945, Lynn Collection.

73 Ruth Lynn Diary, May 19, May 30, and May 22, 1945, Lynn Collection.

74 *Alleghany News*, March 24, 2005; Ruth Lynn Diary, June 1, 1945, Lynn Collection.

75 Ruth Lynn Diary, July 6 and July 14–15, 1945, Lynn Collection.

76 Ruth Lynn Diary, August 20, 1945, Lynn Collection; Jacquelyn Dowd Hall, James Leloudis, Robert Korstad, Mary Murphy, Lu Ann Jones, and Christopher B. Daly, *Like a Family: The Making of a Southern Cotton Mill World* (Chapel Hill and London: University of North Carolina Press, 1987), 312; Betty Hoyle Interview, May 20, 2012.

77 Col. G. M. Nelson to Mrs. Evelyn L. Lynn, May 3, 1945, Lynn Collection.

78 Ruth Lynn Diary, May 31, 1945, Lynn Collection; Capt. C. C. Pierce to Mrs. Evelyn R. H. Lynn, July 27, 1945, Individual Deceased Personnel File, Felmer Lonzo Lynn, U.S. Army Human Resources Command, Alexandria, VA; copy also in Lynn Collection.

79 Ruth Lynn Diary, July 20, 1945, Lynn Collection.

80   George Clarence Smith Personnel Record, National Personnel Records Center, St. Louis. The Smiths lived a long life together. George died in 1989 and Mae in 1994.
81   Atkinson, *Guns at Last Light*, 640.
82   Lt. R. T. Brown to Mrs. Evelyn R. H. Lynn, August 4, 1945, Lynn Collection; Lt. R. T. Brown to Mrs. Evelyn R. H. Lynn, Individual Deceased Personnel File, Felmer Lonzo Lynn, U.S. Army Human Resources Command, Alexandria, VA.
83   Inventory of Personal Effects of Lynn, Felmer L., February 24, 1945, Individual Deceased Personnel File, Felmer Lonzo Lynn, U.S. Army Human Resources Command, Alexandria, VA; Army Effects Bureau Inventory, Felmer L. Lynn, July 21, 1945, Individual Deceased Personnel File, Felmer Lonzo Lynn, U.S. Army Human Resources Command, Alexandria, VA; Ruth Lynn Diary, August 13, 1945, Lynn Collection. The effects were shipped from Kansas City on August 8, 1945.
84   Mrs. Evelyn R. H. Lynn to "Dear Sirs," August 16, 1945, and Lt. R. T. Brown to Mrs. Evelyn R. H. Lynn, November 23, 1945, both in Individual Deceased Personnel File for Felmer Lonzo Lynn, U.S. Army Human Resources Command, Alexandria, VA; Lynn Collection. The wallet with Pete's name on it was evidently one he had left behind, for only one wallet was listed in his effects. Potts was actually from Oklahoma, not Alabama, and died on March 11, 1945. He is buried in Normandy American Cemetery. World War II Enlistment Record for Ernest R. Potts, RG 64, NA; "Ernest R. Potts," www.findagrave.com.
85   Lt. J. L. Closson to Mrs. Ruth Lynn, November 26, 1945; Lt. Howard J. Kisinger Jr. to Mrs. Ruth Lynn, December 8, 1945, Lynn Collection.
86   Sgt. Charlton R. Vincent to Mrs. Ruth Lynn, December 4, 1945, Lynn Collection.
87   Ruth Lynn Diary, December 31, 1945, Lynn Collection.

Chapter 10: Home Before Thanksgiving
1   Ruth Lynn Diary, January 2, 1946, Lynn Collection.
2   Ruth Lynn Diary, January 16, 1945[6], Lynn Collection; Doris Eaker to Dear Mrs. Lynn, January 15, 1945[6], Lynn Collection. The diary entry and letter must be misdated since Pete's body was not recovered until February 1945.
3   Ruth Lynn Diary, January 27, 1945, Lynn Collection.
4   Maj. Gen. Edward F. Witsell to Mrs. Ruth Lynn, February 13, 1946, Lynn Collection. The addresses Ruth received included those of Mrs. Lorine Clark of Globe, Arizona, wife of S/Sgt. Arvil Clark; Mrs. Hazel R. White of Memphis, wife of PFC James K. White; Mrs. Medra O. Floyd of Sans Souci, South Carolina, mother of Cpl. Thomas M. Floyd Jr.; and of 1st Lt. Elsie D. Nelson, wife of Colonel Nelson, who was stationed at the 22nd General Hospital. The Maddens lived at 436 Oneida St.
5   Maj. Gen. Edward F. Witsell to Mrs. Ruth Lynn, February 13, 1946, Lynn Collection.
6   Mary Madden to Ruth Lynn, February 27, 1946, Lynn Collection.
7   Mary Madden to Ruth Lynn, April 7, 1946, Lynn Collection. Another example is Mrs. Mary Madden to Dearest Ruth, May 25, 1946, Lynn Collection.
8   *Pittsburgh Press*, February 3, 1981; Press Release, Obituary of Fr. Alan Madden, February 1981. Copy courtesy of Fr. Francis Fugini, Archivist of the Capuchins. After

being ordained, Madden served as pastor of St. Peter and Paul Church in Cumberland, MA, and then as a missionary. After the war, he attended Harvard University and then worked in ministries for deserters and malcontents. He also served at the Toner Institute in Brookline before becoming a Capuchin Franciscan friar at the St. Augustine Monastery in 1970. Madden died in February 1981 a few days after suffering a heart attack. He was buried in the Friar's Plot of St. Augustine's Cemetery in Millvale, Pennsylvania.

9   Capt. Alan P. Madden to Ruth Lynn, April 4, 1946, Lynn Collection.

10   Capt. Alan P. Madden to Ruth Lynn, April 4, 1946, Lynn Collection; Extract from General Orders Number 3, Section I, Award of Silver Star, Headquarters 28th Infantry Division, January 10, 1945. Copy courtesy of Fr. Francis Fugini, Archivist of the Capuchins.

11   Capt. Alan P. Madden to Ruth Lynn, April 4, 1946, Lynn Collection.

12   Capt. Alan P. Madden to Ruth Lynn, April 4, 1946, Lynn Collection. For more details on Madden's activities in the forest, see http://history.amedd.army.mil/booksdocs/wwii/Schmidt2/SchmidtCh8.htm.

13   Capt. Alan P. Madden to Ruth Lynn, April 13, 1946, Lynn Collection.

14   Order of Service, Springfield Baptist Church, February 4, 1945; Ralph E. Maness to Mrs. Ruth H. Lynn, May 10, 1946, Lynn Collection. The February 4, 1945, Order of Service, which Maness sent to Ruth, is for a prayer service for Maness after it became known that he was missing in action in Luxembourg as of December 20. Maness, who was awarded a Bronze Star in Normandy, died on October 24, 1981, and is buried in Greene Lawn Cemetery in Walnut Grove, Missouri. Entry for Ralph E. Maness at findagrave.com.

15   Col. Charles D. Carle to Mrs. Ruth Lynn, May 1, 1946, Lynn Collection.

16   Ruth Lynn Diary, January 1, 1947, and March 12, 1946, Lynn Collection; Betty Hoyle Interview, May 20, 2012.

17   Maj. Martin G. Riley to Commanding Officer, American Graves Registration Command, December 8, 1946[?], Individual Deceased Personnel File, Felmer Lonzo Lynn, U.S. Army Human Resources Command, Alexandria, VA; Burial Records Correction, Individual Deceased Personnel File for Felmer Lonzo Lynn, U.S. Army Human Resources Command, Alexandria, VA.

18   Brig. Gen. George A. Horkan to Mrs. Evelyn R. H. Lynn, January 3, 1947, Individual Deceased Personnel File for Felmer Lonzo Lynn, U.S. Army Human Resources Command, Alexandria, VA.

19   Erna Risch and Charles L. Kieffer, *The Quartermaster Corps: Organization, Supply, and Services*. Vol. 2. *U.S. Army in World War II* (Washington, DC: Center of Military History, 1995), 392, 402, 404; "Plans for Returning War Dead to United States Completed," unprovenienced newspaper article, Lynn Collection; http://members.trainweb.com/bedt/milrr/batbtww2repat.html. Before the program ended, about 56 percent of American families elected to have the remains of their loved ones returned home.

20   Maj. Gen. Thomas B. Larkin to Mrs. Evelyn R. H. Lynn, March 14, 1947, Individual Deceased Personnel File, Felmer Lonzo Lynn, U.S. Army Human Resources Command, Alexandria, VA; Request for Disposition of Remains, Individual Deceased Personnel File for Felmer Lonzo Lynn, U.S. Army Human Resources Command,

Alexandria, VA; Rick Atkinson, *The Guns at Last Light: The War in Western Europe, 1944–1945* (New York: Henry Holt and Company, 2013), 638–39.

21   Risch and Kieffer, *The Quartermaster Corps* 2, 402.

22   "U.S. Dead Honored at Henri Chapelle," unprovenienced Newspaper Article, Lynn Collection; Atkinson, *Guns at Last Light*, 638–39; Risch and Kieffer, *The Quartermaster Corps* 2, 402; David P. Colley, "Safely Rest," http://www.memorialdayfoundation.org/info.asp?id=1975; http://www.abmc.gov/cemeteries/cemeteries/hc.php. The cost per body for this repatriation process would be estimated at $564.50.

23   Disinterment Directive, Individual Deceased Personnel File for Felmer Lonzo Lynn, U.S. Army Human Resources Command, Alexandria, VA; Joseph T. Layne and Glenn D. Barquest, *Margraten, U.S. Ninth Army Military Cemetery, Margraten, Holland*, National World War II Museum, 16–18; Atkinson, *Guns at Last Light*, 638–39. Each casket was valued at $182.30, while Pete's date of death was incorrectly estimated as January 15, 1945.

24   "Record of Custodial Transfer," Individual Deceased Personnel File, Felmer Lonzo Lynn, U.S. Army Human Resources Command, Alexandria, VA; Atkinson, *Guns at Last Light*, 639.

25   *Time*, October 13, 1947; "Tribute Paid American Dead," unprovenienced Newspaper Article, Lynn Collection; Atkinson, *Guns at Last Light*, 639; *New York Times*, October 5, 1947; Risch and Kieffer, *The Quartermaster Corps* 2, 402. At about the same time, a ship bearing nearly 3,000 dead from the Pacific began its journey home. The ship, the *Honda Knot*, arrived on the west coast on October 10, 1947. (These were the first war dead returned to the states since the war began, except for two marines that had been sent to St. Louis by mistake.) Twenty more ghost ships would follow before the program concluded.

26   Atkinson, *Guns at Last Light*, 639; *New York Times*, October 5, 1947; "Plans for Returning War Dead to United States Completed," unprovenienced newspaper article, Lynn Collection; "Bellhalla/SS Joseph V. Connolly," retrieved from "SS_Joseph_V._Connolly," http://en.wikipedia.org/wiki/SS_Joseph_V._Connolly (no longer available). This would be one of the ship's last voyages. A few months later, it caught fire from an oil leak and sank in the North Atlantic.

27   *New York Times*, October 5, 1947; Atkinson, *Guns at Last Light*, 639; *Time*, October 13, 1947; "Tribute Paid American Dead," unprovenienced Newspaper Article, Lynn Collection; *Charlotte Observer*, October 26, 1947.

28   *New York Times*, October 5, 1947; Atkinson, *Guns at Last Light*, 639; *Time*, October 13, 1947; "Tribute Paid American Dead," unprovenienced newspaper article, Lynn Collection. One of the caskets aboard held the remains of four men. Only one contained the body of a woman.

29   *New York Times*, October 27, 1947. Ruth was under the mistaken impression that Pete's body actually came home on the *Queen Elizabeth*. Ruth Lynn Diary, November 16, 1947, Lynn Collection.

30   *New York Times*, October 27, 1947; http://www.memorialdayfoundation.org/articles/safely-rest.html; Risch and Kieffer, *The Quartermaster Corps* 2, 402.

31   *New York Times*, October 27, 1947; http://www.memorialdayfoundation.org/articles/safely-rest.html.

32   *New York Times*, October 27, 1947; http://www.memorialdayfoundation.org/ articles/safely-rest.html.

33   *New York Times*, October 27, 1947; http://www.memorialdayfoundation. org/articles/safely-rest.html; David P. Colley, "Safely Rest," http://www. memorialdayfoundation.org/info.asp?id=1975.

34   *New York Times*, October 27, 1947.

35   "Plans for Returning War Dead to United States Completed," unprovenienced newspaper article, Lynn Collection; *New York Times*, October 27, 1947; Atkinson, *Guns at Last Light*, 639; http://www.memorialdayfoundation.org/articles/safely-rest.html; photos at http://members.trainweb.com/bedt/milrr/batbtww2repat.html. Some sources say that the ship docked at the Brooklyn Navy Yard, but the evidence points clearly to the Army Terminal.

36   "Record of Custodial Transfer," Individual Deceased Personnel File, Felmer Lonzo Lynn, U.S. Army Human Resources Command, Alexandria, VA; "Plans for Returning War Dead to United States Completed," unprovenienced newspaper article, Lynn Collection; *New York Times*, October 27, 1947; Atkinson, *Guns at Last Light*, 639.

37   *Charlotte Observer*, November 4, 1947; "The Sergeant Comes Home," *Life*, November 17, 1947, 37. The *Life* article poignantly describes the return of another deceased soldier, Sgt. Arnold B. Werner, to his home in Nebraska. Pete's train left New Jersey on November 1.

38   *Charlotte Observer*, November 4, 1947.

39   http://www.cmstory.org/homefront/places/qDepot.htm. The depot was opened in 1941 and deactivated in 1949. It stood in the V-shaped block formed by Statesville Ave. and N. Graham St., bounded on the north by Woodward Avenue and on the south by Davies St. Today, its buildings form part of an industrial park.

40   *Charlotte Observer*, November 4, 1947; http://members.trainweb.com/bedt/ milrr/batbtww2repat.html; Risch and Kieffer, *The Quartermaster Corps* 2, 402, 404. The *Observer* reported the presence of 319 bodies at the depot. Since only 202 sailed on the *Connolly*, the balance surely came from passengers on the *Honda Knot* from the Pacific Theater. Before the program ended, the depot would return 5,170 bodies to next of kin in the Carolinas, Virginia, Tennessee, and Georgia.

41   "Messageform," Charlotte Quartermaster Depot to Mrs. Evelyn R. H. Lynn, n.d., Individual Deceased Personnel File, Felmer Lonzo Lynn, U.S. Army Human Resources Command, Alexandria, VA; Mrs. Evelyn Ruth Lynn to American Graves Reg Div, October 24, 1947, Individual Deceased Personnel File, Felmer Lonzo Lynn, U.S. Army Human Resources Command, Alexandria, VA.

42   *Charlotte Observer*, October 26, 1947.

43   "Resume of Telephone Conversation," Individual Deceased Personnel File, Felmer Lonzo Lynn, U.S. Army Human Resources Command, Alexandria, VA. The Sisk building still stands and continues to serve as a funeral home but under a different name, Withrow's Funeral Home.

44   "Receipt of Remains," Individual Deceased Personnel File, Felmer Lonzo Lynn, U.S. Army Human Resources Command, Alexandria, VA; Disinterment Directive, Individual Deceased Personnel File for Felmer Lonzo Lynn, U.S. Army Human Resources Command, Alexandria, VA.

45 http://www.cmstory.org/homefront/places/qDepot.htm; "Plans for Returning War Dead to United States Completed," unprovenienced newspaper article, Lynn Collection; *New York Times*, October 27, 1947; Atkinson, *Guns at Last Light*, 639. The Graves Registration Division was assigned to the depot in August 1946; *Charlotte Observer*, October 26 and November 4, 1947.

46 *Disposition of World War II Armed Forces Dead*, War Department: Office of the Quartermaster General, 10–11, Lynn Collection; "Linwood P. Comer," www.findagrave.com; *Calhoun Times*, February 22, 1978; Linwood Polk Comer, *The Cup Will Fill . . . A Book of Poems* (Atlanta, GA: Linwood, 1970), 2. Comer went on to serve in the Korean conflict and late in life published a book of poetry. He died on February 18, 1978, and is buried in Gordon Memorial Gardens in Calhoun, Georgia.

47 Ruth Lynn Diary, November 13, 1945, Lynn Collection.

48 Ruth Lynn Diary, November 14–15, 1947, Lynn Collection; Bill Lynn Interview, April 3, 2011.

49 "Kings Mountain Vet's Rites Set," unprovenienced article in Lynn Collection, dated November 14.

50 Memories Scrapbook, Lynn Collection. Pete's sisters were identified as Mrs. John Michem, Mrs. Austin Barrett, and Mrs. George Stroupe; Ruth Lynn Diary, November 16, 1947, Lynn Collection.

51 "Lynn Services in Kings Mtn.," unprovenienced article in Lynn Collection.

52 Ruth Lynn Diary, November 16, 1947, Lynn Collection.

53 Ruth Lynn Diary, November 16, 1947, Lynn Collection; Disinterment Directive, Individual Deceased Personnel File for Felmer Lonzo Lynn, U.S. Army Human Resources Command, Alexandria, VA; Restricted Report of Burial, Individual Deceased Personnel File for Felmer Lonzo Lynn, U.S. Army Human Resources Command, Alexandria, VA. The government pledged to contribute up to $50 toward the defrayment of burial expenses for each repatriated body, but Ruth was reimbursed $75 for the costs "in connection with the interment" of Pete's remains. *Disposition of World War II Armed Forces Dead*, War Department: Office of the Quartermaster General, 10–11, Lynn Collection; "Return of Remains—World War II Dead, Certificate of Interment Expenses," November 16, 1947, Individual Deceased Personnel File, Felmer Lonzo Lynn, U.S. Army Human Resources Command, Alexandria, VA.

Epilogue: Wishing on a Star

1 War Department Report dated March 19, 1945; Restricted Report of Burial; Report of Death, March 19, 1945, all in Individual Deceased Personnel File, Felmer Lonzo Lynn, U.S. Army Human Resources Command, Alexandria, VA; Col. Charles D. Carle to Mrs. Ruth Lynn, May 1, 1946, Lynn Collection.

2 Ruth Lynn Diary, November 2, 1945, Lynn Collection; Petie Bass to Albert Burghardt, n.d., Lynn Collection.

3 Morning Reports, Company B, 112th Infantry Regiment, 28th Infantry Division, November 5, 1944, National Personnel Records Center, St. Louis; Combat Interview, T/Sgt. Roy Littlehales and Sgt. Clarence J. Skains, File 328 Inf (112) 0.1, Entry 427, RG407, NA; copy also in Lynn Collection.

4 http://www.in-honored-glory.info/html/stories/ifspaans.htm, accessed December 31, 2013.

5 Morning Reports, Company B, 112th Infantry Regiment, 28th Infantry Division, November 5, 1944, National Personnel Records Center, St. Louis; Combat Interview, T/Sgt. Roy Littlehales and Sgt. Clarence J. Skains, File 328 Inf (112) 0.1, Entry 427, RG407, NA; copy also in Lynn Collection.

6 "Disinterment Directive," Individual Deceased Personnel File, Felmer Lonzo Lynn, U.S. Army Human Resources Command, Alexandria, VA; Col. G. M. Nelson to Mrs. Evelyn L. Lynn, May 3, 1945, Lynn Collection; Restricted Report of Burial, Individual Deceased Personnel File for Felmer Lonzo Lynn, U.S. Army Human Resources Command, Alexandria, VA; Lee Kennett, *G.I.: The American Soldier in World War II* (Norman: University of Oklahoma Press, 1987), 177, 179.

7 George Wilson, *If You Survive: From Normandy to the Battle of the Bulge to the End of World War II, One American Officer's Riveting True Story* (New York: Ivy Books, Random House Publishing Group, Kindle Edition, 1987), 144; Caddick-Adams, *Snow and Steel*, 199; Michael D. Doubler, *Closing with the Enemy: How GIs Fought the War in Europe, 1944–1945* (Lawrence: University Press of Kansas, 1994), 40, 256–57; Kennett, *G.I.*, 175.

8 Individual Deceased Personnel File, Ralph W. Spaans, Johnny Gregorio, and Guy Hardaway. U.S. Army Human Resources Command, Alexandria, VA. Hardaway's skull was reportedly crushed. His effects included a ring and fountain pen. His body was permanently buried on December 18, 1947, in the Greenwood Baptist Church Cemetery in Lincolnton, Georgia. His wife, Bessie, died in 1963 after being thrown off a horse. Their son, James, went on to serve in the U.S. Marines. *Augusta Chronicle*, March 17, 1945, and December 18, 1947; Author's Correspondence with Cliff and Julie Hardaway, October–November, 2014; "Guy Hinton Hardaway," www.findagrave.com, accessed September 27, 1944; World War II Enlistment Record for Guy H. Hardaway, RG 64, NA. Gregorio's skull was fractured and his maxilla was missing but otherwise the body was complete. A few pictures, a ring, souvenir shoes, a wallet, some cards, some badly eroded souvenir money, and a souvenir medal were later shipped home to his wife at 6038 North Phillips St., Philadelphia, PA. Gregorio remains at Henri-Chapelle. Maj. Gen. Thomas B. Larkin to Mrs. Beatrice Gregorio, September 13, 1948, Individual Deceased Personnel File, Johnny Gregorio, U.S. Army Human Resources Command, Alexandria, VA.

9 Morning Reports, Company B, 112th Infantry Regiment, 28th Infantry Division, November 5, 1944, National Personnel Records Center, St. Louis; Alphabetical Listing of Deaths, 28th Infantry Division, NA. Bodies of 112th Infantry men have been found in the Hürtgen Forest as recently as September 2008.

10 Major Jade E. Hinman, *When the Japanese Bombed the Huertgen Forest: How the Army's Investigation of Pearl Harbor Influenced the Outcome of the Huertgen Forest, Major General Leonard T. Gerow and His Command of V Corps 1943–1945* (Fort Leavenworth, KS: School of Advanced Military Studies, United States Army Command and General Staff College, 2011), 1; James M. Gavin, "Bloody Huertgen," *American Heritage*, December 1979, accessed at www.americanheritage.com/print/53860?page+show, 8.

11   Ruth Lynn Diary, June 11–13, June 29, and June 15, 1945, Lynn Collection.

12   *Alleghany News*, March 24, 2005. Lester Moss's wife Rosanell did remarry, to Mr. Eugene Mahue (http://www.harrisfunerals.com/fh/print.cfm?type=obituary&o_ id+1245279&fh?id+12915, accessed on August 8, 2013).

13   Mrs. Cornelia Moss Davis, telephone interview with the author, March 30, 2014. Rosanell died on August 24, 2011.

14   Cleveland County Register of Deeds office; www.arcgis.webgis.net/nc/cleveland for 122 Dixon School Road (Parcel #11783); Notice of Settlement, National Service Life Insurance, Lynn Collection. The value of the purchase is derived from Ruth's payment of $5.50 for a real estate stamp on the deed. At that time, stamps cost 55 cents per $500 worth of property, which translates into a $5,000 cost. According to online calculators such as www.dollartimes.com and www.measuringworth.com, that would be about $50,000 today, while Pete's life insurance policy of $10,000 is the equivalent of about $128,000 in today's money.

15   *Alleghany News*, March 24, 2005; Mrs. Bobbie Blake, interview with the author, July 6, 2013; Ruth Lynn Diary, June 17, 1945, Lynn Collection; "Macedonia Holds Dedicatory Rites," Unprovenienced Newspaper Article, Lynn Collection. The mural no longer exists since the sanctuary was replaced later.

16   *Alleghany News*, March 24, 2005.

17   *Alleghany News*, March 24, 2005.

18   April 7, 1946, Lynn Collection; Petie Lynn to the author, April 2, 2016. The other congregation was David Baptist Church.

19   Davyd Foard Hood, "Margrace Mill Village Historic District," May 6, 2009. National Register of Historic Places Nomination, North Carolina State Historic Preservation Office, 23, 1, 2, 4, 22–23, 25; Hayne Neisler, e-mail to the author, June 5, 2013.

20   *Alleghany News*, March 24, 2005.

21   "Listen, World," Unprovenienced newspaper clipping, n.d., Lynn Collection; *Alleghany News*, March 24, 2005. The column appears to have been published in 1945.

Bibliography

Manuscript Sources

Dwight D. Eisenhower Library and Museum, Abilene, KS
    Norman D. Cota Papers
Library of Congress, American Folklife Center, Veterans History Project
    Howard Adler Collection
    Benjamin Alvarado Collection
    Charles L. Crain Collection
    Marion Bedford Davis, Jr. Collection
    Elzo Newton Dickerson Collection
    Leslie Stewart Ellis Collection
    Charles A. Haug Collection
    Donald H. Hogle Collection
    Edward Brandt Hipp Collection
    Paul William Johanningmeier Collection
    John M. Kozlosky Collection
    Phillip Walter LaForce Collection
    Joseph H. Mack Collection
    Roy Nix Collection
    Lacy A. Sciame Collection
    Gordon Frederick Smith, Jr. Collection
    Graydon Henderson Woods Collection
Mauney Memorial Library, Kings Mountain, NC
    Letters to Service Men, World War II, 1942–1945
National Archives, College Park, MD.
    RG 319, Records of the Army Staff
    RG 407, WWII Operations Reports
    RG 498, HQ European Theater of Operations, U.S. Army
National Oceanic & Atmospheric Administration, Washington, DC
    "Record of Climatological Observations," Gastonia, NC area, 1944–1945.
National Personnel Records Center, St. Louis.
    J.C. Lynn Personnel Record
    George Clarence Smith Personnel Record
National World War II Museum, New Orleans, LA.
    William P. Shaw. *Fellowship of Dust: The WWII Journey of Sergeant Frank Shaw.*
    Joseph T. Layne and Glenn D. Barquest. *Margraten, U.S. Ninth Army Military Cemetery, Margraten, Holland.*
North Carolina State Archives, Raleigh, NC
    Cleveland County Marriage Register, 1870–1945
    Record of Incorporations, Cleveland County, NC, 1888–1950
Pennsylvania National Guard Military Museum, Annville, PA.
    Headquarters, 28th Infantry Division (Record of Events, 3rd Battalion, 112th Infantry)

Historical File – 28th Division, Personal Stories
  The Invader
Carl L. Peterson Papers, in the custody of Mr. William Snider, Matthews, NC
Pete Lynn Collection, in the custody of Mrs. Petie Lynn Bass, Sparta, NC
Rutgers University, Oral History Archives
  Stuart T. Brandow
  Vincent J. Gorman
  Joseph Parisi Jr.
  David Sive
University of North Carolina at Charlotte, Special Collections, Atkins Library,
    Charlotte, NC
  Biberstein, Bowles, Meacham & Reed Records
U.S. Army Human Resources Command, Alexandria, VA
  Individual Deceased Personnel File for Felmer Lonzo Lynn
U.S. Army Military History Institute, Carlisle Barracks, Carlisle, PA
  Papers of Benjamin A. Dickson
  Gen. Maj. Rudolf-Christoph Freiherr von Gersdorff, *The Battle of the Huertgen Forest,
    Nov.–early Dec. 1944*
  Siegfried von Waldenburg, *Report on 116th Panzer Division (1–9 November 1944)*

Newspapers and Magazines
The Age
The Alleghany News
American Heritage
Augusta Chronicle
Austin-American Statesman
The Daily Courier
Kings Mountain Herald
Life
Monthly Weather Review
The New York Times
The New York Times Magazine
The (Charleston, SC) *News & Courier*
Philadelphia Inquirer
The Pittsburgh Press
The Saturday Evening Post
The State
Time
The Washington Post
World War II

Interviews
Mrs. Bobbie Blake, interview with the author, July 6, 2013.
Mrs. Cornelia Moss Davis, interview with the author, January 3, 2014; March 30, 2014.

Mr. Bill Lynn, interview with the author, April 3, 2011.
Mrs. Betty Hoyle, interview with the author, May 20, 2012.
Mr. William F. Meller, interview with the author, February 12–13, 2013.
Mr. Robert C. Pearson, interview with the author, November 15, 2015.
Mr. Leroy Schaller, interview with the author, February 16, 2013.
Mrs. Clydene Sparks, interview with the author, August 3, 2015.

Books, Articles, and Pamphlets

28th Infantry (Keystone) Division (Mechanized): 125 Years of Service. Nashville, TN, and Paducah, KY: Turner, 2005.

Ambrose, Stephen E. *Citizen Soldiers: The U.S. Army from the Normandy Beaches to the Bulge to the Surrender of Germany, June 7, 1944–May 7, 1945.* New York: Simon & Schuster, 1997.

Anderson, J. T., compiler. *Industrial Directory and Reference Book of the State of North Carolina.* Durham, NC: Christian Printing Company, 1938.

Andrews, Mildred Gwin. *The Men and the Mills: A History of the Southern Textile Industry.* Macon, GA: Mercer University Press, 1987.

Atkinson, Rick. *The Guns at Last Light: The War in Western Europe, 1944–1945.* New York: Henry Holt, 2013.

Baedeker, Karl. *Belgium and Holland, Including the Grand-Duchy of Luxembourg: Handbook for Travellers.* Leipzig: Karl Baedeker, 1910.

Baedeker, Karl. *The Rhine from the Dutch to the Alsatian Frontier: Handbook for Travellers.* Leipzig: Karl Baedeker, 1926.

Bailey, Ronald H. *The Home Front: U.S.A.* Alexandria, VA: Time-Life Books, 1997.

Baity, Dave. *Tracks through Time: A History of the City of Kings Mountain, 1874–2005.* Charlotte, NC: Josten Books, for the Kings Mountain Historical Museum Foundation, 2005.

Baker, Carlos. *Ernest Hemingway: A Life Story.* New York: Charles Scribner's Sons, 1969.
———. *Ernest Hemingway: Selected Letters, 1917–1961.* New York: Charles Scribner's Sons, 1981.

Balkoski, Joseph. *From Brittany to the Reich: The 29th Infantry Division in Germany, September–November 1944.* Mechanicsburg, PA: Stackpole Books, 2012.

Barnett, Correlli, ed. *Hitler's Generals: Authoritative Portraits of the Men Who Waged Hitler's War.* New York: Quill/William Morrow, 1989.

Barnwell, Mildred Gwin. *Faces We See.* Gastonia, NC: Southern Combine Yarn Spinners Association, 1939.

Best, Mary, ed. *North Carolina's Shining Hour: Images and Voices from World War II.* Winston-Salem, NC: Our State Books, 2005.

Black, Conrad. *Franklin Delano Roosevelt: Champion of Freedom.* New York: Public Affairs, 2003.

Blakeslee, Clarence. *A Personal Account of WWII by Draftee #36887149.* Rockford, MI: Rockford Squire, 1998.

Boesch, Paul. *Road to Huertgen: Forest in Hell.* Houston, TX: Gulf, 1962.

Bolger, Maj. "Daniel P. Zero Defects: Command Climate in First US Army, 1944–1945." *Military Review* 71 (May 1991): 61–73.

Bradbeer, Thomas. "General Cota and the Battle of the Hurtgen Forest." *Army History* 75 (Spring 2010): 18–41.

Bradley, Omar N., with Clay Blair. *A General's Life: An Autobiography by General of the Army Omar N. Bradley.* New York: Simon & Schuster, 1983.

———. *A Soldier's Story.* New York: Modern Library, 1999.

Butler, Daniel Allen. *Warrior Queens: The Queen Mary and Queen Elizabeth in World War II.* Mechanicsburg, PA: Stackpole Books, 2002.

Caddick-Adams, Peter. *Snow & Steel: The Battle of the Bulge, 1944–45.* New York: Oxford University Press, 2015.

Carpenter, Iris. *No Woman's World.* Boston, MA: Houghton Mifflin, 1946.

Chernitsky, Dorothy. *Voices from the Foxholes: By the Men of the 110th Infantry, World War II.* Uniontown, PA: Dorothy Chernitsky, 1991.

Clark's Directory of Southern Textile Mills. Nineteenth Edition. Charlotte, NC: Clark, January 1, 1921.

Clarke, Jeffrey J., and Robert Ross Smith. *Riviera to the Rhine.* Part of the United States Army in World War II series. Reprint. Atlanta, GA: Whitman, 2012.

Comer, Linwood Polk. *The Cup Will Fill . . . A Book of Poems.* Atlanta, GA: Linwood, 1970.

Crist, Robert Grant, ed. *The First Century: A History of the 28th Infantry Division.* Harrisburg, PA: 28th Infantry Division, 1979.

Currey, Cecil B. *Follow Me and Die: The Destruction of an American Division in World War II.* New York: Stein and Day, 1984.

Davis, Anita Price, and James M. Walker. *Images of America: Cleveland County in World War II.* Charleston, SC: Arcadia, 2005.

Davis, M. Bedford, M.D. *Frozen Rainbows: The World War II Adventures of a Combat Medical Officer.* Elk River, MN: Meadowlark, 2003.

Doubler, Michael D. *Closing with the Enemy: How GIs Fought the War in Europe, 1944–1945.* Lawrence: University Press of Kansas, 1994.

Eisenhower, Dwight D. *Crusade in Europe.* Baltimore, MD, and London: Johns Hopkins University Press, 1948.

Fitzpatrick, Edward A., ed. *Selective Service in Wartime: Second Report of the Director of Selective Service, 1941–1942.* Washington, DC: Government Printing Office, 1943.

Fleig, Lt. Col. Raymond E. *707th Tank Battalion in World War II.* Springfield, OH: Raymond E. Fleig, 1993.

Gavin, James. M. *On To Berlin: Battles of an Airborne Commander, 1943–1946.* New York: Bantam, 1978.

George, Emily. "Fort George G. Meade, Maryland." *On Point: The Journal of Army History* 21, no. 1 (2015): 44–47.

Glass, Brent D. *The Textile Industry in North Carolina: A History.* Raleigh: North Carolina Division of Archives and History, 1992.

Goldbaugh, Jack. *The Bloody Patch: A True Story of the Daring 28th Infantry Division.* New York, Washington, Hollywood: Vantage Press, 1973.

Grady, Frank R. *Surviving Combat: Hurtgen Forest, Germany, World War II. N.P.* Fort Indiantown Gap, PA: 28th Infantry Division Association, 2002.

Hadden, Alexander H. *Not Me! The World War II Memoir of a Reluctant Rifleman.* Bennington, VT: World War II Historical Society, 1997.

Hall, Jacquelyn Dowd, James Leloudis, Robert Korstad, Mary Murphy, Lu Ann Jones, and Christopher B. Daly. *Like a Family: The Making of a Southern Cotton Mill World.* Chapel Hill and London: University of North Carolina Press, 1987.

Handbook of Information: Infantry Replacement Training Center, Camp Fannin, Texas.

Herr, Michael. "Dispatches: 1967–1975." In *Reporting Vietnam: Part Two, American Journalism, 1969–1975*, 555–764. New York: Library of America, 1998.

Hinman, Major Jade E. *When the Japanese Bombed the Huertgen Forest: How the Army's Investigation of Pearl Harbor Influenced the Outcome of the Huertgen Forest, Major General Leonard T. Gerow and His Command of V Corps 1943–1945.* Fort Leavenworth, KS: School of Advanced Military Studies, United States Army Command and General Staff College, 2011.

Historical and Pictorial Review of the 28th Infantry Division in World War II. Indiantown Gap, PA: 28th Infantry Division, 1946.

Hood, Davyd Foard. *Margrace Mill Village Historic District.* National Register of Historic Places Nomination, North Carolina State Historic Preservation Office, May 6, 2009.

———. *Southern Railway Company Overhead Bridge.* National Register of Historic Places Nomination, North Carolina State Historic Preservation Office, April 19, 2007.

Hogan, David W. Jr. *A Command Post at War: First Army Headquarters in Europe, 1943–1945.* Honolulu, HI: University Press of the Pacific, 2006.

Hogzett, Donald D. *Recollections of an Infantry Lieutenant, WWII.* Oakland, IA: Donald D. Hogzett, 1996.

Holt, Maj. Jeffrey P. *Operational Performance of the U.S. 28th Infantry Division, September to December 1944.* Fort Leavenworth, KS: Master's Thesis, U.S. Army Command and General Staff College, June 1994.

Huie, William Bradford. *The Execution of Private Slovik.* Yardley, PA: Westholme, 1954.

Huston, James A. *Biography of a Battalion: The Life and Times of an Infantry Battalion in Europe in World War II.* Mechanicsburg, PA: Stackpole Books, 2003.

Irving, David. *The War between the Generals: Inside the Allied High Command.* New York: Congdon & Weed, 1981.

Johns, Glover S. *The Clay Pigeons of St. Lo.* Mechanicsburg, PA: Stackpole Books, 2002.

Kemp, Harry M. *The Regiment: Let the Citizens Bear Arms! A Narrative History of an American Infantry Regiment in World War II.* Austin, TX: Nortex Press, 1990.

Kennedy, David M. *Freedom from Fear: The American People in Depression and War, 1929–1945.* New York and Oxford: Oxford University Press, 1999.

Kennett, Lee. *G.I.: The American Soldier in World War II.* Norman: University of Oklahoma Press, 1987.

Kershaw, Alex. *The Longest Winter: The Battle of the Bulge and the Epic Story of World War II's Most Decorated Platoon.* New York: Da Capo Press, 2004.

King, Spencer Bidwell, Jr. *Selective Service in North Carolina in World War II.* Chapel Hill: University of North Carolina Press, 1949.

Lefler, Hugh Talmage, and Albert Ray Newsome. *North Carolina: The History of a Southern State*. Chapel Hill: University of North Carolina Press, 1954.

Lemmon, Sarah McCulloh. *North Carolina's Role in World War II*. Raleigh: Division of Archives and History, North Carolina Department of Cultural Resources, 1964.

Lerwill, Leonard L. *The Personnel Replacement System in the United States Army*. Washington, DC: Department of the Army, 1954.

Linguiti, Paschal, and Michael DeMarco. "Subject: Evacuation of Wounded from Vossenack Kommerscheidt and Schmidt Areas, 2–11 November 1944." Medical Detachment, 112th Infantry Regiment, APO 28, U.S. Army, 15 November 1944. http://history.armedd.army.mil/booksdocs/wwii/Schmidt/DemarcoLinguitiRept. htm, accessed March 20, 2010, courtesy Charlie Oelig.

Lowitt, Richard, and Maurine Beasley, eds. *One Third of a Nation: Lorena Hickok Reports on the Great Depression*. Urbana and Chicago: University of Illinois Press, 1981.

MacDonald, Charles B. *The Battle of the Huertgen Forest*. New York: Jove, 1963.

———. *The Last Offensive (United States Army in World War II: The European Theater of Operations)*. Washington, DC: Office of the Chief of Military History, Department of the Army, 1993.

———. *The Siegfried Line Campaign (United States Army in World War II: The European Theater of Operations)*. Washington, DC: Office of the Chief of Military History, Department of the Army, 1963.

MacDonald, Charles B., and Sidney T. Matthews. *Three Battles: Arnaville, Altuzzo, and Schmidt*. United States Army in World War II. Washington, DC: United States Army Center of Military History, 1952. Reprint, 1999.

McBurnette, Voris Weldon. *The 108th Training Command: A History of Embracing Innovation and Shaping the Future, 1946–2010*. Charlotte, NC: Palette Communications, 2010.

McManus, John C. *September Hope: The American Side of a Bridge Too Far*. New York: NAL Caliber, 2012.

Meller, William F. *Bloody Roads to Germany: At Huertgen Forest and the Bulge— an American Soldier's Courageous Story of World War II*. New York: Berkley Caliber, 2012.

Merriam, Ray, ed. *True Tales of World War II: "We Were There."* Bennington, VT: Merriam Press, 2011.

Miller, Edward G. *A Dark and Bloody Ground: The Hurtgen Forest and the Roer River Dams, 1944–1945*. College Station: Texas A&M University Press, 1995.

Miller, Edward G., and David T. Zabecki. "Tank Battle in Kommerscheidt." *World War II* 15, no. 4 (November 2000): 42–48, 88.

Miller, Robert A. *Division Commander: A Biography of Major General Norman D. Cota*. Spartanburg, SC: Reprint Company, 1989.

Morris, Hillard. *A View From the High Point of Hell: Memoirs of S/Sgt Hillard Morris, 81mm Mortar Observer, 196 Days Combat, Normandy to the Rhine River, July 1944– April 1945*. Privately published, not dated.

Palmer, Robert R., Bell I. Wiley, and William R. Keast. *The Procurement and Training of Ground Combat Troops. In U.S. Army in World War II*. Washington, DC: Center of Military History, 1948.

Peterman, Ivan H. *Pennsylvanians on the Western Front*. Philadelphia, PA: Philadelphia Inquirer, 1944.

Pogue, Forrest C. *George C. Marshall: Organizer of Victory, 1943–1945*. New York: Viking Press, 1973.

———. *Pogue's War: Diaries of a WWII Combat Historian*. Lexington: University Press of Kentucky, 2001.

———. *The Supreme Command. Part of the United States Army in World War II*. Washington, DC: Center of Military History, United States Army, 1989.

Pope, Liston. *Millhands and Preachers: A Study of Gastonia*. New Haven, CT: Yale University Press, 1942.

Ratliff, Thomas G. *I Can Hear the Guns Now: A World War II Story of Love and Sacrifice*. Carlisle, OH: Thomas G. Ratliff, 1999.

Reporting World War II. Part II, *American Journalism, 1944–1946*. New York: Library of America, 1995.

Rhyne, Jennings J. *Some Southern Cotton Mill Workers and Their Villages*. Chapel Hill: University of North Carolina Press, 1930.

Risch, Erna, and Charles L. Kieffer. *The Quartermaster Corps: Organization, Supply, and Services*. Vol. 2. *U.S. Army in World War II*. Washington, DC: Center of Military History, 1995.

Rush, Robert Sterling. *Hell in Hurtgen Forest*. Lawrence: University Press of Kansas, 2001.

Schmidt, Gunther. "The 272 VGD in Action in the Eifel, 1944–1945." Translated by Ron van Rijt. http://www.dererstezung.com/272ndInAction/272ndInAction(3).htm, accessed on July 27, 2013.

Schrijvers, Peter. *The Crash of Ruin: American Combat Soldiers in Europe During World War II*. New York: Washington University Press, 1998.

Shlaes, Amity. *The Forgotten Man: A New History of the Great Depression*. New York: Harper Perennial, 2007.

Shomon, Joseph James. *Crosses in the Wind*. New York: Stratford House, 1947.

Shytle, Tom. *Carolina Roots: From Whence I Came*. Privately Published, 2008.Smith, Robert L. *"Medic!": A WWII Combat Medic Remembers*. Berkeley, CA: Creative Arts Book, 2001.

A Soldier Remembers: The 112th Infantry in the 20th Century. Erie, PA: 112th Infantry Regiment Association, 2001.

Stahel, David. *Operation Barbarossa and Germany's Defeat in the East*. Cambridge, MA: Cambridge University Press, 2009.

Suggs, George G., Jr. *"My World is Gone": Memories of Life in a Southern Cotton Mill Town*. Detroit, MI: Wayne State University Press, 2002.

Sumner, H. C. "North Atlantic Hurricanes and Tropical Disturbances of 1944." *Monthly Weather Review* 72 (December 1944): 237–40.

Sylvan, Major William C., and Captain Francis G. Smith. *Normandy to Victory: The War Diary of General Courtney H. Hodges and the First U.S. Army*. Edited by John T. Greenwood. Lexington: University Press of Kentucky, 2008.

Taylor, Lt. Col. Benjamin G. "Operation Schmidt." *Military Review* (August 1954): 30–39.

Tomlinson, Tommy. "Kings Mountain." http://www.ourstate.com/articles/ kings-mountain.

Tracings: Schools and Schooling, a History of Black Schools and Cleveland County, Kings Mountain District, and Shelby City School Systems, 1800–1970. Volume 1: Series 1–4. Shelby, NC: Westmoreland Printers, 2009.

V Corps Operations in the ETO: 6 Jan. 1942–9 May 1945. Washington, DC: U.S. Army, 1945.

Wade, Gary, transcriber. *Conversations with General J. Lawton Collins.* Fort Leavenworth, KS: Combat Studies Institute Press, 1983.

Walton, William. "The Battle of Huertgen Forest." *Life* (January 1, 1945): 33–36.

Weaver, Michael E. *Guard Wars: The 28th Infantry Division in World War II.* Bloomington and Indianapolis: Indiana University Press, 2010.

Weigley, Russell F. *Eisenhower's Lieutenants: The Campaign of France and Germany, 1944–1945.* Bloomington and Indianapolis: Indiana University Press, 1981.

Wilson, George. *If You Survive: From Normandy to the Battle of the Bulge to the End of World War II, One American Officer's Riveting True Story.* New York: Ivy Books, Random House Publishing Group, Kindle Edition, 1987.

Wiltse, Charles M., ed. *Physical Standards in World War II.* Washington, DC: Office of the Surgeon General, Department of the Army, 1967.

Zeta Psi Fraternity of North America: Double-Diamond Jubilee, 1847–1997. Paducah, KY: Turner, 1997.

Abbreviations

DDE – Dwight D. Eisenhower Library and Museum
USAMHI – U.S. Army Military History Institute, Carlisle Barracks, Carlisle, PA
RG – Record Group
NA – National Archives II, Landover, MD

ACKNOWLEDGMENTS

While writing this book, I have been blessed to have the help of many wonderful people. Indeed, the men and women I have met along the way may have been the best part of the whole process. I could not have finished this project without them, and I offer each my deepest thanks.

I will start with family, for if nothing else that is what this book is all about. Pete and Ruth Lynn's daughters, Petie Bass and Bobbie Blake, are both gracious ladies who were of tremendous help, along with their supportive husbands Norman and Steve. Petie even read my manuscript, offered many helpful suggestions, and showed me the Kings Mountain she remembered, although I'm sure the process dredged up some memories she was reluctant to recall. My father-in-law, Bud Connor, and other members of the Connor clan, assisted in many ways with their own knowledge and recollections of Kings Mountain. He and his wife Joan also read the manuscript and caught some errors. So did my brother-in-law and Pete's grandson, Chris Connor, his wife Kristen, and my other sister-in-law, Kristy Tyndall. My wife Laurie was as usual my shining light, sounding board, encourager, editor, and most of all wife and fabulous mother to Caroline and Taylor Ann. They are all part of Pete and Ruth's story. I love you and I'm proud to be a member of this family.

The family of the late Bill Lynn, Pete Lynn's brother, was also most gracious. One of the most delightful moments of my entire journey was interviewing Bill. He was ninety-one and hard of hearing at the time, but as he sat in his easy chair, wearing a Bud Light T-shirt, he flashed a quick smile and told stories about his brother that made this book better. He has since passed on and is missed greatly.

Cornelia Moss Davis, who appears in these pages as a little girl named Butch, was also ready to assist. She shared memories and photos her mother took that added much color to this book. Bill Snider, grandson of Lt. Col. Carl Peterson, was equally helpful in providing a photo, assistance with sources, and discussing the Hürtgen Forest fighting with me.

Others that I would like to thank include Kathy Barry of the Textile Heritage Museum; Norma Drewery of the Kings Mountain Historical Museum; the staffs of the Pritzker Military Library and National World War II Museum, and especially Eric Rivet with the latter; Tom Hanchett, staff historian at the Levine Museum of the New South; Jeff Pruett and Regan Brooks of the Gaston County Museum; Dr. Roxanne Newton, dean of the Humanities and Fine Arts Division, Mitchell Community College in Statesville; Marilyn Schuster of the Special Collections Department of Atkins Library at UNC Charlotte; Charles B. Oelig, director and curator of the Pennsylvania National Guard Military Museum; Stacie Johnson with the Office of Veterans' Affairs at Fort Indiantown Gap; Fr. Francis Fugini of the Province of Saint Augustine of the Capuchin Order; Leslie Kesler of the Robinson-Spangler Carolina Room at Charlotte Mecklenburg Library; and John Cope of the North Carolina Museum of History.

I would also like to thank John "Jack" Wilson, Hayne Neisler, Julie and Cliff Hardaway, the late Mrs. Clydene Sprinkle Sparks, Jim Ferrell, Mark Moore, Liz Bailey, Henri Mignon (who guided me to the battlefield where Pete Lynn died), Mark Ragan, Robert Doyle, Elisabeth Kimber, Gary Mock, and Ted Savas.

A special salute goes to Mr. Robert C. Pearson. Pearson grew up and worked at both of the mills that figure in this story, so his memories were treasures. Despite being in his nineties and dealing with health issues, he answered many questions and also used the 1940 census, modern maps, and an aerial photo he took to sketch the layout of Park Yarn in those days. His work informed the map of the mill villages in this book.

Along the way, I was most fortunate to receive the assistance of several esteemed historians. As usual, my friend Dr. Mark Bradley was my go-to resource. It seems like I always ask him for help on my projects, and he never fails to come to my aid. Mark connected me with Dr. Robert Rush. Currently historian to the Office of the Surgeon General of the Army, Dr. Rush is the author of the seminal book *Hell in the Huertgen Forest*. He was tremendously helpful to me in offering source suggestions, fielding questions, and reviewing my manuscript. He is a gifted and knowledgeable historian. I would also like to recognize the equally talented John C. McManus, esteemed professor and author of several groundbreaking books about World War II, for his help with research suggestions, connecting me to veterans, and reviewing my manuscript. My thanks also go to Edward G. Miller, author of *A Dark and Bloody Ground*, which is an excellent account of the Hürtgen Forest fighting. Ed read and commented on my manuscript. Other authors and historians who encouraged me or answered inquiries include my friend and mentor Dr. Gary Freeze and Rick Atkinson.

This narrative is certainly better because veterans of the Hürtgen Forest helped too. I truly appreciate the support and most especially the service and sacrifice of both William F. Meller and Leroy Schaller. Men like Meller, Schaller, and Pete Lynn gave so much, and we owe them dearly.

Finally, thanks to the team at Stackpole Books, and especially Dave Reisch and Stephanie Otto, for trusting in the vision and bringing it to reality.

Soli Deo gloria.

Chris J. Hartley
Pfafftown, North Carolina
January 16, 2018

Index